HYPNOSIS
AND SUGGESTION
IN THE
TREATMENT OF PAIN

A Clinical Guide

HYPNOSIS AND SUGGESTION IN THE TREATMENT OF PAIN

A CLINICAL GUIDE

Joseph Barber, Ph.D.

With contributions by

Christel J. Bejenke, M.D.
John J. Bonica, M.D.
William C. Fowkes, M.D.
Samuel LeBaron, M.D., Ph.D.
John D. Loeser, M.D.

Roseann Mulligan, D.D.S.
David R. Patterson, Ph.D.
Donald D. Price, Ph.D.
Sari Roth-Roemer, Ph.D.
Karen L. Syrjala, Ph.D.

Lonnie K. Zeltzer, M.D.

Foreword by
Ernest R. Hilgard, Ph.D.

W.W. Norton & Company • New York • London

Manufacturing by Haddon Craftsmen, Inc.

For information about permission to reproduce selections
from this book, write to
Permissions, W.W. Norton Company, Inc., 500 Fifth Avenue,
New York, NY 10110

Library of Congress Cataloging-in-Publication Data

Hypnosis and suggestion in the treatment of pain : a clinical guide /
  [edited by] Joseph Barber ; with contributions by Christel J.
  Bejenke . . . [et al.] ; foreword by Ernest R. Hilgard.
      p.   cm.
  "A Norton professional book."
  Includes bibliographical references and indexes.
  ISBN 0-393-70216-2
  1. Hypnotism – Therapeutic use.   2. Mental suggestion – Therapeutic
use.   3. Analgesia.   I. Barber, Joseph, 1948-   .   II. Bejenke,
Christel. J.
  [DNLM: 1. Pain – therapy.   2. Hypnosis.   WL 704 H998 1996]
RB127.H97   1996
616′.0472 – dc20
DNLM/DLC
for Library of Congress   96-6382   CIP

W.W. Norton & Company, Inc., 500 Fifth Avenue, New York, NY 10110
                    http://web.wwnorton.com
W.W. Norton & Company Ltd., 10 Coptic Street, London WC1A 1PU

                2   3   4   5   6   7   8   9   0

To the scientists and practitioners who have devoted their working lives to the relief of pain and suffering

And to Kenneth S. Bowers, Ph.D., my friend and mentor, who has cast his wise and benevolent influence upon the professional lives of so many colleagues, including my own

FOREWORD

This book is a very welcome and thorough account of hypnosis and suggestion in the treatment of pain. During the past four decades, hypnosis has become much better understood due to the extensive laboratory and clinical research. While much about hypnosis still remains to be explored and understood, there is a need to more accurately describe the practical applications of hypnosis and imagination. Clinicians who care for patients in pain have benefited greatly from theoretical work that has advanced our knowledge about hypnosis. At the same time, some of the most important questions in this field have been studied by clinicians, who are concerned primarily with practical applications.

This book brings together experimental and clinical knowledge regarding the treatment of these very real problems. Clinicians who read this book will appreciate the detail and thoroughness with which practical clinical questions are explored. At the same time, experimentalists will develop a deeper understanding of the world of those who treat pain.

The literature on psychological factors involved in the treatment of pain is a rich one, but it has been incomplete. There is an unfortunate abundance of exaggerated claims for the efficacy of various psychological methods in treating pain. There are few serious and careful reports of methods that integrate a compassionate exploration of pain problems with the rigorous approach required by the scientific method. This book is a significant contribution to the field, a valuable resource to clinicians and experimentalists alike.

Over the years, Josephine Hilgard and I, along with others in the Stanford Hypnosis Laboratory, observed the wide variability of experimental subjects' experience. This variability helped us realize, with guidance from clinical colleagues, the importance of bringing a flexible approach into the experimental setting. We benefited greatly from this clinical point of view in our design and execution of laboratory studies on pain. A great source of rich detail in these experimental studies was the clinical interviews that Josephine and her associates conducted to explore the experience of both the subject and experimenter. From our work with experimental subjects we learned some valuable lessons that we hoped would be applicable in the clinic. After all, the primary purpose of this experimental work was to benefit actual patients in pain. The first major test of our ability to integrate experimental and clinical methods was the investigation of pain in children with cancer, conducted by Josephine and her colleague, Sam LeBaron. This investigation confirmed that, as we expected, the complexities of clinical work were far greater than we had ever seen in the laboratory. Fortunately, this research also demonstrated the relevance of scientific method in clinical inquiry. The present volume is a demonstration of the genius and creative spirit of many clinicians and their work that has continued in this same manner.

Clinicians who attempt to relieve the suffering of patients in pain know far more about it than the experimental researcher can learn in the laboratory. But in order to truly study the clinical phenomenon and be able to communicate it requires an integration of clinical skill and experimental method. Reading through these chapters, I am deeply gratified to see that Joseph Barber and his colleagues have brought together a fine integration of clinical and experimental methods in approaching the treatment of pain.

Clinicians who wish to know how to treat a specific kind of pain problem with hypnosis or suggestion have had few sound, comprehensive resources. With the publication of this volume, at last the clinician has access to a variety of specific methods accompanied by thoughtful case discussions. This volume is especially valuable for the attention paid to very wide-ranging pain problems.

These cases include preparation for painful medical procedures, pain associated with dentistry, burns, cancer, common pain syndromes such as headache or arthritis, the pain of children, and the pain of the elderly. In short, this book encompasses the pain problems likely to be faced by most clinicians. The reader will also find interest in the unusual and helpful discussion of the occasional failure of treatment and subsequent attempts to understand what went wrong.

In Section I, Barber creates a context for the book by introducing the theoretical position that underlies this work. While the introductory chapter on hypnotic analgesia was thorough and clear, I was particularly intrigued by the discussion of hypnotic responsiveness and clinical outcome. This complex question of the clinical relevance of hypnotic responsiveness has needed further discussion and elaboration. I am particularly pleased that this book on hypnotic treatment includes the very relevant chapter by Bonica and Loeser on the medical evaluation of the patient. Price's chapter is particularly noteworthy for its clear discussion of the importance of neurophysiological experiments pertinent to this domain, as well as for the author's very interesting theoretical contribution.

The chapters in Sections II and III explore and discuss a wide range of pain syndromes and patients in pain. Previous discussions in the literature have tended either to be limited to theoretical concerns or make clinical claims that are not borne out in practice. I particularly appreciate the carefully reasoned clinical discussions found in these chapters. It has been suggested for some time that the pain of burns can be significantly improved with hypnotic treatment. Patterson's chapter further convinces us of the value of this treatment. Finally, let me take this opportunity to remark on the special satisfaction I feel when I read the chapter on children in pain by my young colleagues, LeBaron and Zeltzer, who have contributed a fine example of clinical treatment based on empirical research. It was a particular pleasure for Josephine and me to observe the important contributions made by them over the years.

There are some clinicians whose writing suggests that their methods are so effective that all their patients are cured. Yet common experience tells us this cannot be so. In the Afterword, Barber and LeBaron give us a rare and compassionate view of the clinician's thinking when he or she is confronted with patients who do not improve with treatment. I am confident that this chapter will afford an opportunity for other clinicians to discuss their experiences of treatment complications and failure.

Experienced scientists, clinicians, and students will find much of value within these pages. I am pleased to have this opportunity to participate in this excellent book.

ERNEST R. HILGARD, PH.D.
Stanford, California
December, 1995

CONTENTS

Foreword   *Ernest R. Hilgard*   vii

Acknowledgments   xiii

Preface   xv

Contributors   xxi

I. ORIENTATION TO BASIC ISSUES

1   A Brief Introduction to Hypnotic Analgesia   3
    Joseph Barber

2   Medical Evaluation of the Patient with Pain   33
    John J. Bonica and John D. Loeser

3   Psychological Evaluation of the Patient with Pain   50
    Joseph Barber

4 Hypnotic Analgesia: Psychological and
   Neural Mechanisms   67
   Donald D. Price

5 Hypnotic Analgesia: Clinical Considerations   85
   Joseph Barber

II. SYNDROMES OF SPECIAL INTEREST

6 Cancer Pain   121
   Karen L. Syrjala and Sari Roth-Roemer

7 Headache   158
   Joseph Barber

8 Dental Pain   185
   Roseann Mulligan

9 Painful Medical Procedures   209
   Christel J. Bejenke

10 Burn Pain   267
    David R. Patterson

III. POPULATIONS OF SPECIAL INTEREST

11 Children in Pain   305
    Samuel LeBaron and Lonnie K. Zeltzer

12 Elders in Pain   341
    Samuel LeBaron and William C. Fowkes

Afterword: When We Fail   367
   Joseph Barber and Samuel LeBaron

References   383

Name Index   401

Subject Index   406

ACKNOWLEDGMENTS

Susan Barrows Munro, the editor, organized and clarified this manuscript, which it sorely needed.

I deeply appreciate the generosity of my colleagues who have contributed chapters to this volume; their expertise greatly enriches the value of this book as a reliable resource. I am especially grateful to Ernest R. Hilgard, Ph.D., whose work has profoundly influenced by own, and who has once again graciously taken up his pen to contribute the Foreword.

The following friends and colleagues read the manuscript at various stages; their candid, informed responses were extremely helpful: Cheri Adrian, Ph.D., Sheryll Daniel, Ph.D., B. C. Dashiell, M.S.W., Sureyya Dikmen, Ph.D., Judith Fleiss, Ph.D., Fred Frankel, M.B.Ch.B., D.P.M., Mark Jensen, Ph.D., Sam LeBaron, M.D., Ph.D., Leonard Lewenstein, M.D., Elaine Litton, Ph.D., John Loeser, M.D., Clorinda Margolis, Ph.D., Thurmon Mott, M.D., Michael Nash, Ph.D., Donald Price, Ph.D., Joan Romano, Ph.D., George Sargent, Ph.D., Mark Scott Smith, M.D., Mark Sullivan, M.D., Ph.D., and Bjørn Wormnes, Ph.D. I take credit for any errors and omissions.

Mary Anne Fordyce generously lent me her Macintosh PowerBook 180, which allowed me to continue writing while I was traveling, and to meet the deadline.

My collaboration with Sam LeBaron has contributed greatly to my enjoyment of this project. It's such a pleasure to work with a friend.

Mary Pepping, Ph.D., my wife, has patiently and lovingly tolerated my lengthy absorption with this project, has generously read several versions of the entire manuscript, and has contributed greatly to whatever lucidity and cohesiveness you find here.

My patients have taught me most of what I know about the treatment of pain. I am grateful for the lessons I have learned in the process of trying to relieve their suffering.

PREFACE

One day last year, toward the end of a brief course on the hypnotic treatment of pain that I was teaching in Heidelberg, Germany, a student asked "where all of this is written." The question made clear that, though I'd given these students a series of journal publications on the topic, most of what I was teaching about the practical implementation of hypnotic treatment was taken from clinical experience – my own and that of colleagues with whom I've discussed clinical cases. I realized that this material, central to an understanding of hypnotic treatment for pain, was not available in the literature.

Further consideration of the student's question focused my thinking, and I began to examine topic areas that might fill this lacuna in the literature. While my own knowledge and experience do not extend throughout the full range of pain populations and pain treatment, I have colleagues whose knowledge and experience complement mine. Happily, they were willing to contribute to this clinical guide, for which I am very grateful.

FOCUS OF THE BOOK

This book takes as its focus the treatment of patients who are suffering pain from a variety of recurring syndromes, and whose nervous systems continue to be bombarded by noxious stimulation. We will not be discussing patients who are suffering chronic benign pain syndrome (Sternbach, 1982a), for which hypnotic treatment is not usually helpful, and for which multidisciplinary pain treatment programs probably offer the best treatment.

Recurring pain syndromes represent a broad range of injuries or illnesses that create ongoing noxious stimulation – perhaps daily, as might be the case with the pain of cancer or arthritis, or perhaps less often, as might be the case with the pain of migraine or trigeminal neuralgia. Obvious examples of diseases or syndromes that create recurring pain include, in no particular order: cancer; headaches of many kinds (migraine, cluster, tension, vascular, and posttraumatic); facial pains; arthritis, both rheumatoid and osteoid; postpolio syndrome; irritable bowel syndrome; burns; various neuralgias, including postherpetic and trigeminal; temporomandibular joint (TMJ) syndrome; phantom limb; sickle cell anemia; low back pain caused by the compression of nerves, and many, many more injuries or illnesses that produce intense, sometimes intractable pain.

Except in the chapters covering painful medical procedures, burn pain, and dental pain, the term "pain patients" refers to patients who have been suffering pain over several months.[1] While effective treatment of acute pain tends to resolve the patient's suffering, persistent or recurring pain creates other changes over time, both physiologically and psychologically. Consequently, aside from whatever injury or disease continues to generate the pain, the pain is now a syndrome to be treated, in and of itself.

As you read, please keep in mind that this book explores only those approaches to pain treatment that utilize the imagination of the patient.[2] As I discuss in Chapter 1, "hypnosis" is a word laden with some unfortunate associations, and I have attempted, throughout this book about hypnosis, to avoid its use. I prefer, instead, to refer when possible to "hypnotic process," "hypnotic methods," or other alternatives. This struggle against historical baggage and toward greater precision of experience and expression sometimes yields more awkwardness than accuracy; occasionally, then, I have reverted to the use of "hypnosis." You will notice, though, that this reverting does not extend to the word "trance," which is even more heavily laden with wrong-headed connotations.

---

[1]Names and other identifying features have been altered to disguise the identities of patients whose cases are discussed in this book.

[2]Notice, also, however, that use of these methods does not preclude use of medications. Frequently, a combination of the two provides a satisfying intervention to a complex problem.

The fact that we have confined our exploration of pain treatment methods to "hypnosis and suggestion" should not be construed as a dismissal of other treatments, which, in any particular case, may be more appropriate and effective. I risk belaboring this point because of my observation that clinicians trained in hypnotic methods often develop a narrow perspective on clinical treatment, perhaps even forgetting their broader clinical training as they become fascinated by hypnotic phenomena. However, when a patient suffers from pain, hypnotic treatment is rarely the first choice that occurs to the experienced clinician. Only after adequate evaluation of the patient and the patient's symptoms can we make a well-informed treatment choice.

ORGANIZATION OF THE BOOK

Though I hope this book will be a useful reference to those who wish to be reacquainted with a particular issue or technique, my primary goal is to comprehensively explore the domain of pain treatment by hypnosis and suggestion.

Section I, which provides an orientation to this complex domain, begins with an introduction to hypnosis and suggestion and to their application in the clinical treatment of pain.

When a patient first presents with the complaint of pain, the clinician's task is to identify the nature and source of the pain. Does the pain signal the presence of injury or disease that needs timely treatment? A patient complaining of abdominal pain, for example, might be experiencing a painful inflammation of the appendix, requiring immediate surgical treatment. Beyond these emergency questions, is the pain caused by disease or injury that can be effectively treated? This question is especially pertinent, given that most long-term pain conditions represent inadequately treated disease or injury. If the cause of the pain had been adequately treated acutely, perhaps there would be no long-term pain to treat. There are also many patients, suffering from a variety of conditions, whose suffering does not seem amenable to medical treatment.

Clearly, then, the initial evaluation of a pain complaint must be primarily a medical, not a psychological, process. In Chapter 2, "Medical Evaluation of the Patient with Pain," John Bonica and John Loeser describe the principles and techniques that guide a physician through the process of examining a patient and determining the nature of the patient's pain.

Effective treatment also depends upon adequate psychological evaluation of the patient, which is explored in Chapter 3, and on realistic understanding of the nature of the treatment. To this end, in Chapter 4, Donald Price distills his considerable knowledge of the neurophysiological substrates of hypnotic analgesia, gained from long experience as an investigator of both pain and hypnotic phenomena. He offers a clinically meaningful, cogent explanation of the psychological and neural mechanisms that underlie the phenomenon of hypnotic analgesia. Understanding this model can be very helpful in formulating imaginative and effective hypnotic treatment plans.

Particular hypnotic induction techniques, treatment plans, and the process of choosing appropriate suggestions are discussed in Chapter 5. However, for the reader not yet trained in hypnotic methods, the contents of this book should not be seen as an alternative to formal clinical hypnotic training. Such training is essential to use these methods safely and effectively.

Section II explores pain syndromes most clinicians who treat pain are likely to confront. Surely one of the most painful syndromes is associated with various forms of metastatic disease. Cancer carries with it an enormous emotional loading of fear and dread, and so particular sensitivity is required in the treatment of cancer pain. Karen Syrjala and Sari Roth-Roemer bring substantial clinical experience to bear on their discussion of the management of cancer pain in Chapter 6. Since the hypnotic treatment of headache particularly interests me, and it is well-suited to hypnotic treatment, I provide an account of these methods in Chapter 7. Roseann Mulligan provides the reader with a rare exploration of the world of dental pain, and how it can be psychologically managed, in Chapter 8. A remarkable anesthesiologist who enjoys listening to patients as well as talking with them (even when they are anesthetized), Christel Bejenke brings her broad experience to us in Chapter 9. She discusses the complex problem of helping patients manage anxiety and pain, as she shares techniques for preparing patients who must undergo painful medical procedures. David Patterson has been at the forefront of the relatively modern innovation of hypnotic treatment of the pain associated with burns and their care; he discusses this challenging work in Chapter 10.

Section III concerns the clinical treatment of particular populations of patients. Samuel LeBaron once worked as a pediatric psychologist. After early research with Josephine Hilgard, his collaborations with Lonnie Zeltzer enriched the experimental and clinical literature over a number of years. They work together again in Chapter 11, as they explore the treatment of children in pain. LeBaron, now also trained as a physician, joins with Stanford colleague William Fowkes in Chapter 12 to give readers a splendid view of the humane care of those who have grown beyond childhood, through adulthood, and now suffer the particular pains associated with growing old.

Despite our best efforts, sometimes we fail – the patient leaves our care, still suffering from pain. In the Afterword, Samuel LeBaron and I take up the difficult inquiry of how such failure happens and what we might learn from it.

The treatment of pain with hypnosis and suggestion was once considered an "alternative" treatment, at best, and an example of quackery, at worst. As a consequence of the years of productive research, careful clinical approaches, and the training that has resulted from both, we now know quite a lot about how best to treat pain in this way. This volume is intended as a clinically useful guide to the practical knowledge and skill that has developed from this research tradition, organized so that you can use it as a guide your clinical judgment.

The treatment of pain is one of the most intellectually challenging and personally demanding clinical tasks we can undertake. I hope the material in this book will serve to make this task easier.

Joseph Barber, Ph.D.
Seattle, Washington

CONTRIBUTORS

Joseph Barber, Ph.D.
Associate Clinical Professor, Departments of Anesthesiology and Rehabilitation Medicine, University of Washington School of Medicine. Consultation practice in clinical psychology, Seattle. Past President and Fellow, The Society for Clinical and Experimental Hypnosis. Diplomate, American Board of Psychological Hypnosis.

Christel J. Bejenke, M.D.
Private Practice in Anesthesiology, Santa Barbara, California. Fellow, The Society for Clinical and Experimental Hypnosis.

John J. Bonica, M.D. (1917–1994)
Founding Chair, Department of Anesthesiology, University of Washington School of Medicine. Founder, The University of Washington Pain Service. Founder, The International Association for the Study of Pain.

William C. Fowkes, M.D.
Professor and Co-chief, Division of Family Medicine, Stanford University School of Medicine.

Ernest R. Hilgard, Ph.D.
Professor Emeritus, Department of Psychology, Stanford University. Co-founder, Past President and Fellow, The Society for Clinical and Experimental Hypnosis.

Samuel LeBaron, M.D., Ph.D.
Associate Professor, Division of Family Medicine, Stanford University School of Medicine. Fellow, The Society for Clinical and Experimental Hypnosis.

John D. Loeser, M.D.
Professor, Departments of Neurological Surgery and Anesthesiology and Director, Multidisciplinary Pain Center, University of Washington. President, the International Association for the Study of Pain.

Roseann Mulligan, D.D.S., M.S.
Professor and Chair, Department of Dental Medicine and Public Health, and Associate Dean, University of Southern California School of Dentistry. Fellow, The Society for Clinical and Experimental Hypnosis.

David R. Patterson, Ph.D.
Associate Professor, Department of Rehabilitation Medicine, and Chief Psychologist, Harborview Burn Treatment Unit, University of Washington School of Medicine.

Donald D. Price, Ph.D.
Professor and Director of Human Research, Department of Anesthesiology, Medical College of Virginia.

Sari Roth-Roemer, Ph.D.
Acting Assistant Professor, Department of Psychiatry and Behavioral Sciences, University of Washington School of Medicine, and Associate in Clinical Research, Fred Hutchinson Cancer Clinic, Seattle.

Karen L. Syrjala, Ph.D.
Associate Professor, Department of Psychiatry, University of Washington School of Medicine, and Associate Member, Fred Hutchinson Cancer Clinic, Seattle.

Lonnie K. Zeltzer, M.D.
Professor, Department of Pediatrics, and Chief, Pediatric Pain Clinic, UCLA School of Medicine. Fellow, The Society for Clinical and Experimental Hypnosis.

HYPNOSIS
AND SUGGESTION
IN THE
TREATMENT OF PAIN

A Clinical Guide

Section I

ORIENTATION TO BASIC ISSUES

1

A BRIEF INTRODUCTION
TO HYPNOTIC ANALGESIA

Joseph Barber

HYPNOTIC ANALGESIA is one of the most dramatic of all hypnotic phenomena. To observe the tranquil face of a patient undergoing a painful medical procedure, with no anesthetic agent except words, is a remarkable, perhaps even unbelievable, experience. To watch the power of his or her imagination bring a sigh of relief to a patient who has been suffering the pain of a disease is a welcome and satisfying sight. This book explores the ways in which we can use suggestion and hypnotic techniques to treat patients who are suffering from pain. In this chapter I will introduce you to the domain of hypnosis and to its use in the treatment of pain.

"Hypnosis" is a troublesome word. It conjures a variety of images, generated by decades of stage hypnotists, novels and films – each more strange in its portrayal of "hypnosis" than the next. It was not so long ago that a predominant image associated with hypnotic phenomena was that of a mustachioed, dark-eyed man, focusing with a fixed stare upon a vulnerable young woman, conveying by the intensity of his stern visage the plan to coerce and perhaps harm this helpless young person. Although this image of "hypnosis" is well over a hundred years old, it continues to cling strongly to our contemporary associations of hypnosis – even in the context of medical or psychological care.

Another common image is that of a fast-talking, shiny-suited stage hypnotist, compelling audience participants to perform a variety of weird and embarrassing acts – as if they had no choice but to obey his every command. The notion that hypnotic techniques are a means of controlling another person's will is a deeply rooted one. Even today, hypnotic phenomena can be a source of public entertainment. "Hypnotists" entertain by encouraging members of the audience to act in ways that are, to varying degrees, foolish and, apparently, amusing to those watching. The sight of a stage hypnotist commanding an audience member to crow like a rooster or to hallucinate the audience as undressed is, unfortunately, a common one. A witness to such antics might conclude, reasonably enough, that this can only happen if one person's will has been overcome by another's.

Is this really the case? Do hypnotic processes involve the control of a person's will? You can find interesting and pertinent discussions elsewhere about the nature of hypnosis and about the nature of social coercion (Bowers, 1983; Orne, 1959, 1962; Shor, 1959, 1962). There is ample evidence that human beings can be induced to behave in foolish, even harmful ways – without recourse to hypnotic techniques. While participants do sometimes experience hypnotic phenomena, this is not necessary for the success of the show. It is well demonstrated that the ingredients for "stage hypnosis" include many parts show business and little genuine experience of hypnosis (T. Barber, 1986).

Although some of the foolishness we witness in "stage hypnosis" may, at times, represent genuine hypnotic phenomena, much of "stage hypnosis" depends very little on actual hypnotic effects. It relies, instead, on other social psychological processes. However, no matter what the context, it is still the case that there is something unusually compelling about the true hypnotic experience – something about the involuntary quality commonly experienced by the hypnotic subject. There is also something unusual about the compelling influence of hypnotic suggestions and the feeling of being affected by them.

Although our understanding of and, consequently, our associations to hypnotic phenomena are evolving over time, it has been only very recently that the domain of hypnosis has begun to be systematically explored and demystified.

A BRIEF INTRODUCTION TO THE
DOMAIN OF HYPNOSIS

Since very lucid explorations of the domain of hypnosis already exist (Bowers, 1978; Fromm & Nash, 1992; Hilgard, 1965a, 1965b; Lynn & Rhue, 1991), it is not my purpose here to add to that literature. However, for the reader not yet familiar with this domain, the following discussion is intended to create a useful context for the clinical principles and techniques that will comprise the rest of the book.

The Nature of Hypnosis

It is one of the peculiarities of the study and application of hypnotic phenomena that the definition of hypnosis and an understanding of its basic nature remain in some dispute. In Chapter 4, Don Price explores the fundamental controversy within the domain of hypnosis: whether or not the hypnotic experience includes an alteration of state of consciousness—the state vs. nonstate issue. One's view of this issue depends, I think, less on one's interpretation of the data than on one's fundamental view of human psychology (and, I think, upon whether one has had a hypnotic experience).

The discussion of hypnosis and hypnotic treatment in this book rests on the assumption that hypnotic experience is a complex phenomenon and a function of the dynamic interaction between an alteration in state of consciousness and social psychological forces. You can find a fuller description of this assumption in Barber (1991). For a further exploration of contemporary theories of hypnosis, there are various sources, two of which may be very helpful—Fromm and Nash (1992) and Lynn and Rhue (1991).

The Definition of Hypnosis

Hypnosis is an altered condition or state of consciousness characterized by a markedly increased receptivity to suggestion, the capacity for modification of perception and memory, and the potential for systematic control of a variety of usually involuntary physiological functions (such as glandular activity, vasomotor activity, etc.). Further, the experience of hypnosis creates an unusual relationship between the person offering the suggestions and the person receiving them. Shor (1962) referred to this special relationship as "archaic involvement," by which he meant that the person being hypnotized experiences a form of transference. This involves feeling and to some extent acting as he or she did with an early caregiver. It may be, in fact, that this transferential quality of the hypnotic experience is a powerful determinant of clinical effectiveness.

All of these features of altered functioning can be useful in the control of pain, but clearly the most important are alterations of perception and physical functioning. With respect to alterations in perception, individuals who are hypnotized can experience both positive and negative hallucinations. Positive hallucination refers to the capacity to perceive something that one would not otherwise perceive. Negative hallucination refers to the capacity to not perceive something that one would otherwise perceive. Such hallucinations can occur in any sensory modality. As will be illustrated in the following text, it is the capacity to alter perception (though not necessarily to hallucinate) that allows the development of hypnotic analgesia or anesthesia. (Anesthesia refers to the absence of sensation; analgesia refers to the absence of pain, but not of sensation.)

A prevalent misunderstanding is that hypnotic methods are effective in treating pain only because they produce relaxation; in fact, some believe that a hypnotic induction is merely an exercise for creating muscular relaxation. Muscular relaxation is not a useful treatment for pain – unless, of course, the pain is specifically caused by muscle tension (McCauley, Thelan, Frank, Willard, & Callan, 1983); even then, such relaxation is likely to have only a temporary effect.

Moreover, hypnosis is not necessarily a relaxed condition (Banyai, 1980). The two phenomena can occur quite independently. Their association is largely the result of the fact that relaxation suggestions are so often a part of hypnotic inductions. Far from being merely relaxation, the hypnotic experience involves a sometimes dramatic shift in consciousness. It is this shift, apparently, that subserves the change in awareness of pain (Orne, 1976; Shor, 1965). Relaxation suggestions can play a very useful role in helping the patient to "relax" the usual level of scrutiny, critical thought, and/or "mind chatter" that may interfere with his or her wish to become absorbed in the experiences that are suggested.

Hilgard's neodissociation theory proposes that an essential feature of the cognitive process that underlies the hypnotic experience is dissociation (Hilgard, 1973, 1977). The neodissociation theory further proposes that hypnotic analgesia is a function of the disruption – the dissociation – of sensory information on its way to conscious awareness.

Utilization of the capacities made available by the dissociative shift in consciousness distinguishes hypnotic methods from cognitive strategies for pain control. Hypnotic treatment is not cognitive therapy, in the sense that a cognitively oriented clinician teaches a patient how to think differently about a problem. A patient who experiences hypnotic analgesia or anesthesia feels both the change in perception of pain (either the sensory or affective component, or both[1]) and, usually, the automaticity of that change.

[1]See page 10 for a definition and discussion of the components of pain experience.

Sometimes patients who experience hypnotic anesthesia or analgesia do not even believe they have been hypnotized (for reasons that may relate to false expectations about the experience, as well as to the automaticity of the response). Such patients may actually have no awareness of any change in their cognitions or in any other aspect of their experience except for the reduction or absence of pain.

For instance, one patient who endured an ordinarily painful dental procedure (root canal treatment of a vital tooth) with hypnosis as the sole anesthetic believed he was not hypnotized ("because I can't be hypnotized") and explained to his surprised dentist that he was not hurting because "you didn't do anything to me that would hurt." Another patient, being treated for long-term back pain, came to the first appointment insisting that he needed to be hypnotized and that he could not be. At the termination of treatment (after six appointments, during which he had shown ample evidence of his capacity to experience hypnotic phenomena), he was relieved of his pain. He left, declaring that his only disappointment was that he had never been hypnotized. Though conscious cognitive changes may be part of hypnotic treatment for pain, they are not essential to it and may be entirely unnecessary to pain relief. (The question of why a patient would seek hypnotherapy believing he or she cannot be hypnotized is an interesting psychotherapeutic issue, but is beyond the scope of this chapter.)

Suggestion

It is unfortunate that the distinction between hypnosis and suggestion has been partially lost. Often, upon hearing a suggestion made to a patient in a normal waking state, colleagues remark something like, "That's an example of hypnotic language." Of course, making a suggestion to a person in a normal waking state is not an example of hypnotic language. It is an invitation to an experience – a suggestion. Such suggestions are ubiquitous in our lives. When we say to a friend on a winter's evening, "Isn't it a little cold in this room?" we are communicating our discomfort and perhaps inviting our friend to put another log on the fire. It is not a hypnotic suggestion, and our friend's subsequent fire-building activity does not represent hypnotic behavior. (If, in a different circumstance, we were to hypnotize this friend and suggest, "After you awaken, you will notice that it's cold in here, and you will feel compelled to put another log on the fire. And you won't remember that I've told you this," it would be a hypnotic suggestion. And our friend's subsequent behavior, if it were experienced as compelling or involuntary, would be an example of a hypnotic behavior.)

If we blur the distinction between suggestion and hypnosis, thereby including all influential communication within the concept of hypnosis, the special meaning of hypnosis is lost. Advertising, for instance, is an example not of mass hypnotic techniques but of a set of suggestions that influence our waking perceptions and desires.

Clinically, suggestions occur all of the time, with all patients, by all practitioners, both witting and unwitting of the influence of a suggestion. This is not an example of clinical hypnotic intervention – except in those cases in which a patient's vulnerability is so great and suggestibility so high that the circumstance of injury or illness and the anxiety and dread that accompany it evoke an altered state of consciousness. This special circumstance, which is not uncommon in the medical setting, is discussed by Christel Bejenke in Chapter 9 and David Patterson in Chapter 10. It can occur in any setting, of course, even the psychologist's office. However, if we do not recognize that suggestions can have even greater impact in the context of a hypnotic experience, we lose the particular benefits of such interventions.

THE NATURE OF PAIN

Some pain conditions are not amenable to amelioration or cure by either medical or cognitive-behavioral treatment. Certain recurrent pain syndromes, such as migraine headache, trigeminal neuralgia, or osteoarthritis, involve ongoing noxious stimulation. When the best medical care cannot significantly reduce pain, psychological intervention is often undertaken to help the patient function while suffering with an ongoing pain problem. Although cognitive-behavioral treatments may be critical to the rehabilitation of patients, these approaches do not – and are not intended to – eliminate pain itself, but rather to modify its dysfunctional behavioral analogues.

The majority of patients who undergo comprehensive cognitive-behavioral programs at pain clinics are diagnosed with *chronic benign pain syndrome* (see below). Such patients learn to be more active, to return to work, to take less medication; generally, they are rehabilitated to good function (Fordyce, 1976; Fordyce et al., 1983).

For patients who do not have benign pain syndrome, but who suffer from recurring pain accompanying an injury or disease process, such cognitive-behavioral programs may be of some help, but the problem of suffering from pain persists. Giving such patients mood-altering analgesics (e.g., opioids), even if such medication could continue to ameliorate the pain, which it generally cannot, is clearly undesirable because of the side-effects of such medications (e.g., psychological dependence, physical dependence, tolerance, dysphoria, constipation, pruritis etc.).

For patients who suffer recurring pain what is needed is an intervention that:

1. eliminates or at least significantly reduces pain;
2. does so without untoward psychological side-effects, such as operantly increasing the level of perceived pain or reducing activity levels;
3. enhances the other treatments patients are receiving; and
4. enables patients to learn to use the treatment themselves so that they become more self-reliant and less dependent on the health-care system.

Hypnotic treatment offers such a clinical intervention. No other psychological technique is as efficacious in creating comfort out of discomfort, with none of the adverse side-effects associated with medical treatments of comparable efficacy. Using hypnotic approaches effectively in the management of a recurring pain condition, however, requires more than a simple application of a hypnotic induction followed by suggestions for analgesia.

Many patients – and some clinicians – turn to a hypnotic method with the expectation that it is a magical treatment for pain, just as many regard it as the primary or even sole treatment for compulsive problems, sexual problems, or anxiety. Such use is misguided and, consequently, fraught with disappointment. To be effective for such complex problems, hypnotic methods must be thoughtfully incorporated into a broader psychotherapeutic model (Barber, J., 1982, 1986, 1991; Edelstien, 1981). When so incorporated, these methods can be a satisfying aspect of treatment.

Types of Pain

Acute pain is the pain that results immediately from noxious stimulation (injury or medical procedure or disease process). Examples of acute pain include appendicitis, bone fracture, lumbar puncture, and meningitis.

Recurring pain results from injury or, more likely, disease, which produces repeated noxious stimulation over time. Although I am calling it "recurring pain," these conditions can sometimes involve almost constant pain. Examples of recurring pain include arthritis, cancer pain, migraine (and other headaches), phantom limb pain, thalamic pain syndrome, irritable bowel syndrome, sickle cell pain, tic doloreux and other facial pains.

Chronic benign pain syndrome is distinguished from the first two by the fact that the patient experiences pain and suffering that endure beyond the noxious stimulation produced by the injury or disease process that resulted in the original pain. Examples of chronic benign pain syndrome include low back pain and most other pain that persists even after healing has occurred.

Psychogenic pain is a variant of somatoform disorder, and is a condition rarely seen in pain clinics.

The Experience of Pain

It is worth considering here the distinction between the sensory-discriminative (or, simply, *sensory*) and the motivational-affective (or, simply, *affective*) components of pain. All pain experience involves both of these components simultaneously. This is true even though the sufferer is not likely to recognize each of them separately, unless asked to do so, just as the more complex experience of vision simultaneously includes the components of shape, texture, color, and intensity.

The sensory component of pain provides basic information to the sufferer about the location and the sensory quality of the pain. For example, it tells us if our pain is lancinating or dull, cold or burning, tingling or aching, persistent or intermittent.

The affective component of pain provides quite different information, namely, how much the pain bothers. The two components do not necessarily correspond. For instance, the birth pain of a welcome child may involve very intense sensations for the mother. However, this high intensity pain may not *bother* her in the same way as a pain of similar intensity, but of different origin, might. She *hurts*, but she may not *suffer*. At the other end of the spectrum of human experience, consider the pain of cancer. Even when the cancer pain is not intense, it can be extremely bothersome – ominous and frightening, even – and the patient suffers. This affective component is what determines the overall experience of suffering.

How much we are bothered by pain – how much we suffer – is a function of what the pain means to us – what it tells us about our life and our relationship with the world. If the pain, by virtue of its location or severity or cause, raises the question of our *existence*, as Bakan (1976) has said, then we are likely to be very bothered and to suffer substantially. If the pain does not signal danger to our good functioning or our life, then even if it is intense it need not cause us to suffer. (For a full discussion of this very important issue, see Price, 1983, 1988; Price & Harkins, 1992a.)

Measuring Clinical Pain

When asking a patient to make the distinction between the sensory and affective components of pain, I often find the following analogy is helpful: Imagine you are listening to music on the radio. How loud is the music? How loud it is – how *intense* – corresponds to the sensory component of the pain experience. How pleasant or unpleasant is the music? How *bothersome* the music is corresponds to the affective component of the pain experience.

I then ask the patient to rate the sensory component of pain, using either a visual analogue scale (VAS)[2] or an imaginary numerical scale, in which "0" corresponds to no intensity at all, and "10" to "as intense a pain *as you can imagine*" (Price, Long, & Harkins, 1994).

Next I ask the patient to rate the affective component, using the same VAS or imaginary numerical scale, now anchored by "0," which corresponds to "not bothersome at all," and "10," "being bothered as much as you can imagine."

A clear understanding of the meaning and distinction between these two components is not only important to our apprehension of the theory of pain but also crucial to effective pain treatment and to the evaluation of treatment progress, as we shall see later.

HYPNOTIC ANALGESIA

A Brief History of Hypnosis as Used for Analgesia

Although the human capacity to experience hypnotic phenomena has probably been used in pain management for as long as there has been clinical treatment of any kind (since most medical treatment prior to the twentieth century was largely dependent upon expectation and suggestion), the modern history of medical hypnosis begins with the work of the Austrian physician Franz Anton Mesmer (1734–1815). Mesmer's explanation for the phenomenon of cure by his method, "animal magnetism," was later discarded in favor of an explanation supported by the scientific evidence. This preferred theory then led to the development of the concepts of suggestion and hypnosis (Bloch, 1980).

---

[2]The visual analogue scale is a simple, reliable measure of a variety of psychological experiences, including the experience of pain. The VAS is a horizontal line (usually 10 cm long), drawn on a sheet of paper, anchored at each end by a defining word or phrase. For instance, to measure the intensity of pain, the two ends of the VAS are defined, respectively as "not intense at all" and "as intense as I can imagine." Instead of a horizontal line, a slide algometer (Price, Long, & Harkins, 1992b) may also be used.

The use of hypnotic treatment in medicine slowly developed throughout the nineteenth century, most dramatically in the operating room. Because the development of chloroform and ether anesthesia was still in the future, painless surgery was impossible. As early as 1850, James Esdaile (1957), an English surgeon working in India, successfully used hypnoanesthesia for a variety of major surgeries. This development was met with both astonished disbelief and astonished hope, since it meant an alternative to the agony of nonanesthetized surgery. Since then, there have been numerous accounts of surgery performed with hypnotic analgesia – some involving self-hypnosis (Rausch, 1980) – as the sole anesthetic. Almost simultaneous with these initial reports of hypnoanesthesia was the independent development of chemoanesthesia.

Contemporary applications of chemoanesthesia are so successful, of course, that we no longer need to promote the use of hypnotic analgesia as a surgical anesthetic. Though the initial accounts of hypnoanesthesia demonstrated its potential and promised a role in medicine, the lack of a scientific method or model for understanding hypnotic phenomena contributed to its limited application in medicine. Without a credible scientific model, hypnotic methods remained largely in the hands of entertainers and lay healers. Medical practitioners who did use these methods were limited to a few pioneers.

The Scientific Birth of Hypnosis

As the science of psychology developed in the nineteenth century, interest in hypnotic phenomena among psychological researchers naturally grew. Severely abbreviating this history, we leap forward to the middle of the twentieth century and the work of Ernest R. Hilgard. After establishing his reputation as a reliable researcher in the field of human learning, Hilgard established the Hypnosis Laboratory at Stanford University in 1957. It is fair to say that the most substantial advances in understanding hypnotic phenomena in general and in understanding hypnotic analgesia in particular resulted from investigations made under Hilgard's direction at the Stanford Hypnosis Laboratory (Hilgard, 1965a, 1965b, 1967a, 1969; Hilgard & J. R. Hilgard, 1994; Hilgard & Morgan, 1975; Hilgard, Morgan, & MacDonald, 1975; Weitzenhoffer & Hilgard, 1959). By establishing standards for evaluating hypnotic procedures and for measuring hypnotic analgesia, Hilgard and his coworkers demonstrated hypnotic phenomena could be scientifically investigated.

The results of Ernest Hilgard's research at the Stanford Hypnosis

Laboratory stimulated research by other investigators, including his wife, Josephine R. Hilgard, Kenneth Bowers, Perry London, Martin Orne, Andre Weitzenhoffer, Ronald Shor, Frederick Evans, and many others. Consequently, the clinical use of hypnotic methods in medicine, in dentistry, and in psychological treatment has become more commonplace. In recent years, hypnotic methods have been increasingly employed in the treatment of a multitude of pain problems and psychophysiologic disorders, including the acute pain of burns, surgery, and malignant disease, as well as pain syndromes as widely divergent as arthritis, sickle-cell anemia, trigeminal neuralgia, migraine headaches, peripheral neuropathies, and thalamic pain syndrome (Barber, 1990; Barber & Adrian, 1982; Crasilneck & Hall, 1985; Hilgard & Hilgard, 1994).

Neurophysiological Mechanism of Hypnosis [3]

Many attempts have been made to understand the neurophysiological mechanism by which hypnotic processes operate to produce analgesia. Although such a mechanism has yet to be identified, certain hypotheses have been tested; none has been confirmed. Goldstein and Hilgard (1975), Barber and Mayer (1977), Finer and Terenius (1981), and Spiegel and Albert (1983) each independently found that hypnotic analgesia is apparently not subserved by the endorphin system. Sternbach (1982b) was unable to confirm another possible hypothesis, that acetylcholine underlies hypnotic analgesia. Presumably the mechanism is more complex than can be understood by reference to the action of a single neurotransmitter. More recently, Kiernan, Dane, Phillips, and Price (1995) demonstrated that hypnotic analgesia involves suppression of activity in spinal sensory neurons, emphasizing the complexity of this phenomenon.

Whatever the underlying mechanism, it is clear that the rate and degree to which the hypnotic process enables the modification of pain perception and/or suffering can be quite dramatic. The hypnotic elimination of both experimental and clinical pain, whatever its nature, history, or intensity, has been fully documented (Barber, 1977; Crasilneck & Hall, 1985; Hilgard & Hilgard, 1994, J. Hilgard & LeBaron, 1984; Melzack & Wall, 1973; Olness & Gardner, 1988). Further, the elimination of pain can occur immediately in response to hypnotic suggestion.

Research over the past 30 years has demonstrated that hypnotic

[3]A more thorough discussion of this issue is taken up in Chapter 4.

subjects (including college students, children, and older adults) are able to reduce or eliminate a variety of experimentally-induced pain, including ischemic, cold-pressor, electric, and thermal (Hilgard & Hilgard, 1994). Careful investigation has established that such hypnotic pain control is superior to that achieved by other psychological means (Hilgard & Hilgard, 1994; Orne, 1980; Turner & Chapman, 1982). However, outside the laboratory setting, there has been no significant investigation of hypnotic analgesia. For example, while there is a substantial case report literature suggesting that hypnotic methods can be effective in the treatment of long-term pain conditions, there is very little rigorous research which speaks to this issue of effectiveness. The research that does exist often involves treatment that on the face of it cannot be expected to be effective (so interpreting the data is difficult). Undertaking controlled investigations that take into account the psychological complexity of these chronic conditions is a difficult but necessary task.

Hypnotic Responsiveness

Under what conditions can hypnotic methods be used to achieve elimination of suffering? Recent research has explored the conditions under which such methods are clinically useful. Neither gender nor intelligence is relevant to the development of the hypnotic state (Hilgard & Hilgard, 1994). Nor is age a factor; much work has been done with the hypnotic treatment of children in pain (Olness & Gardner, 1988; J. Hilgard & LeBaron, 1982, 1984; Kellerman, Zeltzer, Ellenberg, & Dash, 1983; Schafer, 1975; Wakeman & Kaplan, 1978; Zeltzer, Dash, & Holland, 1979).

Unfortunately, there is no substantive literature which addresses this issue in the growing population of elders. Perhaps because of this, there exist misconceptions about the inefficacy of hypnotic methods in the elderly. This belief is not supported by my own clinical experience – nor that of Samuel LeBaron and William Fowkes, as they describe in Chapter 12.

Individual differences is a domain that is interesting to explore, but one that can also be frustrating to understand when trying to investigate hypnotic processes. It is well-known that individuals differ in the degree to which they respond to hypnotic suggestion in general and to hypnotic treatment in particular (J. Hilgard, 1975; Hilgard & Hilgard, 1994). In my view, an issue that remains unresolved is the clinical relevance of measured hypnotic responsiveness (Hilgard & Hilgard, 1994). Experimental investigations of this issue have yielded differing results. Whether a particular patient can benefit from hypnotic treatment is, of course, an important clinical issue, so let us explore what we know.

The belief that only some individuals are responsive to hypnotic suggestion is based partly on the old and clearly unsupportable belief that only persons of inferior intellect or "weak personality" could be hypnotized (and on the corollary assumption that the hypnotic experience requires giving control of one's mind over to the hypnotist). More important than this old misunderstanding, however, are contemporary experimental and clinical investigations that seem to suggest that only a minority of individuals can achieve clinically significant hypnotic analgesia (Hilgard & Hilgard, 1994).

In the typical study, hypnotic responsiveness is measured by reference to an individual's performance (referred to in this chapter as "responsivity" but elsewhere, variously, as "hypnotizability" or "susceptibility") on a standardized test, such as the Stanford Hypnotic Susceptibility Scale (Weitzenhoffer & Hilgard, 1959), the Harvard Group Scale of Hypnotic Susceptibility (Shor & E. Orne, 1962), or the Hypnotic Induction Profile (H. Spiegel, 1974). Such tests create a circumstance in which an individual has the opportunity to respond to a hypnotic induction and to several suggestions for hypnotic behaviors. The number of behaviors the individual demonstrates then becomes the numeric measure of hypnotic responsiveness.

Hilgard and Morgan (1975) demonstrated that the correlation between such measures and an individual's ability hypnotically to reduce experimental pain is significant ($r = .50$). However, Hilgard and Morgan also reported that 44% of low-susceptible individuals were able to reduce their pain by 10% or more and concluded:

> This means that the relation between pain reduction and hypnotic responsiveness is probabilistic, with a greater probability of successful pain reduction for those highly responsive to hypnotic suggestions. The data do not mean that those unresponsive to hypnotic suggestion as measured by the scales, have no possibility of help through suggestion. (Hilgard & Hilgard, 1994, p. 68)

Research Reports vs. Clinical Reports

Just as it is clear that there is a wide range of hypnotic responsiveness among individuals, so there is also evidence that another significant variable in determining clinical effectiveness of hypnotic treatment is the clinician's particular approach to the patient (Alman & Carney,

1981; Barber, 1977, 1980, 1982, 1991; Fricton & Roth, 1985; Gfeller, Lynn, & Pribble, 1987; Price & Barber, 1987). We can infer from these reports that an approach based on suggestions offered in the context of a meaningful relationship is more likely to be successful with individuals performing poorly on tests of responsivity than would be predicted simply on the basis of these tests.

Although such an approach has been characterized in the past as "indirect" as distinct from "direct" (Alman & Carney, 1981; Barber, 1982; Fricton & Roth, 1985), such a characterization is simplistic and misleading. It misses the fundamental difference between suggestions communicated in a standard way, e.g., through a test of responsivity – whether or not the suggestions are formulated in a direct or an indirect manner – and those communicated in a nonstandard but more individualized way (Price & Barber, 1987). Moreover, such a characterization neglects the crucial importance of the relationship that develops between clinician and patient (or even between experimenter and subject).[4]

One explanation for the disparity in research findings, at least with respect to the analgesic capacity of those individuals with low responsivity to hypnotic suggestion, might be that those with high responsivity are better able to reduce the sensory-discriminative component of pain, while those with low responsivity are able to reduce the motivational-affective component (Price & Barber, 1987). If these two components are not independently measured, it is entirely possible that some patients' measures reflect the sensory component, while others' reflect the affective component. The disparate findings might be explained by this lack of precision in pain measurement.

Price and Barber (1987) sought to assess this possibility. In their experiment, thermally induced pain was measured independently on both the sensory-discriminative and the affective-motivational dimensions, using a visual analogue scale (from Price, 1983). Highly responsive subjects were better able to reduce the sensory component of pain. However, subjects with low hypnotic responsivity were as able to reduce the affective component of pain as were subjects with high hypnotic responsivity. This finding confirms reports that hypnotic responsiveness predicts the capacity to hypnotically reduce pain perception. However, this finding also suggests that hypnotic responsiveness is not related to the capacity to reduce suffering (i.e., the affective-motivational component of pain).

[4]For a fuller discussion of this theoretical issue, see Barber, 1991. See also Diamond, 1984, and Gfeller, Lynn, and Pribble, 1987, for a discussion of the relationship as a determiner of the hypnotic process.

Another unresolved issue is that of the experimentally verifiable effects of hypnotic suggestion compared with clinical reports of effectiveness. Most of the clinical literature shows hypnotic suggestion to be more effective as an analgesic (and more frequently so) than experimental reports would predict (Crasilneck & Hall, 1985; Haley, 1967; Hilgard & Hilgard, 1994). Part of the explanation for this difference lies in the obvious differences in motivation of the subjects and patients. Experimental subjects are significantly less motivated to experience a hypnotic effect than are clinical patients who are seeking relief from suffering. There are also significant differences in the behavior (and motivation) of experimenters and clinicians. Experimental protocols usually require rigid adherence to a well-operationalized, standardized induction and set of suggestions. Rarely is the purpose of an experiment the search for optimum hypnotic effect. However, that is precisely what is involved in the clinical situation. Effective clinical use of hypnotic suggestion requires an individualized approach. Rarely is a standardized set of procedures followed, and the clinician, normally focused only on doing what is effective, may vary or repeat procedures until success is obtained. While this may lead to successful clinical outcomes, it is usually impossible to assess the causal link between treatment and results.

In this regard, Orne (1980) suggests that effects of the context of the situation, both direct and indirect, must account for at least part of what would otherwise be taken to be the hypnotic effect. For instance, the meaning of the clinician's attention is very different from that of the experimenter's. As Diamond (1984) suggests, the relationship between the clinician and patient is a powerful determiner of the hypnotic effect (or any clinical effect). The relationship between an experimenter and a subject is significantly less personal (sometimes the hypnotic induction is even conveyed by a tape recorder) than the well-developed, intimate and more potent relationship of a concerned clinician and a suffering patient. Whatever the explanation for the disparity of reported hypnotic effect between experimental and clinical contexts, it is clear that clinical success with hypnotic suggestion requires innovative, personalized, clinically sophisticated procedures. It is difficult to compare such procedures with experimental procedures.

It is essential that clinical research be done if we are to understand the nature of hypnotic treatment and to be honest in the interventions we offer to patients. The questions we have before us are not particularly difficult ones and they do not require especially sophisticated research designs. If we do not support the thorough scientific exploration of hypnotic treatments, I think we risk eventual dismissal of this domain by reasonable people. The pitfalls I have described above can all be avoided by careful attention to detail and by our interest in placing our clinical interventions on the record. The very least we can do is to simply make careful records of the patients we see, of the interventions we make, and of the results we find. This information would be of substantial advantage to our understanding of hypnotic processes and to our effective utilization of them for the benefit of our patients.

The Locksmith Metaphor

The variation in responsiveness, even in the same individual on different occasions, has led me to a hypothesis that I call the "locksmith metaphor." This hypothesis assumes that most individuals are able to experience hypnotic phenomena, at least to some degree, given the appropriate circumstances, and that psychological defensiveness (both healthy and neurotic) largely accounts for lack of observed responsiveness on some occasions. Moreover, the hypothesis supposes that there may be ways around an individual's defensiveness in any given circumstance. The key to "unlocking" the individual's defenses depends on a high degree of sensitivity and flexibility on the part of the clinician.

We know that in clinical circumstances the sincerity of our compassion, as well as our willingness to utilize the patient's language and style of communication in conveying our compassion, is important in the formation of a trusting alliance that supports the therapeutic work. So it is also in the context of hypnotic treatment. Our capacity for empathy, for intuiting what the patient needs in order to be open to an altered state of consciousness, is primary in discovering the appropriate hypnotic approach.

We may perceive that one patient needs a paternal, even authoritarian approach in order to feel properly supported, or that another patient needs a sense of equality with us. We need to sense what will enable the patient to relinquish "the cares of the day," as Hilgard once described the phenomenon, and to become profoundly absorbed in responding to our suggestions. If we are sufficiently fortunate to accurately sense what the patient needs, and if we gracefully convey to the patient those qualities that will satisfy those needs, then we may enable the patient to respond to hypnotic suggestions that would otherwise be defended against. A more complete treatment of the locksmith metaphor is found in Barber (1991).

Clinical Screening for
Hypnotic Responsiveness

Though the issue of what best predicts hypnotic responsiveness is still far from resolved, I think there are very good reasons not to use responsivity tests to "screen" patients for potential hypnotic treatment. Even if hypnotic responsiveness is a good predictor of *hypnotic* response to suggestion, it does not predict *clinical* response to the therapeutic context in which the suggestions are given. Recall that in the Price and Barber experiment, subjects showing low responsivity were quite able to reduce suffering. The evidence suggests that such assessment does not measure actual capacity for response to optimal clinical treatment. Also, because of the potentially discouraging effects of such tests (for both clinician and patient),[5] I would argue that such screening should be done only under very carefully considered circumstances. Finally, the decidedly unclinical stance required when administering most such tests is a further reason not to use them in the psychotherapeutic context. (The Hypnotic Induction Profile [H. Spiegel, 1974] is a notable exception in this regard.) In order to establish a reliable measure of hypnotic responsiveness, it is necessary to administer the test more than once. Commonly, the first score an individual obtains will be lower than that obtained on a second or third administration. This phenomenon, called "plateau hypnotizability," may reflect the development of comfort with the hypnotist and with the altered state experience. For the clinician, this necessity for multiple administrations involves a substantial amount of time and effort simply to obtain an idea of the patient's *likely* response to hypnotic suggestions.

If the patient obtains a low score, how does this guide the clinician in treatment? Even low responders sometimes benefit from hypnotic treatment, so denying such treatment on the basis of a low score is not justified. The argument that this benefit is from nonspecific aspects of treatment is relevant, but it is also relevant when the patient is highly responsive.[6]

It has been suggested, on the other hand, that a responsiveness score may be clinically useful because it indicates a particular ap-

---

[5]Note the case of Francisco, in Chapter 5.

[6]Remember that, because responsivity scales offer only probabilistic information, no scale can accurately predict a particular person's responsiveness to hypnotic suggestion.

proach to a clinician. For example, a low score may suggest that the clinician emphasize the reduction of suffering, as opposed to the reduction of intensity (Nash, 1995).

An exception to my disinclination toward measures of hypnotic responsivity in my own clinical practice is the use of Tellegen and Atkinson's (1974) Tellegen Absorption Scale (TAS). The TAS is a brief and clinically unobtrusive means of obtaining an *impression* of a patient's openness to the experiences of altered states of consciousness. While the TAS does not permit *prediction* of hypnotic responsiveness, it does provide a clinician with a sense of how readily a patient may respond to suggestions.

CLINICAL USE OF HYPNOTIC PHENOMENA IN PAIN MANAGEMENT

Effectively using hypnotic methods in the treatment of a pain condition requires individualizing the hypnotic treatment and integrating that treatment into the larger psychotherapeutic intervention. (This can be said of any clinical treatment, of course, but perhaps bears mentioning because of common misconceptions about the "standardized" use of hypnotic procedures.) This means that the first step is to assess the patient's personal style, expectations, and attitudes toward hypnotic treatment, and to choose hypnotic induction procedures and suggestions for pain relief accordingly. In general, a patient's pain can be reduced by hypnotic means. (Hypnotic suggestion is generally less effective in the treatment of psychogenic pain.) How hypnotic suggestion is used for such treatment, however, is a very complicated issue and requires assessment of the likely consequences of pain reduction for the patient.

Criteria for Choosing Hypnotic Treatment

In my clinical practice, I would use hypnotic methods to initiate pain reduction if the following criteria were met:

1. *The patient will not be harmed by this treatment.* Will the patient experience the use of hypnotic treatment as permission for risking harm in some way? Some relatively disturbed patients, for instance, might use the opportunity to ignore pain that signals bodily harm and might thereby injure themselves further.

Such patients might also neglect to comply with necessary medication regimen. In extreme cases, such patients might behave in a "trance-like" manner in inappropriate circumstances (e.g., while crossing the street).

In general, if a patient tends to have more than the usual side effects from medication or has a history of developing unexpected complications from medical procedures, it is wise to defer the use of hypnotic treatment.

2. *The patient will be able to accommodate the emotional intimacy often associated with hypnotic treatment.* If the patient is not likely to feel comfortable with such intimacy, problems of trust may arise. It is important that the clinician will be able to help the patient if this particular difficulty should arise.

3. *The patient's condition will be improved.* Aside from doing no harm, will we help? Is the patient likely to experience pain reduction without significant loss (of self-esteem, compensation, other secondary gains, stability of the family system, etc.)? If such pain reduction is likely to facilitate such loss, the use of hypnotic treatment ought to be deferred until treatment addresses the patient's other needs.

4. *The patient is willing to take responsibility for initiating his or her own treatment.* Use of hypnotic methods for pain reduction requires significant effort on the part of the patient, often requiring frequent and repeated use of self-hypnosis, perhaps far into the future. Inability to initiate and maintain such effort renders the effective use of hypnotic treatment unlikely.

Patients' Concerns about Hypnotic Treatment

Our patients and our colleagues – and ourselves – have all been influenced by the popular cultural characterizations of hypnosis. We need to acknowledge the effect of such influence if we are to successfully evolve through it and if we are to adequately understand patients' attitudes about hypnotic treatment. Patients are frequently wary, sometimes even quite afraid, of the prospect of hypnotic treatment. They fear the possibility of being made to do something embarrassing, as they have seen or heard about from others. Perhaps they fear behaving at odds with their usual sense of themselves. In the context of the ethical use of hypnotic methods this fear is groundless. But how is a patient to know this? As odd as it sounds, I have often been asked by a patient when we discussed the possibility of hypnotic treatment if he or she would need to act like a chicken. The pervasiveness of this image, apparently gained from years of stage hypnosis, is an important reminder of the potential disparity between a patient's expectations and our own.

A more realistic fear of the patient, however, is that he or she will experience emotions that are ordinarily kept suppressed or repressed. In my experience this is particularly so when a patient is unfamiliar and uncomfortable with his or her own emotions and lives with the habit of suppressing or repressing them. When a patient expresses wariness about hypnotic treatment, we need to respectfully consider this perhaps unexpressed fear of emotional release.

There are many reasons why people feel a hesitation about being hypnotized including some of the following:

1. Concern about giving up control and responsibility for his or her experience or actions. Individuals who have a healthy interest in exerting control and direction over their own lives express concern that being hypnotized will render them out of control of their feelings and their behavior. When need for control is a preoccupying theme in the person's life, the concern about being hypnotized becomes greatly enlarged.
2. Concern about submitting to authority. People sometimes express concern that being hypnotized will place them under the authority of another person.
3. Concern about the competence of the clinician. Who is this clinician? What training does she have? How responsible is he? Can I trust her to take adequate care of me when I am in this vulnerable condition? Does he know what he is doing?[7]

These concerns can usually be effectively managed by respectfully acknowledging them, openly discussing the issue from the patient's point of view, providing useful information about hypnotic phenomena and how we use them in the clinical context, and remaining clear about the relative importance of hypnotic methods in this particular patient's case. Though hypnotic interventions often greatly facilitate effective treatment, they are rarely indispensable. In the case of a

---

[7]To the extent that we harbor misconceptions about hypnotic processes, we may contribute to this concern by behaving in clumsy, insensitive, or incompetent ways.

patient whose concerns about hypnotic treatment cannot be readily managed, we should be prepared to consider other treatment methods.

Describing Hypnotic Treatment to the Patient

Because the word "hypnosis" may have such frightening and unrealistic connotations and because it does not ordinarily convey an accurate idea of what the patient is likely to experience in the clinical context, it is generally helpful to discuss the treatment in more operational terms. This obviates the use of the word "hypnosis" altogether. There are accurate ways of describing the treatment without using the word "hypnosis." The intention is not to deceive or obfuscate but, rather, to communicate clearly and to avoid a misunderstanding. Therefore, if the patient uses the word "hypnosis" or raises a question about "hypnosis" we need to be honest and clear, and we may need to use the word "hypnosis" and explain what we mean by it. If a patient has had prior experience with hypnotic treatment – especially if the experience was a pleasing or satisfying one – we can utilize this experience.

Here is an example of what we might say to introduce the topic of hypnotic treatment:

"You probably know that the relationship between mind and body is a powerful one. I can show you how to use the power of your imagination, for instance, to help you feel better."

Or, "Let's use your ability to fantasize, now, to help you feel better."

Or, "Mental imagery can be very helpful in retraining your nervous system so that the nerves that carry the useless information about your pain will do so less and less in the future."

Or, "Your ability to become deeply absorbed by your imagination can be really helpful now. May I ask you to close your eyes right now, take a very deep breath, and begin to notice how really relaxed your mind can become?"

In each example, the guiding principle is: Convey to the patient that there is a means – a technique, a mental capacity, a clinical tool, etc. – which can naturally be used for his or her benefit. By communicating in this way we may diminish the unrealistic concerns about the patient's losing control over his or her mind. We should be mindful, though, that merely asking a patient to close his or her eyes – and, implicitly, to be "open" to one's imagination – can provoke anxiety (Reyher & Smeltzer, 1968). Also, using this approach requires that the hypnotic techniques we use are consistent with the language we have used to introduce them.

Dangers and Contraindications in the
Use of Hypnotic Methods

... a medicament is not really potent unless it is able to be dangerous on occasions; and it is very difficult to think of any method of treatment which would be efficacious although it could never by any possibility do harm. (Pierre Janet, 1860, in Nahum, 1965, p. 221)

Any clinical technique that has the capacity to help must also have the capacity to harm. Among clinicians who use hypnotic methods, there is a lot of claptrap to the effect that these methods can only help and can do no harm. There is no evidence to support this naive claim. On the contrary, there is evidence that hypnotic interventions can be harmful to patients, depending upon their use. In Chapter 6, Karen Syrjala and Sari Roth-Roemer describe a case in which misguided use of hypnotic interventions led to sad consequences. I have explored this issue at some length elsewhere (Barber, 1996), and there is no need to do so here, except to make these brief remarks.

While the experience of being hypnotized per se is probably harmless, how that experience is used determines its beneficial or harmful effects. In principle, the hypnotic methods can be harmful when:

1. The clinician's motives are not in the patient's best interest. The clinician may or may not be aware of this.
2. The clinician does not have an adequate understanding of the patient's needs and proceeds with treatment anyway.
3. The patient's capacity for coping with deep absorption in fantasy, or with intense contact with the clinician, is insufficient.

The best insurance against harmful hypnotic treatment is appropriate clinical training. This training includes not only technical skill in making hypnotic interventions, but also thorough knowledge of psychological phenomena, including psychopathology, that the clinician may encounter. Equally important, however, this training should include experiences of personal growth, such that the clinician's own unresolved psychological issues have become known to him or her; moreover, the clinician should be open to future opportunities for such personal development.

HYPNOTIC INDUCTION

Hypnotic treatment begins with the "hypnotic induction." This is a process that involves the communication of suggestions not for clinical treatment per se but for the change in state of consciousness, leading from ordinary wakefulness to the hypnotic state that supports the acceptance of clinical suggestions. A hypnotic induction provides both information and time (to respond to the information) to the patient about how to begin the alteration in experience. (The induction also provides time for the clinician, since he or she also begins to shift to a quieter, calmer demeanor.) Time is necessary for the neurophysiological and psychological changes that both create and are created by the hypnotic experience.

To illustrate this point, I think it is useful to see the parallel in the process of going to sleep (at the risk of creating the mistaken impression that the hypnotic condition is like physiological sleep). We know that the length of time it takes an individual to fall asleep is highly idiosyncratic—some people characteristically fall asleep very quickly and easily, while others do so much more slowly, perhaps with interruptions in the process. Even in an individual who characteristically falls asleep quickly circumstances can impede the process: for example, if he is not really sleepy, if he does not feel sufficiently secure, or if the environmental events (e.g., loud noises) interrupt. In the context of developing a hypnotic state, many variables interact to facilitate or impede the process, such as the individual's motivation or sense of need, the degree to which the individual feels safe, and environmental factors. It is only by observing the patient's responses to suggestion, and by talking with the patient about his or her experience, that we can determine how effective the induction is and how much longer we need to continue it.

Steps of the Induction Process

Simply stated, the induction of a hypnotic experience involves the following steps, and they occur approximately in this order:

1. *Eliciting the patient's attention, interest, and cooperation.* This may be accomplished by saying something like, "Now we will begin to use your capacity for imagination." At this stage there is also an implicit agreement on the patient's part to respond to the clinician's suggestions—at least to some extent.
2. *Reducing the patient's range of attention.* This may be accomplished by suggesting, for example, "You can pay attention to the sound of my voice, and you can notice that nothing else really matters right now, as I continue to speak to you."
3. *Suggesting an increasingly narrow focus of attention, and direct-*

ing that attention inward. For example, you may suggest, "Feel each breath, as you inhale, and as you exhale notice the feeling of deep relaxation. Feel each breath, feel the relaxation, and notice that nothing else matters right now."

4. *Suggesting dissociation.* In my view, this is the crucial step. It distinguishes the experience from normal wakefulness and supports the unusual and dramatic capacities associated with hypnotic processes. It is somewhat misleading to separate this stage from the others, insofar as this phenomenon tends to occur naturally as a function of the other stages. I emphasize this aspect of the experience, though, because of its clinical importance. I would even go so far as to suggest that much of what people interpret as the lack of efficacy of hypnotic intervention is a result of the failure to actually develop the dissociative processes inherent in the hypnotic experience. I believe that it is not reasonable to expect hypnotic effects in the absence of dissociative processes.

You might facilitate dissociation by saying, "You can hear the sound of my voice without really listening to my words." Or, "You are aware of my voice, and yet you can allow yourself to feel more and more absorbed in [whatever experience has already been suggested – relaxing in a pleasant place, for example] and less and less aware of anything else."

Moving beyond the actual induction involves the following elements:

1. *Offering therapeutic suggestions.* Once the patient has begun to experience the fullness of dissociation, suggestions can be offered for whatever therapeutic change is desired. If the goal is analgesia, for example: "You notice more and more comfort with each passing moment. The sensations that were bothering you seem to be farther and farther away." Posthypnotic suggestions may also be offered at this stage: "Whenever you take a deep breath [or whatever cue you determine to be appropriate], you might notice how curiously comfortable you feel, with nothing to bother you, and nothing to disturb you."

2. *Providing suggestions to end the experience.* Normally, you will offer suggestions for feeling well, for being alert, and so on: "As your eyes open, you notice how alert and how energized you are, almost as if you've just awakened from a very refreshing nap."

Duration of Induction

How much time should a hypnotic induction take? My glib answer would parallel that of the professor in answer to the student's query about how long the essay needs to be: as long as is necessary, and no longer. But let us explore this issue further.

I do not know if anyone has measured the difference in induction length between experimental and clinical settings, but my experience leads me to believe that clinical inductions tend to be both longer and shorter — depending on the patient's needs. Does an induction need to be of a particular length? What is the function of an induction? Is it only to communicate, to convey suggestions?

You will notice that the examples of hypnotic inductions offered in this book tend to be longer than inductions you will find in many textbooks on hypnosis. The extended length of these inductions, by psychologists and physicians alike, reflects our belief that, aside from being sufficiently long to contain the desired suggestions, the induction needs also to contain sufficient time to allow the alteration in consciousness that distinguishes the hypnotic experience from other experiences.

Since the amount of time needed for such alteration varies among individuals and within the same individual in different contexts, we need to observe the alteration as carefully as possible. Other things being equal, for instance, the most evident disadvantage of using a tape recording to convey the induction is that the recorded suggestions cannot take into account the patient's responsiveness. The tape-recorded suggestions continue independently of when or how the patient responds.

A Brief Word About Children and Hypnosis

Because Samuel LeBaron and Lonnie Zeltzer discuss the induction of the hypnotic experience in children, I will not take this space for such a discussion. It is worth mentioning, however, in this exploration of hypnotic inductions, that children often respond very rapidly to both hypnotic and nonhypnotic suggestion — usually requiring very little or no actual induction.

Observing the Patient's Responses

When you intend to hypnotize a patient, watch carefully to observe whether or not the patient responds to each suggestion. Since most responses are relatively invisible, taking place only within the patient's imagination, it is helpful to include suggestions for which the response can be observed. For example, the initial suggestions made to a patient about how to sit comfortably provide an important opportunity to observe the patient's responsiveness. While this responsiveness is not hypnotic, it provides information about how initially responsive the patient is to your suggestions.

Next, we can suggest that the patient close his or her eyes. I tend to do this very simply and directly, since if there is to be initial resistance it might well be about closing the eyes. Rather than taking time to create a compelling experience of eye closure, I simply ask the patient to close his or her eyes. If the patient responds, I continue. However, if, as sometimes happens, the patient remains staring, wide-eyed, I comment on this fact. I might say, "I asked you to close your eyes, but I notice that you haven't. Is it OK if you close your eyes now?" The patient's response to this query might be very informative. For example, he or she might say, "No, I feel worried about closing my eyes." This provides an opportunity for us to discuss discomfort about the process in general (since eye closure is probably the focus but not the actual cause of the discomfort). This resulting conversation may be more important than any hypnotic effect I was hoping to obtain. It may be an important opportunity to discuss the patient's fears about the hypnotic experience, or about losing control, or about trusting me – or a variety of other concerns.

The Usefulness of Motor Responses

In addition to evaluating a patient's ongoing responses to my suggestions, I often find it helpful to elicit hypnotic phenomena that may have no direct clinical benefit but serve as opportunities to evaluate responsiveness. Then I observe the response and perhaps inquire about the experience. For example, catalepsy is a hypnotic phenomenon which can usually be easily elicited and incorporated within the therapeutic relationship (so that the experience does not seem odd or inappropriate). It can be monitored for the purpose of understanding the extent to which the patient is experiencing hypnotic processes – in contrast to merely complying with the therapist's request.

Teaching the Patient How to Talk

We talk with the patient during the hypnotic induction to better understand his or her experience. Because most patients will probably not have had previous experience in talking while hypnotized, it may be helpful to provide suggestions to simultaneously inform and guide the patient through the process:

"While you continue to remain comfortable and relaxed, and to remain deeply absorbed in [whatever experience has been occurring], I also want you to allow the muscles of your voice – the muscles of your breathing, of your larynx, of your jaw, of your tongue, and of your lips – to become independent and active, so that you can talk to me, even while you remain deeply absorbed."

You can now ask the patient what he or she is experiencing and determine the fullness and degree of reality of the experience – in short, the extent to which the experience is *hypnotic*. For example, if you have suggested arm catalepsy and the patient's arm seems cataleptic (the classic "waxy flexibility" – when you attempt to move the patient's arm, it feels as though it is waxen and able to be easily moved – as opposed to being voluntarily held in the air), you can ask the patient, "What do you notice about your arm?" If the patient's remarks suggest that he or she is primarily aware of holding the arm voluntarily, so as to comply with your suggestions, this is probably not a hypnotic phenomenon. If, however, the patient's remarks suggest that he or she is primarily aware of the lightness of the arm, of the lack of awareness of the arm, of the involuntariness of the experience, this is probably a hypnotic phenomenon. Or suppose you have suggested that the patient imagine being in a particular place – a sun-filled meadow, for instance. You can ask the patient, "What are you aware of?" If the patient talks about the meadow and indicates that this experience feels "real" as opposed to imagined, this suggests the experience is a hypnotic one.

Of course, these determinations are not only subjective with respect to the patient, but also, unfortunately, subject to our own needs and expectations. It is helpful if we can remain open to the possibility that the patient will not respond (despite our best efforts) and that this eventuality is interesting in itself. If we so deeply need a patient to respond to our hypnotic methods, our judgment about the reality of the experience to the patient may become impaired. If this is the case, we are probably less helpful and more frustrated (and perhaps frustrating to the patient).

SAMPLE INDUCTION

This induction should be read as an *example*, not as a template. It reflects my own personal style, which may not be the most effective one for you. This is a somewhat abbreviated induction: many repetitions have been omitted.

1. *Eliciting the patient's attention, interest, and cooperation.*

Now you might feel ready to begin to use some of the talents we've been discussing, in order to retrain your nervous system. Why not just rest back in your chair, and allow your body to be as comfortable as you know how. That's right. . . .

2. *Reducing the patient's range of attention.*

Close your eyes, and take a very deep, relaxing breath, and . . . hold it . . . hold it . . . and now, let it all the way out, as you sink deeper and deeper into the chair.

3. *Suggesting an increasingly narrow focus of attention, and directing that attention inward.*

As you continue to allow yourself to breathe comfortably and restfully, as you notice the pleasant heaviness that can become more and more a part of your awareness . . . as you notice these things, I will be talking to you, and you can notice how easily you hear the sound of my voice, without having to listen. And you can understand what I say to you without any particular effort.

And all the while, the sounds around you . . . all the sounds you can hear . . . can become more and more a part . . . of your experience of comfort and well-being . . . with nothing to bother you . . . and nothing to disturb you.[8] Just notice your breathing, pay attention to your breathing, and notice how easily you can discover that nothing else matters . . . nothing at all . . . just your comfort.

4. *Suggesting dissociation.*

As you allow yourself to become more and more absorbed by the comfort of your breathing, you can also notice that it is more and more interesting to continue . . . to continue to feel each

[8]If the patient is experiencing pain during the induction, of course, this induction is not appropriate, and should be replaced by one that incorporates the experience of pain. Such an induction is described in Chapter 5.

breath . . . as you breathe in, and as you breathe out. It's almost as if your breathing, and your awareness of your breathing, is all that matters. As if there really *is* nothing else at all . . . just your breathing, and your comfort.

You might also have begun to notice the interesting tingling sensations in the tips of your fingers. A pleasant, glowing sensation . . . and this interesting sensation can radiate up your fingertips, and into your hands . . . almost all of the way up into your wrists. A tingling sensation that seems to remind you of how deeply absorbed you can be . . . how deeply comfortable you can be.

You might notice a similar tingling sensation around your mouth and lips . . . and perhaps, too, in your lower back. You might even notice this pleasant tingling sensation in the soles of your feet. You might begin to feel almost as if you are *glowing* with energy. Glowing, tingling, breathing, all in a comforting rhythm. Allowing the sound of my voice to continue to be a part of your comfort.

Assuming the patient is now absorbed in a hypnotic experience, the following steps can occur:

5. *Offering therapeutic suggestions*:[9]

As you continue to feel more and more absorbed by the sensations of your breathing, I'm going to talk to that part of you that controls the sensations in your nerves. You can listen to me, or you can just float so comfortably, knowing that your nervous system is hearing everything that I'm saying to you.

It is so curious, and so very interesting . . . that you have the capacity to increase or decrease the sensations throughout your body. And I imagine you will feel very interested in the *way* that you decrease the sensations in just that one part of your face. You won't really know how you do it . . . at least, at first. You can be curious, you can be surprised . . . and you can simply notice that, whenever those electrical feelings begin to shoot down your face . . . for some reason, they will just stop. Almost like a sneeze that never quite happens.

The first few times, you'll have the sense that a pain is coming,

[9]The following is an example taken from a case of trigeminal neuralgia, a condition producing excruciating neuropathic pain.

but, somehow . . . you won't know how, at first . . . somehow, the sensation just seems to stop, almost before it can quite get started. Almost as if your nervous system is beginning, already, to retrain those nerves to no longer send those awful, painful messages across your face.

And, sometime later today . . . I don't really know when that will be . . . maybe ten minutes before five this afternoon . . . or maybe it will more likely be ten minutes *after* five this afternoon . . . but I really don't know when it will be . . . that you will suddenly notice . . . how really well you are feeling . . . but then, again, I don't really know. It may not be so much the time on the clock that's important here. It may be that what you are doing at that time is what is important.

Maybe you will be lifting a cup to your lips. Or, I don't know . . . maybe you'll be turning the pages of a book . . . I really can't know what you'll be doing, when you will suddenly . . . turn your head very slightly, almost as if you're trying to catch sight of something just out of your awareness . . . and, at the same time, notice how much better you're feeling than you ordinarily expect you will feel.

And you won't know how . . . you won't know why, really. You'll just know how you feel. *Better . . . just better.*

And tomorrow morning, after you awaken, you can feel really surprised at how well you've slept, and how really rested you feel . . . with nothing to bother you, and nothing to disturb you.

6. *Providing suggestions to end the experience.*

So, in a moment, when I ask you to, you can notice how really easily you find yourself breathing just a bit differently. As if each breath begins to feel more and more refreshing, more and more energizing. And, then, as your eyes open, you'll notice how really clear and awake you feel . . . and, maybe, how ready you are to feel surprised.

That's right, really deep breaths . . . more and more refreshed. Notice, now, as your eyes open, how alert . . . how refreshed you are. Almost as if you've just had a very restful nap.

2

MEDICAL EVALUATION OF
THE PATIENT WITH PAIN

John J. Bonica
John D. Loeser

UNDERSTANDING THE underlying medical cause of the patient's pain is essential to both an adequate appreciation of the patient's complaint, as well as the patient's suffering and pain behavior, and the development of a realistic and effective treatment plan.

An individual suffering from pain first presents to a physician or, if oral pain is involved, a dentist. The first goal of the clinician is to determine the cause of the pain. The protection of the patient's health and well-being is at stake. Sometimes a serious condition such as appendicitis may present with pain; then it is the condition creating the pain, not the pain itself, that requires treatment. The importance of the initial medical evaluation cannot be overemphasized.

In this chapter, we discuss the general principles of the medical evaluation of patients with pain, with emphasis on patients with complex pain problems. In the context of the initial medical evaluation in the physician's office, we cover:

1. objectives of the medical evaluation
2. general method of approach
3. characteristics of the pain

4. eliciting a detailed history
5. performing a comprehensive physical examination

The medical evaluation of patients with complex pain problems is time-consuming and often psychologically and physically taxing to both the physician and the patient. In addition to the medical evaluation, a psychological evaluation, preferably by a clinical psychologist, is essential for establishing the diagnosis and developing the most therapeutically beneficial strategy. This is described in detail in Chapter 3. These tasks are most efficiently achieved within the setting of a multidisciplinary or interdisciplinary pain program, but are often accomplished in a variety of clinic or private office settings.

OBJECTIVES OF THE MEDICAL EVALUATION

The medical evaluation of the patient's pain involves making a correct diagnosis that permits the development of the most appropriate therapeutic strategies. An initial objective is the determination of whether the patient is suffering from acute, recurring, or chronic pain, and if the pain is recurring, whether it is a result of cancer or of some other, nonmalignant disease process. Management strategies for acute pain and for cancer or other recurring pain are dramatically different from those used for nonmalignant chronic pain. It is also important to determine if a major injury or disease process was actually overlooked or arose during the course of the patient's pain complaint, which might have been inappropriately rated as hypochondriasis or somatoform disorder.

An important objective of the evaluation and treatment process is to avoid fragmentation of care. Often, patients with chronic pain have already had multiple contacts with health-care systems through various, often simultaneous, physician visits. It is sometimes erroneously assumed that the patient has been and is receiving coordinated and monitored comprehensive care, complete physical examination, coordinated medication management, and the necessary psychological assessment and treatment. This is often not the case, unfortunately, not only among pain patients but also among patients with other disorders who receive fragmented care from multiple physicians. The serious consequences of such a mistaken assumption are explored in the case of Fritz in Chapter 3.

Another important objective of the medical evaluation is the development of sufficient rapport with patients to be able to convince them that a psychological and psychosocial evaluation is essential. Without adequate information and psychological preparation, many patients reject the recommendation that they be examined by a clinical psychologist, a social worker, or any other mental health professional. This reaction often reflects a concern that they have already been diagnosed as having a psychological problem and that their physical complaints have not been taken seriously. It is important, then, that this recommendation be made with sensitivity and empathy, in order to avert this reaction.

METHOD OF APPROACH

Instilling Confidence

During the patient's initial visit, several things should be accomplished, the most important of which is for the physician to instill confidence in the patient. The necessity of establishing a rapport between the physician and patient to gain full cooperation of the patient and to achieve optimal results cannot be overemphasized. As a result of previous therapy failures, many patients with chronic or recurring pain come to the physician discouraged and pessimistic. Others are angry, bitter, and resentful. Unfortunately, many have been told that "your pain is in your head" or that "nothing can be done for the pain."

The difficult task of cultivating the confidence and faith of the patient can be accomplished in several ways. First, the referring physician should convince the patient that the pain specialist is, in fact, a specialist in the management of pain and has special skills that can help to solve the pain problem. During the initial visit, the pain specialist should strengthen the patient's belief in this by employing and developing to the fullest extent those intangible attributes that we include in the phrase "the art of medicine." The physician should bring to the pain patient a quiet, considerate humanity, as well as confidence and security based on the conviction that all that can be done to help will be done.

All patients must be made to feel that their individuality is recognized and that understanding their problem is meaningful not only to them but also to the physician. A sympathetic attitude, consideration, affectionate care, and a deep interest in the patient's problem greatly enhance the cooperation of the patient during the evaluation procedure and help to create confidence in patients that they can be helped with their pain problem.

Informing the Patient

The next objective is to inform the patient about the various steps and procedures to be followed during the evaluation process. Even if this has been done by others, the physician should describe the entire plan of assessment and management. The evaluation process and treatment are likely to require a great deal of time and either repeated office visits or a stay in the hospital. The patient's cooperation is essential. The patient should agree to follow through either verbally or, as Sternbach (1974) prefers, by signing a management contract. As mentioned, such cooperation is usually obtained without difficulty, provided the physician discusses the problem fully with the patient, explaining the entire management plan with sensitivity to the patient's concerns and in language that can be understood.

Reviewing the Initial Diagnosis

Several points should be made with regard to the diagnosis. First, it is necessary to confirm or reject any diagnosis made by the referring physician. In some cases, the former diagnosis, when critically examined, is found to be inappropriate or outdated or to be merely a description of an initiating disease that might have little or no relation to the patient's present pain problem. Even if the diagnosis was made correctly by a respected physician who referred that patient to the pain specialist[1] for management, it is essential to investigate the problem fully. Often, additional information can be obtained that aids in the treatment plan. A detailed history and a comprehensive physical examination are therefore essential. Generally, the medical evaluation of the patient's pain is based to a major degree on the history, to a lesser degree on the physical examination, and least of all on the laboratory data. Indeed, in most patients with chronic pain, it is essential to await the results of the psychological and psychosocial evaluation, as well as those of consultation with other specialists, before reaching a definitive diagnosis.

Taking the History

Taking a detailed history constitutes one of the most important parts of the evaluation of the pain patient. When a history is carefully and meticulously elicited, skillfully interpreted, and carefully analyzed, it

---

[1]A pain specialist is a clinician specially trained in methods of the evaluation and treatment of pain.

provides important information not only about the possible mechanisms and pathophysiology of the pain syndrome but also about the emotional and psychological status of the patient (De Jong, 1979). The history often affords the physician such a clear picture that diagnosis can be largely established from the reported symptoms alone, even before physical, neurologic, and laboratory examinations have been undertaken. In other cases, the history might not necessarily be decisive, but it can so limit the diagnostic possibilities that it suggests a logical program of investigation. Finally, and just as importantly, the history affords the physician an unequalled opportunity to establish rapport with the patient. This is an opportunity for the physician to demonstrate his or her caring for the patient by being friendly, understanding, and courteous, by being visibly interested in the patient's problem, by expressing eagerness to help, and by centering all attention on the patient.

A comprehensive history consists of a history of the pain problem, a past medical history, a general psychological and psychosocial history, and a family history. These are elicited as for any other medical condition and need no elaboration here except in regard to matters that are of special concern in patients with chronic pain syndromes. The patient with chronic pain is frequently fatigued, irritable, and nervous, so the history is best taken in privacy, with the patient as comfortable as possible. There are, however, times when the presence of the patient's spouse or significant other can facilitate the process of obtaining an accurate history.

During the process of history-taking, the physician should avoid haste and use language readily understood by the patient. Although a regular sequence is valuable in obtaining and recording the history, both for ensuring completeness and facilitating future reference, the clinician should never follow a stereotyped form or repeat a memorized list of questions. If the physician's questions seem arbitrary or otherwise unrelated to their particular problems, patients may become understandably resentful.

The history should be recorded clearly and concisely in a logical, well-organized manner. Each statement must be considered in its relationship to the whole. It is important to stress the more significant manifestations and to keep irrelevancies to a minimum; essential factual material must be separated from extraneous information. Diagnosis involves the careful sifting of evidence and the art of selecting and emphasizing pertinent data. It is a good idea to record negative as well as positive findings, so that later examiners understand that the historian inquired into certain aspects of the disease.

The initial step of the history is to let patients tell their stories in their own words. The importance of this part of the examination of patients with pain was stressed by Leriche (1949), who wrote that the physician who really wishes to investigate pain and to find some means of abolishing it ought to give great attention to the patient's complaints. The physician should listen to the story of the patient's sufferings, however long and tedious it may be. Although some patients do appear to exaggerate subjective sensations, they should be given an opportunity to express their feelings anyway, since the conversation may reveal important information. While the patient is talking, the physician should intervene as little as possible and only then to lead the story into directions where useful information can be obtained – to exclude obviously irrelevant material or to obtain amplification of statements that seem to be vague or incomplete. The use of open-ended questions is essential; closed questions can distort the patient's history and obscure diagnosis.

Whereas the patient's spontaneous narrative affords the examiner valuable information, rarely is it complete. Only exceptional patients recall all particulars of their illness and repeat them accurately and in chronological order without confusing symptoms and their interpretation of symptoms (De Jong, 1979). Furthermore, if the patient's mind is focused on a particular manifestation, he or she might fail to mention others of equal importance. Thus, it is usually necessary to augment the patient's account by tactfully asking leading questions. It is often necessary to go into detail regarding specific factors, many of which patients might not relate to their present condition but whose presence or absence could be significant. Especially in cases that involve compensation for medical or legal problems, an accurate, detailed record of events is essential.

Patients should be allowed to use their own words. The clinician should avoid suggesting symptoms or diagnosis, particularly when obtaining the history from suggestive and hypochondriacal patients (De Jong, 1979). Certain types of individuals require modified tactics. The garrulous person might have to be stopped from getting lost in a mass of irrelevant detail, while the timid, inarticulate, or worried patient might have to be helped by sympathetic questions or reassuring comments. The fearful, antagonistic, or paranoid patient should be questioned with particular respect, so as not to arouse fears or suspicions; the patient with multiple vague complaints must be kept to specifics, and the evasive or undependable patient should be questioned more searchingly. Such individual variations are important to consider in taking the history of any illness, but especially when appraising the pain patient's complaints.

While taking the history, the physician has an opportunity to study the patient as a whole—that is, the patient's manner, attitude, behavior, and emotional reactions. The patient's tone of voice, bearing, facial expressions, any gesticulations, restlessness, delay or hesitancy of speech, and emotional responses to description of certain events or facts about marital or work history reveal his or her character, personality, and emotional state.

CHARACTERISTICS OF THE PAIN

In eliciting the history of the pain and examining the painful part of the body, we obtain a detailed description of the location and distribution of the pain, the quality of the pain, the severity or intensity of the pain, and the periodicity and duration of the pain.

Location and Distribution

The value of localizing the site and distribution of the pain in diagnosing its cause is universally recognized, but it should be remembered that the accuracy of such localization begins to diminish from the moment the pain ceases and so it is best to obtain this information while the pain is actually present. Moreover, pain arising from the skin or mucous membranes, and from the innervation of these tissues, is localized with almost negligible error, but pain arising from deep somatic or visceral structures can be referred remotely or localized only with difficulty. Such referred pain might be accompanied by hyperalgesia, hyperesthesia, and deep tenderness. Pain with a segmental distribution can arise from dysfunction of the nerve roots or deformed spinal nerves. Pain can be classified as localized, projected (transmitted or transferred), or referred, of reflex (sympathetic) distribution, or it can be a manifestation of a somatoform disorder (De Jong, 1979; Lewis, 1942).

Localized pain. Localized pain remains confined to its site of origin without radiation. Cutaneous hyperalgesia and hyperesthesia and deep tenderness can be present, but are also confined to the site of the disease. Examples of these are bursitis, tendonitis, and arthritis.

Projected (transmitted or transferred) pain. Projected pain is perceived to be transmitted along the course of a nerve, either with a segmental (dermatomal and sclerotomal) or peripheral distribution, depending on the site of lesion. Examples of projected pain with segmental distribution are radiculopathy caused by herpes zoster or other diseases involving the nerve root or nerve trunk before it divides into its major peripheral branches. Examples of projected pain with peripheral distribution include trigeminal neuralgia, brachial plexus neuralgia, and meralgia paresthetica.

Referred pain. To the person who is not medically trained, referred pain, like projected pain, can seem mysterious, since the actual source of a pain many not be in the region that hurts. Referred pain is referred from a deep somatic or visceral structure to a distant region within the same segment, with or without hyperalgesia and hyperesthesia, deep tenderness, muscle spasm, and autonomic disturbances. No changes are seen, however, in the reflexes, and no muscle weakness or atrophy is present. This type of pain is found in visceral disease and deep somatic disorders. In patients with this type of pain, the segments involved are identified, and all somatic and visceral structures innervated by these segments are carefully examined for a pathologic process. Shoulder pain seen with an abscess of the subphrenic region is an example of referred pain.

Reflex sympathetic pain. Reflex sympathetic pain does not conform to any segmental or peripheral nerve distribution or to any other recognizable pattern; it is associated with hyperalgesia, hyperesthesia, and vasomotor and tropic changes. It is best exemplified by causalgia[1] and other reflex sympathetic dystrophies.

"Psychological" pain. The location and distribution of pain caused primarily by psychological or psychiatric disorders (included in the somatoform disorders) usually do not fit normal neuroanatomical patterns. The etiology may vary, but often psychological pain is a somatic representation of an unresolved conflict. Obvious examples of psychological pain include pain with glove or stocking distribution, pain involving the entire body, or various pains scattered all over the body.

Quality

The quality of pain indicates whether the causative factor is superficial or deep. Pain associated with a superficial lesion is usually sharp, burning, and well localized, whereas pain caused by deep somatic or visceral disease is dull, diffuse, and poorly localizable.

[1]Causalgia is a syndrome of sustained burning pain following traumatic injury.

Severity or Intensity

The severity or intensity of pain is perhaps the most difficult aspect to evaluate, because it cannot be measured precisely (compared with blood pressure, heart rate, sedimentation rate, or other physical variables). Evaluation of the intensity of pain must rely on the patient's statements and on the examiner's ability to appraise the patient's personality and physical status. In the usual clinical setting the patient is asked to rate the pain intensity on a 0 to 10 scale, "0" representing no pain and "10" representing the most severe pain imaginable. Others use descriptors such as mild, moderate, severe, very severe, and excruciating. It is possible to discriminate between the sensory and the affective components of pain with a variety of standardized tests, such as the McGill Pain Questionnaire, and the Visual Analogue Scale (VAS), as Barber describes in Chapter 1.

Duration and Periodicity

The duration and other temporal characteristics of the pain suggest its mechanism, thus aiding the diagnosis. The patient should be asked whether the pain is continuous, intermittent, pulsing, or characterized by a wave-like rise and fall in intensity. Determination of the length of the interval between painful episodes is important. In connection with these temporal factors, Lewis (1942) has suggested the use of a time-intensity curve. The curve portrays the manner in which pain starts, the rapidity of its cumulation, the duration and smoothness at its height, and the manner of its decline. Pain can be experienced in various ways: a very brief flash, as in tic douloureux; in rhythmic pulses, as in inflammation of dental pulp or migraine; in longer and less rhythmic phases, as in intestinal colic; rising gradually or suddenly to a plateau that is maintained for a long period without any fluctuation before vanishing, as in angina pectoris or burns; and/or continuous but fluctuating in intensity, as in aches that arise from the musculature of the limbs. In addition to the time-intensity curve, the relation of the pain to the time of day, week, or season, to weather conditions, and to emotional stress or environmental cues is revealing.

GENERAL OUTLINE
OF THE HISTORY

The history of the pain, as for all clinical histories, usually begins with obtaining certain data (if they are not already available), including the patient's name, address, gender, age, marital status, occupation, race, nationality, and religion. A statement of the patient's major or presenting complaint, which in this case is pain, is then obtained. This is followed by a description of the symptoms and course of the present illness, with a chronologic account of its development.

History of the Pain

Pain at onset. Detailed information should be obtained regarding the precise date of onset and the circumstances contributing to the causation of the pain. The location and distribution, quality, intensity or severity, and duration of the first pain should be ascertained. The type of onset – gradual or sudden – should be determined. If the pain was motion-related, patients should be asked to demonstrate the position they were in and the action they were performing when the pain first occurred. For example, if the patient says pain began while lifting something, we ask whether the pain occurred during bending or raising of the trunk. Was the pain sharp and localized or was it dull and aching? How long did the pain last at the time of onset? Was the patient able to continue activities that day, or was the pain immediately disabling? If the injury was job-related, we ask about interpersonal relations in the work setting at the time. In addition, the patient should be questioned regarding any associated sensory (e.g., numbness), motor, or autonomic disturbances when the pain was first noticed. The patient should be questioned about the treatment received at the time of onset of pain and its effect.

Pain during the interval. We explore the course of the pain during the interval between the onset and time of evaluation. Did the pain get better or worse with time? Did the location and spread of the pain change or remain the same? Were the quality, severity, and temporal characteristics of the pain and associated disturbance modified during the interval?

It is essential to obtain detailed and precise data about the diagnostic and therapeutic procedures that have been carried out and the results achieved. Whether the pain following surgery or any other therapy was the same as the pain before the procedures must be carefully and precisely determined. Iatrogenic complications caused by inappropriate or unnecessary procedures (as well as appropriate ones) add to the pain and suffering of many patients. For example, multiple abdominal surgeries, whether properly indicated for diagnosed organic disease or carried out because of the patient's complaints of persistent pain, can lead to the formation of more adhesions and thus more pain.

In other cases, chronic use of medication over a long period can produce unwanted physical and psychological side-effects.

Special care should be exercised early in the interview to determine whether the patient is taking significant amounts of medication. Many chronic pain patients are confused and have impaired memories because of drug-induced cognitive defects. If such is the case, the patient should be placed in a detoxification program before a diagnostic evaluation is continued and completed.

Present pain. The patient should be asked to describe in detail the quality, site, distribution, intensity, and temporal characteristics of the pain at the time of evaluation and to indicate if any of these factors has changed since the onset or during the interval. The patient is then asked what factors aggravate the pain, relieve the pain, and have no effect on the pain.

Also, the patient should be asked what effect emotional disturbances, movement of the part, exercise, local pressure, heat or cold, coughing, sneezing, straining, and deep breathing have on the severity, quality, and distribution of the pain. The physician should be especially sensitive to the patient's description of the present pain and should record this description. If the patient describes the pain in unusually colorful terms that make no anatomic sense or implies some external and unusual causative factor, the likelihood of the pain resulting from a pathologic lesion decreases. Such phrases as "fishhooks in the mouth," "red hot poker," or pain "traveling down the leg and jumping to the opposite knee" should alert the physician to expect significant psychological factors in the maintenance of the patient's pain. When the pain is constant and does not fluctuate with any physical or emotional activity, it is again likely that a structural lesion is not the primary cause of the patient's complaint. Another clue that a specific lesion is unlikely to be found is when the patient states that the pain levels are always 9 or 10, or even higher!

We want to know about the impact of the pain on the patient's activities, the amount of time the patient is up and about ("up time"), and the amount of time the patient spends sitting or lying down ("down time") while awake. This type of information is best elicited through the use of a two-week diary in which the patient records the physical activities, medication taken, and intensity of the pain during each waking hour. We inquire about the effect of pain on sleep. Does the pain make it difficult to fall asleep? Does the pain awaken the patient from a sound sleep?

In order to insure our reliable understanding, this part of the history involves asking the same questions repeatedly, which can tax the patient as well as the physician. Patients should be encouraged to sustain their efforts during this long and tedious part of the evaluation. The physician must allow ample time to unravel these patients' complex medical, psychological, and social problems, often associated with multiple areas of pathology.

Medical History

The medical history is especially important in evaluation of the patient with long-term pain in regard to developing the therapeutic strategy and predicting the outcome. The general health of the patient prior to onset of the pain is elicited and recorded, followed by a history of past illnesses, operations, and accidents or injuries sustained, with the date and nature of each, period of disability, and sequelae (De Jong, 1979). If the patient's health was normal prior to the onset of the pain problem, a return to normality can be expected with effective therapy. If, however, the patient has had many serious physical or psychological illnesses and problems and has a long history of seeking health-care during times of stress, it is unrealistic to expect improvement beyond the previous best level of functioning.

In relating past illnesses and injuries, the patient might list serious or outstanding ones and fail to mention individual symptoms that might be of diagnostic significance (De Jong, 1979). Consequently, any symptoms referable to the various organs and systems should be investigated.

Family History

Since evidence exists that "modeling" is an important factor in the development of chronic pain behavior (Craig, 1986), we inquire about the health of the parents and siblings, and whether they suffered frequent painful disorders and disability. Proceeding tactfully and considerately, we ask whether the patient was abused as a child. The development of chronic pain behavior is often a sequela of such abuse.

Psychological and Psychosocial History

The psychological and psychosocial part of the history helps to determine the contribution of affective or environmental factors to the patient's pain complaint. Often the factors generating pain at the onset of the disease are not those that are present when the patient is eventually seen by the pain specialist. This aspect of the patient's evaluation is dealt with in more detail by Joseph Barber, in Chapter 3, so we will proceed with medical aspects of the evaluation.

THE PHYSICAL EXAMINATION

Because pain in general and chronic pain in particular have widespread effects, an appraisal of the general physical, neurologic, musculoskeletal, and mental status of the patient is essential to a proper diagnosis. In addition, a thorough physical examination indicates that the physician has an appropriate level of concern for this particular patient and is taking his or her complaints seriously.

The physical examination of the pain patient is often a demanding and lengthy process. It involves not only a general physical examination but more extensive neurologic and musculoskeletal studies than are indicated for most other types of medical patients. Clinical assessment of the patient's functional abilities is also required; this is usually a tiring procedure for the patient and invariably involves maneuvers that exacerbate the pain. If the patient appears to be fatigued after the lengthy history-taking, we advise carrying out a superficial preliminary examination and postponing a more definitive study to a later date.

General Physical Examination

The general appearance of the patient is noted. The observations made during the taking of the history are correlated with those made after the patient has disrobed. Any outward manifestations of pain should be noted in particular. The appearance and color of the skin, distribution of fat and hair, evidence of weight loss, emaciation, weakness, abnormal attitudes, contractions, contractures or deformities, atrophies or hypertrophies, enlarged glands, and presence of vasomotor or trophic changes are observed and recorded. One should observe the posture of the patient and note the presence of lordosis, scoliosis, kyphosis, rounded shoulders, ptotic abdomen, flat feet, and if one shoulder or hip is lower than the other.

The facial expression and presence of flushing or paleness, sweating, pupillary dilatation, tears, tremors, muscular tension, or the appearance of anxiety, fear or depression are all significant manifestations of pain, which should be noted. The gait is observed by having the (disrobed) patient walk in a straight line, backward, sideways, and on the toes and heels, and also run. The temperature, pulse, respiratory rate, blood pressure, height, and weight of the patient are recorded.

The skin and mucous membranes should be examined, and their appearance, color, temperature, consistency, texture, elasticity, and any abnormalities noted. Nails of the patient whose history suggests a diagnosis of reflex sympathetic dystrophy (RSD) should be closely examined, with particular attention paid to texture, smoothness, and presence of fissures. The hair of such patients should also be examined with regard to amount, distribution, and color, and particularly texture, since hair changes are common manifestations of RSD.

Examination of the Painful Region

After this general inspection, the specific region of the pain complaint is examined. This is done before proceeding with the rest of the physical examination, primarily because the patient expects the investigation to begin in the area in which the discomfort is located. Many patients understandably feel resentful when the initial examination involves areas other than the painful region. The examination consists of inspection, palpation, and percussion, and sometimes auscultation of the region.

Visual inspection of the area provides definitive data that can be correlated with the story given by the patient and with the information obtained by palpation, percussion, and special tests (De Jong, 1979). The appearance and color of the skin overlying the painful area are observed closely, and any trophic manifestation, hypertrichosis (excessive hair growth), hyperhidrosis (excessive sweating), cyanosis or flushing, cutis anserina ("goose flesh"), or visible evidence of muscle spasm is noted.

Palpation of the region provides further information about the pain. Deep tenderness is best elicited by digital palpation, using the middle finger to exert firm deep pressure on the painful site. The area of tenderness is mapped out and the segments involved are ascertained. If any doubt regarding the existence of a pathologic basis for the complaint is present, the findings can be confirmed or discounted by repeated palpation, approaching the region from a different direction each time. If this is done while the patient is distracted, evocation of pain in the same region is some indication of a pathologic process. During palpation of the region, these evocations of pain should be correlated with subjective and objective manifestations of the painful disorder, and a determination made of whether any discrepancy exists between them. Subjective pain behavior includes grimacing, groaning, shouting, writhing, and other verbal and nonverbal expressions.

The degree of such subjective behavior expected for a particular condition varies greatly across cultures and ethnicities and among individuals; writhing and groaning on the part of an ordinarily stoic individual can signify a more noxious condition than the same behavior from a customarily flamboyant person. Likewise, such behavior can be more marked in an anxious or depressed person with a given condition than in someone without these emotional problems. Objective signs associated with some painful conditions, which are not wholly under the voluntary control of the patient, include manifestations of automatic discharge, such as sweating, flushing, tachycardia, elevated blood pressure, and muscle spasm.

In a patient with a pathologic process, palpation provides not only a qualitative reaction but also quantitative data proportionate to the stimulus used. Therefore, the response of the patient when the opposite symmetric nonpainful side is palpated in exactly the same manner should be noted for differences. This also provides important information regarding the sensitivity of the patient to noxious and nonnoxious stimuli, as well as information about the sensitivity of the painful region.

To determine whether the tenderness and pain provoked by palpation are caused wholly or in part by overlying skin hyperalgesia and hyperesthesia, the pinch test, prick test, and scratch test are used. The pinch test consists of simply pinching the skin between the thumb and index finger, applying pressure along close parallel lines beginning over the adjacent nonpainful area and continuing over the painful part and then beyond to the farther asymptomatic area. The pin prick and pin scratch tests are used similarly to examine superficial pain sensibility.

These procedures should also be carried out over the opposite and corresponding nonpainful areas to obtain an index of the patient's response to stimuli, to show the patient what to expect, and to provide a subtle, subconscious basis of comparison when the affected side is examined. Response should be evaluated by noting any wincing, groaning, or voluntary complaint by the patient, or by the onset of reflex muscle spasm. The patient is asked only neutral and nonsuggestive questions. These tests should always be used as complementary procedures to maneuvers intended to elicit, reproduce, or evaluate pain and tenderness by percussion, jarring, or pounding, because such percussive tests are positive in the presence of cutaneous hyperesthesia, which contributes greatly to misdiagnosis if unrecognized. The presence of objective signs tends to suggest a significant organic or pathologic substrate underlying the patient's pain complaint, whereas excessive subjective signs tend to indicate a major psychological component to the patient's complaint.

In addition to palpation, factors or circumstances that reproduce, aggravate, or relieve the pain are determined, particularly the effects of motion, application of heat and cold, exercise, walking up steps, deep breathing, coughing, sneezing, straining, digital pressure over the regional arteries, assumption of the prone, supine, and upright positions, and the Valsalva maneuver. In addition, effects of barbiturates, narcotics, and other analgesics such as aspirin should be ascertained, not only as a rough index of the intensity of the pain but as a guide to differentiating pathologic from nonpathologic pain.

In all but the most obvious and simple cases, the rest of the physical examination should be completed, because it frequently reveals pertinent data. The head, neck, chest, abdomen, back, and extremities are carefully examined and evaluated; these are discussed elsewhere (Bonica & Loeser, 1990).

Neurologic Examination

Though the neurologic examination is an essential part of the thorough physical examination of the patient in pain, its details are more complex than the other parts of the physical examination and have not been included here. The reader interested in those details can refer to Bonica and Loeser (1990).

Examination of the Musculoskeletal System

A screening examination of the musculoskeletal system indicates or excludes functional impairment of this system. If an abnormality is revealed, a more detailed examination of that region is indicated. Excellent texts on the examination of the musculoskeletal system have been written by Clawson et al. (1980) and Spangler (1982).

First, the disrobed patient must be observed for posture and extremity abnormalities. Next gait and accessory motions are observed. Then strength, muscle mass and tone, and range of motion at all major joints are ascertained. The mobility of the spine and any regional tenderness should be assessed.

SUMMARY

An accurate history and carefully conducted physical examination are the cornerstones of the diagnosis and treatment of the patient with pain. No matter what form of therapy is contemplated – including psychological – these evaluations must be performed to rule out diseases that should be directly treated. Furthermore, relevant pain-generating factors that may lie in the affective, cognitive, or environmental spheres can often be elicited by the history and physical examination. The neurological and musculoskeletal examinations are usually the most relevant to chronic pain problems, but other special evaluations may occasionally be required. Clinicians who treat patients with pain would be well advised to be certain that an appropriate medical evaluation has been undertaken before embarking upon psychological therapies.

3

PSYCHOLOGICAL EVALUATION OF THE PATIENT WITH PAIN

Joseph Barber

UNTIL RECENTLY, pain was thought to be a natural concomitant of various ailments. By and large, physicians and other health-care practitioners did not treat pain in and of itself as a problem for which intervention was necessary or appropriate. Needless to say, psychological treatment for pain was not even considered.

Beginning in the 1950s, anesthesiologist John Bonica pioneered anesthetic interventions (most notably the epidural) to treat pain. Almost single-handedly, Bonica founded the International Association for the Study of Pain, the first organization to focus on the science and practice of pain treatment. In 1960, Bonica established the world's first clinic devoted entirely to the investigation and treatment of pain, the University of Washington Pain Center. This clinic was among the first to integrate both medical and psychological evaluation and treatment. Its success was partly a result of similar pioneering work of such psychologists as Wilbert Fordyce (a colleague of Bonica) and Richard Sternbach, whose research and treatment methods led to our contemporary appreciation of the psychological dimensions of pain.

The seminal contribution of Fordyce, Fowler, Lehmann, and De-Lateur (1968) demonstrated the effective rehabilitation of pain patients by behavioral methods, stimulating more interest in the substantial role to be played by psychologists in the evaluation and treatment of pain. Bonica's recognition and support of that role, demonstrated by his inclusion of psychologists on the staff when he developed the first pain clinic, provided inspiration to a new generation of psychologists, who have now been trained in the clinical evaluation and treatment of pain. It is now accepted that the experience of pain and suffering, like the experience of pleasure, is a psychophysiological phenomenon, not a purely physiological phenomenon to be treated by purely medical approaches.

PSYCHOLOGICAL EFFECTS
OF PAIN

Let us briefly review the types of pain presented in Chapter 1: *Acute pain* is the pain that results immediately from noxious stimulation. *Recurring pain* results from injury or disease that produces repeated noxious stimulation over time. *Chronic benign pain* is distinguished from both of these by the fact that, although the patient experiences pain and suffering, this experience endures beyond the noxious stimulation itself. *Psychogenic pain* is one of the somatoform disorders and, among all the syndromes causing pain, is rare. (An example of this disorder is that of Nero, which I describe later in this chapter.)

When acute pain is properly treated, it tends to resolve and does not usually have enduring psychological effects. On the other hand, both recurring pain conditions and chronic benign pain syndrome produce enduring psychological effects, reflected in alterations in the patient's mood and behavior. In part, the purpose of psychological evaluation is to uncover those effects in the patient who has suffered pain over a period of time.

A thorough and comprehensive psychological evaluation can provide information essential to understanding why some patients' pain persists beyond normal expected healing time, as well as to the planning and implementation of successful treatment. (Turner & Romano, 1991, p. 595)

One can assume that an organic basis for pain exists or did exist, in nearly every case of chronic pain, even when current organic sources cannot be found. In any case of pain that persists over time – no matter what the nature of the pain – psychological factors tend to have significant influence on the degree of suffering and the extent of disability experienced by the patient. Except in cases of acute pain, medical treatment of the pain does not tend to ameliorate these psychological factors, and when these factors are sufficiently influential the medical treatment does not satisfactorily resolve the pain syndrome.

In recognition of these issues, it is now common for psychologists to be an integral part of the staff of most pain clinics. Additionally, psychologists in private practice are increasingly called upon to evaluate and/or treat pain patients.

One reason why physicians and psychologists refer pain patients to a multidisciplinary pain clinic is because such a clinic has greater interdisciplinary resources than private practitioners usually have, including the capacity for extensive psychological evaluation. Although it is more difficult for private practitioners to provide such psychological evaluation, it is certainly possible to do so. This chapter is intended to be a guide toward such an evaluation.

THE PSYCHOLOGICAL EVALUATION – BASIC ISSUES

The details of how to do a complete psychological evaluation are described elsewhere (Turner & Romano, 1991); here we will focus on the principal issues of the psychological evaluation: what constitutes adequate evaluation, how it is done, and what the consequences are of adequate and inadequate evaluation.

The process of psychological evaluation reveals the extremely complex interplay between psychological variables and the patient's experience of suffering from long-term pain. Personality variables, as always, interact with situational variables (in this case, the experience of hurting and probably some loss of participation in life's activities) to generate what is sometimes a bewildering array of symptoms. Fortunately, the energies of researchers and clinicians who have gone before us have led to a satisfying means to clarify what might otherwise only confound us.

It is important to keep in mind that the goal of psychological evaluation of the pain patient is to identify those psychological factors that are associated with pain, suffering, and disability. For example, depression is often though not always present to some extent in pain patients. It is useful, then, to determine the extent to which the patient's pain and suffering have resulted in that depression. Conversely, it is important to determine, for example, what aspect of a patient's premorbid depression may be serving to exacerbate the pain, suffering, and disability. Similarly, overattentiveness to health issues is usually found in patients with pain. It is important to know if such "hypochondriasis" existed prior to the pain condition. Evaluation will identify such psychological qualities and pertinent treatment goals.

There are other psychological factors that play a powerful role in the prognosis of a pain patient; these should also be evaluated. A history of alcohol or substance abuse is associated with frustrated pain treatment. Patients with certain personality disorders (especially borderline and antisocial) have much greater difficulty achieving treatment success than others, since their goals are likely to conflict with clinicians' goals. In elderly patients, dementia can be an important prognostic influence, because, to the extent that the patient has difficulty understanding or remembering treatment requirements, treatment gains will be especially difficult and frustrating to achieve.

An adequate evaluation also takes into account social and environmental factors. How the patient's spouse or children or other family members cope with the patient's symptoms is a powerful determinant of the patient's own coping patterns. The system of monetary compensation for illness and disability that rewards what Fordyce (1976) has coined "pain behavior" further complicates the problem. Exploration of the role of such rewards is essential to understanding any patient's pain problem.

(As an aside, it is worth noting that such variables need to be seen in context. I have evaluated patients who live in countries where the cultural expectations around disability and its compensation are different from ours. For instance, if a worker lives in a culture where it is simply assumed that pain complaints following injury should be unquestionably granted substantial monetary compensation for the rest of the worker's life, the clinician's options are severely limited.)

As Turner and Romano (1991) have described (and as experienced clinicians know), pain patients tend to be resistant to the prospect of psychological evaluation, believing that such evaluation implies that they are either crazy or faking their symptoms. Clearly, then, your first conversation with the patient about such evaluation needs to address the patient's needs. The patient needs to be taken seriously, to receive compassion and sympathy for his or her suffering, and to be told that all humans – even mentally healthy ones – are affected psychologically by the experience of suffering. It can be surprisingly salutary to explain to the patient that, whatever the source of the pain and suffering, your purpose is to reduce that pain and suffering. A thorough evaluation will make that possible.

Respectful discussion with the patient of the clinical reasons for the evaluation ("to really help you as quickly and as fully as possible") is essential. Equally crucial is your ability to listen to the patient's fears or frustrations about evaluation, in order to better understand how to fully meet the patient's needs.

As Fordyce (1976) and others have revealed, noxious stimulation causes pain, but the way the patient experiences and responds to that pain is substantially determined by environmental contingencies. Essential to this process is to clarify the nature of such environmental forces upon the patient. It is clear that the dynamic interplay of economic, social, familial, and personal forces tends to create pain behaviors in patients who suffer from pain. Even if a patient seems to have an exaggerated response to symptoms or seems less than enthusiastic about some aspects of rehabilitation, this does not mean that the patient is malingering, nor does it mean that the patient is intent on manipulation. It is unfortunate that the phrase "secondary gains" has come to connote manipulation or malingering. Perhaps the current usage of the term "social and financial disincentives" will help us to recognize that, as organisms capable of learning, all humans – even pain patients – are susceptible to influence by environmental contingencies. It would be a strange and unusual (and perhaps uneducable) patient who was not affected by the ways his family and friends respond to symptoms, by the prospect of monetary reward without returning to a perhaps unattractive job, or by the compassionate attention of clinicians.

When a patient does not respond well to treatment, it is easy for us to conclude that the patient is resistant to treatment or is manipulative, malingering, or otherwise cause for hostile and untherapeutic attitudes on our part. As we describe in the Afterword, the interaction between environment, patient, and treatment variables is complex and dynamic. Therapeutic failures cannot always be attributed to patient characteristics – even in patients who seem troublesome!

When a patient presents for psychological pain treatment, these basic psychological issues need evaluation:

1. Depression, including suicidality
2. Anxiety, including posttraumatic stress disorder (PTSD)
3. Mental status, especially in patients who are elderly, who have suffered head injury, or whose history includes alcohol or substance abuse
4. Pain behaviors, including reinforcers and punishers
5. Presence of ongoing substance abuse

THE INTERVIEW

Most evaluations begin with interviews of the patient and family members (and, if appropriate, coworkers and friends). Details of such interviews have been widely published over the years. A succinct and detailed discussion can be found in Turner and Romano (1991).

Where Does it Hurt?

When the patient is asked specifically about the nature of the pain experience, the distinction is made between the pain's sensory and affective components (see Chapter 5 for discussion of this issue). In most cases, it is valuable to ask the patient to keep a "pain diary" (Fordyce, 1976), which documents the level of pain, noting both sensory and affective components throughout the day. In this way, both you and the patient can become aware of antecedents and patterns in the waxing and waning of pain. It is very helpful for the patient to discover what activities or events tend to make the pain better or worse. (And it is the rare patient who can correctly identify these antecedents before using the pain diary.) Such a diary can also help a patient determine if the medications he or she is taking are effective in relieving the pain, and if so, for how long and to what extent.

We ask the patient to evaluate the sensory and affective components of the pain using either the VAS or a numerical scale, as described in Chapter 1, to determine the felt intensity and bothersomeness of the pain – at this moment, at its worst, and at its best. This assessment provides substantial information not only about the pain but also about the patient's attitude toward it – his or her readiness to evaluate it and render it treatable. (We also learn if the patient tends to evaluate the pain in a straightforward or an exaggerated fashion. For instance, if a patient rates the intensity or the bothersomeness of the pain as "10," we might carefully explore with the patient what it means for something to be as much as we can imagine it to be.)

What Does it Mean?

The implications of the pain powerfully determine both the extent of the patient's suffering and the patient's readiness for treatment. Discussion with the patient and with the patient's spouse, partner, or close family member should reveal, among other things, what the pain means (e.g., for future good functioning), what illness means, and what recovery will mean. How the patient evaluates the affective component also tells us something about the meaning of the pain.

What Medications Are Being Taken?

It is essential to know what medications the patient has been taking and specifically whether the patient takes a medication that affects mood (e.g., tranquilizers, muscle relaxants, opioids). While such medications can be very beneficial in the treatment of acute pain, they can exert a maleficent influence on the course of long-term pain (Monks, 1991). There are two very important exceptions: (1) the use of analgesics for recurring pain (including but not limited to cancer pain, migraine headache, and arthritis pain) when tolerance is not an issue; and (2) the use of antidepressant medications, which can have a substantial beneficial effect on both pain and depression (Monks, 1991).

What Are the Possible Consequences of Pain Reduction?

What are the likely consequences if the patient's pain experience is changed (made better or worse)? Sometimes exploring this question will uncover a rich lode of expectations (realistic or fantastic) and attributions of life's dissatisfactions to the pain (rather than to all of the other sources of dissatisfaction with which we are familiar). This will facilitate your understanding of how the patient may be affected, for good or ill, by a reduction in pain and suffering.

Will There Be Litigation?

If you learn that the patient is likely to become involved in litigation concerning the pain, explore this issue carefully. Although the evidence is mixed and indicates that some patients benefit from treatment even when they are involved in litigation, I find that generally patients tend to achieve little relief from their pain and suffering if they are simultaneously working to establish a legal case that depends upon the stability of that same pain and suffering. I have encountered the occasional patient who is willing to forego litigation in favor of pain treatment; such a patient is likely to benefit from treatment. However, if the patient is not willing or able to forego litigation, it is likely that treatment will be unsuccessful and frustrating for all concerned. It has been my practice to explain this to the patient and to offer treatment *after* litigation has been finally settled. Frequently, patients experience substantial relief from their suffering upon the successful outcome of litigation. Fordyce has referred to this as the successful application of "the green poultice." This does not mean that such patients did not suffer from pain; however, it does reflect the complex and powerful interaction between external reward systems and internal suffering.

There are important exceptions to my equation of litigation with treatment failure. In any case that involves litigation, I would recommend a full evaluation of this issue; unless the evaluation strongly suggests otherwise, a treatment trial may be undertaken to see if this case is an exception. It is important to keep in mind, however, that early indications of unresponsiveness to treatment may reflect the influence of the litigation.

What Is the Patient's Attitude Toward Hypnotic Treatment?

To evaluate the patient's attitude toward and expectations about hypnotic treatment, we ask: What does the patient expect of hypnosis? Are his or her expectations realistic? Has the patient had experience with hypnotic treatment? Was that experience satisfactory or disappointing? If the patient has a recurrent pain syndrome, is he or she prepared to use self-hypnotic methods for the foreseeable future?

Some argue that the conscientious clinician should also evaluate the patient's hypnotic responsivity; while I believe otherwise, I find it helpful to administer the Tellegen Absorption Scale (Tellegen & Atkinson, 1974) as a way of gaining an impression of the patient's readiness for the general experience of altered consciousness. Of course, as for any patient for whom one is considering the use of hypnotic treatment, evaluation of the appropriateness of this treatment is also indicated at the earliest opportunity; this is discussed in Chapter 5.

PSYCHOLOGICAL TESTING

In addition to the interview, a minimal psychological assessment includes administration of the Minnesota Multiphasic Personality Inventory (MMPI), the Symptom Check List 90 (SCL-90), and perhaps one of the depression inventories (e.g., the Beck Depression Inventory [Beck, Ward, Mendelson et al., 1961]).

Sometimes pain patients are referred to a mental health practitioner who correctly identifies a psychiatric syndrome. However, the presence of psychiatric difficulties is not prima facie evidence that the patient's pain is not organically based. Psychiatric patients may also sometimes suffer from chronic pain. Of course, if the syndrome is identified as a somatoform disorder or if significant depression is present (especially if the patient has a premorbid history of depression), then effective treatment may well focus on the psychiatric syndrome.

BENEFITS OF ADEQUATE
EVALUATION

The evaluation process is often a source of dissatisfaction, even frustration, for a patient. It is unwise, however, to act hastily because the patient insists that the evaluation be curtailed and treatment begun. This can be especially challenging when the patient is suffering greatly while being asked questions that seem to have no relevance to the pain. Only after you are confident of the thoroughness of the evaluation, and after the information gained from that evaluation has been understood and integrated into a treatment model, is it likely that the subsequent treatment will benefit the patient.

It is worthwhile here to remember that, while formal evaluation takes place prior to treatment, such evaluation is never truly complete or accurate. Pretreatment evaluation cannot, of course, take into account the information available about the patient's responses to treatment. The effective clinician is constantly making informal, often subtle evaluations throughout the course of treatment. It is the openness of this ongoing evaluation that provides for "course corrections" in the process of treatment.

CASE EXAMPLE: ARCHIE, 26, INJURED AT WORK

Archie was a factory worker, married and the father of two young children. A mishap with a manufacturing machine very nearly took his life. He was frequently to remark, later, that he sometimes wished he had died that day, rather than suffering chronic pain and disability. At the time of this evaluation, two years post-accident, he was referred for treatment of chronic headaches (a consequence of head injury) by his neurologist.

What was remarkable about Archie's initial interview was his lack of guile, his sweet smile, and, more to the point, the unusual degree to which he remained a passive recipient of care — jobless, almost totally sedentary, and deeply depressed (despite several trials of antidepressants).

He reported that the intensity of his pain was 10 (out of 10), but that it only bothered him 2 out of 10. Yet, despite this denial of suffering, each and every time he was asked about the possibility of increasing his activity, he replied that he was not able to because of the pain.

He received Social Security compensation, but this was sufficient only to maintain a minimal standard of living — not the comfortable life he and his family had enjoyed while he worked. He was anticipat-

ing the successful outcome of a lawsuit brought against the manufac-
turer of the machine that had injured him. (My interview with his wife
revealed that she was far less optimistic about the likely outcome of
the lawsuit; she was confident only that the attorneys "will get most
of the money.")

Archie was superficially very cooperative, yet he found it impossible
to comply with even the simplest therapeutic directives. He was unwilling to maintain a pain diary, for example, because he said the pain
was unvarying, so there was no point to such a diary. He was unwilling
to undergo physical therapy or even to begin undertaking incremental
increases in his activity level, because "my head hurts too much." (Curiously, he also refused to take analgesic medication offered by the
neurologist, because "it doesn't help.")

After four meetings, it was suggested to Archie that he defer treatment of his pain until his lawsuit was settled. He took this advice with
the same equanimity as he did all of the other advice offered him, and
he agreed to call me at the completion of litigation.

Fifteen months later, to my surprise, Archie did call. His lawsuit
was settled, he said, and so he was calling, as he said he would. He had
had a satisfactory resolution of the case, so that there was a substantial amount of money available to him and his family even after the
attorneys' fees were paid. Archie reported the same level of pain as he
had more than a year before, but he now seemed more prepared to
follow through with treatment.

A treatment plan was created that combined a variety of approaches, including a behavioral program to facilitate his increased
activity, exploration of vocational opportunities, and hypnotic treatment of his pain.

Within two weeks, Archie was working out daily in a gym and
was responding sufficiently well to hypnotic interventions so that the
intensity of his pain showed a steady decrease to a level between 1 and
3 (out of 10).

One year later, Archie was physically more fit, continued to work
out almost daily in the gym, and experienced pain intensities rarely
greater than 2. More important, he was now a full-time student in the
business school at the university. Over the next year, Archie continued
to report that the pain no longer bothered him and successfully completed his first year at the university.

Archie's case demonstrates the usefulness of gathering appropriate
information early on to prevent frustration and, perhaps, therapeutic
failure. This case also may represent confirmation of the value of
applying Fordyce's "the green poultice." It is difficult, in this case, to

distinguish between the benefit of having no further stressful litigation to cope with and the benefit of no further financial requirement
for the pain and suffering.

CASE EXAMPLE: NERO, 48, WITH HEART PAIN

Nero, a very pleasant man and a successful dentist well-known in the
community, was referred to me by his cardiologist, who could find no
organic basis for the pain that troubled Nero. For some months now,
Nero had suffered increasingly from an intense, aching pain in his
anterior chest wall. While his cardiologist was convinced that Nero
had no heart disease, Nero was very concerned that he did, and that
the chest pain warned that he was in danger of a heart attack. It
was only because Nero was a somewhat obedient man, concrete in his
thinking, that he accepted his cardiologist's recommendation that he
see me, since Nero believed the problem was cardiac, not psychological.

After reviewing his medical records and discussing the symptoms
with Nero, I was reasonably certain that his pain was not caused by
either damage to tissue or disruption of the pain transmission system—it was neither nociceptive nor pathogenic pain. Rather, his
pain—or, at least, his fear about it—reflected an as yet unidentified
psychological issue. Nero was most aware of the pain when he lay in
bed, sometimes before falling asleep, and sometimes after awakening.
The pain was of moderate intensity (varying from 4 to 6), but it was
extremely worrisome to him (varying from 9 to 10), since it meant to
him that he was dangerously ill.

As I continued to listen to Nero's description of the pain, it became
clear to me that Nero was desperately afraid of dying. In order to
understand better what dying meant to him, I asked, "What do you
believe will happen to you when you die?"

He looked at me very gravely as he paused for a moment, and then
he said, "I am Catholic. When I die, I will go to Hell."

His reply confirmed that Nero was feeling substantial guilt about
something, and it was this guilt that had been converted into his
experience of life-threatening pain.

"What have you done, that you will be so damned?" I asked, after a
moment.

Nero's face reddened with shame. He sat silently for a moment, not
looking at me any longer, and then said, very quietly, "I am a homosexual, and as a Catholic I know that is a mortal sin. When I die, I will go
to Hell."

I did not know anyone who still believed such a thing. But I wanted to understand his circumstances better, to see why he was so troubled. "Do you have a lover?" I asked.

"Yes, and we have lived together for ten years. We are both Catholic, we both know it's wrong, and we have tried to stop being lovers. We have separated several times over the years, each time trying to stop being homosexual, but we really love each other, and we can't stand living apart." There were tears in Nero's eyes as he spoke.

As I asked him more about his circumstances, I learned that Daniel, his lover, was a surgeon, that the two were devoted to each other, that they enjoyed respect in their community, where they both played active roles in civic functions. I gently asked Nero more about the details of his life. His modesty made him reluctant to talk about himself; nonetheless, it became apparent that these men contributed substantially to the benefit of their friends and community. Nothing he told me suggested that either Nero or Daniel deserved punishment, but clearly my own values were not relevant to Nero's concerns.

I said, "You believe that God will punish you for your love affair with Daniel. I cannot tell you what God will or will not do, of course. But I have a friend, a gay Catholic priest, who may be in a better position to discuss this matter with you."

Nero looked suddenly astonished. "There are no gay priests!"

"Well, my friend is a Jesuit priest, and he has talked with me about his sexuality, so I am convinced that there is at least one gay priest. From what my friend tells me, there are many. In any case, would you be willing to talk with him?"

Nero could barely recover from his astonishment at my words. But he agreed that I would call my friend (who was both a Jesuit priest and a psychologist), relate Nero's story, and ask if they could meet. As he left, Nero did not look relieved; however, he did look very, very thoughtful.

Later that day I telephoned my friend Cramer, the priest-psychologist, and told him about my meeting with Nero. It was arranged that the two of them would meet.

One week later, Nero came for his appointment with me. He looked well, and he reported that he no longer had any chest pain. When I asked him about his conversation with Cramer, he smiled, saying it had been one of the most amazing conversations he'd ever had. He related their conversation, which essentially involved Cramer's assertion that God loves people who lead homosexual lives even as he loves people who lead heterosexual lives. Cramer further told Nero that homosexual behavior was not a mortal sin.

Just as Nero's simplicity of character had led him to accept the Church's assertion that his behavior would lead to eternal damnation, so this same quality now led him to readily accept Cramer's contradictory assertion. This acceptance gave him substantial relief from the guilt and shame — and growing anxiety — he had been carrying for so many years.

Nero's case demonstrates the importance of understanding the nature of the problem before proceeding to treat it. Clearly, any attempt to directly treat the pain, hypnotically or otherwise, would have failed, since the pain was a symptom of an existential problem of profound importance to Nero. We often think of the role of a symptom as protecting a patient from change. In Nero's case, however, the symptom was a somatization of his anxiety, the root of which was Nero's fear of eternal damnation. His anxiety was warning him of the need for change. It turned out, of course, that he did not have to change his behavior, though he did need to reevaluate his beliefs.

Nero maintained occasional contact with me, letting me know that he continued to do well.

CASE EXAMPLE: LILY, 35, WITH JOINT PAIN

Lily, an attorney, suffered from pain in her elbows, wrists, and knees. She referred herself for treatment of this pain. According to Lily, this pain had become more and more intolerable over the course of the past three years. Oddly (for someone with her level of education and social awareness), she had not consulted a physician about this pain. During the initial interview it was evident to me that she was severely depressed and had apparently been so for much of her life. Subsequent review of the MMPI taken that same week confirmed my impression.

At the second visit I shared with Lily my judgment that she had an arthritic condition that needed evaluation and treatment by a physician, and that she was also depressed, a condition that might respond best to a combination of antidepressant medication and psychotherapy. With evident relief that someone was able to offer her care, she agreed to see a rheumatologist whom I recommended, to consult with a psychiatrist whom I recommended to evaluate for medication, and to begin psychotherapy with me for the purpose of treating her depression.

Three months later, Lily had already benefited from anti-inflammatory medication prescribed by the rheumatologist, to the extent that her joints were visibly less inflamed and she reported substantial relief of her pain. She was also working well with me and taking an antidepressant medication; she was significantly less depressed. I am confident that if I had simply attempted to treat Lily's pain, I would have failed. (Even if she had not required medical attention for her arthritis, her deep depression would have presented a challenging obstacle to pain relief.)

REVIEW OF MEDICAL RECORDS

If you undertake to treat pain, you must be sufficiently trained in the medical evaluation of pain problems that you can read a medical record and determine the nature of the problem, what tests and procedures have been done, and what the findings or results imply about whatever treatment plan you might devise. As we learned in Chapter 2, the medical evaluation of a pain complaint usually identifies the nature of the problem, but not always. When an organic basis for pain is not identified, it can be very tempting for the physician to suggest that the problem must be psychogenic. While this may be the case, we must recognize that absence of evidence is not evidence of absence: Sometimes an organic cause lurks beyond our ability to search for it. It helps to remember the ridiculous drunk in the classic joke: He preferred to look for his lost keys under the convenient (and comforting) illumination of the street lamp, although the keys had been lost elsewhere (in the inconvenient darkness). We, too, may prefer to look in "well-lighted places," when the source of the problem may be in the unpleasant darkness.

What follows are two very different clinical examples that illustrate why it is essential for a nonmedical clinician who treats pain problems to routinely review not only psychological, but also medical, records.

Case Example: Sol, 72, with Arm Pain

Sol was a retired businessman who telephoned me, asking for an appointment to "cure my arm pain." He lived in a distant city and had been referred by his internist. He declined referral by me to someone near him, so I made an appointment with him and arranged that his medical records be sent to me. From his description of his pain, given to me during this telephone conversation, I tentatively hypothesized that he suffered from postherpetic neuralgia. This syndrome can be very satisfactorily treated with hypnotic methods.

So it is good that I asked for his medical records. When the records arrived from his internist about a week later (a day before his scheduled appointment), I began to review them. What I read pointed to the obvious solution to his pain. Sol had begun to complain to his internist about the arm pain about three months previously. For reasons not entirely clear to me, his internist referred him to the Mayo Clinic for evaluation. In his chart was a summary letter from the physician at the Mayo Clinic, who indicated that Sol was suffering from syphilitic neuropathy and recommended a course of penicillin. Again, for reasons not entirely clear to me, there was no indication that Sol had been seen subsequently by his internist, and there was no indication that he had begun the course of penicillin treatment.

I telephoned Sol and told him it was unnecessary for him to travel the next day to see me, but that he should make an appointment with his internist, who would be able to treat his arm pain. Sol was very reluctant to take this advice, saying that his internist really wanted him to see me. I prevailed, however, and suggested that I would also speak with his internist.

Subsequent telephone conversation with his internist satisfied my wish that the Mayo Clinic physician's recommendation would be followed by the internist. The internist indicated to me that he thought Sol was "a crock," that he had not taken his complaint of arm pain seriously ("He's always been strong as a horse, but he complains a lot"), and that he had thought this would be an interesting opportunity to "see what you could do with him."

Two months later, when I telephoned Sol to follow-up, I was pleased to learn that he had been well treated and no longer had arm pain.

CASE EXAMPLE: FRITZ, 58, A HYPOCHONDRIAC

Fritz, a 58-year-old writer, was referred to me by his internist after an extensive medical workup, which had identified no organic basis for intense abdominal pain that had begun about four months previously. In our first discussion about his pain, Fritz described it in unusual, florid ways, thus introducing me to his customarily imaginative turn of mind. His style of relating to his pain also confirmed his internist's view that this was psychogenic pain. He described the pain variously as "angry," "hurt," "lonely," and "frightened." Only when pressed was he likely to describe its physical attributes: "burning," "cramping," or qualities of physical sensations. He also told me, not once but several times in the first conversation, that he was a hypochondriac.

Fritz's pain was relatively constant, and he rated its intensity as 9 out of 10 most of the time, with occasional ratings of 10 out of 10. His pain was least intense in the morning and worst in the middle of the night. He reported that pain medication made no difference and that the only effective remedies were taking a hot bath and playing the piano.

Fritz was wryly amused that his hypochondriac personality style had "chosen" such an excruciatingly painful symptom. His MMPI profile also indicated a hypochondriac profile. Every bit of information seemed to point in the direction of a somatoform disorder, and no information tended to contradict this. Fritz talked like a hypochondriac, acted like a hypochondriac—and no organic explanation could be found as the cause for his pain.

Assuming that Fritz's pain was of a somatoform type and that hypnotic treatment would be beneficial in confirming this and perhaps facilitating a readiness for effective psychotherapy, I undertook hypnotic treatment. Fritz, to my surprise, experienced substantial pain relief during the treatment and for an hour or so afterward. Not surprisingly, though, the pain returned unabated, as before.

At the second treatment appointment, the next day, I initiated hypnotic treatment again. This time, however, I concurrently said to Fritz that this pain might represent some psychological difficulty and inquired about things that might be bothering him. For the next two weeks we had daily conversations that seemed productive and were reasonably satisfying to Fritz, but the pain in his abdomen did not change, except, temporarily, with hypnotic treatment. Fritz experienced occasional significant relief from pain and occasional significant insights; however, his suffering was still substantial, and he frequently called me after hours to ask for my help or to contribute a newfound insight that he thought might be helpful to our work. Because I had no serious doubt about the diagnosis, I felt confident that the treatment would eventually bring relief to Fritz. I did not know when this would occur, but I believed that relief was imminent.

Two weeks after treatment began, Fritz abruptly traveled to the Mayo Clinic and sought further medical evaluation. It seemed to me that he was acting out of his need to defend against the psychological conflicts our work had been raising.

Physicians at the Mayo Clinic interpreted the CT scan he'd initially had and diagnosed Fritz with pancreatic cancer. They repeated the scan and confirmed their diagnosis.

Only in retrospect did I realize that all of us—the various medical consultants who had seen Fritz and myself—had placed our confidence in the "psychogenic" diagnosis primarily on the basis of one radiologist's report. Although Fritz sought many "second opinions," none of these consultants reviewed the original CT scan itself; rather, each read the lone radiologist's report of a negative finding.

This case is instructive because it involves a tragic and unnecessary mistake. My familiarity with Fritz's internist gave me substantial confidence in her conclusion that Fritz's pain was psychogenic. As a consequence, I did not seriously reconsider this diagnosis. Moreover, Fritz's psychological evaluation confirmed this diagnosis. What was lacking in this otherwise rational process was the opinion of a second radiologist. Each consultant was less likely to look more thoroughly into this particular medical diagnosis because Fritz so clearly demonstrated the qualities of a hypochondriac. Sadly, Fritz is a painful example that even hypochondriacs can become ill.

CONCLUSION

Psychologists have a crucial role to play in the evaluation of pain patients. Since the experience of pain both influences a patient's psychology and is influenced by it, effective treatment of the pain must be informed by this evaluation.

While the hypnotherapeutic approach to pain benefits from additional information gained by such evaluation, all treatment benefits from such information.

4

HYPNOTIC ANALGESIA: PSYCHOLOGICAL AND NEURAL MECHANISMS

Donald D. Price

THOUGH THERE IS no question that the phenomenon of hypnotic analgesia is real, there continue to be intriguing questions about its nature: How does hypnotic analgesia work? What is the psychological mechanism of its action? What is the biological mechanism of its action? What does knowledge of the mechanisms tells us about its use in clinical circumstances? Inquiry into these questions has absorbed and challenged investigators for some time. Their work has been fruitful and their questions have begun to yield answers. This chapter explores these questions, the method of their scientific investigation, and the clinical implications of answers that have emerged thus far.

Studies of hypnotic analgesia have labored under a double burden. Both the independent variables of hypnotic treatments and the multiple components of pain experience, which are the dependent variables, are subjective phenomena. Partly as a consequence, measurements of subjective independent and dependent variables of hypnotic analgesia experiments are seen as lacking the precise control that may be present in physiological or pharmacological studies.

This chapter presents an alternative view of the possibility of precise analysis and measurement of both the independent and dependent variables of hypnotic analgesia studies. In the context of providing this alternative view, a preliminary explanation of the neural and psychological mechanisms that may underlie hypnotic analgesia will be presented. Finally, the implications of understanding the neural and psychological mechanisms of hypnotic analgesia for the treatment and management of clinical pain will be elaborated.

THE INDEPENDENT VARIABLES OF HYPNOTIC ANALGESIA

The logistics and intent of hypnotic analgesic interventions are sometimes quite simple, particularly for acute pain. The clinician induces a hypnotic state in the patient, makes suggestions for reduced pain or the absence of pain, and then both the clinician and patient enjoy the consequences of hypnotically induced pain control. The problem becomes enormously complicated the moment one begins asking questions about the factors that evoke and maintain pain reduction, as well as about the nature of the pain reduction itself. The factors that evoke pain reduction range from psychosocial, including interactions between clinician and patient, to psychophysiological ones that influence the actual transmission of pain signals within the patient. The factors that maintain pain reduction differ; they seem to be largely dependent on an interaction among the patient's personality, environmental contingencies, and the efficacy of treatment. It is these factors and their relationships that effective treatment must address, even more than basic factors such as nociception.

The following discussion will consider: (1) the demand characteristics of the hypnotic analgesia situation; (2) the role of the hypnotic state; and (3) the possible interactions between hypnotic state and incorporation of hypnotic suggestions.

This discussion will be followed by a consideration of how hypnotic interventions influence the multiple dimensions of pain and, at least in a general sense, the neurophysiological processing of pain.

Demand Characteristics and Role Enactment Theory

One school of thought about the nature of hypnotic analgesia is that this phenomenon merely represents compliance with demand characteristics of the experimental or clinical situation and does not involve a genuine alteration in an individual's experience of pain. This model suggests that, after being given hypnotic induction and suggestions, subjects or patients cognitively relabel their reports of pain as less intense not because they perceive them to be less intense but because social expectations require that they act in the role of someone who has less pain (Spanos, 1986). In other words, while they continue to feel pain, they pretend that they do not.

There are two interrelated claims in this explanation. The first is that the hypnotic situation does not create a change in state of consciousness and that such a change is not required to respond to hypnotic suggestion. The second related claim is that there is nothing special about the hypnotic response of reducing one's pain rating. This response does not necessarily involve an actual reduction in pain, but rather a willingness to invent lowered ratings to describe unaltered sensory pains, in order to behave "as if" one were actually experiencing less pain. According to the "role enactment" theorists, the elaborate process of hypnotic induction serves only to strengthen the demand characteristics of the situation and encourage subjects to follow instructions and emit the desired behavior. (A corollary assumption underlying this theory is that self-report is an unreliable means of knowing what an individual is experiencing.)

Support for the claim that change in state of consciousness is neither necessary for nor contributory to hypnotic analgesia comes from studies that show no difference in analgesia levels between two groups of subjects given analgesia suggestions, with and without an induction of a hypnotic state (T. Barber & Hahn, 1962; T. Barber & Wilson, 1977; Evans & Paul, 1970). On the other hand, there are considerably more studies that demonstrate that greater analgesia occurs when subjects experience a hypnotic state, and that hypnotic responsivity is at least somewhat predictive of hypnotic analgesia (see references in Hilgard & Hilgard, 1994).

The related claim that hypnotically induced reports of reduced pain do not necessarily reflect actual reductions in perceived pain is perhaps best supported by observations that physiological responses to pain, such as increased heart rate and blood pressure, often still occur at the same time hypnotized subjects provide reports of greatly reduced pain (Hilgard & Hilgard, 1994). This issue will be further discussed when we consider dependent variables of hypnotic analgesia.

The Role of a Hypnotic State
in Hypnotic Analgesia

If a hypnotic state is not required to evoke reductions in pain report, and if subjects of hypnotic analgesia experiments are simply enacting an elaborate role, then subjects who are deliberately instructed to simulate analgesia—to pretend not to hurt—should be able to tolerate intense pain—while pretending that they do not hurt—as well as those who undergo the allegedly unnecessary ritual of hypnotic induction.

An elaborate experiment designed to test this hypothesis was carried out by Greene and Reyher (1972). They randomly assigned highly responsive subjects to the hypnotized and simulating groups. They instructed the simulators to remain unhypnotized, while deceiving the experimenter into believing they were hypnotized. They were also told to react to the painful stimulus as if they were analgesic. Increasing intensities of electric shock served as the painful stimuli, and pain tolerance and pain intensity reports served as dependent measures.

Despite the attempt to behave like hypnotized subjects while not, in fact, hypnotized, the simulators were clearly less tolerant of the pain during each of the several experimental conditions than were the hypnotized subjects. For example, the hypnotized and the simulators increased their tolerance of pain by 45 percent and 16 percent, respectively, a difference that was statistically highly reliable. Apparently, the shocks were more bearable for the hypnotized than for the equally responsive, but unhypnotized, role enactors. This experiment and similar others cast doubt on the idea that hypnotized subjects feel pain but report less pain to satisfy the demand characteristics of the situation.

Interactions Between a Hypnotic State and the Incorporation of Hypnotic Suggestions

Since it is clear that a hypnotic state is not in itself sufficient to produce analgesia, and since there is reasonable evidence that analgesia is greater in the context of a hypnotic state than without one (Hilgard & Hilgard, 1994), it is reasonable to conclude that a hypnotic state facilitates the analgesia induced by suggestions. This brings us to the general question of *how* a hypnotic state does this.

Two investigations have directly addressed this question. In the first (Price & Barrell, 1990), a group of 21 graduate students and faculty members participated in an experiential-phenomenological study of the common elements that comprise the experience of a hypnotic state, using the approach and method the investigators had previously described (Price & Barrell, 1980). First, through direct experience of several hypnotic inductions, each participant-observer identified the common elements that were present in most or all inductions used for analysis. Second, a group consensus identified the common elements that were necessary or sufficient for a hypnotic state. These elements included the following:

1. a feeling of relaxation (a letting-go of tensions or becoming at ease)
2. an absorbed and sustained focus of attention on one or a few targets
3. an absence of judging, monitoring, and censoring
4. a suspension of usual orientation toward time, location, and/or sense of self
5. experience of one's own responses as automatic (i.e., without deliberation and/or effort)

It was evident from descriptions of the observers' direct experiences of the hypnotic state that some of the common elements were necessary for the emergence of other elements and that, in general, strong interrelationships existed among these elements. Thus, element 1 ("relaxation, becoming at ease") appeared to provide a supportive general background for element 2 ("absorbed and sustained focus"), which in turn appeared to affect elements 3 ("absence of judging, monitoring, censoring") and 4 ("suspension of usual orientation toward time and location"). The latter two elements, in turn, appeared to maintain element 5 ("automaticity"). Finally, it was agreed by all observers that elements 4 ("suspension") and 5 ("automaticity") directly contributed to perceived hypnotic depth. A tentative model of these interrelationships was then formulated as shown in Figure 4.1A.

This model was subsequently tested in a second study in which 62 participants rated their perceived magnitudes of these elements on visual analogue scales during normal waking, mild, and deep hypnotic states (Price, Barber, & Harkins, 1988). As can be discerned from Figure 4.1B, path analysis provided at least a general statistical confirmation of the validity of the model. Only the hypothesized influence of element 3, "lack of monitoring," on element 4, "disorientation," was not confirmed. The experiential and conceptual basis for this model is generally supported by the work of others who have independently arrived at many of these same common elements (Bowers, 1978; Pekala & Kumar, 1984).

Returning then to the question of how a hypnotic state facilitates the incorporation of suggestions for analgesia, this model implicitly provides a basis for *increased responsiveness to suggestion* that is unique and distinguishable from other types of psychologically mediated increases in responsiveness to suggestion (e.g., placebo). This basis is directly evident in the phenomenology of the interrelationships between the common elements of this model and can be described as follows:

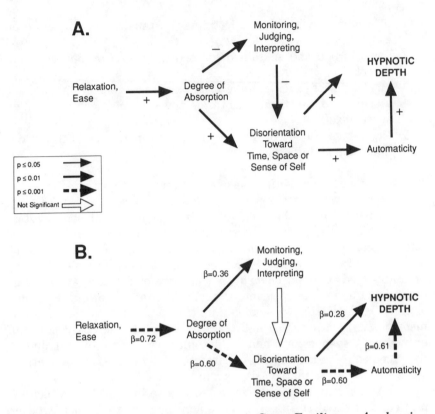

FIGURE 4.1. *Models of How a Hypnotic State Facilitates Analgesia Induced by Suggestions*

A hypnotic state begins with an absorbed and sustained focus on something. It can occur naturally during periods of fascination, for instance while watching an absorbing movie or ripples in a stream. The experience captures us. At first, it may take effort to develop this absorption. With time, however, one proceeds from an *active* form of concentration to a relaxed, *passive* form.

There is often (though perhaps not necessarily) an inhibition or reduction in the peripheral range of one's experience. At the same time, this relaxation and/or reduction in range of attention supports a *lack of monitoring and censoring* of that which is allowed into one's experience. Hence, inconsistencies are now more tolerable. Contradictory statements, which once arrested attention and caused confusion or disturbance, now no longer do so. The uncensored acceptance of what is being said by the hypnotist is not checked against one's own associations. Consequently, one no longer chooses or validates the correctness of incoming statements. This allows thinking and meaning-in-itself that is disconnected from active reflection.

From this way of experiencing, there emerges the sense of *automaticity*, wherein thought doesn't precede action but action precedes thought. Thus, if the hypnotist suggests a bodily action, a sensation, or a lack of sensation (e.g., analgesia), there is no experience of deliberation or effort on the part of the subject. The subject simply and automatically identifies with the suggested action, sensation, or lack of sensation, whatever is suggested. The possibility of not carrying out the action or experiencing the suggested changes in sensation is not considered, or is considered very little. In this way, a hypnotic state *facilitates* the incorporation of suggestions, including that of analgesia.

It must be noted that the automatic identification with the suggested action or sensation (or lack thereof) that occurs during the hypnotic experience shares some common principles with other types of psychologically mediated forms of responses to suggestion. To take just one of many possible examples, Kojo (1988) has suggested that the imagination of heat evokes actual increases in blood flow and skin temperature by creating a psychological set wherein the subject *allows* the feeling of warmth to be there without deliberation or effort.

It may well be that what is unique about hypnotic suggestions is not the effect of the suggestions themselves, such as pain relief, but the way in which the suggestions implicitly or explicitly refer to the source of experiential change – it is both effortless and automatic. This deceptively simple idea may, in fact, provide a rich source of understanding by clinicians of how to create effective suggestions for analgesia.

This uniqueness can perhaps be illustrated by comparing the nature of hypnotic suggestions with those that occur during placebo administration. The "suggestion" provided in the case of placebo analgesia can readily be distinguished from that provided during hypnotic analgesia, in that the former refers to an outside authoritative source as the origin of the pain relief. For example, injections or tablets provided by a health-care professional indicate that the agency of therapeutic relief comes from a medicine and a person experienced in the knowledge of the efficacy of the treatment. Within the placebo literature, there exists considerable evidence that greater placebo effects are achieved by more believable and technically convincing agents. Thus, placebo injections are more effective than placebo pills, and placebo morphine is more effective than placebo aspirin (Traut & Passarelli, 1957).

Implicit in the overall suggestion inherent to a placebo analgesic manipulation is the idea that in the absence of this outside authoritative agent there would be unrelieved pain. The nature of hypnotic suggestions for analgesia, on the other hand, refers to a more innate and *self-directed* capacity to alter one's own experience, often to the effect that one can experience sensations differently and including the possibility that there is no pain to be experienced (Barber, 1982). The source of experiential change, in the case of hypnotic analgesia, is perceived as occurring automatically and from within.

This experiential distinction between hypnotic and placebo analgesia may at least partly account for the complete lack of relationship between the magnitude of hypnotic analgesia and the magnitude of placebo analgesia tested in subjects of both high and low responsiveness (Hilgard & Hilgard, 1994). It has been determined that, for subjects not responsive to hypnotic suggestions, about the same modest degrees of analgesia are achieved through hypnotic suggestion and placebo administration. For highly responsive subjects, pain reduction evoked by hypnotic suggestion is far greater than the negligible or even negative effects produced by placebo. Therefore, hypnotic analgesia is more than a placebo and very likely different with respect to psychological mechanisms.

The considerations raised so far indicate that multiple factors within the psychosocial context and within the experience of subjects influence the alteration of pain as a result of hypnotic suggestions for analgesia. The influences of individual factors on responses to various types of hypnotic suggestion – other than hypnotic responsiveness per se – have received relatively little explicit recognition. However, the relative influence of elements within the hypnotic state on analgesic responses to suggestions could be tested in experiments wherein participants provide judgments of their experienced magnitudes. For example, self-ratings of such elements as "automaticity" and "depth of hypnotic state" could constitute independent variables in investigations of the relationship between depth of hypnotic state and responsiveness to analgesic suggestions.

THE DEPENDENT VARIABLES OF HYPNOTIC ANALGESIA

The suggestions for alteration of the experience of pain in studies of hypnotic analgesia relate closely to the dimensions of pain and to the psychological stages of pain processing. Thus, there are suggestions that specifically target the affective dimension of pain as distinguished from the sensory dimension. These include suggestions for *reinterpreting* sensations as pleasant rather than unpleasant or for reducing or eliminating the implications of threat or harm from the sensations. Then there are suggestions designed specifically to alter the quality and/or intensity of sensations so that they become less painful, not at all painful, or absent altogether. These include suggestions for *substituting* sensations of numbness, warmth, or other sensations for that of pain and suggestions for the complete absence of sensation. The latter include suggestions for *dissociation*, wherein subjects do not feel parts of their bodies that would otherwise be painful or subjects experience themselves in another location and context altogether. In addition to studies to assess the role of hypnotic depth and individual components of hypnosis on pain, we need studies of differential effects of various types of suggestion on sensory and affective dimensions of pain experience. For example, what are the effects on pain of suggestions exclusively designed to reinterpret the meanings of the sensations so that they are less threatening or unpleasant?

Just as there exist multiple psychological dimensions that contribute to hypnotic analgesia, analgesia itself is also likely to be comprised of multiple dimensions. As Barber described in Chapter 1, the experience of pain has both sensory and affective dimensions. The strategy discussed above for characterizing and measuring the factors in hypnotic treatments could be interfaced with one that assesses how these factors influence the different dimensions of pain, as well as the different neurological stages of pain processing (i.e., spinal, cortical, etc.).

Maximizing this strategy requires accurate, sensitive, and valid methods of pain measurement. This may be accomplished by using pain measurement methods that fulfill criteria for ideal pain measurement (Gracely & Dubner, 1981; Price & Harkins, 1992b). Direct magnitude scaling of sensory and affective dimensions of pain would seem essential, especially if hypnotic suggestions differentially influence the two dimensions of pain. Tursky (1985) has recommended the use of more sophisticated scaling methods and has identified the deficiencies of certain quantitative methods as they relate to the assessment of analgesia.

Since pain is comprised of sensory and affective dimensions, a number of questions can be raised about how a hypnotic intervention influences the various dimensions and stages of pain processing:

1. Does hypnotic analgesia reduce the affective dimension more than the sensory dimension of pain?
2. To what extent does hypnotic analgesia involve descending inhi-

bition of pain transmission at spinal cord levels or intracortical mechanisms that prevent awareness of pain?

3. Does hypnotic analgesia utilize an endogenous opiate system?

As surprising as it may seem, these questions are at least partly answerable in experiments that utilize multiple measures of pain experience and, in some cases, physiological indices of pain processing at different levels of the nervous system.

Differential Effects of Hypnotic Suggestions on Sensory and Affective Dimensions of Pain

The question of whether hypnotic suggestion has differential effects on *sensory* and *affective* dimensions was addressed in an investigation of the factors that contribute to the magnitudes of reduction in pain following indirect hypnotic suggestions (Price & Barber, 1987). Two groups of human volunteers made responses on extensively validated visual analogue scales of sensory pain intensity (sensory VAS) and pain unpleasantness (affective VAS) to noxious skin temperature stimuli (44.5 to 51.5 °C) before and after hypnotic suggestions were given for analgesia. Group 1 was given suggestions for developing a hypnotic state only once, just before analgesic testing, and did not have significantly reduced VAS responses to experimental pain after hypnosis. The experimenter remained with Group 2 and provided cues for maintaining a hypnotic state during their analgesic testing session. This group developed a 44.5 percent mean reduction in sensory pain intensity and a 87.4 percent mean reduction in affective pain. As shown in Table 4.1, the reduction in affective pain was much larger and more consistent across Group 2 subjects than the reduction in sensory pain intensity. A small but statistically reliable correlation was found between hypnotic responsiveness and overall magnitude of reduction in VAS sensory ratings but not VAS affective ratings.

It is not immediately apparent why hypnotically induced reductions in VAS affective ratings to experimental pain were greater and more consistent than reductions in VAS sensory ratings. Affective responses to experimental heat pain were reduced even in participants who had low responsivity scores and who showed very little change in perceived sensation intensities (see, for example, subjects 2 and 5 in Table 4.1). A possible answer to this question may be obtained through consideration of the nature of sensory and affective responses to experimental pain and of the degree of hypnotic involvement required to experience alterations in these pain dimensions.

Table 4.1

Hypnotic Susceptibility and Analgesia in Group 2

Subject	Hypnotic Susceptibility	% VAS Sensory Change	%VAS Affective Change
1	1	56.8	74.5
2	1	9.0	90.0
3	1	65.5	100.0
4	1	63.1	100.0
5	1	3.6	100.0
6	1	60.0	100.0
7	2	17.8	91.4
8	2	17.5	78.6
9	2	20.7	51.5
10	3	28.3	78.0
11	3	24.7	74.6
12	3	50.0	100.0
13	3	46.0	100.0
14	4	82.7	99.1
15	5	83.9	62.5
16	5	81.7	98.7
Mean	2.4	44.5	87.4
R_s		.4	−.2

Affective responses associated with pain are more influenced by the perceived context of the experimental situation than are sensory responses (Price, 1988). Thus, factors related to the psychological context of the person can selectively and often powerfully reduce affective responses to experimental pain (Price, 1988; Price, Barrell, & Gracely, 1980). Hypnotic suggestions in this experiment were directed toward

1. experiencing the testing situation as more pleasant.
2. experiencing the heat stimuli as more pleasant.
3. experiencing the heat stimuli as less intense.

It is clear that these three alterations in experience would require different degrees of hypnotic involvement (Shor, 1965; Weitzenhoffer, 1957). Experiencing the testing situation and test stimuli as less unpleasant would require less hypnotic involvement than experiencing direct reductions in sensations evoked by noxious heat stimuli. In some instances, selective reduction in affect could occur without a hypnotic state. Therefore, one component of a hypnotic intervention may involve responses to suggestion for reduced unpleasantness that do not require a hypnotic state. This explanation is consistent with the result that reductions in unpleasantness were not at all correlated with hypnotic responsiveness.

The reduction in pain-related unpleasantness beyond that accountable by a simple reduction in sensory pain intensity, and in some cases without any reduction in sensory pain, is not likely the result of reduction of the pain signal at peripheral or even spinal levels. Rather, it is likely the result of alteration in the *meanings* that normally attend painful experience. As such, the selective reduction in affective pain by cognitive mechanisms is likely to reflect neural events at higher levels of pain processing, including intracerebral mechanisms.

MECHANISMS OF REDUCTIONS IN SENSORY PAIN INTENSITY

Although it is clear that hypnotic suggestions may exert a more powerful reduction of affective pain than of sensory pain, it is also quite apparent that both dimensions are reduced. This has been amply demonstrated in several experimental laboratories (see Hilgard & Hilgard, 1994, and Price, 1988, for reviews). Moreover, it is the reduction in sensory pain itself that is statistically correlated with hypnotic responsivity, albeit at modest levels. Therefore, the hypnotic intervention that relies on hypnotic ability and a hypnotic state is the one most influential in reducing sensory pain intensity. Interestingly, the correlation becomes stronger with increasing levels of pain intensity, as shown in Table 4.2.

It makes sense that reduction of more intense pain requires more hypnotic ability than reduction of less intense pain. However, the overall modest strength of correlation between hypnotic responsivity and sensory analgesia and the complete absence of a significant correlation

Table 4.2
Hypnotic Susceptibility and Analgesia

Stimulus Temperature	Spearman Correlation Coefficient	
	Sensory Analgesia	*Affective Analgesia*
44.5°C	+0.04	−0.23
47.5°C	+0.21	−0.11
49.5°C	+0.43*	−0.08
51.5°C	+0.56*	+0.10

*P < 0.01

between hypnotic ability and reductions in affective pain ratings (Table 4.2) strongly indicate that multiple factors are involved. When analgesia results from a hypnotic intervention, it can also include factors that are unrelated to hypnotic responsivity and even to a hypnotic state. Such potential multiple factors are closely related to different proposed mechanisms of hypnotic analgesia as discussed below.

Neodissociation and "Intracerebral" Mechanisms

At present, there are two general mechanisms by which sensory pain can be reduced in intensity during hypnosis. The neodissociation theory (Hilgard & Hilgard, 1994) proposes that during hypnotic analgesia there is reduced awareness of pain, which normally occurs when nociceptive information has reached higher centers. According to this theory, pain is registered by the body and by covert awareness during hypnotic analgesia, but it is masked by an amnesia-like barrier between dissociated streams of consciousness. This dissociation in awareness has been demonstrated through "automatic writing" and through the phenomenon of the "hidden observer" (Hilgard, 1977; Hilgard & Hilgard, 1994; Hilgard et al., 1975).

Hilgard and his colleagues (1975) instructed subjects to report covert levels of cold pressor pain through automatic key pressing ratings of pain while their overtly experienced pain produced by the same cold pressor was reported through magnitude estimation. The result was that during *nonhypnotic* suggestions for analgesia there was about a 40 percent reduction in *both* overtly and covertly reported pain intensity. Suggestions for analgesia after inducing a hypnotic state produced an additional reduction in overtly reported pain, but not in covertly reported pain. This additional reduction is said to reflect dissociative mechanisms that are available for manipulation only when a hypnotic state is induced. A component of the perception of pain may be immediately forgotten or otherwise diverted from conscious awareness.

This interpretation of hypnotic analgesia as a dissociation in consciousness suggests an explanation for the paradox that physiological indices of stress often continue during hypnotic analgesia, even though the subject consciously feels little or no pain. Interestingly, Hilgard and his colleagues found that, with highly responsive subjects, the rise in heart rate caused by cold pressor pain was somewhat less during the hypnotic experience than during waking nonhypnotic control conditions, but that some increase in heart rate still occurred

(Hilgard & Hilgard, 1994). This partial reduction is consistent with Hilgard's observation of two components of pain reduction (sensory and affective). The reduction of pain during nonhypnotic conditions may be accompanied by reductions in autonomic and reflex responses to pain, whereas the reduction in pain associated with dissociative mechanisms would not likely be accompanied by decreases in autonomic responses.

Descending Spinal Cord Inhibitory Mechanisms

A second general mechanism by which hypnotic suggestions could reduce pain is by activation of an endogenous pain inhibitory system that descends to the spinal cord, where it prevents the transmission of pain-related information to the brain. There are multiple lines of indirect evidence for and against such a mechanism.

The question of whether hypnotic analgesia involves a brain-to-spinal-cord descending control mechanism is indirectly related to another question: whether endogenous opiates mediate hypnotic analgesia. If they do, then it would be likely that a descending control system is involved, since it has been well established that opiate analgesic mechanisms rely heavily on a brain-to-spinal-cord descending control system. A number of observations indicates that hypnotic analgesia does *not* depend on endogenous opiate mechanisms. First, different groups of investigators have found that naloxone hydrochloride, an opiate antagonist, does not reverse analgesia produced by hypnotic suggestions. For example, Barber and Mayer (1977) found that hypnotic suggestions elevated pain thresholds produced by tooth-pulp stimulation, and that these elevations in threshold were completely unaffected by naloxone hydrochloride. Similar negative results were obtained by Goldstein and Hilgard (1975).

Other characteristic differences also exist between opiate analgesia and hypnotic analgesia. Once it is repeatedly established in a highly responsive subject, hypnotic analgesia can be induced again very quickly (sometimes within seconds) in the same subject, and can also be very quickly terminated. Endogenous opiate mechanisms, by contrast, typically have a delayed onset to maximum effect (e.g., several minutes), and the effect is predictably slow to dissipate.

However, the lack of demonstration of an endogenous opiate mechanism involved in hypnotic analgesia does not exclude the possibility of a descending control system, only the possibility of an *opiate* descending control mechanism. Nonopiate brain-to-spinal-cord descending control mechanisms are known to exist (Price, 1988).

Although physiological investigations have addressed the possibility that hypnotic analgesia involves a brain-to-spinal-cord descending inhibitory mechanism, nearly all studies have focused on autonomic (T. Barber & Hahn, 1962), neurochemical (Barber & Mayer, 1977; Goldstein & Hilgard, 1975; Mayer, Price, Barber, & Rafii, 1976), or electrocortical changes associated with hypnotic analgesia (Crawford & Gruzelier, 1992).

A limitation common to all of these studies is the difficulty of identifying the general neuroanatomical sites at which the relevant modulatory mechanisms take place. Evidence that hypnotic analgesia involves a descending inhibition at spinal levels could be simply provided if some measure of spinal nociceptive function and pain perception could be simultaneously provided during hypnotic analgesia. The feasibility of such an approach is strongly indicated by Willer (1977, 1984, 1985), who has demonstrated that different types of somatosensory stimulation and attentional manipulations simultaneously reduce pain and the electrically evoked flexion reflex. He has also demonstrated that graded doses of morphine reduce the electrically evoked flexion reflex and pain intensity on a near equal percentage basis, thereby providing a standard for assessing descending pain inhibitory mechanisms. All of these observations suggest the possibility of simultaneous measurement of pain and the flexion reflex during hypnotic analgesia. Indeed, this idea may have originated in Hagbarth and Finer's (1963) preliminary demonstration of marked suppression of the flexion reflex in a few subjects during hypnotic analgesia. Though this result is very interesting, its meaning is difficult to interpret, partly because the suppression of the reflex was demonstrated in subjects who were aware of the physiological response that was being measured (and may have, unwittingly, complied in a nonhypnotic fashion).

A more recent and extensive analysis of the question of a possible descending inhibitory mechanism of hypnotic analgesia was made by examining changes in the R-III, a nociceptive spinal reflex, during hypnotic reduction of sensory pain and unpleasantness (Kiernan, Dane, Phillips, & Price, 1995). The R-III was measured in 15 healthy volunteers who gave VAS sensory and VAS affective ratings of an electrical stimulus during conditions of resting wakefulness without suggestions and during hypnosis with suggestions for hypnotic analgesia. A critically important feature of this study was that subjects were blind to the physiological index being measured and, later, when informed that measurements were being made of the R-III flexion reflex, failed to intentionally reduce the magnitude of this reflex. (This controls for both expectancy and compliance effects that had not been controlled in the earlier demonstration by Hagbarth and Finer.)

Hypnotic sensory analgesia was partially, yet reliably, related to reduction in the R-III (R^2 = .51, p < .003), suggesting that hypnotic sensory analgesia is at least in part mediated by descending antinociceptive mechanisms that exert control at spinal levels in response to hypnotic suggestion. Hypnotic affective analgesia was not quite significantly related to reduction in R-III (p = .053). Reduction in R-III was 67 percent as great as reduction of sensory pain, and accounted for 51 percent of the variance in reduction in the affective component. In turn, reduction in sensory pain was 75 percent as great as, and accounted for 77 percent of the variance in, reduction of unpleasantness.

The results suggest that three general mechanisms may be involved in hypnotic analgesia: The first, implicated by reductions in R-III, is related to spinal cord antinociceptive mechanisms. The second, implicated by reductions in sensory pain over and beyond reductions in R-III, may be related to brain mechanisms that serve to prevent awareness of pain once nociception has reached higher centers, as predicted by Hilgard's neodissociation theory (Hilgard & Hilgard, 1994). That the percent reduction in sensory pain intensity was greater than that of the R-III is consistent with Hilgard's and others' finding that some autonomic responses to pain remain even under conditions of profound hypnotic analgesia. The third, implicated by reductions in unpleasantness above and beyond reductions in sensory pain, may be related to selective reduction in the affective dimension, possibly as a consequence of reinterpretation of meanings associated with the painful sensation, as previously suggested by Price and Barber (1987).

This study by Kiernan and his colleagues provides crucial confirmation that hypnotic analgesia (1) is a measurable psychophysiological phenomenon and (2) has measurable effects on spinal reflexes.

The analytic strategy provided in this study is very useful for two reasons: (1) It conceptualizes the possible multiple actions of a hypnotic pain control intervention; (2) it provides a strategy for independent evaluation of multiple stages of pain processing. Similar to the work of Hilgard and Hilgard (1994), this study shows that multiple components of pain reduction are produced by a single hypnotic intervention. Most critically, the study demonstrates that the hypnotic experience has some measurable effect on a person beyond that suggested by role-enactment theory.

CLINICAL IMPLICATIONS

Taken together, investigations about the psychological and neural mechanisms of reduction of pain by hypnotic interventions strongly indicate the existence of multiple factors and mechanisms. These mechanisms include factors that evoke the development of a hypnotic state and incorporation of suggestions for analgesia, as well as multiple dimensions of pain experience and behavior.

Future studies of hypnotic analgesia should be designed to better assess the experiential factors and psychosocial contextual factors that influence changes in self-reported pain intensity that occur as a result of a hypnotic intervention. New approaches and methods are available to measure experiential factors such as "perceived automaticity" and "degree of absorption" (cf. Bowers, 1978; Pekala & Kumar, 1984; Price & Barrell, 1990). Using these methods, the factors that optimally influence responses to hypnotic suggestions for analgesia could be identified and utilized by both patients and clinicians. The concept of "hypnotic therapeutic manipulations" could shift in emphasis from reliance on outside authority to the patient's active participation in developing psychological conditions for therapeutic effects. (Many effective clinicians already utilize this concept, if only intuitively.)

More precise analysis of different components of hypnotic analgesic effects also has important therapeutic implications. These components include:

1. Selective reduction of pain-related affect (i.e., unpleasantness) through changes in the meaning of sensations and of the contexts in which they occur. It is possible that little or no hypnotic state is required for this type of influence, even though it may be an integral part of a hypnotic intervention.
2. Reductions in sensory pain by mechanisms that divert pain from conscious awareness once nociceptive information has reached higher centers. To the extent that this component is manifested within an individual, the normal somatomotor reflexes and autonomic, neuroendocrine, and neuroimmunological consequences of pain are *not* attenuated. Thus, stress-related reponses associated with pain still occur, often to the physiological detriment of the individual.
3. Inhibition of pain signals at the spinal level of processing. In contrast to the mechanism just described, negative physiological consequences of pain would be attenuated by this mechanism, since inhibition of pain signals would interrupt the supraspinal activation of brain structures involved in autonomic and neuroendocrine responses to pain.

Different individuals may utilize different proportions of these mechanisms, as has been suggested previously (Kiernan et al., 1995;

Price, 1988). For example, considerably different proportions of reduction in both affective pain and sensory pain were found among subjects in the Price and Barber experiment (1987), as indicated in Table 4.1.

Knowledge about the prevalence of these multiple mechanisms and the factors that influence them has far-reaching implications for treatment of various medical conditions, as well as pain. For example, the discovery that reductions in affective pain are larger and more prevalent than reductions in sensory pain, and that such reductions in affective pain are unrelated to hypnotic responsiveness, suggests that a large percentage of people could benefit from a hypnotic intervention (rather than only highly responsive individuals). Furthermore, hypnotic responsiveness does not appear to be a critically limiting factor in determining which patients could benefit from a hypnotic intervention.

To take another example, suppose certain types of hypnotic suggestions or treatments optimally activate cognitive dissociative mechanisms, whereas others activate descending spinal inhibitory mechanisms. The latter may be accompanied by reduced physiological consequences of pain, such as reduced immune response and reduced healing time. This specific type of hypnotic intervention may have a significant therapeutic advantage over hypnotic mechanisms that only involve cognitive dissociative mechanisms or selective reductions in affective pain, since the latter two mechanisms would not reduce the centrally mediated physiological responses that accompany pain, such as release of stress-related hormones and cardiovascular response. Clearly, further precise analysis of factors that contribute to hypnotic analgesia, as well as the components of analgesic responses themselves, offer possibilities for improved therapeutic effects of hypnotic interventions.

5

HYPNOTIC ANALGESIA: CLINICAL CONSIDERATIONS

Joseph Barber

THE OLD MAN reminded me of my grandfather, as he talked about his pleasure in riding his horse around the perimeter of his farm. But his conversation was frequently interrupted by spasms of pain that shot through his left shoulder and arm, momentarily taking his breath away. An auto accident, ten years before, had severely torn his left shoulder ligaments and left him with traumatic evulsion of the left brachial plexus, an injury which continued to stab him with pain, several times each hour, every day.

In that decade, John had been all around the medical world, figuratively and literally – he'd traveled to several of the world's most renowned clinics in search of relief. The neurosurgical treatments he'd been given had, unfortunately, left him in worse pain, and with less control of the muscles of his left side.

He looked me in the eye, a grim look on his face, which was reddened and sweating from the most recent wave of pain. "Just tell me the truth, young man. If you can help me, I'll appreciate it. If you can't, please tell me so, and I won't look any further."

"If it turns out that I can't help you, what will you do?"

John hesitated before he answered, which made me think he was going to give me a truthful answer to my question. With the same grim expression on his face, he said, "I've had a good, long life. If you can't take away this. . . . " Yet another stab of horrific

85

pain momentarily stifled his ability to speak. After a several seconds, he released his breath, relaxed his body a bit, and continued, now more quietly, "If you can't fix this pain, then I'll go home and use my shotgun to give me some peace."

Pain patients, by and large, are individuals whose medical condition has not been successfully managed. Though not all pain patients' circumstances are as dramatic as John's, there is always significant suffering from recurring pain for which there has been no effective treatment. Because these patients suffering from pain over time have usually been evaluated and treated, often by a number of clinicians, with no success, they can readily become worried that there is something psychologically amiss with them. They are particularly vulnerable to the notion that their pain is all in their head—that they are merely imagining it. (While this is especially likely to be a concern of patients with chronic benign pain syndrome, it is common in other pain patients, as well.)

When a patient is referred by his or her physician to a psychologist or psychiatrist—even if the referral has been thoughtfully and compassionately discussed with the patient—it is highly likely that the patient will feel confirmed in his or her worst fears about the "real" nature of the problem. The referral implies that the problem is psychological, which might mean that the patient has a troublesome personality or is actually "crazy." Sometimes it is believed that pain patients are just unable to tolerate the usual aches and pains tolerated by the rest of us. (This belief persists in spite of the fact that pain patients' ability to tolerate pain is, perhaps by necessity, significantly higher than that of the rest of the population.)

In order to allay a patient's fears of not being taken seriously and to evoke a more trusting relationship, we discuss, at the earliest opportunity, why the referral to a psychologist has been made and what our clinical task will be. We want to convey the appropriateness of the referral, while simultaneously educating the patient about the nature of pain, the nature of the interface between our mind and our body, and the reasonableness of a psychological approach to a pain problem. I might tell a patient, for instance, that I am going to help him or her retrain the nervous system, so that he or she will no longer have to be "notified" of the presence of the pain.

If a physical cause for the pain has been found, the discussion generally makes sense to the patient. When a physical cause has not been found, the patient may have a difficult time understanding why he or she is having pain. Patients nearly always have an organic basis for the pain, though the cause may be neither identifiable nor physically treatable. Something is stimulating the pain transmission system of these patients. The pain is not all in their head.

The change in a patient's self-image and the dramatic increase in confidence that occurs when a patient experiences hypnotic analgesia for the first time can itself be salutary. The experience can also, paradoxically, confirm the patient's fear that the pain was all in his or her head. If there is a hint that the patient's success at hypnotic analgesia will be interpreted as denial of the pain's reality, this must be addressed before continuing with treatment.

Among all psychological treatments, hypnotic techniques are uniquely capable of bringing about dramatic relief from suffering. How that capability is channeled and how the relief is integrated into the patient's life is, as we shall see, a profound and unavoidable clinical issue. We need to be flexible in our approach, choosing feedback from the patient about what is effective over our own preconceptions. In the pages that follow, I identify principles that can guide you in selecting effective treatment approaches to particular patients.

TECHNIQUES FOR CREATING HYPNOTIC ANALGESIA

As documented in Chapter 4, hypnotic treatment can alter either the sensory or the affective components of pain. Thus, a variety of hypnotic techniques may be effective, depending upon the circumstances. As in other clinical circumstances, we should choose a particular hypnotic technique for a given situation on the basis of what will best meet the needs of the patient. It helps, of course, to have a large repertoire of approaches. Although it is sometimes difficult to interpret the effects of his methods, I gathered some of my approaches from reading Milton Erickson's reports of his inventive hypnotic treatments for pain (Erickson, 1982; Haley, 1967). You may also refer to the rich literature of hypnotic analgesia for descriptions of clinical treatment for pain; see, for example, Barber (1982, 1990), Brown and Fromm (1987), Erickson (1982), Erickson, Hershman, and Secter (1990), Hartland (1971), Hilgard and Hilgard (1994), J. Hilgard and LeBaron (1984).

Although my clinical work was initially influenced by the classic techniques described below, when I reviewed the clinical cases I've treated over the past twenty years, I noticed the development of a distinct preference for two particular hypnotic approaches. I believe that these approaches, used singly or in combination, can be very effective in relieving suffering from a wide variety of long-standing conditions: (1) reinterpreting sensations so that the patient can incorporate them into his or her life in a benign fashion; and (2) developing the expectation that suffering is no longer a necessary part of life.

First, however, let us look at some well-established techniques: anesthesia; direct diminution of pain; sensory substitution; displacement of pain; and dissociation.

Anesthesia

Hypnotic suggestions can evoke a perception of anesthesia that renders a body area insensitive to feeling, including pain, just as though a local anesthetic had been administered, blocking neural transmission in that region. The fidelity with which this hallucination mimics actual anesthetic numbness can be quite dramatic.

Anesthesia can be suggested quite simply, as for example:

> It can begin to feel as if [the painful area] is becoming numb, with no sensation at all.

This experience requires a positive hallucination of numbness and, in my experience, this is a relatively difficult phenomenon to achieve, compared with the following techniques.

Direct Diminution of Sensations

Direct diminution of sensations is a simple technique for reducing sensory pain. A suggestion might be made, for example:

> You can continue to enjoy feeling increasingly well, with each breath you take . . . almost as if the discomfort is somehow gradually going away . . . as if, somehow, the feelings are getting smaller and smaller and smaller, or, perhaps, getting farther and farther and farther from your awareness.

Suggestions focus on the diminution of the intensity of pain. One might suggest, for example, that the "volume" or the "intensity" or the "brightness" or the "heat" of the pain can be turned down. Metaphors for turning down volume, reducing intensity, dimming brightness, cooling heat, and so on are most effective when matched to the patient's own phenomenology of pain intensity or quality. Asking the patient to scale pain intensity and then to discover the apparent change in that intensity level is another diminution technique.[1] It is essential that you be able to imagine such imaginary possibilities, and then convey them clearly and compellingly to the patient.

Sensory Substitution

Hypnotic suggestions can be used to create sensory substitution, or a reinterpretation of sensations. A sensation of intolerable burning, for instance, can be substituted by another sensation. It may be preferable that the substituted sensation not be pleasant, but merely more tolerable than the original sensation. You might suggest sensations such as itching, or coldness, or tingling. Such a substitute sensation has several virtues:

1. The patient knows the pain is still present (so the cancer patient, for instance, does not have to be concerned that he or she will forget that cancer still persists and thereby fail to seek proper medical attention).
2. The substitute sensation is not particularly pleasant, so it is more plausible—more expected, even—than, say, a sensation of pleasure.
3. If the patient is still feeling uncomfortable, but not in agony, many financial and social incentives ("secondary gains") that require the maintenance of pain can still be obtained without the patient's needing to suffer. Used initially and only temporarily, this strategy establishes the patient's confidence that there is little to lose in cooperation. Eventually, of course, treatment goals are likely to include the diminution of debilitating rewards for disability.

Sensory substitution might be accomplished with the following kind of suggestion (successfully used with a 42-year-old paraplegic patient suffering burning dysesthesia in the legs):

The feelings that you describe [needles stabbing into his thighs] can begin to change, very slightly. Oddly enough, it may begin to seem as if the needles are becoming more and more blunt . . . broad . . . almost as if they have become tiny, massaging fingers. What an interesting sensation you can begin to have: thousands

[1] It is important to re-visit the patient's pain rating throughout treatment, as a means of evaluating treatment progress.

of warm buzzing fingers, massaging your legs. Not entirely pleasant, of course, but perhaps a welcome relief.

Again, suggestions are most likely to be effective if they incorporate
qualities of the patient's personal experience of pain and suggest a
plausible modification of sensory quality.

Displacement

Displacement of the pain from one area of the body to another can
be accomplished with well-localized pain that is primarily intolerable
because of its location (e.g., abdominal pain is less tolerable than limb
pain). This technique can also serve to increase the confidence of a
patient who is skeptical about his or her abilities to alter the pain. A
suggestion for creating displacement, for example, is:

> You may have already noticed that the pain moves, ever so
> slightly, and you can begin to notice that the movement seems to
> be in an outwardly spiraling, circular direction. As you continue
> to attend to that movement, you may not notice until some time
> later that the pain has somehow moved out of your abdomen and
> seems to be staying in your left hand. It seems to be very much
> the same sensation . . . yet, for some reason, it seems less bother-
> some.

The effects of such suggestions may be enhanced if patients are left
free to choose the direction or location of movement or if the phenomenon is made more plausible by some discussion of the complex inter-
connections of the nervous system. The primary goal of this approach
is to render the pain less disabling, threatening, or frightening, and
thus more tolerable – by changing the locus of pain experience. An
important implication of such modification, however, is that, if pain
can change in location, perhaps it can be modified in other dimensions
(and, ultimately, eliminated entirely). This implication should be conveyed with clinical sensitivity.

Dissociation

In addition to creating the kinds of sensory alterations just described,
hypnotic suggestions can evoke dissociation from the pain. The patient is able to accurately describe the still persisting pain, but as from
a distance and with no suffering, no concern. That is, the pain is still

perceived, but the patient no longer suffers from it. Dissociation is often useful when the patient is relatively immobile (e.g., during surgery or some other painful procedure, or when a patient is bed-ridden). A suggestion to evoke dissociation might be the following, used with a 49-year-old woman with life-threatening metastatic disease:

> It isn't necessary for you to stay here, in bed, conscious of all the hospital routine that occurs. I wonder if you might prefer to enjoy a kind of vacation from this room. You might like to imagine yourself, for instance, stepping out of the room, moving down the hall, and settling nicely into the solarium. Or, later today, you might prefer to feel as if you are enjoying a lovely sunny afternoon resting on the beach at Maui. [Maui was not my choice; she had suggested it during our previous conversation.] Your body can remain here, in bed, to insure that all the routine things can be done for you; but your mind can take you far away, and you can enjoy whatever you'd like, with nothing to bother you.

By describing the circumstances in the hospital room as "routine," I imply that nothing important—nothing serious, nothing catastrophic—would be happening to her. This suggestion, if accepted, can help alleviate the anxiety felt by the patient about being in the hospital, with all the implications that location had for her.

SPECIAL CONSIDERATIONS

When the Patient Is Experiencing Pain during the Induction

In order to be helpful to the patient, suggestions must be credible; that is, they must match the patient's current experience. Moreover, they must be heard and understood. If the patient is currently feeling pain, it is not helpful to offer suggestions based on how comfortable the patient is. In fact, the patient's pain may be sufficiently absorbing that it makes it difficult to pay attention to your suggestions.

When a patient is feeling substantial pain during the hypnotic treatment, it is often not practical to offer suggestions that are intended to distract. Rather, the pain sensations themselves can be utilized as the target of attention during the hypnotic induction. This conveys to the patient that you know he or she is hurting and that you are not frightened by the pain. Further, you raise the possibility that the pain can change simply as a function of paying careful attention to it.

John, 66, with Excruciating Shoulder and Arm Pain

Let us return to John, the farmer I described at the beginning of the chapter. His injury had left him with excruciating, stabbing pain throughout his left shoulder and arm. He experienced the pain in waves of intensity, usually several minutes apart. During the onset of a wave of pain, he was forced to stop whatever he was doing and to double over in agony, holding his breath until the pain passed, several seconds later.

The doubling over was a futile resistance to the pain and, I thought, tended to further intensify the pain, rather than to help John endure it. I believed that if he could accept the pain, as terrible as it was for now, and not resist it, he would be less terrorized by it and it would take up less of his attention. Here is an excerpt from an early hypnotic induction (fourth treatment) with John:

> Now, John, when the pain comes, I want you to notice how easily it can move right through you. Right now, take a very deep breath, hold it for a moment, and let it all the way out. . . . That's right. Now, just breathe . . . with your eyes comfortably closed. Don't relax too much, so the pain won't be too much of a surprise. Just breathe, comfortably, with your eyes closed. . . .
> . . . Now, as it comes, take a deep breath, and let it go . . . just as you let the pain go through you . . . like water through a pipe. That's it . . . just breathe it through you, like water through a pipe. Now, let yourself breathe comfortably . . . it's gone now. Just breathe, and relax just a bit more than you were. When it comes again, just take a deep breath and don't hold onto it . . . just let it go, just as you let my words go through you . . . just like water through a pipe. That's right.

In this way John was able to encompass the experience of the pain, while at the same time begin to suffer less. Ultimately, this induction strategy facilitated his absorption in pleasant imaginings. Even though pain continued to attack him periodically, his response to it continued to wane until he was able to experience a sense of comfort even when the attack came over him. We were able to use hypnotic methods more effectively after this successful experience.

Extending Relief with
Posthypnotic Suggestions

My own preference when treating pain patients is to use posthypnotic suggestions frequently. I believe that the most helpful consequences from hypnotic intervention rarely occur from a patient's conscious intent; rather, they seem to the patient to be automatic events that happen *to* him or her. My work has been most successful when I have been able to facilitate the patient's perception that the pain is "going away" as a function of its own time course (rather than because of something specific that the patient or I have done). Whether this is an example of superstitious learning on my part or a reliable clinical finding, I do not know. In the absence of compelling evidence to the contrary, however, I would cautiously recommend this practice to you (and do, in fact, teach this practice to my students).

The fact that a patient can be comfortable during a hypnotic treatment is clinically meaningful, as well as pleasant for the patient. As a clinical outcome, however, it obviously has limited usefulness. What, then, are the uses for posthypnotic suggestions?

For the patient whom we would like to rehabilitate, we use posthypnotic suggestions as a means of extending the duration of the hypnotic effect. *A posthypnotic suggestion is one that is intended to have effect after the hypnotic experience is over and the patient has regained normal waking consciousness.* In general, posthypnotic suggestions include a cue that evokes the suggested experience (or behavior).

For instance, one could suggest that, "Whenever I gently touch your arm, like this, you will discover, at that moment, how really comfortable your arm feels." If successful, this suggestion would create analgesia whenever I touch the patient's arm. This strategy has instructive value for the patient because this effect can be generalized to other experiences. For example, if the patient's arm can become analgesic, then potentially any area of the patient's body can become analgesic, including the area affected by pain. If it can become analgesic when I touch his arm, then perhaps it can become analgesic at other times as well.

The cue can also be made a function of context. For example, one might say, "Whenever you need to feel relief from this pain, you'll suddenly notice that, in fact, you *are* beginning to feel better. And you will feel better throughout the day." In this way, the patient's own recognition of the need for comfort is the cue, and no behavior on my part is necessary. The patient's experience can be that of noticing a natural fluctuation in the intensity of the pain. In this case, though, the "natural fluctuation" tends to involve progressively less intensity of pain, for progressively longer periods of time.

Different patients may need different kinds of cues, some more elaborate than others. For instance, an independent individual can discover that she can create her own cues and can create hypnotic analgesia in a variety of ways you may not have described. A less independent patient may need more circumscribed suggestions, such as, "When you are in your bedroom, lying in your bed, you can know that just closing your eyes and taking a deep breath will allow you to suddenly notice how really comfortable you have become."

Self-Hypnotic Management

Ultimately, the most effective means of creating both independence for the patient and long-lasting pain relief is through self-hypnosis. Most patients can learn self-hypnosis quite readily and apply their skills to the development of analgesia over increasingly greater lengths of time (Barber, 1982; Sachs, Feuerstein, & Vitale, 1977). However, as is true for most processes of personal development, this is easier said than done.

A patient's interest in learning self-hypnosis and willingness to use it provide a valuable index of his or her motivation for actively participating in recovery, as well as a means of assessing broader psychological issues concerning self-esteem, willingness and ability to undertake self-care, attitude toward the pain or disability, and so on. If not effectively managed, this complex issue of assessment and management of motivation can become an obstacle to therapeutic success.

In my experience, most patients, even when successful at experiencing a profound reduction of their pain resulting from hypnotic treatment, are resistant to initiating and maintaining such treatment for themselves. When you encounter this obstacle, it must be addressed. Because resistance may be associated with complex psychological conflicts, we proceed in a way that conveys concern for the difficulty and respect for whatever may be the cause. We want to identify both the nature of the patient's resistance to self-hypnosis and possible means of resolving it.

One psychological issue that often emerges indirectly when exploring this resistance is the patient's preference for being taken care of by the clinician, rather than initiating this kind of self-care. Most people enjoy being nurtured and cared for by someone else, and hypnotic treatment often feels like being deeply cared for. This enjoyment may be threatened by the demand for self-care. Exploring this obstacle with patients, I have found that:

1. While hypnotic treatment is a pleasurable experience of being taken care of, self-hypnotic rehearsal may feel emotionally empty and aversive.
2. While hypnotic treatment reminds patients, however sublimi-

nally, of earlier experiences of nurturing and care, self-hypnotic rehearsal may feel like abandonment.
3. While hypnotic treatment feels virtually effortless, self-hypnotic rehearsal may feel uncomfortably effortful.

For many patients the difference between feeling cared for and feeling left to care for oneself is sufficiently unsatisfying, if not actually aversive, that it hinders their otherwise conscientious efforts to follow through with treatment recommendations. Consequently, they avoid learning self-hypnotic methods.

While exploring these issues, you may determine that self-hypnotic methods are not appropriate in a particular case. Sometimes, though, discussing the patient's disinclination will result in a sufficient change in her perceptions to support a renewed, sometimes successful effort. More often, the issue will not be quickly resolved; the discussion will need to be continued over time and will be accompanied by supportive coaching in learning self-hypnotic methods.

There are many ways to teach self-hypnotic techniques to a patient. My own preference is to use a principle described by Erickson and Erickson (1941). Essentially, through a posthypnotic suggestion I convey that the patient will have control of the posthypnotic cue and that the suggested posthypnotic behavior is the act of developing a hypnotic experience. For example, I might say:

Whenever you want to feel this kind of relaxation and comfort, all you have to do is . . . rest back, in a chair, or sofa, or bed . . . and take a very deep, very satisfying breath, and hold it . . . hold it for a moment. Then, as you let it all the way out, these feelings . . . of comfort and well-being . . . will automatically come washing over you . . . just like water in a hot tub . . . with nothing to bother you, and nothing to disturb you.

In this instance, the posthypnotic cue is taking the deep breath, and the posthypnotic behavior is feeling the experience of comfort and well-being, unbothered and undisturbed—the experience, in effect, of analgesia.

Since self-hypnotic methods involve learning a skill, competence can be improved by practice. Sometimes it is helpful to make an audiotape for the patient to use at home as an aid to practicing these methods. I always recommend a regular practice schedule for a patient, as a means of rapidly and effectively developing self-hypnotic skills. I also emphasize that the development of this skill, like any skill, requires a substantial commitment of time and effort.[2]

As a patient's improving condition permits greater independence from you, and as his or her mastery of self-hypnotic skills increases, less frequent treatment is necessary. At this point clinical follow-up becomes increasingly important. I make clear to patients that, in addition to whatever follow-up appointments we schedule, I want them to ask me for additional help if they find at some point that their self-hypnotic skills are no longer effective. Sometimes, many months pass during which a patient successfully uses self-hypnotic management of pain. Then, for a variety of reasons (e.g., sudden onset of environmental stressors, reinjury, or worsening of a medical condition), he or she finds managing the pain increasingly difficult. At such times, an appointment may make a substantial difference. A "booster" treatment may be all that is necessary to return the patient to independent functioning. It may also be helpful to identify, with the patient, the antecedents to the present difficulty in using self-hypnosis, so they can be better managed in the future. Sometimes more intensive treatment is necessary to help the patient cope with a worsening condition.

THE TREATMENT OF
RECURRING PAIN

The use of hypnosis for the recurring pain of various headache syndromes, cancer, burn injury, and dental pain is explored in other chapters. Here we take up the question of how to effectively use hypnosis in the treatment of other recurring pain syndromes.

Strictly speaking, hypnosis can effectively reduce awareness of any pain, independent of the location, the intensity, and the underlying cause of the pain. In any given case, however, these factors may powerfully affect how hypnosis can best be used and its ultimate effectiveness.

The Vital Importance of the
Meaning of the Pain

The power of meaning cannot be overemphasized. It is precisely the patient's understanding of the nature of the pain and of the meaning

---

[2]Many piano students, for example, devote at least an hour a day to practicing. Surely, learning the effective use of self-hypnotic methods requires a similar dedication of time and intellectual focus (Holroyd, 1996).

of the pain that determines how much the patient will suffer from the pain – and how the pain can best be treated. As Karen Syrjala and Sari Roth-Roemer emphasize in Chapter 6, cancer frightens us more than other disease. Consequently, the pain of cancer generates suffering even greater than might be experienced with equally noxious but less feared stimulation. Likewise, the pain that accompanies a debilitating illness may cause more suffering than other pain. Effective treatment of such pain depends upon confronting the meaning of the pain for the patient. This may be done explicitly or implicitly, depending on the patient's readiness for discussion and need for clarity.

CASE EXAMPLE: DAGNY, 63, WITH TERRIBLE HEADACHE

The severe headache of Dagny, a 63-year-old business executive, was found to be caused by an inoperable cerebral aneurysm. Aside from the headache, the aneurysm was asymptomatic. The patient knew, of course, that there was a risk – a likelihood, in fact – that the aneurysm would one day burst, with catastrophic results.

Dagny was a highly successful woman, accustomed to focusing on practical aspects of whatever problems confronted her. In this case, however, her habitual way of coping was obstructed by the realization that there really was nothing she – or anyone else – could do to reduce the likelihood that sometime in the future the aneurysm would suddenly, unpredictably explode in her brain. And the headaches were a cruel reminder of the "time bomb" in her head (as she characterized the aneurysm).

Four treatments with hypnotic suggestion, over three weeks, were ineffective in relieving either Dagny's pain or her worry over it. It was difficult for either of us to imagine a benign reinterpretation of the meaning of this pain. I am sure that my clinical ineffectiveness was partly a result of our inability to find a benign view of this pain. But I reluctantly and regretfully acknowledged that I did not know anything further to do for Dagny. Although I profoundly wished that I could offer her treatment, there was nothing I could offer except my empathy.

Fortunately, in most cases, pain is not so lethal in its implications. Perhaps because the mechanism of hypnotic action has not been understood, we are vulnerable to magical beliefs about its efficacy. For instance, a colleague, believing that hypnotic treatment can produce magical cure, seriously suggested that I attempt to reduce the aneurysm by hypnotic means. I did not follow his suggestion.

Your Anguish about Your Patient's Pain

A colleague recently described to me how deeply troubled she felt when a patient left her office, after a treatment, still obviously suffering a lot of pain. She did not want this, yet she did not know what more to do at that point. As a psychologist who has treated thousands of pain patients over the past 20 years, and not all of them successfully, I could easily identify with her anguish. Perhaps it is easier for a psychologist to feel sanguine when an emotionally troubled psychotherapy patient leaves the office, because we know that he can cope with his troubles until we see him again. (This is not the case, obviously, with an acutely disturbed psychotherapy patient – and we ordinarily make special arrangements for such a patient.)

I am aware that our compassionate concern, however real and vital, must be held at a safe distance from our clinical judgment, so that we can effectively plan treatment without being unduly affected by the patient's suffering. This implicitly communicates to the patient that, while we care about his or her pain, the pain does not deeply disturb us, and we are not afraid of it. This is the attitude we hope the patient will adopt.

Additionally, it is unwise for either clinician or patient to hold expectations about when or how much the pain will be relieved. Such expectations can be deadly to morale. Because we do not know how posthypnotic suggestions will affect the patient's pain – when he will notice feeling better, how much better, and for how long – we can maintain our curiosity and hopefulness about their future effect. That said, I admit that I usually begin with the optimism that the patient can become sufficiently comfortable, and I communicate this optimism to my patient. This optimism does not carry a guarantee, however, nor promise specific improvements.

Frequency of Treatment

If a psychotherapy patient is acutely distressed, we are likely to make special arrangements, ranging from being more available on the telephone or increasing treatment frequency to hospitalization. These same kinds of arrangements are helpful in the case of the acutely distressed pain patient. I usually see such patients frequently – once a day or at least every other day – until therapeutic momentum is established and I have evidence that the treatment is beginning to be effective.

Appropriate Use of Analgesic Medications

Using hypnotic methods does not preclude the use of other treatments, particularly analgesic medications. While supporting the patient's use of appropriate medications, including analgesics and antidepressants, I stress time-contingent, rather than need-contingent, medication schedules (Finer, 1982; Fordyce, 1978; Sternbach, 1982a). Sometimes it is necessary to consult with the prescribing physician to insure that everyone involved understands the efficacy of time-contingent medication.

Often, patients do not understand they are receiving various treatments. I educate them about the appropriate integrated use of analgesics, antidepressants, physical therapy, and other treatments. I also listen to their concerns or objections, sometimes acting as ombudsman between patients and their physicians. This fosters patient cooperation in the whole of treatment.

CLINICAL EXAMPLES

AYN, A 77-YEAR-OLD TEACHER WITH THALAMIC PAIN SYNDROME

Ayn presented with a two-year history of excruciating hemicorporeal pain secondary to cerebrovascular accident (CVA). Her diagnosis was thalamic pain syndrome, for which the only medical remedy is thalamotomy — a neurosurgical procedure which she was unwilling to undergo because of the likely untoward consequences. She had traveled to several pain centers on the East Coast of the United States, and in the Midwest, and had received a variety of treatments, including hypnosis, physical therapy, analgesic medications (including some experimental ones), acupuncture, and transcutaneous electrical nerve stimulation (TENS), all to no avail. In addition to the pain, the CVA had left her with hemiparesis, so walking was very difficult for her. She was, however, an extraordinarily vivacious individual. She hoped that she would eventually find curative treatment. A retired college professor, she had filled her life prior to the CVA with travel and friends. Now, with movement difficult and every waking moment filled with the perception that the left side of her body was "being squeezed in a red-hot vise," she was virtually housebound.

She was taking no analgesic medication, since none affected the pain. She simply endured the pain and suffered mightily. She was unable to enjoy any activity, because the pain was so intense that it took up most of her conscious awareness. Significantly, the stroke and its sequelae meant to Ayn that she was aging. This was a shocking realization, one she preferred to deny as best she could.

The first appointment was occupied primarily with assessment of Ayn's psychological status, with a particular focus on her pain, how she coped with it, and what relation it bore to her life, and a review of her medical history pertinent to the rehabilitation treatment she had received. It was clear from Ayn's demeanor that she was quite depressed. She was fatigued, sad, sometimes crying during the interview, but she expressed an unusual (and, I thought, unrealistic) degree of hopefulness about my successful treatment of her pain. A magazine article had led her to conclude that I would be able to successfully return her to a pain-free life.

Curiously, in spite of Ayn's otherwise lively optimism (or perhaps *because* I experienced it as unrealistic and too demanding of me), my own reaction to Ayn, including my response to reading her medical records and to recognizing her profound depression, was one of hopelessness. She was clearly distressed by the high level of intense pain and seemed highly motivated for relief. Her life had become increasingly constricted by her disability, so that she now spent most days sitting at home watching television.

My immediate impulse was to recommend that she return to her own town and find someone there who could care for her on a long-term basis. She had said that she planned to be in my city for two weeks and would be able to see me throughout that time.

Persisting in my pessimism, I told her two weeks would not be sufficient time to properly treat her and began suggesting alternatives for care back home. She quickly discounted that possibility, and said she would make arrangements to stay as long as necessary.

Feeling no choice but to try to help Ayn, despite my own hopelessness, I suggested that we make an appointment for the following day, at which time I would begin showing her "how to retrain your nervous system and begin feeling more human again." I explained that I would use hypnosis to alter her sensory processing and that it might not be immediately effective.

At the second appointment Ayn was hypnotized, given an explanation of the nature of her pain based on the understanding of the consequences of an infarct to the thalamus, and told that over time her nervous system could "reroute" nervous impulses through other pathways, just as her motor system had done. (In the two years following her CVA her paresis had improved markedly, though it was not stable, and she walked with the aid of a cane.) This suggestion for diminution was intended to counter her belief – and fear – that her pain was merely imagined. Since Ayn was highly educated and valued education, this suggestion was also intended to increase the plausibility of treatment success.

I suggested that she could not reasonably expect full relief from pain to last throughout the day and certainly she could not expect full relief to last until the next appointment (two days hence). However, I said that *some* relief could be expected during that period of time. (Of course, being told that "full relief" could not be expected to last a particular amount of time implies that full relief is to be expected for some amount of time.) Suggestions were also given to increase her confidence in her ability to endure, no matter what the outcome of treatment. Posthypnotic suggestions were given to facilitate the re-development of the hypnotic state at the next appointment.

At the termination of the hypnotic treatment, she expressed some surprise that her arm and chest didn't seem to hurt as much as usual. (I was also pleasantly surprised.) I asked in what way they felt different. She indicated that both the temperature and pressure of the vise had somehow decreased. We arranged for her to return in two days for the next appointment.

Ayn next arrived looking significantly more cheerful and reporting that she had been hurting less. Specifically, she reported that her arm and chest had felt unencumbered and comfortable following the previous treatment and that this relief had lasted throughout the day. She reported having slept comfortably and without sedatives for the first time since her CVA. The next day, however, she awoke feeling nearly as much pain as usual. The pain had remained unchanged throughout that day, she had taken medication to sleep that night, and she was now feeling her usual intense pain.

As part of the hypnotic induction process, I suggested that she imagine sitting at a lakeside (an image she had suggested when describing enjoyable vacations at a particular lake). Later I sought to deepen her dissociative experience (dissociated both from the experience of being in the office with me and, more importantly, from her body awareness) by suggesting catalepsy in her unaffected (right) arm. I then discussed the importance of the analgesia she had created two days previously and emphasized the implication of that: She had the power to alter her pain experience. If she could do it for a day, I continued, then a day and an hour wouldn't be too much to expect. And a day and an hour isn't so much less than a day and an hour and a half, of course. . . . In this way, within a few minutes suggestions were given for increasing the amount of time she could expect comfort. I then reinforced the previous suggestion that she could retrain her nervous system to reroute sensory processing through other pathways, isolating the damaged pathways and thereby avoiding the need for processing "painful impulses." In order to begin the process of independence for Ayn, I also gave her posthypnotic suggestions such as the following:

> This experience, right now, of comfort and peace, is your experience . . . not mine. And the ability to create this experience is your ability . . . not mine. And you can enjoy learning how to use your ability to create this experience whenever you need to. For instance, whenever you're feeling very fatigued, or uncomfortable, and would really like to reexperience this pleasant comfort, all you need to do is lie down in a bed, close your eyes, and recall to your mind this lovely lakeside setting that you know so well. I'm going to stop talking right now, and I want you to just enjoy as fully as you like the comfort and peace you can bring yourself from just sitting here, looking out at the water, or enjoying the scent of flowers from that garden over there.

At the end of this second treatment session, Ayn was excited and surprised that she had no awareness of any discomfort at all. As she left, I suggested that it would make for a more pleasant stay in the city if she were to remain relatively comfortable over the next four days until our next appointment.

At the third treatment appointment, Ayn reported that she had had no pain since she left my office four days previously. She was quite dramatic in her expression of delight and gratitude at this turn of events. She had slept well without medication as well. Hypnosis was used at this appointment to reinforce the gains that had been made and to reemphasize the importance of her own independent use of this skill, so that she could remain comfortable back home, far from my office.

The fourth, fifth, and sixth treatment appointments were used to consolidate these gains and to increase Ayn's confidence in her own hypnotic abilities, independent of my clinical intervention. She had six treatment appointments in two and a half weeks and was now ready to return home. Although I tried to refer her to someone near her home for follow-up care, she declined this, and we agreed that we would keep in touch by telephone and correspondence.

Follow-up contact revealed that she maintained her pain-free condition for over seven months, at which time she suffered a serious fall, spraining an ankle and, curiously, causing a return of her thalamic pain to nearly pretreatment levels. We arranged that she would return for treatment, which she did. Her return occurred one year after the first series of treatments.

Continued treatment of Ayn's pain syndrome was complicated by other factors. Although the first treatment alleviated her pain, it was clear that Ayn was now quite depressed—more than she had been a year ago. Her fall had meant to her that she really was becoming "old and weak and helpless."

She remained for two more weeks, and treatment for her depression was initiated as well as hypnotic reinforcement of her successful analgesia. I attempted to refer her for continued treatment of her depression to a psychiatrist near her home, but she declined. Follow-up contact was again maintained by telephone and through the mail, and Ayn's condition remained relatively stable. She was "comfortable enough," although her depression continued, with only occasional relief. Despite my urging that she obtain treatment near her home, she continued to resist. I maintained contact with Ayn, and she returned for treatment once more, two years later.

Her phone conversations and letters had reflected what I thought to be a growing dementia—increasingly poor memory, increasingly misunderstood communications, growing paranoid ideation—and her visit clearly indicated the presence of depressed mood and sometimes confused thinking. Her pain was no longer a serious problem, and she continued to resist anyone's help with depression and with the increasing difficulties of living as an elderly, now somewhat infirm, person. Ayn died a year later following another CVA.

This case illustrates the complexity of treating pain and the unique value of hypnosis in such treatment. Ayn's hypnotic treatment included: (1) suggestions for directly reducing the sensory dimensions of her pain (e.g., by imagining a rerouting of the sensory signals); (2) suggestions for reducing the affective dimension (e.g., not being bothered by whatever sensations she did notice); and (3) training in self-hypnosis so her relief could be maintained independently. Perhaps equally effective was the trust she had in our relationship and her belief that I would help her.

FRANCISCO, 56, A SURVEYOR WITH OSTEOARTHRITIS

As with any psychological treatment, the application of hypnotic treatment principles varies considerably, depending on the patient and the nature of the pain problem.

Francisco was referred to my care by his rheumatologist. Francisco suffered greatly from pain in his left hip, radiating down his leg into his ankle. A civil surveyor by trade, Francisco was highly intelligent and well read; he was very much a self-educated man. He had been unable to work for six months due to his increasingly debilitating pain, for which he took aspirin with codeine, about three tablets a day, when the pain became unbearable. He spent each day actively; most of his time he was in his garage-shop, fashioning a cello, which he intended to learn to play. (He had taught himself to play the piano some years previously, and he enjoyed playing classical music.) He was happily married; his children were grown, living away from home. From his report, Francisco's wife was a supportive friend who also lived an independent and active life.

His rheumatologist had recommended that Francisco have hip replacement surgery, believing that such a procedure was the only satisfactory treatment for the very severe degeneration of the head of the femur. Meanwhile, he recommended that Francisco take anti-inflammatory medication.

Francisco refused to take anti-inflammatory medication, however, because when he had taken it previously it had caused very severe gastric side-effects (including gastrointestinal complications that required emergency surgery). Understandably, then, he was afraid of being harmed by this medication. Francisco also actively resisted the idea of surgery. He reasoned that, because of his relatively young age, the prosthesis would need to be replaced two, possibly three times over his lifetime—and he did not want to risk that much surgery. Despite the reasonableness of his intellectual argument against surgery, I perceived Francisco to be quite afraid of what he considered to be dangerous medical intrusions into his life.

Francisco's rheumatologist hoped that I would at least convince Francisco to take the anti-inflammatory medication. At best, he wished that I would convince Francisco to have the surgery. Francisco, however, had a different agenda: He wanted me to hypnotize him so he would no longer have pain in his hip. His very strong wish was to be able to return to work, not take medication, and not have surgery.

I knew upon first seeing Francisco that he and I would have trouble. As I opened my office door to greet him in the waiting room, he was standing, glaring at me, his pipe in hand. He said to me with unconcealed ire, "What am I supposed to do with this?" He was referring to his pipe, which he held in his hand, and to the fact that my secretary had told him smoking was not permitted in the office.

Francisco was a severe man, suspicious of the medical community (perhaps with reason because of his ordeal with the anti-inflammatory medication, but probably predating that unfortunate experience). During the history-taking, I noticed his increasing agitation: frequent sighing and other expressions of irritation in response to my dogged questioning of him about work history, family history, and other questions not obviously related to his pain.

I explained that I needed to know a lot about him in order to know how best to help him. He responded, somewhat impatiently, that he was willing to cooperate fully and that I should continue. Nonetheless, with subsequent questions – about his family's health history, his wife's employment, his children's circumstances, and where he went to high school – he became more convinced than ever that I was not going to help him.

He said that it was only because he had been told, for over two years, by several different people (including his wife, whose opinion he valued), that he should come to see me, and that I could probably help him – only because of this had he endured my obviously irrelevant and absurd questions. Throughout the hour, we developed a kind of rhythm, in which he would tolerate my questioning for several minutes, then express frustration, whereupon I would sympathize with his frustration, he would be temporarily satisfied, and we would continue the intake interview.

Francisco believed that hypnosis could reduce his pain, but he also believed that he could not be hypnotized. His interest had led him to take a course in hypnosis at the community college. During the course, he and his fellow students were given a hypnotic responsivity test and Francisco was found to be clearly unresponsive. He had later gone to a psychologist for the purpose of being hypnotized to relieve his pain and it was, he said, "a total waste of time" – he did not respond to the psychologist's suggestions for hypnotic induction or for pain relief. Nevertheless, Francisco was quite articulate and emphatic in his belief that hypnosis would be able to help him under the right circumstances. He did not specify what those circumstances were, but I assumed they would be related to his trust in the competence of his clinician. Francisco had been told independently by three friends over the past two years that he should be treated by me, he said. So, he had finally concluded, he would "give [me] a try."

It seemed clear to me that Francisco was a healthy, highly functioning man, motivated to be rid of his pain, and eager to return to his work. Francisco also had a strong streak of skepticism and was unwilling to be hoodwinked by some mysterious, mystical force (while at the same time, perhaps, wishing unconsciously he could be). I thought it

best to be clear and straightforward with him and to educate him
about the nature of hypnosis – in order to defuse his skepticism, provide him with needed information, and avoid supporting his wariness
of me as a clinician.

Although the agreed-upon treatment goal was the reduction of his
pain, I hoped – and intended – that such reduction would ultimately
inspire Francisco to follow his rheumatologist's recommendations for
surgery. (Successful hypnotic treatment could only relieve his suffering from the pain, not the increasing dysfunction of his hip joint.) I
recommended that Francisco read *Hypnosis for the Seriously Curious*
(Bowers, 1983) and made an appointment for the first treatment.

The following week, Francisco was hobbling due to particularly severe pain. I asked him why he didn't use a cane to relieve some of the
pressure on his beleaguered hip joint; he replied, "I'm not a cripple."
He was particularly sour on this day, responding to any comment or
request with a scowl and unpleasant muttering.

I looked at him for a long moment without speaking, long enough to
get his attention. I could see that he was really irritated and frustrated – and, like many patients, did not know how to express himself.
I also had the impression that Francisco was a tough man who might
not take well to soft treatment. So I didn't smile when I then said,
evenly, "You're a grumpy old bastard, aren't you?"

My rude confrontation and his shock and amusement in response
felt to me like the first authentic contact we'd had. "Well, you'd be
grumpy, too, if you felt like I do," he finally replied.

I was relieved to see his amusement and, recognizing the sincerity
of his reply, said, equally sincerely, "I'm sure you're right. And I'd
want someone to get through my grumpiness and help me to feel
better. I actually like your grumpiness, but I suspect it gets in the way
of your getting help."

His anger seemed to have given way to curiosity and an openness
to needing my help, as his next question suggested a vulnerability I
had not yet seen in him. He asked very quietly, "Do you think you can
hypnotize me?"

I did not think Francisco's capacity to experience hypnosis was the
essential problem. Rather, I thought his fear of dependence, along with
his associated fear of being hurt by me (and other clinicians) was a
major obstructive defense. I thought quietly for a moment before I
said, "I have no doubt at all about your ability to experience hypnosis.
I don't know if I'm the one you'll want to be with while you're hypnotized, but we'll see."

Because Francisco had had previously disappointing experiences
with hypnosis, I began an induction that would be too verbally compli-

cated for him to monitor and criticize and doubt in his usual way – and thus might give him an opportunity for less habitual, more spontaneous responses. This induction was also intended to engage his monitoring abilities in an innocuous way. (In this case, I asked him to count his breaths.) And I hoped to confound his understandable tendency to maintain control of the conversation, thus freeing him to be more receptive to suggestions.

Francisco, I want you to close your eyes as you settle back in the chair now, so that I can talk to you without interruption. I don't really expect much to happen today, given the kind of experiences you've had previously. It might take many, many appointments for you to get any benefit. I know that will be expensive, but you are very persistent. [This suggestion was intended, paradoxically, to stimulate Francisco's already existing concern about the cost of treatment, and thus increase his motivation for rapid success.] Today you can expect to be appropriately disappointed that you haven't been hypnotized, but that can afford you the opportunity of experiencing some other kind of relief without knowing how or why. [The relief of not having been hypnotized – of not having been overtaken by me.]

It is very important that you pay as much attention as you possibly can to the experience of your breathing. I know you can attend to whatever you want, and I want you to pay attention right now to your breathing. Really notice what it feels like, each time you breathe in, each time you breathe out. Notice the rising and falling of your chest, notice the change in tension of the material of your shirt as your chest fills with air with each inhalation, notice that the air is cool as it enters your nose, and warm as it leaves. It has been warmed by the very process of your life.

And in a moment, I want you to begin counting your breaths ... each one ... either as you inhale or as you exhale ... it doesn't really matter. I'm going to keep talking to you for a while, but I want you to pay direct and complete attention to counting your breaths.

Begin now. Count each breath. If you become distracted and forget, that's all right ... just bring your attention back, and resume counting. If you don't remember at which number you forgot ... that's OK ... just start over again at the beginning. Just keep counting ... don't pay attention to me, I'm not saying anything important at the moment anyway, and it will be difficult to determine when I do, so just keep counting.

And while you're counting, I'm going to talk to you about some

> experiences you might have, if you knew how, and you do; and
> I'm going to suggest various experiences to you . . . and you can
> respond to those suggestions in a variety of ways. You might
> respond fully, or partially. You might respond quickly, or with
> some delay. You might respond predictably, or you might sur-
> prise yourself. I don't know how you'll respond, and I hope you'll
> allow yourself the opportunity of responding in more than one
> way. And keep counting. . . .

I continued to suggest that Francisco could ignore my suggestions or
could respond. In general, I emphasized his independence from me,
because I believed he would more readily respond to suggestions if he
were secure in his sense of independence.

Next, I also suggested that he couldn't reasonably expect much to
happen that day. I did this because in the past he had expected results
and gotten none. With no expectations, he could not be disappointed.
Further, this would allow room for novel responses. I believed that his
characteristic vigilance and monitoring of his own responses were at
least partly responsible for his previous lack of hypnotic success.

Then I offered suggestions to allow for a possible pleasant surprise
(e.g., pain reduction would certainly be a pleasant surprise). Francisco
knew intellectually that hypnosis could reduce pain. He also "knew"
that he had not been able to be hypnotized and that his responsivity
score was low. However, he must, at some level, in some way, have had
some idea that he could get satisfactory results; otherwise he would
not have come to my office. I needed to capitalize on that hope while
disarming his skepticism. I proceeded:

> You know how to explain a lot of things. And some things you
> don't know how to explain, but you can enjoy them just the same.
> For instance, you don't need to understand principles of optics in
> order to know how to be absorbed by the beauty of a sunset. You
> don't have to know anything at all about reflection or refraction
> or spectra in order to really enjoy the vivid golds and reds and
> pinks and purples and blues of a sunset.
> And you certainly don't have to be able to explain why it hap-
> pened in order to enjoy the comfort you can feel later today.
> Because later today, and I don't know precisely what time it will
> be – How can I know precisely what time it will be? – later today,
> you will have the opportunity to suddenly discover how really
> well you are feeling – without any need to explain *how* it hap-
> pened. It might be 2 o'clock this afternoon, or five minutes after

3, or fifteen minutes after 4, or perhaps exactly 5 o'clock. I don't know what time it will be – in fact, it may not have to do with the actual time on the clock, it may seem more related to what you are doing at that time. You might be untying a shoe, or lifting a glass to your lips, or turning the page of a magazine – I don't know what you will be doing – when you'll have the sudden awareness that you are feeling better than you expected. And you will not have any way to explain it, nor will you need to. For some reason, you'll just realize you're feeling better, with nothing to bother you, and nothing to disturb you.

And you won't even have to memorize the fact that I've told you this. And you won't even have to believe that you've been hypnotized. After all, who's to say that you were? In fact, if you are asked, later today, if you were hypnotized, you can take comfort in the fact that you can say you really don't think so. You really don't think you were hypnotized. And who is to say that you were? The fact that you are feeling better might be accounted for in a number of other ways. And you don't even have to think about it. But when I see you next time, I'll be really interested in any surprises you have had . . . particularly pleasant surprises.

Now, in a few minutes, I'm going to suggest that you take a very refreshing breath, or even two, and open your eyes and enjoy how very wide awake you feel. And when you leave my office, although you will certainly feel alert and awake, it is possible that you might also feel very dry and thirsty, just as if you have been working out in the hot sun all morning. Because you have been working hard. And you can enjoy how easily you can get a drink of cool water. And when you are lifting the glass to your lips, you can really enjoy how nice it is that you can quench your own thirst, that you can satisfy your own needs. [I am not certain that such metaphoric suggestions are therapeutic, but I hoped they might be.]

Francisco was aroused without discussion of his experience and left looking somewhat distracted. A few minutes later he returned, excitedly saying that he had no pain in his hip or leg. Because I did not yet want to support hopeful expectations, I replied noncommittally and told him I looked forward to seeing him in a few days. I also suggested that he begin using a cane.

When he returned for his second treatment appointment, Francisco reported that he had felt pain-free from the moment he'd left my office, even driving home (and driving was normally quite painful). Although some pain had returned later in the evening, he had generally felt much better throughout that day. The pain had returned the next morning, however, and had remained unabated – for two days – until this morning. This morning he forced himself to mow the yard – another painful activity – almost in defiance of the pain. As he bent over to empty the grass-catcher, however, he suddenly noticed that he was, once again, entirely pain-free. And he had remained pain-free throughout the morning and was still pain-free, now, in the early afternoon. "But how can that be," he asked, now in my office, "since I wasn't hypnotized last time?"

I responded by asking him how he would determine if he was hypnotized or not. He replied that arm levitation (a dissociative phenomenon that many regard as classically hypnotic) would be sufficient. Then, using a posthypnotic suggestion I had given at the previous appointment,[3] I showed him how really easy it was for him to accomplish arm levitation and suggested that he could develop a very absorbing and pleasant hypnotic state even though he was already feeling quite comfortable. Francisco demonstrated a very well-developed hypnotic response.

From that time on, Francisco felt increasingly confident in his hypnotic abilities and was increasingly able to control his pain. During that second treatment appointment, I revived the discussion of surgery. If his hip joint was becoming increasingly deteriorated with use, so that movement was causing injury to the joint, wouldn't it make sense, I wondered, now that he'd shown his ability to cope with the pain, to have the surgery his rheumatologist had initially suggested?

Francisco's answer was a definite "no." He did not want surgery; he wanted to perfect his hypnotic abilities and to continue to control the pain. I explained that he might not be able to continue to control his pain, over time, if by doing so he was further contributing to his injury. Curiously enough, he began to be less and less able to control his pain. Within a week it was clear to him that he could be hypnotized, but that he could no longer relieve his hip pain. Over a month of determined effort went by before Francisco decided to consult the orthopedic surgeon recommended by his rheumatologist.

After Francisco had made plans for surgery (which was to take place a month later), he again became able to control his hip pain. He

---

[3]The details of this suggestion are not pertinent here; the interested reader can learn about such posthypnotic suggestions from hypnosis texts or from clinical training programs.

(and I) understood this to mean that he was unconsciously controlling his analgesic ability so that he did not contribute to further injury of his hip joint. However, now that he was going to get proper treatment, he was able again to reduce his pain. Francisco underwent hip joint replacement surgery a month later and, following suggestions from me in this regard, was pleasantly surprised that he had little postoperative pain. (He had no analgesic medication except for the day of surgery.) Francisco is now functioning well, free of pain, and back at work, walking comfortably with the aid of his "high-tech hip," as he calls it.

Francisco's case is an important example of the power of *meaning* in pain control. When his pain meant injury (and further injury without treatment), Francisco was unable to control it. However, when his pain became an irrelevant signal (when he had decided to have surgical treatment), it was controllable. Although this premise has never been experimentally verified, anecdotal accounts (Erickson, 1976; London, 1975) suggest that the survival value of pain is an important determiner of its hypnotic modification. My own clinical experience suggests that the issue is a very complex one. This idea assumes, incorrectly I believe, that the patient will always reliably interpret the correct signal value of his or her pain—as if there is a homunculus on duty, objectively aware of whether the pain requires our attention or not. On the contrary, I do not rely upon the biological warning value of pain as a criterion for choosing hypnotic treatment. In Francisco's case, our substantial discussions about the nature of his pain and the benefits of surgery must have influenced Francisco's readiness, in effect, to now ignore the pain that had been so important not to ignore previously.

RAGNAR, 54, A LAWYER WITH METASTATIC DISEASE

Ragnar first developed testicular cancer, which was treated by surgical removal of his testicles and follow-up hormone suppression therapy. A year later it was discovered that he had metastases in his spine. He sought treatment from me for his back pain, which had over the past two months rapidly become debilitating. At his first visit, Ragnar was visibly depressed and in pain. He was a stoic man, not readily given to expression of pain (or other) complaints. He did not take medications for pain. Although his oncologist had prescribed morphine sulphate tablets for him, he had also warned him about the "dangers" of dependence on opioids and counseled him not to take the medication.

Because such advice was inconsistent with my own understanding, I suggested that Ragnar get another opinion, from another oncologist, about the appropriateness of using opioids for pain relief. He declined to do so, at least for the present time. His wish and hope were that I would be able to use hypnosis to reduce his pain. He had had previous experience with hypnosis, when he learned self-hypnosis for the purpose of enhancing his immune system response to the cancer. He had a very optimistic attitude with respect to his hypnotic capacities and the potential of hypnotic methods to reduce his pain and augment the strength of his immune response. [4]

At the first treatment appointment, we discussed the details of the sensations of his back pain and of what the pain meant to him. (It was significant that the back pain prevented him from playing tennis, an activity that he greatly enjoyed.) Because he was satisfied and confident with his use of self-hypnosis, I suggested that he induce himself by the means with which he was most familiar. He proceeded to use the eye fixation induction that he had learned previously and which he used daily. I watched quietly, interested in assessing the effectiveness of his own methods. I then spoke to him, offering him suggestions for pain control. These suggestions communicated the following ideas:

1. You can alter your sensory experience. You can reduce the input from your sensory nerves. You can alter the way your nervous system processes the input. There are thousands and thousands of switches, or gates, that your mind can turn off, so that the sensations won't be able to be communicated to your mind and won't be able to be noticed.
2. Painful sensations will bother you less and less. You won't have to know why, you won't have to explain or justify the phenomenon to anyone, but you will be less and less bothered.

At the next appointment, two days later, Ragnar reported that he felt emotionally much better, and that his back felt significantly more comfortable for a few hours following our previous appointment, but that it had begun hurting again, so he had taken one tablet of morphine sulphate[5] which had helped significantly. I supported his use of the medication and suggested more hypnosis.

[4] I know of no evidence that hypnotic methods can affect the immune response, so I would not be willing to promote this possibility to a patient. However, I do not know what is actually possible, so, while not encouraging Ragnar's hope about this, I did not discourage it.

[5] Ragnar finally sought consultation with another oncologist, which led to a more appropriate use of opioids.

At this appointment, the suggestions given in the context of hypnosis were:

1. Restatement of suggestions given previously.
2. Suggestions intended to encourage Ragnar to be more aware of his thoughts and feelings about his disease and to freely discuss those thoughts and feelings with me.

At the next appointment, five days later, Ragnar reported using morphine sulphate more regularly, one tablet each morning and one at night. He also reported feeling less depressed. It appeared, though, that whatever pain reduction he had felt had been a function of the medication, not the hypnotic treatment. Although there was no problem, from my point of view, with Ragnar's use of medications, I wanted to satisfy his wish to use his hypnotic skills to reduce his pain. However, it seemed to me that Ragnar was not developing an adequate hypnotic state using his own methods. In fact, it seemed to me that he was only succeeding at relaxing, not actually altering his state of consciousness.

On the premise that he might respond more authentically to an unfamiliar induction, I asked Ragnar to let me use a different induction technique at this visit. I used an eye-roll induction combined with suggestions for progressive physical relaxation and emotional placidity. On this occasion, Ragnar seemed to actually develop a hypnotic state. His subsequent arousal from this experience indicated a greater degree of disorientation, and he reported feeling substantially different this time. He reported that his pain was significantly reduced, and he felt excited and hopeful.

Three days later, Ragnar reported that he still felt significantly better and had not needed to use morphine. He was, of course, pleased with the results and felt confirmed in his belief in hypnotic treatment. Follow-up one week, one month, and three months later confirmed the persistence of this analgesic effect. I did not follow the outcome of Ragnar's case, although I recognize that his prognosis was not a hopeful one.

Unless the noxious stimulation from the tumor coincidentally reduced during the hypnotic treatment, an unlikely possibility, Ragnar's case is a very interesting demonstration of the efficacy of hypnotic analgesia.[6]

[6]The circumstances of this case also seem to disconfirm the social psychological hypothesis for hypnotic analgesia, which asserts that the individual merely behaves "as if" there were no pain or suffering, even while feeling pain or suffering.

THE MEANING OF PAIN,
REVISITED

Hypnotic treatment of pain is not a simple treatment. It is not simply a matter of hypnotizing a patient and offering suggestions for analgesia. The particular way an individual patient's pain is integrated into his or her life—the meaning of the pain to the patient—will determine some of the twists and turns that treatment must take if it is to be effective.

Ayn's distress, for instance, was primarily a function of unusually severe central pain. At certain points in treatment, however, her depression and mental confusion contributed significantly to her distress. Hypnotic suggestion was not likely to reduce Ayn's depression and certainly not her mental confusion (and, in fact, hypnotic treatment was difficult to use because of her sometimes confused state).

Surgery was recommended for Francisco's pain syndrome. However, Francisco's fearful refusal of surgery rendered that treatment impossible, at least temporarily. One could conceptualize Francisco's treatment as having increased his self-confidence by reducing his pain. Perhaps more particularly, hypnotic treatment reduced his fear of dependence by demonstrating the "painlessness" of hypnosis—so that he was able to summon the courage to undergo the best treatment.

NONHYPNOTIC COMPLICATIONS

As is frequently the case with medication, hypnotic effects are not as reliable or predictable as one would like; consequently, it is necessary to be persistent when treating pain. If your most brilliant clinical strategy is not succeeding, then it is time to try another. Your creativity is as important in hypnotic treatment as it is in any other treatment. If the pain is somewhat reduced in intensity, but is not eliminated (if that was the goal), this is not a treatment failure. Rather, this result can be used to demonstrate the modifiability of the pain—and perhaps the advisability of reexamining the patient's needs, in order to revise the treatment approach. (The clinical example of Dominique, below, illustrates this principle.)

While it may be appropriate in a given case to focus on the alteration of the sensory dimension of pain, it may also be valuable—and necessary—to focus on alteration of the affective dimension of pain. A strategy that succeeds only temporarily may need to be subsequently replaced by yet another strategy and sometimes yet another . . . and another.

DOMINIQUE, 56, A WRITER, WHO NEEDED HER PAIN

Sometimes, concomitant psychological issues render the treatment of pain quite puzzling and complicated. Dominique, a very likable professional writer, had endured significant pain for 44 of her 56 years. She had contracted polio when she was two, and her lower body was consequently very weakened. When she was 12 she started to experience the painful symptoms of post-polio syndrome. She was now confined to a wheelchair, but nonetheless professionally and socially quite active. Largely as a consequence of post-polio syndrome (a form of myofascial syndrome), combined with the rigors of sitting in a wheelchair for most of her life, her upper body musculature and joints were increasingly painful. There was no medical treatment that would reliably reduce the pain. She normally avoided taking analgesics but found it increasingly necessary to take oxycodone for pain relief.

Dominique was very adept at developing hypnotic analgesia. Literally within seconds of beginning a hypnotic induction, Dominique was totally free of pain. However, this pain-free condition was unsettling, even frightening, to her. "This isn't me," she explained, unhappily. Her identity, established over her lifetime of pain, was to a large extent dependent upon experiencing constant, unrelenting pain. So she found it ego-dystonic to feel such relief. Subsequently, we found that the best solution to this dilemma was to reduce her pain hypnotically, but only to a point that was tolerably low and not altogether absent. Her most comforting experience was to feel some pain, but not at such a high level that it interfered with her life.

Dominique also received physical therapy (Feldenkrais treatment) to address the actual physical debilitation of her post-polio syndrome. Therapeutic success for Dominique involved continuing to live with some level of pain, although her suffering was no longer substantial.

LILLIAN, 50, A FILM DIRECTOR, WHO NEEDED TIME TO HEAL

Lillian, who was referred for treatment of pelvic pain, was almost totally disabled by pain, which had begun three years previously and apparently was the result, initially, of a bladder infection. The problem had been exacerbated by numerous invasive medical procedures and by three years of reflexive muscular contraction, a natural defense against pain. Lillian's condition was not well understood by a score of highly competent physicians who had examined and treated her. This was not an uncommon case (Reading, 1982), but it was a difficult one to treat, because medical treatments — even "routine" investigations —

tended to exacerbate the chronic inflammatory response, which naturally increased the pain, in a positive feedback loop.

Lillian responded well to hypnotic suggestions for decreasing suffering from her bladder pain. She also cooperated with my primary goal, which was that she avoid further invasive medical procedures for at least a few months. (Even when medical evaluations have not been fruitful and do not suggest reasonable avenues for treatment, it is easy for a patient in pain to find physicians who will be curious about the cause of the pain and willing to perform yet more invasive procedures.)

Although Lillian required continuing follow-up hypnotic treatment, she remained free of substantial suffering, was able to avoid further medical procedures, and was able to resume her professional and social life. For Lillian, then, effective treatment was primarily aimed at the temporary relief of pain – long enough to allow physical healing to occur. Perhaps equally important, this temporary relief gave Lillian time to attend to other issues in her life and to unlearn the habit of constant vigilance concerning the sensations in her bladder.

KIRA, 32, AN ATTORNEY WITH PELVIC PAIN

Kira suffered from the same pain syndrome as Lillian. She, too, was diagnosed with pelvic inflammatory disease; she, too, had a three-year history of unsuccessful medical treatments; and she, too, was severely disabled by her pain and by her ceaseless search for a physician who could relieve it. Although Kira, too, was referred to me by her urologist, unlike Lillian's urologist, Kira's had described her as a "crock."

The intake interview revealed the extent of Kira's constant involvement with her pain and with the search for its solution (perfectly understandable, of course, but in this case futile). Psychological testing identified a substantial hypochondriacal element in Kira's personality. This finding, however, must be tempered by our acknowledgment that anyone with a health problem naturally expresses more than average concerns about health. Psychological testing also suggested that Kira's dependent style of relating to caretakers might complicate treatment.

I explained to Kira that her pain was real, that it no doubt was the result of changes in tissue, but that, from the medical evidence gained thus far, it was unlikely that any physical treatment would be effective. However, I went on, pain is a psychological as well as a physical phenomenon, and the power of her mind could make a tremendous difference to the amount of suffering she experienced. I suggested that hypnotic treatment would be a very good way to illustrate for her the power of her mind to "retrain" her nervous system, so that the nerves that had developed "the habit of carrying pain messages" to her brain could be redirected in more comfortable ways.

Kira was very responsive to hypnotic suggestions and developed substantial relief from her pain. The next time we met, several days later, however, Kira expressed disappointment that the relief did not extend for more than a couple of hours following the first treatment.

In subsequent treatments, the temporary relief sometimes extended throughout the day of the treatment—but never, unfortunately, beyond that time. Moreover, Kira continued to exhibit an obsessiveness about her pain, which I thought made long-lasting relief unlikely. Also, because of her impatience with only temporary relief, because of unresolved issues relating to the control in her marriage she achieved by virtue of her pain, and because of her continued attentiveness to her pain, hypnotic treatment was of only limited usefulness.

For example, as with nearly all pain patients, I made a tape recording of one of our early hypnotic treatments and recommended that Kira listen to it once in the morning and once again in the evening, each day, for a week. She was never able to follow through with this recommendation, saying that she did not have time. My view was that, in effect, Kira was not yet ready to do what was necessary to obtain relief. I believe that she needed prolonged contact with me to meet her dependency needs. The tape recording was, for her, an insult. She wanted to be cared for by a live human being.

Unable to extend her relief more than we had obtained in the first week, I recommended that Kira be evaluated at a pain clinic. She declined this recommendation and decided to seek treatment elsewhere. Kira was already being treated in long-term psychotherapy, so it was inappropriate for me to enlarge the focus of my work with her and we terminated treatment.

WHY ARE HYPNOTIC METHODS NOT MORE WIDELY USED?

Hypnotic intervention offers a powerful alternative to surgery and analgesic medication in the treatment of pain. Since this is so, it is puzzling that this treatment is not more widely used. Although I do not know of a systematic survey, it is my impression, based on conversations with colleagues, that the use of hypnotic interventions in pain treatment programs is the exception rather than the rule.

This may be the case largely because training in the clinical use of hypnotic methods has not commonly been part of the curriculum of either medical, dental, or psychological training. Competent use of hypnotic methods requires mastery of the same interpersonal skills necessary to effective psychotherapy, but with a somewhat different elaboration. Additionally, hypnotic methods require the capacity and comfort of the clinician with imaginal techniques.

Also, one of the factors influencing the success of hypnotic treatment is the clinician's ability to observe and to make calculated guesses about what the patient needs. The observations of the patient's behavior and inferences about what the patient needs are then used in the development of hypnotic strategies.

Perhaps another reason why hypnotic treatment is not more widely used is the particular combination of sustained imaginal focus required, coupled with close monitoring and observation of the patient's affective state. This often results in an intensification of transference and countertransference issues. This can be both emotionally affecting and draining to the clinician, especially in the context of a busy daily practice. Many competent clinicians may prefer to not be additionally burdened.

Effective hypnotic treatment requires an unvaryingly high level of this interpersonal contact. It is difficult to be effective when using these methods if we find it awkward to develop and maintain such close psychological relationships with our patients.

Additionally, hypnotic methods can be misused when the therapeutic relationship feels too overwhelming, complex, intimate, or otherwise threatening. It may be tempting for us to reach for hypnotic tools as a way to regain a sense of control or to counter feelings of helplessness. Rather than narrowly focus our attention on hypnotic techniques or hypnotic responsiveness, we need to be mindful of the "neglected importance" of the therapeutic relationship and how the relationship should guide our use of hypnotic methods (Diamond, 1984). As we develop in our sophistication of thinking about therapeutic contact, in either a medical or psychological context, the use of hypnotic methods in pain management may become more common. And we are more likely to be more effective in the treatment of patients who suffer from pain.

We need to keep in mind, however, that the hard work and emotional investment often involved in this treatment leave clinicians vulnerable to discouragement if the treatment is not successful. The experienced clinician evaluates the progress of treatment along the way in order to correct misconceptions and judgments and improve the efficacy of the treatment. Nevertheless, we have to accept the fact that, regardless of how skillful we are, regardless of how committed we are to helping our patients, we will still make errors, and our treatments will not always succeed. This is usually easier said than done.

Section II

SYNDROMES OF
SPECIAL INTEREST

6

CANCER PAIN

Karen L. Syrjala
Sari Roth-Roemer

ANNA HAD BEEN treated for metastatic breast cancer with chemotherapy and radiation over the past two years. She was referred by her oncologist for treatment of isolation and depression, as well as assistance with managing her gut pain. At the time of the consult she was hospitalized for anorexia. She had been unable to eat, due to nausea and gut pain resulting from tumor infiltrates and possibly because of the effects of her radiation therapy. She had lost more than 30 pounds, but while this had taken much of her physical energy, she remained quick witted and acutely observant of her surroundings.

A retired army nurse, Anna, now 63, had always been a very independent person with few close friends. Her family lived across the country, she had only one friend available for some assistance, and she did not feel emotionally close to anyone. Anna no longer had the energy to seek interactions with others; yet, having become increasingly isolated since her diagnosis, she experienced acute loneliness.

This work was supported by National Cancer Institute grants CA57807 and CA63030.

In therapeutic interactions, she grieved for her losses and explored her feelings about dying alone. She grieved for what she had not had in her life, but also experienced a sense of comfort and competence from her recognition of the choices that she had made that she felt were best for her, such as her work in taking care of other people, even in difficult times such as combat.

More than any other disease, cancer and its treatment bring a multitude of pains and discomforts that rarely occur in isolation from other symptoms. A cancer diagnosis brings with it immediate concerns, which may become, in effect, internal suggestions to the patient. Foremost among these are loss of control over the physical body and uncertainty about the future, for which the patient almost certainly had other plans. The clinician who uses psychological approaches with cancer patients needs to understand this interplay of physical challenges and psychological demands. For optimal patient comfort, both phenomena must be integrated into suggestions for pain relief.

In this chapter, we discuss the context in which treatment for cancer pain exists. First, we provide a description of the types of pain reported by cancer patients. Next, we evaluate factors to consider in the integration of hypnosis with the medical management of the disease. Finally, we review some of the techniques that are effective in treating cancer pain.

Pain is one of the most common symptoms reported by people with cancer. Everyone with cancer will have pain from procedures, and many will have pain at some point from treatment. All cancer patients undergo painful procedures that can take between a few minutes to several hours — for example, blood draws, needle aspirations, and imaging. Many patients will have pain from their anti-cancer therapies. Radiation can cause skin burns or gastrointestinal distress; chemotherapies often cause diffuse aching or generalized discomfort or burning from neuropathies.

Although it is the pain of cancer itself that most frightens people, not all patients will have pain related to their disease. Prevalence of disease-related pain ranges from 30 percent to 40 percent for the entire cancer population, and from 60 percent to 90 percent for patients with advanced disease (Cleeland et al., 1994; Grond, Zech, Diefenbach, & Bischoff, 1994; Portenoy, 1989). It is normal for patients with advanced disease to have four to eleven symptoms concurrently. The most frequent symptoms are pain, fatigue, anorexia, nausea, and sleep disturbance (Donnelly, Walsh, & Rybicki, 1995; Portenoy et al., 1994). Gastrointestinal distress, which is particularly common, may include not only nausea and vomiting, but also diarrhea or constipation, difficulty swallowing, mouth and throat ulcers, and abdominal cramping. These symptoms make eating very difficult, contributing to weight loss and fatigue. When patients have pain from their disease, it is not unusual for multiple pains to occur simultaneously, in different locations.

An important distinction needs to be made between pain that is caused by damage to tissue, sometimes called physiologic pain or nociception, and pain that is caused by a disturbance in the neural transmission system, called neuropathic pain. Nociception can be highly variable, but it is often characterized by aching, heavy, or cramping sensations, while neuropathic pain is more characteristically felt as sensations of pins and needles, burning, electrical, shooting pain or numbness. Opioids and other medical treatments are more effective with nociception (Bonica, 1990; Saeger, 1992). Neuropathic pains tend to attack suddenly and unpredictably and, as a consequence, to overwhelm the patient's ability to cope. During each occurrence, the pain tends to last a similar length of time. These are difficult but often rewarding symptoms to work with hypnotically, because patients often benefit from hypnotic treatment when it seems that nothing else is effective.

When treating neuropathic pain, suggestions need to begin with the reminder that the sensation is temporary. It is helpful to have a period of training during which the hypnotic experience can become familiar to the patient and images can be tested and refined to suit the patient. During neuropathic attacks, we use very brief images to transform the pain. These must be suggestions that the patient can use alone so that he or she has strategies available even when the clinician is not.

The cancer patient's history must be considered when designing treatment – whether one considers brief procedures, postsurgical pain, treatment-related pain, or progressive disease-related pain. Past experience is one of the chief influencing factors in the patient's fears and expectations and, therefore, in determining internalized suggestions. Identifying thoughts and emotions that occur with the pain can stimulate valuable metaphors and images to modify the patient's experience.

Research with cancer patients clearly demonstrates an association between depression and pain (Ahles, Blanchard, & Ruckdeschel, 1983; Spiegel, Sands, & Koopman, 1994). Patients with greater distress, specific to their cancer situation or their pain, will also experience greater pain intensity (Syrjala & Chapko, 1995). Thus, treating distress is an important component of pain treatment, although of course it is never the only component.

To be effective in treating cancer pain, you need to understand the context in which most people experience cancer and the issues they face when managing this disease, as well as the types of pain that are caused by cancer and its treatments. With this understanding, hypnosis and suggestion can be immensely helpful, even to those patients who might have been reluctant to try such strategies prior to facing their disease.

TYPES OF PAIN COMMON TO CANCER PATIENTS

Painful Medical Procedures

As Table 6.1 illustrates, patients with cancer experience an assortment of pains with varying etiologies. They may have the briefest pain from a needle stick, or pain from treatment that continues for weeks but gradually resolves, or they may have pain that progressively worsens over months or years as a result of tumor invasion. Images and suggestions vary quite widely, depending on the circumstance of the pain and the concurrent issues a cancer patient is facing.

Acute procedural pain is brief and is treated as one would treat any brief pain situation. An important consideration in a patient with cancer is the repetitive nature of these procedures. A simple blood draw that may initially cause no distress can become wearing or even evoke phobic symptoms in patients whose treatment requires repeated needle sticks. Other procedures, such as bone marrow aspirations, can become so intolerable to patients that they refuse further life-promoting treatment rather than expose themselves to the excruciating pain of additional aspirations.

We emphasize procedures here because they tend to be ignored as sources of distress by a medical system focused on curing the disease. Patients, wishing to be cooperative and to be strong, often do not express their distress to health-care providers who are in a position to help them. As with most cancer pain, medical approaches can ease many of the procedural discomforts if staff recognize the level of patient discomfort and act to prevent or provide treatment for these symptoms. It has been demonstrated that hypnotic intervention is effective for treating pain from procedures (Genuis, 1995; Wall & Womack, 1989). Procedural discomforts are particularly responsive to hypnotic intervention, in part because they are temporary. Due to the repetitive aspect of procedures, we train the patient and/or a family member to use these methods without the presence of a clinician. Although most work on procedures has been done with children, we find these methods equally effective and immensely appreciated by adults.

Table 6.1
Types of Pain Common in Cancer Patients

Duration of Pain	Source of Pain	Examples
Brief	Procedures	Blood draws
		Needle aspirations (e.g., breast, bone marrow, liver)
		Angiographs and other imaging
		Bronchoscopies
	Unpredictable events	Neuropathies
		Gastrointestinal distress
	Incidental, movement-related	Activity exacerbates a constant bone pain
Persistent treatment-related	Post-surgical	
	Oral mucositis	Mouth and throat ulcers with pain
	Radiation burns	Raw or burned skin, gastric distress
	Chemotherapy caused pain	Joint aching or burning pain in extremities
	Gastrointestinal distress	Chemotherapy induced gastric upset
Chronic, progressive disease-related	Nociception	Bone pain
		Tumor invasion or obstruction of viscera
	Neuropathic	Nerve root invasion
Chronic, residual	Lymphedema	Massively swollen arms
	Fractures	
	Phantom limb	
	Post-herpetic neuralgia	
Concurrent, non-disease related	Arthritis	
	Low back pain	
	Muscle aches	

To illustrate these ideas, we will discuss a case that demonstrates the effectiveness of hypnotic management of procedural pain. Most patients tell us that bone marrow aspirations are the most painful procedures they endure. Other patients are very discomforted by magnetic resonance and other imaging procedures that require isolation in closed chambers and immobilization for long periods of time. In addition, some patients have needle phobias or other aversions that can make even blood draws or transfusions intolerable to them. These procedures are routine for medical staff whose focus is on "getting the job done." For the most part, clinicians and patients share the same contradictory cultural beliefs about pain and suffering. These attitudes communicate, on the one hand, that no one should have to endure pain and suffering. On the other hand, society is permeated with messages that suffering is a virtue. This incongruity, in effect, leaves both patient and medical staff confused and wishing simply to escape from dealing with an insolvable quandary. In addition, no caring person wishes to cause another to suffer. Thus the medical staff may deny the importance of the pain to the patient or respond to a patient's concern by suggesting that he or she is overreacting. For their part in this complex and difficult interaction, patients may wish to appear strong and thus win the respect of staff. As a result, they may not clearly communicate their distress.

When we are assisting with a procedure, our first step is always to assess the nature of the physical sensations that will be involved, the time each sensation normally lasts, and what sounds are commonly heard during the procedure. This helps us to incorporate references to these sounds and to suggest alternative sensations into our repertoire of suggestions.

Bone marrow aspiration procedures involve several intense physical stimuli: the cold liquid of the antiseptic wiping, stinging of the local anesthetic, very heavy pushing of the large needle into the bone, and a long, sharp pulling feeling throughout the hips and legs as the marrow is aspirated. (Samuel LeBaron and Lonnie Zeltzer describe this procedure fully in Chapter 11.) We consistently find that if we counter these intense sensations with either energetic physical activity or strong (but tolerable) sensations incorporated into our suggestions, patients are more likely to remain comfortably absorbed as the otherwise compelling procedure and the talking of staff continue around them.

The more invasive the procedure or the less absorbed a patient is likely to be, the more likely we are to have the patient talk to us, telling us what she sees and experiences.

CASE EXAMPLE: KRISTY, 23, ENDURING A
BONE MARROW ASPIRATION

Kristy was referred to me [KS] by her physician for treatment of acute anxiety. Her mother was also quite anxious, fearful of losing her only child, and unable to tolerate the distress she could see her daughter experiencing. This prevented her mother from being able to comfort Kristy and, in fact, left Kristy feeling that she needed to reassure and comfort her mother. Consequently, this left Kristy with no place where she could express her own fears and anger.

My primary therapeutic role was to provide Kristy with a safe place to experience and to explore her own feelings. This was helpful to her; fortunately, her mother was also relieved and grateful. (Sometimes parents who have not allowed their grown children to separate are resentful of a therapeutic relationship. In a cancer setting, where family is so essential in providing the emotional support and assistance a patient needs, meeting the therapeutic needs of a patient while not alienating a parent can be a difficult balance to achieve.)

When Kristy needed a bone marrow aspiration she asked me to be present. She said her mother could not tolerate being in the room, that she would "pass out" from seeing the blood and hearing Kristy yell. I rehearsed with Kristy a routine hypnotic induction leading to deep relaxation. I then suggested she imagine her favorite activity – exploring the farm where she grew up.

While Kristy had previously been able to be absorbed in the hypnotic experience, she was not as deeply absorbed during this procedure and was very vigilant about the people and sounds around her. To facilitate her absorption, I periodically asked her to tell me what she saw or felt in her imagination.

When the antiseptic was being wiped on her back, I asked her to "find some coolness, a breeze or perhaps even a stream that you might run your fingers through, or perhaps there is another coolness somewhere, but it really doesn't matter, wherever it is just enjoy the coolness along with the warmth as you notice all of these sensations just making you that much more aware of how aware you can be, how sharp your vision is today as you enjoy seeing and smelling and hearing the sounds in the field."

At the point of greatest physical pressure during the procedure, when the needle is punched into the bone and the marrow is aspirated, I raised my voice slightly, spoke more rapidly and suggested to Kristy that she begin to:

> ... Run through the field, down a slight hill and up the next, feeling your legs working, the strength and power in your legs as they move smoothly, landing firmly. Notice how your legs listen to the instructions from your mind and follow just where you tell them to go, how your mind moves your body where it needs to

be, feeling the strength in your body as your legs carry you through the field, you feel the breeze in your face, and your mind knows just what your body needs in order to be strong and comfortable and confident. Feeling your lungs expand to take in the air you need, and just how good it feels to breathe out from deep inside. And now begin to slow down . . . coming to a stop . . . and resting. Enjoying the pleasure of feeling how well your body works with your mind, how good it feels to exert your body and then to rest, letting your whole body be quiet now . . . and once again, noticing the fields and hills around you. . . .

There is an additional element to this work that I find very helpful for coping with intense physical sensation, if it is appropriate for a particular patient. With Kristy, I stood near her head and shoulder and let her hold my hand while I put my hand on her shoulder. I let her know that she could squeeze my hand at any time and that I might squeeze her shoulder. At the moment of most intense physical stimulation, or when I felt her squeeze my hand, I squeezed harder on her shoulder. The physical pressure of my hand provided a neutral physical stimulus to compete with the sensations from the procedure; as important, I believe this acted as reassurance that I was there to support her through the experience.

Kristy endured this procedure three times, and after each time, she would turn to me, smile, and say, "That was the best one yet," and then, fall asleep.

Treatment-Related Pain

Treatment-related pain is now managed more effectively with opioids than was the case not long ago. Nonetheless, even aggressive opioid use does not eliminate all discomfort. Hypnotic intervention has significantly reduced suffering from painful procedures in cancer patients (Syrjala, Cummings, & Donaldson, 1992; Syrjala, Donaldson, Davis, Kippes, & Carr, 1995). However, effective hypnotic intervention needs to be started prior to the start of cancer treatment if at all possible, because cancer treatment often impairs cognitive function, causes extreme fatigue, and may cause complications other than pain. In any case, psychological strategies that are provided during treatment must often be brief, since most patients' concentration and attention span are limited. When patients are in the midst of treatment, our typical intervention will last 10 to 30 minutes.

CASE EXAMPLE: PEARL, 61, SUFFERING FROM
TREATMENT-RELATED THROAT PAIN AND NAUSEA

Pearl's physician asked that I [KS] provide hypnotic intervention for Pearl, who was being treated for lung cancer. Pearl needed to eat so that she could leave the hospital after her radiation therapy. But Pearl's pain with swallowing and her continued nausea made it difficult for her to eat. Her physician could find no reason for Pearl's pain or nausea; although he had tried all of the medical treatments he knew, Pearl still could not eat.

When I first saw Pearl, she was lying in bed with her curtains closed. In the initial evaluation, it quickly became clear that she was depressed. Pearl said that she had two personal goals: to get out of the hospital, so that she could return to her job at the burger stand where she enjoyed the companionship of her coworkers; and to return to smoking. Although her daughter came to visit about once a week and called daily, Pearl was otherwise alone. When I asked about her family, she said she had only her daughter and that her daughter was very mad at her because she was looking forward to smoking again. She explained that many people, including her doctor, had told her not to smoke, but smoking gave her great pleasure, and she was still looking forward to smoking. Pearl also had been a heavy drinker, but she had no intention of returning to alcohol. When we explored her difficulties with eating, she indicated that eating most food made her nauseated, and it was hard to swallow, but that ice cream and apple pie were OK to eat. Pearl did not eat only ice cream and apple pie, because "everyone tells me I have to eat more regular meals."

It became clear to me that Pearl was fighting with most of her caregivers about what she should take in. She was a responsible adult who knew what other people thought was good for her and what she wanted for herself. Though I also knew what was and what was not good for her to take in, it seemed most helpful not to jump into this battle, but rather to focus on the healthy reasons Pearl wanted to leave the hospital – to return to her work and to make her own choices about the food she could eat. Often, the diets of cancer patients leave a lot to be desired, but calories become the most important factor, especially when trying to resume eating after a hiatus caused by the treatment. I recognized, too, that Pearl's wish to smoke could be partly an attempt to hold onto some part of herself (even an unhealthy part), when she was losing so much else – including, probably, her life – whether or not she stopped smoking.

Despite her depression and the conflict she was experiencing, Pearl was eager to try hypnotic methods. When I asked for her thoughts on what might be causing her nausea and difficulty swallowing, she had no ideas. She did say, though, that her throat hurt, and that she was nauseated only when she tried to eat. Rather than exploring the etiology of this problem, which her physician had done in detail, I decided to begin by directly addressing the symptoms. She seemed to respond well to my induction and deepening suggestions. I next suggested:

> As you enjoy these feelings of deep comfort and calmness, you may also become aware of feeling this same comfort in your throat and in your stomach. Notice just how comfortable and quiet you are right now. As you experience this comfort, imagine a smooth, protective coating beginning to line your throat, your stomach, all the way down. This can be any protective coating you wish. Perhaps it is like a steel lining coated with Teflon . . . hard and smooth and slick, so that anything that you swallow slides through easily, effortlessly, perhaps even without much awareness on your part . . . no need to even notice it any more than you wish.
>
> You know, there are so many things that we do in a day that it's not possible to remember them all . . . so you don't. Some things just aren't important to remember. Perhaps swallowing a few small bites of your next meal will be like that, just not important to remember. The food can just glide down over the protective coating, without any effort or awareness. So easily, you don't even really need to pay attention, knowing the steel lining will protect you. And at any time, just before you are about to eat, or whenever you wish, you can just close your eyes, remember these feelings of calmness and comfort, you can remember this smooth slick protective coating, and allow the food or liquid to just pass through easily. How wonderful it is to know that you can be in control of your own comfort. You can choose what you take in, and you might be surprised how easy it can be to choose the best ways for you to be as healthy and as comfortable as can be, how natural and easy it is to choose what is best for you and your body now.

After the meeting with Pearl, I spoke with her physician and nurse, who confirmed that they had been telling Pearl that she could not just eat ice cream and apple pie but needed to take in more nutritious food. After our discussion, they agreed to let her eat whatever she liked and to merely praise her accomplishment in taking in calories.

I also spoke with May, Pearl's daughter, who confirmed that she had had many fights with her mother, because her mother insisted that she wanted to continue smoking and May wanted her to stop. May also persisted in suggesting new foods that Pearl should try. As May and I discussed this struggle, I said I imagined this was difficult for both of them. May then expressed her fear that Pearl's wish to smoke was really a sign that she was giving up and wanted to die. After further discussion, May agreed to assume that her mother knew well enough what she could eat and what she needed at the time; she further agreed not to struggle with Pearl about this.

I returned two days later to find that Pearl had begun eating, her affect was brighter, and she said, "The doctor says I can go home in two days if I keep on like this!" In that day's hypnotic treatment, I used the suggestions for protective coating and described her ability to take care of herself and to choose what she eats and takes in so that she will feel as well as possible. Afterwards, she expressed some anxiety about returning home and being able to care for herself. She raised other concerns about being alone and expressed concern for her daughter as well. As a result, we scheduled a follow-up appointment for three days after she returned home.

When she came to see me as an outpatient, Pearl's eating had continued to improve, her pain and nausea had completely resolved, and she seemed to be regaining her sense of competence.

After three additional follow-up meetings, Pearl had returned to work, was getting along better with May, and had not returned to smoking, although she did not say that she had stopped smoking altogether.

Disease-Related Pain

Hypnotic treatment for long-standing, disease-related pain has not been studied extensively, although there are indications that it can be effective (Spiegel & Bloom, 1983; Spira & Spiegel, 1992). Numerous factors interact in the treatment of this type of pain. Although 90 percent of cancer pain can be effectively treated with available medical methods, at least 42 percent of cancer patients with advanced disease do not receive adequate treatment (Cleeland et al., 1994). *Clinicians considering hypnotic intervention for disease-related pain have an obligation to determine whether all available options for improved medical treatment have been used with these patients. Often, patients are unaware of medical options and physicians are unaware of the extent of the patients' pain* (Grossman, Sheidler, Swedeen, Mucenski, & Piantadosi, 1991). *Patients may seek hypnotic treatment, rather than approaching their nurses or physicians for better treatment.*

Even patients receiving excellent pain management are likely to have some residual pain or movement-related or incidental pain for which hypnosis and suggestion can be quite effective. *Hypnotic intervention is an appropriate adjunct to medical treatment with these patients, not an alternative to medication.*

A major issue in using hypnotic treatment with disease-related pain is determining how to maintain a durable effect for a pain condition that is likely to continue for months or even years. While hypnotic intervention can be extremely valuable, it needs to be repeated regularly, or patients need to be taught skills for using the methods on their own.

For a variety of reasons, many cancer patients who seek hypnotic treatment are not able to continue ongoing treatment. Most often, this is because patients have progressive disease, with progressive debility. Moreover, they have many medical appointments and demands; it takes tremendous energy just to meet these demands and endure. Tasks that may simply tire those of us who are healthy can thoroughly exhaust a cancer patient for several days. Since these patients do not want to be burdened by any appointments that are not essential, we find it extremely valuable to provide posthypnotic suggestions and training in brief, self-hypnotic methods that they can use on their own. We include these methods in the hypnotic treatment, and then we help patients to use the suggestions on their own whenever they need to feel better.

We find that hypnotic treatment eliminates most pain for patients during the time spent with us. Additionally, audiotapes can augment this help when the patients are on their own. However, sometimes patients say, "When I do hypnosis on my own, it helps while I'm doing it – but I hurt all the time, and the pain is tiring. I need something that helps when I can't stop what I'm doing, like driving a car, or when I'm too exhausted and I can't even concentrate enough to listen to the tape." Sometimes, the impediment to self-treatment can be explained by just this kind of simple, practical objection. We need to be alert, however, for reasons that underlie these simple objections. (You may want to review this issue, discussed in Chapter 5.)

CASE EXAMPLE: FRIEDA, 72, SUFFERING CONTINUOUS PAIN
FROM DISEASE

Frieda was a retired professional who had developed advanced breast cancer four years before she referred herself for hypnotic treatment.

While there was no cure for her disease, she and her physician expected that she could live several more years. She was a very active person who enjoyed many friends and numerous sports, including biking and sailing.

Initially, Frieda had no pain, but in the past six months she had suffered progressively more bone pain. When she came to see me [KS], she had constant, diffuse, aching pain in her shoulders, ribs, and hips which she rated as "3" on a scale from 0 to 10 when she took her medication, "7" if she did not take her medication, and "8" if she moved in certain ways and when she stood after prolonged sitting. She complained that the pain was making her crabby; moreover, she was reluctant to see friends or commit to any activities because she did not know how she would feel at the time of the activity. She did not like her medication because she felt sleepy when she was on it and, as the sleepiness wore off, the pain returned. As a result, she rarely took her medication. She did not tell her doctor how much she hurt, because she expected he would only tell her to take more medication.

Such reluctance to take analgesic medication is very common in cancer patients. The "Just Say No" campaigns against drugs have worked very effectively on the population of people with cancer, the vast majority of whom have little risk for misusing drugs. The most frequent problem we see is people who are afraid that if they increase medication when the pain increases they will be come addicts. We also commonly see people who have side-effects such as nausea or sedation with an opioid medication like morphine and then assume that all analgesic medications will make them nauseated or sleepy. They stop taking the medication and do not tell their doctor because they do not know that the nausea can be treated, that the nausea or sleepiness may go away in a short time, or that there are many other drugs that may not make them nauseated.

Frieda was one of these people. Clear thinking and remaining active were very important to her, and she felt the medication hindered these aspects of her life. On the other hand, the pain hindered her ability to feel like herself. My first step was to offer her a brief education in analgesic medication. Instead of taking intermittent doses of medication, she tried a sustained release medication that kept her constant pain at a level of 2. She agreed to try the medication for two weeks to see if some of the sedation would wear off. Indeed, after about a week, she found she was not sleepy in the daytime and, because her pain was better controlled and her medication continued to work for eight hours, she was sleeping much better at night. However, she still had substantial increases in pain when she moved. She had immediate-release morphine that she could take when she anticipated movement or when her pain increased, but she also wanted to see if hypnotic methods could help her feel better when she moved.

Although Frieda had an analytical and practical style of thinking, she was also imaginative. She could easily imagine herself on her sailboat, feeling the wind and the waves. She was curious, but she was also skeptical about whether she could be hypnotized. I suggested that this was a very good attitude with which to begin.

You can stay as curious as you like, exploring all the ways to use your mind to find the ways that work best for you to be as comfortable as can be. And you know, when you're sailing you can think of many things – the direction of the wind, the trim of the sails, the point of the boat. Your analytical mind continues to be very sharp and clear, but its focus is somewhere else, very much on the water, the sky, the wind, and the boat. Other concerns are far, far away. If they pass through your mind, they just don't really matter any more, gone with the next wave. . . . And you can take your mind in this same way to another place, anyplace you like, anytime. Just take a deep breath, let your eyes roll up as if to the sky, and then, as you close your eyes and let out that breath, you can feel the light breeze on your face as you fully and completely imagine yourself on the boat, sailing. You know so well how it is when you're sailing, and now you can experience it all again, and examine it as much as you like. Here, there is just the sound of the water, lapping against the sides of the boat, the feeling of the waves around you. And you might become aware of the other feelings here, on the boat. How many things you can feel . . . the boat as it moves slightly under you, your legs, as they adjust smoothly and easily to the shifting sensations, your hand, as it knows just where to rest lightly for the best balance, but mostly, just that feeling of breathing in life all around you in the air, feeling the refreshing and soothing steady breeze, as steady as the strength of the water beneath you. Just taking a few moments to breath in that life and energy, that feeling of renewal that you get from the water and the air. Always free to go in the direction you choose, finding the best direction for you now. And from this place of steady, calm, and easy movement, you can look back on yourself, perhaps from far away, but able to see what would help you to be comfortable as you move, watching as you do that, moving smoothly and easily, changing position, bending and standing, and knowing just how to do it as slowly or gently as needed but sure and steady. Just as you do here on the boat. Just taking a moment to experience this, so that, whenever you like, you can move with this same feeling, sure and calm and steady. And you might like sometimes to just get away on this sailboat to simply move away to where it is easy to look on the horizon and to move easily and comfortably. You can do this when you want to move. In just a few moments, you can take a deep breath, as if you are breathing in that fresh sea air, let your eyes roll up to the sky, let out that breath, and, from that place with steady balance, you can find it easy to move smoothly, from sitting to standing, one hand to balance as you steady, and then, when you've got that steadiness under you, it's easy to just move on.

Afterward, I helped Frieda to practice the suggestions I had given her: She took a breath, looked up, imagined the sailboat and, from this place in her imagination, some distance away, she moved from sitting to standing. We met two more times, during which she said that she used the distancing/sailing suggestions on her own and that they were very helpful. She said she felt much more confident in getting together with friends and she was having an easier time changing positions. She still used medication if she found the pain continued after she moved, but she felt more comfortable using the medication and she was more confident that she could trust herself to be able to do what she wanted to do. And she was no longer afraid to move. She found herself using this distancing technique (a variation of what Barber describes as "dissociation" in Chapter 5) at other times when she was stressed or uncomfortable. She said she would just imagine herself on her sailboat, and then she would look at her troubles from far away and they just didn't seem as big. Sometimes, she said, she was even able to see her problems differently; this helped her to find solutions to some difficult problems. The real joy for Frieda in this sailboat image was that, even though she was no longer actually able to sail because of her illness, she could once again enjoy the experience of sailing through her imagination. This intervention helped her with her pain and also restored one of her great joys in living.

INTEGRATING MEDICAL CARE
WITH HYPNOTIC TREATMENT

*Understanding the Psychological Effects of
the Disease and its Treatments*

Cancer treatment is changing rapidly and patients are living longer, receiving far lengthier courses of more aggressive treatment. When you treat the pain of cancer patients, you need to know not only the expected course of the disease but also the potential effects of various treatments. We consider it part of our standard clinical care to know what medications or treatment the patient is receiving. If the treatment is unfamiliar to us, we either find a colleague to inform us or search the literature to assure that we are aware, for example, of neurologic and somatic toxicities and their likely interaction with psychological intervention. For instance, a patient receiving ongoing interferon injections will have aches and pains as well as depressive CNS effects that can be relieved with pharmacologic treatment. If the patient understands that these symptoms result from treatment, rather than endogenously, his or her interpretation of the pain may be more benign, as we see in the following case.

CASE EXAMPLE: SUSAN, 35, SUFFERING FROM TREATMENT-RELATED DEPRESSION

Susan said, "I just can't go on. I just want to die now. I hurt all over, I'm totally tired all the time and I just don't care anymore, even about my kids. I feel very guilty because I don't care about them, but I just can't get interested." She had been receiving interferon injections daily for three months and had at least three more months of injections. She knew that the injections gave her flu-like symptoms, but she did not know that interferon can also produce depressive symptoms.

Because she attributed her feelings of depression to her "self," rather than to the effects of the interferon, Susan felt not only depressed but terribly guilty for being a "bad mother" and not caring about her children. I [KS] explained to her that depression is a very common side-effect of interferon and that her indifference to her life and those she loved was almost certainly a result of the medication, since this symptom did not predate the medication. We discussed pharmacologic and psychologic options for treating her depression.

As a result of this brief and respectful explanation, Susan felt tremendous relief and immediately stopped telling herself she was a bad mother; instead, she told herself, "I feel terrible, but it's from this medication. As soon as it stops, I'll feel better. Just because I feel bad, it doesn't mean I don't love my family." She gave me permission to speak with her physician, and he began antidepressant treatment that relieved many of her depressive symptoms.

The most powerful suggestions offered to cancer patients, who almost always feel a loss of control over their body, are those that acknowledge the difficulty of the situation and reaffirm patients' competence to manage these difficulties. Such a communication can be met with skepticism if expressed by a well-meaning family member or a clinician who has no knowledge of the disease or treatment. As we see from Susan's example, however, this information can be empowering and gently supportive when it comes from a clinician who can normalize the patient's experience and provide a context that includes the probable course of the symptoms. Often, as in Susan's case, the patient can also be assured that the experience has a time limit.

An important role of any clinician involved in cancer pain treatment is to educate patients and their families about the available medical treatment options (Jacox, Carr, Payne et al., 1994; Syrjala, 1994; Syrjala, Williams, Niles, Rupert, & Abrams, 1993). For moderate to severe pain, patients should request hypnotic intervention as an adjunct to medical treatments but not as an alternative to these treatments. Fear of addiction, reluctance to depend on medication, and concern about side-effects of medications often result in cancer patients' severely underutilizing life-enhancing medical treatments. Regrettably, healthcare providers themselves often share some of these misconceptions. They are often not aware of patients' levels of discomfort and may not have adequate training in the treatment of cancer pain and its side-effects. Consequently, clinicians considering hypnotic treatment for pain related to cancer need to fully evaluate the pain, as well as the ability of the patient to advocate for his or her own needs with healthcare providers.

Misperceptions about the Power of Hypnosis

There is no more common question asked of a psychologist working in oncology than the one about how effective hypnosis, suggestions, or thoughts can be to cure the disease. As we will see, serious damage can be done by well-meaning relatives and patients who believe that cancer can be cured primarily by suggestion or by encouraging or discouraging certain thoughts. Such misconceptions require that we approach with care any expressions of the power of the mind in treating cancer, that we are clear about our own beliefs and how these beliefs may transmitted to our patients.

When we talk with a patient and his or her family, we try to be as clear as possible that hypnosis and suggestion are not known to cure cancer or even to directly affect its course. We further emphasize that, while we know that the mind and body are connected, and that the mind influences the body, no data demonstrate that the mind alone can cure cancer. It is as mistaken to think that the mind totally controls the body as it is to think that the mind has no influence on the body whatsoever. Since this belief in mind supremacy is a reflection of the basic human need for invincibility and immortality, we try to be sensitive to the patient's and family's struggle with mortality even as we discuss these scientific and clinical issues.

When these misconceptions are not confronted, patients who have difficulty with the guaranteed discomforts of medical treatment are naturally more likely to turn to a less painful treatment, such as hypnosis. Their wishes develop into beliefs that hypnosis will be the only treatment they will need, and they do not understand that hypnotic intervention is only one component of their cancer treatment. Other patients, discouraged when their medical treatment seems to be ineffective, may find it difficult to accept that currently available treatments are limited in their effectiveness. And so, they may believe that the failure to improve is their own fault—that their disease is not responding to treatment because of something lacking in their own attitude or personality. We strongly recommend that patients continue all medical care while integrating hypnotic treatment as a part of their active participation in their health. We try to support patients when they are discouraged and help them avoid blaming themselves when treatment is not effective. Because pain and other physical symptoms of cancer and its treatments respond very well to hypnosis and suggestion, we do encourage patients and their families to include these interventions in their overall care.

Communicating congruence with the patient's beliefs is important to developing initial rapport, of course. So, if a patient believes in the "magic" of hypnosis, we do not discourage this belief. If a patient requests "visualization" or "guided imagery" rather than "hypnosis," unless it is necessary to correct a misunderstanding, we simply respond by offering training in "visualization," incorporating the use of suggestion as a potent component of this strategy.

Hypnotic Responsivity

Hypnotic responsivity is rarely an issue when treating cancer patients, although some knowledge of the patient's capacity for imagination and absorption can be valuable. The data are mixed with respect to the issue of hypnotic responsivity and pain management. Some data indicate that highly responsive subjects reduce pain more than unresponsive subjects in laboratory studies (Spanos, Kennedy, & Gwynn, 1984; Spanos, Radtke-Bodorik, Ferguson, & Jones, 1979), while other data do not (Fricton & Roth, 1985; Price & Barber, 1987). Generally, clinicians do not believe that hypnotic responsivity is the best predictor of response to hypnotic treatment (Barber, 1980, 1982, 1991; Price & Barber, 1987). For cancer patients with strong motivation, response on standard measures seems even less useful than with non-cancer patients as a predictor of ability to benefit from these strategies (Barber, 1980; Frischholz, Spiegel, Spiegel, Balma, & Markell, 1981).

Our clinical experience suggests that almost anyone with sufficient motivation can benefit from individualized psychological treatment, although the patient with more responsivity will probably respond more readily to any approach. Rather than focusing on responsivity, we individualize our treatment approach by assessing the cognitive style of the patient and the beliefs or wishes that bring the patient to treatment. We find this assessment to be a useful guide to the development of treatment strategy.

With a skeptical patient who demonstrates little facility for imagination, or indicates some suspiciousness about hypnosis, we begin with phenomena that most patients find comfortable. For example, we may begin with tense-release muscle relaxation training, then move on to imagery, and after that incorporate suggestion. Since these patients often are not in touch with their bodies, they can gain confidence and a sense of personal control merely by becoming aware of the simple shift from tense to relaxed muscles.

It is often helpful to begin the first treatment with a description of what will happen. The concrete physical change and the experience of mental control over that physical change, as well as the patient's greater comfort with feeling in control during the procedure, helps to eliminate his or her skepticism and engender probable success, which may not occur as readily with hypnotic suggestions initiated at this point.

Alternatively, we sometimes use an experiential exercise. For example, we may ask the patient to stand with arms extended and hands against our hands. Patients are instructed to raise their arms straight out in front of them and to continue to hold their arms straight while we press as hard as possible against them. Next, patients are instructed to imagine steel bars through their arms while the exercise is repeated. These demonstrations of the effects of the mind on the body are valuable first steps for patients who are inexperienced in using their imaginations.

Evaluation Prior to Hypnotic Intervention

Before we can responsibly develop a pain treatment plan incorporating hypnosis or suggestion, our patient needs to have a medical evaluation to determine appropriate medical treatments, as described in Chapter

2. While additional evaluation is valuable, the depth of this assessment depends in part on the duration of pain relief being sought. Very brief suggestions for procedural pain may require only a brief evaluation. However, designing a strategy for management of chronic cancer pain requires a more thorough evaluation. Medical and physical status can change suddenly. The evaluation needs to be updated as the patient's needs change, depending, for instance, on the course of the illness and cognitive shifts, as well as input from others, such as the physician or family. Further details on assessment of pain in cancer are available from other sources (Cleeland & Syrjala, 1992). Let us review, now, the factors that need to be considered when we develop a pain treatment plan using hypnosis or suggestion.

A good description of the pain will help in developing hypnotic strategies and suggestions that can be tailored to the individual characteristics of the pain, as well as identifying other needs of the patient. Understanding the etiology and location of the pain is very important in developing an effective treatment plan. Is the pain a result of a procedure, surgery, chemotherapy, radiation, disease progression, muscle overuse, or is it of unknown origin? The answer to this question not only tells us about the targets and goals of treatment but also provides some information about the potential meaning of the pain to the patient and about secondary goals that might be achieved with hypnotic intervention. Is the pain a symbol to the patient of frustration, helplessness, or loss? Is it a cause for anxiety and questions about whether the disease is progressing?

Paradoxically, in a life-threatening illness, patients sometimes see the pain as an indicator of their health status – they are still alive – and may be reluctant to be completely relieved of the pain. We have had cancer patients tell us that they are reassured by staying in touch with the pain and saying to themselves, "The pain is the same today as yesterday so I'm not worse, the disease hasn't spread."

The intensity of the pain is easily measured with a VAS or numerical scale. A baseline assessment and reassessment after the use of suggestion can assist both you and the patient in evaluating the efficacy of treatment. In itself, this assessment can act as an important motivator, reminding the patient that the time spent using the technique has had a measurable effect, even if the pain does not disappear altogether (which, in itself, is probably an unrealistic goal). Continuous pain above "6" (out of 10) needs rapid attention from the medical team to assess options for improved treatment. Once we are assured that the treatment method is appropriate, it is usually best *not* to reassess pain immediately after each session, since assessment draws the patient's attention back to the pain, perhaps undermining the effect of the suggestion. This can decrease comfort and make patients understandably irritated.

TECHNIQUES

Suggestions

As clinicians we recognize the power of our suggestions in all of our conversations with patients and their families, whether or not hypnosis is a component of treatment. While suggested analgesia may be more powerful in the hypnotic state than without it (McGlashan, Evans, & Orne, 1969), suggestion is an extremely powerful tool in any state and may account in large measure for the placebo effect (Turner, Deyo, Loeser, VonKorff, & Fordyce, 1994). Increasingly, clinicians are recognizing that placebo effect should be maximized rather than eliminated. When you simply act as though pain relief *will* be accomplished with treatment, you effectively communicate the suggestion of success to your patient.

Additionally, you can suggest comfort and mastery over physical well-being. For example, you might say:

I'm sure that, as you see how easy this can be for you, you will find a way to use it that will make it automatically more comfortable. Perhaps at first you will think about it when you notice a sensation, just like when you learned to ride a bike. But pretty soon, just like riding a bike, you find yourself doing what it is that makes you feel more comfortable.

For many acute pain situations, analgesic or sensory transformation suggestions are not needed. Relief is obtained by actively moving the patient's mind to comfort and pleasure that is unrelated to symptoms. The suggestion is implicit, since the patient knows that comfort is the goal.

Patients' Self-Suggestion

We also recognize the powerful impact of self-suggestion. For patients with continuous pain or negative self-talk about procedures, we teach the skill of "reframing" to neutral or more positive self-suggestions. (This is related to what Barber describes as "reinterpretation" in Chapter 5.) We have identified four different ways to do this. A major clinical task, of course, is to help patients discover which of these ways best matches their own personal style.

1. Patients can *focus on what they have accomplished*, rather than on what remains to be done. For example, they might remind themselves what hurdles they have already passed, such as completing a course of chemotherapy or a marrow aspiration. They can then be encouraged to congratulate themselves for having gotten through it so well.
2. Patients can be assisted in *finding something positive* that can be gained from the situation and focusing on that. For example, he or she might say, "In coming through this, I have learned what a strong and capable person I am. I couldn't have imagined two years ago that I would be able to do all this, but I've really done it, and done it well. Nothing can ever change that accomplishment."
3. It can also be helpful to encourage patients to *step out of the situation and observe it from a distance*, saying to themselves something like, "When I take a step back and put this in perspective I can see that this is just a small part of my whole life."
4. One of the most effective reinterpretations we can offer patients involves suggesting that they *focus on the temporary nature* of what is difficult or painful. For example, we might encourage a patient to say, "This is difficult, but I know that this will not last forever. In five minutes [or two days], I won't have these feelings."

One of our major goals in working with cancer patients is to identify aspects of their lives that they already can control. We then help them to gain greater control of their own comfort. Sometimes, with patients who feel very out of control, we initially take charge of the situation, and we introduce the seeming magic of the hypnotic experience. But, ultimately, we help the patient to "own" the accomplishment and abilities.

Developing Analgesic Suggestions

In the development of analgesic suggestions, it is essential to hear the patient's description of the *qualities* of the pain and its pattern of occurrence. Is the pain brief, continuous, or intermittent? Is it expected to stabilize indefinitely or to progress in severity? For instance, with a pain that is brief, hypnotic suggestions can focus on active distraction. We can suggest that the patient imagine him or herself in a pleasant place and then suggest a particular physical activity to more fully engage the patient's awareness for the duration of the procedure. For continuous or progressive pain, a sensory transformation method can help the patient to integrate the analgesic suggestion into his or her ongoing life.

Descriptions of the pain (e.g., stabbing, burning, cramping, shooting, aching, pressing) can be incorporated into the sensory transformation experience. For example, for a burning pain, we often use suggestions of freezing Arctic air blowing through the painful sensation:

> Just take a deep full breath, and as you breathe out, breathe the cool air through that feeling. Imagine the air is freezing cold Arctic air and just breathe it through that hot burning place. That's right . . . deep breath in, and breathe that icy cold air through it and watch as it changes, just notice the cooling as the feeling changes. Perhaps the shape changes, or the color might go from red to orange to yellow or even green. However it is, just notice as you feel more comfortable, more at ease. And continue to breathe that cool, comforting air through as long as you like. And whenever you like, or whenever you need, you can just take another cool, deep breath . . . whenever you would like to feel more comfortable.

Alternately, we may use information from the patient's description to suggest that the patient imagine what the pain looks like, and then modify the image, sometimes in surprising ways.

CASE EXAMPLE: ANNA, 63, SUFFERING FROM CONTINUOUS GUT PAIN AND NAUSEA

Anna, whose story was introduced at the beginning of this chapter, was interested in doing all that she could to cope with her cancer and symptoms. When I [SR] raised the option of using hypnotic methods to help manage her pain, she was enthusiastic and eager to begin. While we worked on multiple facets of her emotional and physical discomfort, using a variety of techniques, here I focus on our sensory transformation work.

After the first induction, I asked Anna to focus on her gut and see if she was able to imagine the color of the pain she was experiencing. She did this quite easily, describing it as very dark and black. I then asked her if the "black" had a texture. She responded that the "black" had a "sticky" quality to it. I inquired whether the pain had a shape or form to it; if so, could she describe it for me? The sticky black became a hard, weighty, and sharp-edged geometric object, filling her gut and tearing at it with its sharp edges. As she described this, she expressed a tangible sense of anger and hostility toward the object. I encouraged her objectification of the pain and explored the specific sensations and emotions around it.

I then asked her to see what she could do to this object, using the descriptors she had used, to soften its impact. We began with a transformation of color. Anna imaged the object changing from black to red to orange to yellow, ending with cool blue. She remarked that the temperature of the object changed as she did this, from hot to warm and finally to comforting coolness. As the color and temperature changed, so did the form. The edges softened and the object became a sphere. With each change that occurred I gave suggestions for increased comfort and for her increased control over managing her own comfort.

In subsequent meetings with me, Anna experienced the pain-object as becoming more amorphous and fluid. In the third meeting, she was able to make the pain-object completely dissolve. With each transformation, and in each session, the pain in her gut diminished. By the third meeting, she reported a complete lack of discomfort. The tone of her emotions shifted. She reported actual joy, triumph, and pride in her own strength in conquering the pain.

We audiotaped the second and third meetings so that Anna could learn self-hypnosis. Her sense of control over this part of her cancer experience seemed energizing to her. She said, "I feel like now there is something I can do against the cancer. It's not just the cancer eating at me and the doctors doing things to me, it's also what I can do for myself." Although the pain only rarely completely vanished, she was able to modify it enough to maintain eating and to be discharged from the hospital.

We most often use suggestions about patients' "favorite places" as a part of the hypnotic intervention. For example, a patient may enjoy reliving a particular holiday at a particular beach, while another patient may enjoy remembering being with grandchildren, and still another may enjoy reliving the experience of hiking a favorite woodland trail. While such an experience is not necessary for analgesia, for patients with moderate to severe continuous pain the escape to a comfortable, safe place as a reprieve from the pain is as important as direct analgesic suggestions. We find that patients immensely enjoy this experience, and this pleasure further enhances their readiness to use these methods when needed.

In the pleasant place the patient chooses, we suggest that he or she walk, in order to feel his or her own body as strong, healthy, and whole, knowing how to move and take care of itself, even without conscious thought. To most effectively take the mind away from moderate to severe pain, we include suggestions for physical activity of some type within the images the patient uses. We find that when a physical activity such as dancing, swimming, or skiing is chosen, the patient's affective absorption is much greater than if he or she is more passive (e.g., lying on the beach). Moreover, with a suggestion for activity, the patient is also required to focus on a variety of sensory experiences, including pleasant kinesthetic ones. This type of engaging suggestion is more easily maintained than a suggestion for relaxation by patients who have difficulty focusing on anything other than their severe pain.

Once patients have enjoyed being in their "special place," we incorporate analgesic suggestions developed during our assessment of pain qualities. Often we use the suggestion of ice placed on the painful area. As it melts, we suggest, the cold is absorbed into the area of discomfort until that area is numb or just tingles. Ice works well as an analgesic agent for several reasons. It is familiar and can be brought into any image. In the mountains, snow can easily be found; at the beach, in a warm cozy house, or on the front porch, an ice cold, refreshing drink can be found—the patient imagines taking the ice out of the drink and placing where it helps the most. Remember that there is no limit to the use of suggestion, beyond what the clinician and patient can imagine and comprehend.

Here is an example incorporating suggestions that employ the experience of cold to relieve pain:

> Enjoy being in this pleasant safe place, experiencing it fully. Noticing everything around you in this special place of yours. . . . And I wonder if you might be surprised by any of the sounds your hear around you, or any of the smells in the air . . . perhaps the smells of life or energy or freshness, just taking a moment to smell the air and feel the air against your face. . . . Notice if it is cool or warm or perhaps a bit of both . . . warmth from the sun or a slight cool breeze of fresh air. It doesn't really matter what it is, whatever is there is just fine. And maybe you can enjoy this fresh air as it refreshes your face and body. Taking in a deep cleansing breath, feeling the comforting coolness.
>
> And notice whether you can find something else cool nearby,

something refreshing, icy cold. You may need to move around or look about you. It may be a refreshing drink with ice, a cool lake or stream, or perhaps even the cold of snow, or a different kind of cold. But wherever it is, however it is for you, just explore that feeling of cold in your hand. As you hold it, notice how the sensations change. First cold, then perhaps tingly or maybe numb, no feeling at all. You might even be curious to put that icy cold on a part of your body where you would like to feel more comfort and notice how the feelings change, gradually the coldness seeps in . . . layer by layer . . . a tingling feeling, perhaps . . . and then the feelings become less intense, perhaps even becoming numb, or no feeling at all.

However it is for you, just less noticeable or less bothersome, just cool sensations around the edges perhaps, but soothing cool. And you can hold this coolness there for as long as you like. And know that whenever you would like to come back to this comfort or numbness, you need only to close your eyes, take a deep breath, see this place in your mind, and bring back the feeling of fresh air in your face. Then you can bring this icy cool to any place on your body, as you allow the sensations to change and as you become more and more comfortable. How wonderful it feels to be in control of your own comfort. And you might even be surprised at how easy this becomes for you, when you take a deep breath and see this place and feel this coolness as it brings as much comfort as you need.

Many other analgesic options are available. Some are described in Table 6.2. In situations where pain is long-term, patients need methods for using individualized suggestions on their own.

We have at least two initial meetings with the patient to establish a trusting therapeutic rapport and to identify any problems and solutions that will facilitate the patient's use of these methods on her own. Initially, we often provide an audiotape of the induction that was used and ask patients to practice creating the hypnotic experience between appointments. In the second appointment, problems are reviewed and addressed. For example, for the person who was unable to practice the skills between sessions, we inquire about the reasons and then problem-solve in order to facilitate future practice. We then offer a second induction. Again, patients are encouraged to practice on their own, both in a quiet place and, more briefly, during daily activities when discomfort is likely to occur.

From this point on, interventions are highly individualized. We tai-

Table 6.2
Hypnotic Suggestions for Pain Control with Cancer Patients

Most Frequently Used

1. **Escape or distraction** by going to a favorite place:
   (a) Include action for added intensity or involvement.
   (b) Metaphors for dissociation may include flying above or away from the physical sensations.
   Advantages
   Most enjoyable.
   Takes the least effort from an energy depleted patient.
   Disadvantage
   May provide shorter duration of pain relief.

2. **Blocking pain** through suggestions of anesthesia or analgesia:
   (a) Often uses numbness via cold or anesthetic.
   (b) Can use flipping switches in the brain or spinal cord to disconnect pain messages or changing channels.
   Advantages
   Patients can easily use the images on their own.
   Has potential to extend pain relief past the duration of hypnosis.
   Disadvantages
   Takes more active participation and concentration ability from the patient.
   May require more hypnotizability for full effect.

3. **Sensory transformations:**
   (a) Go to the pain location and explore it; "open to the pain" rather than push it away; watch as the pain changes; usually it diminishes greatly.
   (b) Take the pain description and introduce an image that can change as pain changes:
   find the color of pain and change the color;
   change the intensity of pain (e.g., reduce "8" to "3");
   blow cold Arctic air through a hot burning pain;
   take a knotted, cramping pain and gather the knot into the fist and throw it away or unknot the pain, soften and smooth it.
   Advantages
   Takes less energy and goes with the patient's focus of attention instead of fighting it.
   Can be done quickly without lengthy induction, especially for fatigued patients or those with acute onset, severe pain.
   Can be very effective.
   Disadvantages
   Does not seem to "get rid of the pain."
   Pain may initially seem worse, scaring the patient.

(Continued)

Table 6.2
Continued

___

Less Often Used

4. Increase tolerance of pain or decrease perceived intensity of pain (e.g., use metaphor of dessert: with each bite you are less aware of the taste, by the sixty-eighth taste it isn't bad, you just don't care about the flavor anymore, it's just there, but you don't notice).
5. Move pain to a smaller or less vulnerable area (e.g., hand).
6. Substitute another feeling for the pain (e.g., itch or pressure).
7. Alter the meaning of the pain to make it less fearful or debilitating (e.g., itch, pressure or burning are signs of treatment working, sensations are indications of healing).
8. Dissociate the body from the patient's awareness or move the mind out and away from the body.
9. Distort time so it seems to go by very quickly.
10. Suggest amnesia to forget pain and reduce fear of painful recurrences.

___

lor the number of meetings and the content of suggestions to the needs of the patient and his circumstances. Only a small percentage of patients continue using audiotapes regularly. In large measure this seems to be because the patients' situations change so dramatically over time, and they do not think of the tapes in their new situations. Instead, patients take the points they recall as most helpful from the hypnotic experience and adapt the methods and images to their new situations. Most patients find suggestions that work for them and use tapes or more formal hypnotic inductions less for pain than for particularly tense or stressful periods or to facilitate restful sleep.

With the uncertainty and constant changes patients experience during cancer treatment, the stability of our presence can be a great source of continued comfort and reliability. Many patients reach a point where they do not need further hypnotic intervention but wish to either stop by our office or have us stop by their hospital rooms, just to hear our voices or see a familiar, reassuring person who brings comfort and stability. Other patients will use their tapes in lieu of our presence to simply reexperience the comfort and sense of not being alone.

Coping with Isolation and Dying

Often we invite someone else into the images that we suggest to patients. We ask patients if they can see someone else, someone coming toward them. We suggest that they listen to see if that person has something to say that can be helpful, something that they most need to hear right now. We may ask if the patients would like to reach out and touch that person,

> ... to feel the warmth and energy of the person and perhaps to absorb some of that life-giving energy, to feel the love and connection that flows with that energy. As you absorb that energy, you can feel it flow through your body, bringing strength and renewal.

This can be much more fully elaborated if the patient is pleased and comforted by the experience.

Isolation is one of the most common experiences of cancer patients. Patients tell us that inviting someone else into the image is a powerful support that they carry with them well beyond the induction to feel safe, loved, and less alone in what is often perceived as a lonely battle. The same suggestions that are used to bring someone else into the image can be used to suggest an image of the patient at a future point in recovery. Patients imagine themselves at some specified time in the future, usually at least one year ahead, strong, healthy, and pain-free.

At the time, these suggestions can be powerful motivators and sources of strength, regardless of the actual outcome of the disease. If we know a patient is not likely to live much longer, we emphasize an imagined place of peace where the person can enjoy seeing him or herself strong and healthy. For some people, this is a way to enjoy a health that is now lost in the "real world"; for others, this may bring a very soothing foreshadowing of death. We have not found it to be unsettling to people. As with all work with ill or dying patients, we need to be prepared to work with the issues that emerge and to explore the patient's thoughts and images of death. We need also be prepared for strong feelings, perhaps fear, perhaps sadness, perhaps anger, both in the patient and in ourselves.

This entire process can be done out loud as a conversation between the patient and ourselves. We ask questions or elaborate patient responses, and the patient fills in the details. This keeps us aware of and able to respond immediately to the patient's experience, while the patient is required to stay deeply involved in her imagination to be able to respond to our questions. We are most likely to use this conversational method with patients who have difficulty creating their own images or concentrating without fatigue or tangential thoughts disrupting their focus.

Metaphor Modifications Effective in Clinical Practice

With cancer patients, as with many others, formal hypnotic inductions are often not necessary. It is possible simply to offer acutely distressed patients variations of the images found in Table 6.2. Brief, transforming images, such as seeing the pain as an object and watching as it changes color and shape or moves to a distant location, can be very effective and greatly enhance patient confidence when the pain is brief.

During occasions when concentration and attention are severely limited, helping the patient recall a "snapshot" of his or her pleasant place can take less energy, yet still provide relief. Metaphors and suggestions either with or without formal inductions are effective, particularly when you have established some therapeutic relationship with the patient. As an illustration, a patient who has said that her pain feels as if a metal band is squeezing her tighter and tighter with each new cramping sensation can be asked to describe what might be used to loosen and eventually remove such a metal band. Suggestions can then be developed based on her response. Or you might offer suggestions in the hypnotic context for cutting and gradually loosening the band. Using the patient's own description of the pain is much easier, and is probably much more effective, than using a suggestion that is meaningful to us but perhaps not to the patient.

Telling Stories

Several types of patients respond very well to active storytelling, especially when they are themselves involved in telling the story. This strategy is particularly effective when patients have difficulty concentrating because they have intrusive thoughts, short attention, or severe pain that intrudes into otherwise absorbing images. When using this strategy, it is important to elicit from the patient a story that evokes a pleasant or otherwise ego-enhancing time in his or her life. For example, we may ask a patient to describe the proudest moment in her life, the most joyous or the most at ease. We then encourage the patient to share as much detail as possible. Ordinarily, the patient becomes so engrossed in the reliving of that experience that she is unaware of pain for that moment.

PROBLEMS AND PITFALLS
IN USING HYPNOSIS WITH
CANCER PATIENTS

Perhaps the greatest difficulty in using hypnosis for cancer pain is the requirement that clinicians work through their own fears about death and believe in their own capacity to assist a patient with managing sometimes terrible situations. This does not mean that clinicians do not have feelings. On the contrary, it is the awareness of our own feelings that so often guides us toward apt interventions with the patient. However, in the emotionally taxing environment of cancer care, there is a natural tendency either to take on too much of the feelings of our patients or to distance ourselves excessively from our own feelings. Taking either of these directions can lead to burnout or to sudden overwhelming feelings.

We have seen colleagues who try to overcome their painful feelings by suppressing unpleasant thoughts and emotions. These people often have to leave cancer work because eventually the suppressed pain begins to emerge, and it makes them feel unable to continue to shoulder the burden of this clinical work. Often, these feelings include great anger, partially at our own helplessness and at the unfairness of a world where good people suffer such terrible illness and pain. Not infrequently, the anger takes the form of blaming others. These emotions can be difficult to understand if we are not free to discuss and explore them in a trusting environment.

Many clinicians, of all specialties, are isolated with these feelings, just as patients may be. Understanding this aspect of our working environment enables us to work with other staff, as well as with the patients, effectively. As clinicians, we need to remain accessible to a patient's feelings, yet not take on those feelings. We must stay in touch with our own feelings and know that these can be quite different from the patient's feelings. We need to balance hope and yet plan for the worst. To continue working well with cancer patients, we must come to our own terms with physical deterioration and the intense emotional loss people experience when they are possibly dying of cancer. We realize that these things are not easily done. They take time; even more, they require that we find opportunities where we can safely express and explore our own thoughts and feelings.

One of the greatest difficulties in using hypnosis and suggestion for cancer pain is the requirement that, as clinicians, we need to work through our own fears about dying and about not being able to do enough to help. We need to believe in our own capacity to assist a patient with managing sometimes terrible situations, while knowing that there are limits to what we can do. We sometimes feel inadequate. Accepting these limits is extremely hard, and yet in some ways it reflects valuable growth. Really, this is essential if we are to be helpful to others who are also struggling to make sense of what can be done when one has cancer. Allowing these powerful feelings to go unexamined can interfere with the most basic aspect of patient care – the therapeutic relationship between clinician and patient.

For example, a clinician who is fearful about his own death or who has not come to terms with the death of a loved one is very likely to be drawn into the center of a patient's own struggle when he is confronting his own mortality. As with any type of countertransference, if this issue is left unexplored the needs of the patient become hopelessly confounded with the needs of the clinician.

Once we are aware of and understand our own feelings, we are less likely to minimize the patient's distress or to get caught up in believing that to help patients we must experience what they experience. It can be of immense help to the patient if we can convey the calm optimism that even the barely imaginable can be managed, that even the most intense feelings of the patient can be tolerated and accepted, and they will not harm the clinician.

Having said this, sometimes we must also assertively advocate for the patient to receive greater medical attention to symptom management needs when suffering should not be tolerated. Thorough pain assessment is crucial. For instance, a patient rating his or her usual pain level as greater than "4" (out of 10) is a candidate for more aggressive medical intervention.

Most of the other problems that occur when providing hypnotic treatment to cancer patients do not differ in type or solution from those problems seen in non-cancer patients. These include skeptical patients, religious prohibitions, patients with rigidly biological models for pain, etc. (See Syrjala & Abrams, 1996, for more detail.) In Table 6.3, we list difficulties that we see more often with cancer patients than with other populations, as well as some solutions that we have found.

The most common difficulty occurring when using hypnotic treatment with cancer patients is that patients are exceedingly fatigued or cognitive function is impaired such that concentration and complex processing are very limited. With these patients, we may need to reschedule an appointment or keep the content of the appointment very brief and simple. Otherwise, in the middle of an induction, a patient may say, "I can't do this right now," or she may simply fall asleep.

Table 6.3
Problems and Solutions Encountered with Cancer Patients

Problem	Solutions
Lack of concentration	Use brief images.
	If preoccupied, talk about preoccupations.
	Perhaps try at a later time.
	If medication effects are interfering, may try at a later time.
Unsupportive family	Talk to the family.
	Involve the family in helping the patient.
	Help the patient solve the problem.
Falling asleep	For patients in severe pain with sleep deprivation, encourage to continue with a deep restful sleep.
	Raise the tone of voice and incorporate suggestions for more active imagery.
	If patients complain of falling asleep during home use, suggest practice sitting up and at a time of day when more alert.
Intrusion of pain into trance	Use more active images to more fully engage patient.
	Use sensory transformation images that accept some pain.
	Have patient talk to you to more fully engage the patient's cortical processes.
Fatigued or in severe pain	
First	Use medications for better pain control.
	Consider medication options for fatigue/depression.
Then	Begin simply, do only what is possible, e.g., breathing with an image of pain description changing.
	Use brief images, little induction is needed.
	As appropriate, use touch on the hand, foot or shoulder to help the patient focus, to anchor the patient away from the location of the pain, and to provide a competing sensation to the pain.

Rarely, issues can occur that are more harmful to the patient or the family and require great care from clinicians. The most serious problems we have seen have occurred in families where the power of hypnosis or suggestion was embraced wholeheartedly – and unrealistically. In several situations, patients have taken their training in self-hypnosis and used the techniques to treat severe, post-chemotherapy nausea and vomiting, rather than using medication to relieve most of the symptoms. Because this "treatment" was ill-conceived, these patients have developed strong conditioned responses of nausea and vomiting to future hypnotic interventions and even, in one case, to the presence of the clinician who was associated with hypnosis.

Hypnotic treatment has proven effective in relieving conditioned effects of chemotherapy such as anticipatory nausea (Burish & Tope, 1992). However, in our experience hypnotic treatment will not always work as alternative to anti-emetic medication for treating nausea and vomiting caused directly by severely emetogenic chemotherapeutic agents (Syrjala et al., 1992, 1995). Knowledge of the literature is helpful in developing a realistic treatment plan.

If a patient is receiving chemotherapy and has vomiting, not just mild nausea, it is essential to advocate for early aggressive medication treatment of symptoms. Untreated vomiting greatly increases the risk of nausea and vomiting in future episodes of chemotherapy, as well as the risk of developing anticipatory symptoms (Andrykowski & Gregg, 1992). Furthermore, nausea and vomiting are the most difficult symptoms for patients to tolerate and can cause rapid exhaustion of internal resources.

On the other hand, if a cancer patient has mild nausea, which inhibits eating but permits activity, hypnotic intervention can be quite effective. For example, we might suggest the image of a protective coating, such as Teflon, lining esophagus and stomach, allowing pills and food to pass through easily, effortlessly and even unnoticed, as described in the case of Pearl.

Serious consequences of misusing hypnotic methods have also occurred when family members believe hypnosis will cure the patient when medical treatment has failed. In more than one situation, a family member has asked, after a patient died, whether the patient would have lived if he or she had only practiced hypnosis or suggestion more (or better), suggesting that "something" should have saved the patient's life. Other times, this intervention becomes a method over which the patient has control when so much of the patient's existence is beyond control. In these circumstances, family members may nag the patient to practice, the patient resists, and the resistance serves to divide the family as both sides struggle for an area of control when they are truly struggling with fear of loss. To avoid this possibility when the family is closely involved in a patient's care, we discuss this common occurrence with patient and family. We make it a policy that the patient and family agree that the hypnotic methods belong to the patient. If the patient wishes help from a family member, he can request assistance. If a family member asks about the hypnotic intervention, and the patient does not wish to discuss the topic, we rehearse with the patient a response of simply "It's fine, I don't wish to discuss it." If any further issues arise, the patient is encouraged to discuss them with us.

One additional situation deserves mention – a family looking desperately to hold onto a loved one, and misusing hypnosis in the attempt.

CASE EXAMPLE: NEAL'S MOTHER FOUGHT FOR HIS LIFE

I [KS] received an emergency call to see Neal, a young man who was hallucinating, with tachycardia and hyperventilation. Neal was dying from multiple organ failure, including liver failure and fluid in his lungs, during aggressive chemotherapy to treat his advanced disease. When I arrived at his room, there were two physicians, a nurse, and his mother, all surrounding the bed. I had not seen Neal before, because he had been treated by another clinician who was now on vacation.

The staff reported to me that Neal had become very agitated, shouting, "The plane is going too fast, I can't stop it, help me, help me!" The medical staff were trying to reassure him that he was not in a plane and that he was safe, but his distress continued to escalate. The situation apparently developed while the mother was suggesting the fantasy of sailing with Neal in an effort to calm him during a time when he had difficulty breathing and when his mentation was clouded from multiple medications and from the disease effects. Neal spontaneously began to hallucinate being in an airplane.

As I watched, Neal became increasingly agitated; suddenly he said he was no longer on a sailboat but now he was in a plane. I asked Neal if I could join him in the plane. Then I began to talk about the plane, describing it as strong and safe, able to hold us, and then I asked to hold the control column and the throttle, along with Neal. He agreed. I then began to guide the plane with him, gradually slowing the plane while looking for a safe place to land. When Neal said that he saw a safe, peaceful, grassy place to land, we landed the plane together. I then suggested, now that we had safely landed, that Neal could quiet his heart rate and ease his breathing to a nice steady pace, and he could then leave the plane. I suggested that there would be someone to meet him with whom he could be safe and at peace, so that he could rest for a bit.

During these suggestions, I asked for and received assurance from Neal that he was following the suggestions and that he was responding. He said that he met his aunt and uncle outside the plane, and they would go to a safe, comfortable spot to rest. At this point his heart rate had slowed and his breathing was easier, so the staff and I left him to rest. Outside the room, the mother said to me, "I know what you're trying to do, you're trying to help him die, to give him permission to die. He's never met the aunt and uncle he was talking about. They're dead. I won't let him die. He has to fight!" I assured her that my only intent at the time had been to calm him by bringing him to a peaceful place where he could rest and feel safe from his agitated state. Unfortunately, at that point, I was called away by the staff (who needed guidance about coping with a possible recurrence of this situation). I said to the mother that I would return as soon as I had seen what the staff needed. Unfortunately, there was no more time to talk with her just then.

Ten minutes later, when I returned, Neal's mother was once again encouraging him to imagine that he was sailing. But Neal was now very frightened, shouting, "I'm sinking, I'm going to drown, the boat is going down!" The mother responded with, "Climb the mast! You have to keep climbing! You can't sink, don't let go!" Meanwhile, Neal's heart rate again soared, and his breathing became labored. He lost all consciousness. He was ventilated, but he never regained consciousness. Unfortunately, while his mother was trying everything she could to save her son, she lost the chance to say good-bye to him. She so desperately wanted to save him that she held to the belief that hypnosis and her love could keep her son alive.

When Neal's clinician returned from vacation, I talked with him about this sad circumstance. He told me that he had trained Neal in using self-hypnotic methods prior to the cancer treatment. Neal had enjoyed and benefited from the treatment. As may be surmised, Neal's mother was very close to him and wished to help him in using hypnotic methods, so she listened to his practice tapes, and sat in on some treatment sessions with the clinician in the hospital room. This treatment, along with his mother's assistance, had greatly benefited Neal during earlier phases of his treatment. He and his mother had ably used the strategies for controlling pain. But, while hypnotic intervention could help him to be more comfortable, it could not keep his body functioning against a tide of organ failure.

These regrettable situations are rare, but they provide important reminders to us. Hypnosis is a powerful tool that, like any tool, can sometimes be misdirected out of good intentions by people who do not fully understand the problem they are working to resolve. Further, with cancer patients, the family is integral, and so it cannot be ignored. Increasingly, in today's health-care climate of insufficiency, family members are required to be active caregivers. In many cases, a family member can learn hypnotic techniques along with the patient, in order to facilitate the patient's use when he or she is fatigued or for other reasons prefers assistance when the clinician is not available.

For persistent pain or for multiple procedures, this strategy may be an excellent solution for some patients. It can also be inadvertently misused. Early consideration of the family's role in the hypnotic treatment, as supporters, participants, or resistors, may enable us to anticipate and prevent unfortunate difficulties. In a situation like Neal's, where we anticipate some issues with separation between a parent and particularly a young adult, we are likely to simply ask the parent to step out of the room when we provide hypnotic interventions. We talk with the parent separately to provide some support so she does not feel threatened, but we try to assist the patient in keeping the hypnotic treatment as his or her own domain.

CONCLUSION

Admittedly, the setting in which hypnosis takes place makes a difference to how it is used and often to its efficacy. The clinician who practices outside a medical environment faces a number of challenges not present for those of us who work within the hospital or clinic setting. Clinicians who work within the very setting in which their patients receive treatment have easier access to medical records and can be present for procedures. Practitioners who work outside the oncology setting can also gather the information they need, of course. It is essential to gain information about the medical management of the patient's pain. This may mean obtaining the patient's permission and calling the attending oncologist or oncology nurse to request the information. Regardless of the setting, clinicians who are able to communicate between psychological and medical caregivers will increase their success in controlling their patient's discomforts.

7

HEADACHE

Joseph Barber

"I FEEL LIKE I lose nearly a week out of my life every month. It's like the pain is a monster, consuming me, starting with my head, crushing it in a vise. Taking the medication is like taking water, it just doesn't help. I'm so miserable, I can't stand this anymore!"

When she is not felled by the pain of a migraine, Helen is a charming, optimistic 34-year-old woman, married, with two young children, who writes a popular opinion column for one of the nation's most widely read newspapers. Since the birth of her second child, five years ago, her menstrual cycle has included migraine headaches of increasing intensity.

"I'm afraid I'm going to lose my grip on my life. Not only am I useless during the four days of my monthly headache, but now I am beginning to anticipate those days, feeling increasingly anxious and irritable before the headache even begins. My kids are going to think I'm nuts! My husband is going to run out of patience with me. Please, can you help me?"

Helen's case will be familiar to any clinician who treats patients with headache. What to do for Helen, and patients like her, is the subject of this chapter.

Though the etiology of headache is complex and varied (see Oleson & Bonica, 1990, for a full review of headache), here I am simplifying the problem by collapsing the many headache categories to the following few, which encompass most of the headaches likely to be treated by psychological methods: migraine headache, muscular tension headache, cluster headache, vascular headache, and posttraumatic headache.

MIGRAINE HEADACHE

Migraine headache is a frequent source of disabling pain, producing greater impact on social and work activities than all other headaches. Recent epidemiological studies suggest that between 15 and 30 percent of adults suffer from the blinding, disabling pain of migraine (Oleson & Bonica, 1990, p. 697).

The International Headache Society has adopted the categories "migraine with aura" and "migraine without aura" to indicate the two distinctive types of migraine, although there are other, specific varieties of migraine as well, e.g., hemiplegic, opthalmoplegic, basilar, retinal, and facial.

Although there is a widely held notion that migraine is a result of primarily psychological factors, this belief is not supported by the evidence, which suggests a strong genetic factor in over 50 percent of cases (Selby & Lance, 1960). In women (who comprise about 75 percent of migraine sufferers), hormonal changes associated with the menstrual cycle may be the predominant etiological factor (Oleson & Bonica, 1990, p. 699). Food allergy or food intolerance is also a major source of migraine attacks. Food rich in tyramine (e.g., aged cheese, pickled herrings, red wine) is particularly likely to induce migraine attack in those persons who are susceptible. Although psychological stress facilitates migraine attacks in individuals who are biologically predisposed, it does not seem to be a common primary cause of migraine.

Simply stated, the pain of migraine is essentially the result of over-dilation of vessels in the scalp, meninges, and brain. This over-dilation produces mechanical stretching stimulation of nociceptors that surround these blood vessels, thus producing pain. This is a vastly simplified description, and there is much still to be understood about the pathophysiology of migraine. Nevertheless, this description may be sufficient for clinicians who treat migraine patients with hypnosis and suggestion.

Migraine headache is characterized by pain that is almost always unilateral (which gives the syndrome its name, from the Greek, "hemi-

kranios"), pulses with each heartbeat, can be of severe intensity, and
may be associated with nausea and sensitivity to sensory stimulation
(primarily by light and sound). Persons suffering a migraine attack are
nearly always disabled, for a period ranging from four to seventy-two
hours. In practical terms, when a person experiences a migraine attack, it is likely that he or she will be unable to work that day, and
perhaps the day or two following as well. The patient's family and
social life is, of course, disrupted.

In *migraine with aura* (formerly called classic migraine), the pain
is preceded (usually by less than an hour) by an aura that, though
idiosyncratic, is often characterized by early visual symptoms, which
may involve a sense of flickering or shimmering light and may be
associated with a developing sense of tunnel vision. There may be
other sensory symptoms, including various dysesthesias.

In *migraine without aura* (formerly called common migraine), the
onset of pain is not preceded by such an aura. Compared to migraine
with aura, there are also other differences in the quality of the pain.
However, these differences are not pertinent to our purpose here, of
learning how to treat migraine pain with hypnotic techniques.

There is a wide variety of medications used in the treatment of
migraine, most commonly ergotamine, aspirin, sumatriptan, beta
blockers, calcium-channel blockers, and non-steroidal anti-inflammatory drugs. Although medication is of substantial benefit for most
migraine sufferers, in some cases it is not effective and in others the
side effects are so troublesome that patients are not appropriately
compliant to support their effective use.

Hypnotic Treatment

Assuming the appropriate medical evaluation has been done and that
medical solutions are inappropriate to the case (or that hypnotic treatment will be an adjunct to these medical treatments), I have found
that using posthypnotic suggestions is useful in the treatment of pain,
in general, and migraine pain, in particular. It has been my experience,
and that of colleagues with whom I've consulted, that the only successful way to relieve a migraine is to prevent it. That is, once the migraine
attack begins, sufficient physiological changes have occurred and the
intensity of the pain is such that only medication can provide any
relief at all. In fact, once the attack has reached a certain point, it is
my experience that only substantial doses of opioid medications can
bring relief to the patient.

Using hypnosis to prevent the attack, however, can offer an effective alternative to medications. I encourage the patient to construe the prodromal aura as a signal for two simultaneous events:

1. Reversal of the physiological process leading to the migraine – namely, the gradual reduction in dilation of the vessels involved.
2. A rest period that makes the first event possible.

Special Considerations

Sometimes, of course, patients suffer from migraines without auras. Since the treatment described above depends upon the perception of the aura as a signal (a posthypnotic cue, if you will), I suggest to such patients that they, in fact, do have an aura but that they have not yet noticed it. While this may not be strictly true, it is a useful therapeutic conceit.

Another complication occurs when a patient tends to be awakened from sleep by onset of the painful migraine attack (as happened to Elaine, whom I discuss below). In this case, I suggest to the patient that the aura is there to warn her of the impending migraine, even while she is sleeping; as with other important signals that occur during sleep, she can be awakened by the signal of the aura. I suggest that the aura will awaken the patient and that she will then respond to the aura by initiating the hypnotic procedure, just as if the attack had occurred during a waking period.

Although I have not always succeeded in helping patients relieve other kinds of headaches, all my migraine patients have benefited from hypnotic treatment. Six-month follow-up on twenty-six of my patients revealed that fifteen reported successfully averting migraine attacks each time they experienced an aura, eight had been successful with two episodes of failure each, and three reported success when the headache began while awake but failed completely when the headache occurred during sleep.

CASE EXAMPLE: ELAINE, 35, MIGRAINE WITH AURA

Elaine, a married mother of two children who owns her own business, was referred by her neurologist for treatment. She has suffered for five years, since the birth of her second child, from migraines that are associated with her menstrual period. Menstruation-related migraines are the most common of migraine. (Elaine's case is reminiscent of Helen's, described at the opening of the chapter.) Various medications have been tried, but none with success. When she develops a migraine, she is disabled for about three days. Almost completely unable to function, she remains virtually bedridden for the duration of the attack.

The intake interview was occupied by the usual history-taking and discussion of the problem and how it affects the patient. Because she was highly motivated and her headaches seemed to be uncomplicated by psychological issues, Elaine seemed to be a good candidate for psychological treatment – that is, she had headaches that disabled her and she wanted to be rid of them. In my judgment, Elaine also had realistic and healthy expectations about the role of psychological treatment, including hypnosis.

The first treatment visit involved no particular explanations or discussion, just a fairly rapid initiation of the hypnotic induction. I do not remember, and my notes do not reveal, what kind of induction I used. This, of course, does not matter to this discussion, since the induction can be independent of the therapeutic suggestions offered.

Following the induction, I offered the following suggestions:

You are about to begin a very interesting process of learning how to use your mind's capacity to work toward the greater health and well-being of your body. . . .

In the future, whenever you begin noticing the sensations of the aura, that will be the signal for your body to react in the following way:

When you first notice the sensations of the aura, you will stop whatever it is that you are doing [examples were given here, based on the activities she might be engaged in, including driving her car, working at her desk, etc.], you will find a place to sit back or lie back comfortably. After you are sitting or lying down, take a very deep, very satisfying breath and . . . hold it . . . hold it for a moment. Now, continuing to hold your breath, roll your eyes up as far as they will go, and just hold them there. Then, as you let your breath all the way out, without moving your eyeballs, allow your eyelids to close. Now . . . just allow yourself to sink deeply down into this experience of comfort and relaxation.

Whenever you do this . . . whenever you rest back, on a sofa, or a bed, or a chair . . . and take a deep, satisfying breath . . . and whenever you then roll your eyeballs up, as far as they will go, and, holding them there, slowly lower your lids . . . letting your breath all the way out, and relaxing your eyeballs . . . whenever you do this, you'll find yourself suddenly and pleasantly recreating the experience you are having right now, here with me.

With your eyes closed, breathing comfortably, allowing yourself to become more and more absorbed by the comfort of your inner experience, you prepare your body to reverse the process of the headache. You will begin to notice that you see an image in your mind . . . an image of swollen blood vessels that are now very gently beginning to relax, beginning to reduce the swelling. . . .

Just watch carefully as the blood vessels begin to relax, to reduce that dilation, to promote normal blood flow throughout your body. Continue to breathe comfortably, and just watch the vessels continue to relax. . . .

You may find that, after a while, you drift into restful, restorative sleep . . . or you may find that, after twenty minutes or so, you find yourself sitting up, alert, relaxed, and noticing that the aura has gone away. . . .

By taking this time, by allowing your body to relax, you will be helping those blood vessels to reduce in size, and to reverse the process of the headache. You will not need to have any headache at all. . . .

But it is very, very important that . . . each time you notice the aura, this is the signal for you to automatically begin the process of reducing the dilation of your blood vessels. Always, and without fail, if you notice the aura, you will stop what you are doing, and follow the suggestions I have given to you.

This hypnotic treatment was followed by several minutes of coaching Elaine, so she could practice developing what amounts to a self-hypnotic experience. For example, I would ask Elaine to take a deep breath, hold it, roll her eyeballs up, as high as she could, slowly lower her lids . . . and then follow her inclinations. I would then observe her behavior, adding supportive suggestions to guide her into an experience that could be practically repeated whenever she developed an aura.

I could see that Elaine was able to produce an effective hypnotic experience in this way, based on my observation of her rapid relaxation and her ability to carry out posthypnotic suggestions. A few days later I saw her again to confirm that she could still produce the hypnotic experience. However, because the entire purpose of this treatment is to reduce pain, there was as yet no way to know if she would be successful. Since I wanted her to have an optimal chance to experience success, we made an appointment to meet at about the time that she would otherwise expect, given her menstrual cycle, to be experiencing migraine attacks.

At that next appointment, about two weeks later, Elaine indicated that she had awakened the previous morning, earlier than usual, with the sense that she was having a prodromal aura. She initiated the self-hypnotic treatment we had established for her and experienced much the same feelings as she did in my office. She did not have an attack.

At follow-up of one, two and three months, Elaine reported that she was continuing to avert the migraine attacks. However, seven months later she called to make another appointment, because she had had an attack the day before. At the subsequent meeting, she indicated that she had awakened several days before with an aura and had done what she had learned to do, but had, nonetheless, been unpleasantly surprised by the onset of a painful migraine attack about half an hour later. That attack had kept her bedridden for the day. She was feeling very discouraged, wondering if the hypnotic effect had "worn off."

Upon more detailed discussion, it turned out that Elaine had probably gone back to sleep after awakening, and had not really followed through with the hypnotic procedure. I used hypnotic suggestions to reestablish in her mind what the hypnotic experience was like, and reminded her of the importance of going through the procedure entirely each and every time she thought she was having an aura.

Three weeks later, Elaine called to say she had successfully averted an attack. At follow-up three months later, she continued to be successful, and had not had another migraine.

CASE EXAMPLE: MATT, 55, MIGRAINE WITHOUT AURA

Matt, an accountant, had begun experiencing migraine headaches about two years previously. He had also suffered with them in late childhood and adolescence, but with auras, and they had abated when he was 20. Then, over 30 years later, they had begun to recur, this time without auras. Over the course of the past two years, his neurologist had tried several combinations of medication, but to no avail. About twice a month, with no obvious precipitant, Matt was laid low by severe head pain and photophobia. Matt and his neurologist were interested in the possibility that hypnotic treatment might relieve his symptoms.

Intake revealed his circumstances to be within normal range, with nothing catching my eye. I suggested that we make four appointments to initiate hypnotic treatment. Matt expressed some ambivalence about this. On the one hand, he very much wanted to be free of the headaches; on the other, he was wary about the prospect of being hypnotized. He feared that this would mean surrendering his will to me. I attempted to put his fears at ease by discussing my understand-ing of hypnosis and how it alleviated pain – all without surrendering one's will.

Several days later, I reminded Matt that we were going to use the power of his imagination to affect the physiological process that led to a migraine attack. Although Matt was very clear that he did not experience any prodromal warning of the headache, I suggested to him while he was hypnotized that, while he did not have the kind of aura common to many migraine sufferers, his body was sending him a warn-ing of a more subtle kind. I didn't know what form the warning took, but, I suggested, if he would allow himself to become very absorbed, now, by the process of his imagination, he might begin to remember a signal, however subtle, that had been associated with migraine onset in the recent past.

After repeating these suggestions, I asked Matt to

... take a moment, as I stop talking, and allow yourself to focus deep, deep down within you, to that awareness of yourself that feels most right, most true to you. Allow yourself to become completely absorbed in the sense that you can be aware of your body and its needs.

Now, from this place, allow yourself to remember back to the most recent headache. Remember back, minutes before that last headache. What sensation can you become aware of that signals to you that you were about to have a headache?

After several minutes, Matt was unable to report any significant awareness. I then suggested that he allow himself to remember back to the headache before that one, and the one before that, to discover what might be common to the antecedent conditions of each headache. With continuing support and encouragement, Matt finally reported that he had a vague sense of smelling something metallic. He could not be more specific than that – just a vague metallic smell.

I continued:

That's right. Something about the process that creates each head-ache also inexplicably produces a metallic smell for you. So I want you to know that, in the future, whenever you become aware of that same metallic smell, you will know that this smell is a signal for you to stop what you are doing as soon as possible, and to do the following.

I then gave Matt the same suggestions for developing a self-hypnotic experience for the purpose of averting the headache that I'd given Elaine. I repeated the suggestions, gave other posthypnotic suggestions for the purpose of evaluating his responsiveness, and then asked him to terminate the hypnotic experience.

Our appointment time was now at an end. If his headache frequency could be predicted from his recent history, it was likely that he would again suffer a migraine attack within ten days. I thought further practice would be helpful to insure success, so we made an appointment for three days hence.

At the second treatment appointment I asked Matt to imagine, for a moment, that he was beginning to experience the metallic smell and then to follow his inclinations. After a brief clarifying discussion (because he didn't understand exactly what I meant – he felt odd just closing his eyes and ignoring me, he said), he took a deep breath, held it for several seconds, he rolled his eyes up, and, releasing his breath, closed his eyes and appeared to become quiescent and relaxed.

After two or three minutes, I asked him what he was aware of. He replied that he was feeling deeply comfortable and was observing with curiosity his blood vessels, looking for some that might seem swollen but not finding any.

I asked him to end the hypnotic experience and to find himself feeling alert and awake and well. As we repeated this process three times over the next half-hour, I became more and more confident of Matt's responsiveness to the hypnotic treatment.

We then made an appointment that I thought would take place about when his headache would be predicted to occur. I also encouraged him to call me if he experienced anything out of the ordinary between now and then.

As it turned out, he did not have a headache, or any signal of one, by the next week, so he telephoned to discuss changing the appointment. We agreed to meet four days hence. Two days later, Matt called and told me, with some excitement, that about an hour earlier he had noticed the same metallic smell he'd talked about in my office. At that signal he had stopped his work and gone through the hypnotic procedure; he had developed a slight nauseated feeling but no headache. And he was now feeling fine.

Because he seemed to be doing well, we canceled the appointment and agreed to meet two weeks later. Doing so allowed us to confront a common complication in the treatment of migraines.

It turned out that, about five days after our telephone conversation about the apparent averted migraine, Matt was returning to his office from lunch and thought he noticed the metallic smell. He wasn't sure, though, and waited to see if it became more apparent. By the time he'd reached his office, he was no longer aware of the smell sensation and began work at his desk. About 15 minutes later, he suddenly experienced a full-blown migraine attack. As instructed, he took the oral medication he'd tried previously and lay down in his darkened office. The headache continued to build, however, and disabled him for the remainder of that day and most of the next.

As I listened to Matt's report, I was reminded that this is one of the greatest obstacles to patients' reliable use of hypnosis to avert migraines. The patient isn't certain that he or she is actually experiencing an aura and so ignores whatever had been noticed and continues to work, only to be surprised by the onset of a migraine later. Or, sometimes, particularly in patients whose work lives are very intense, the patient will notice the aura but, because of the press of work, develop a version of denial or put off cessation of work "for just a few minutes." In fact, it is the subsequent onset of the full-blown migraine that causes them to stop working.

In Matt's case, and in others of this type, I patiently but emphatically insist that the headache can only be averted by swift and timely response to the prodromal sign. Sometimes I remind them of Hobson's choice in this context: If they mistakenly think they are experiencing an aura but aren't, they will have unnecessarily stopped work for a while; however, if they mistakenly think they are not experiencing an aura, they will have unnecessarily lost at least a day of work to the subsequent headache. When nothing else has been persuasive, this last characterization often reveals to the patient the wisdom of acting swiftly and decisively, even if he or she is not certain that what is being experienced is a true aura.

Given the severity of migraine pain and the inexorable development of an attack once it has begun, it is a source of some mystification to me that this hypnotic treatment of migraine is so often effective. Even though other headache syndromes may not be so severe, they are not also quite as amenable to successful hypnotic intervention.

MUSCLE TENSION HEADACHE

This is the most common headache type. Muscular tension headache is caused primarily by ischemia and fatigue of scalp muscles held under tension (either by poor posture – including "posture" of the mandible –

or psychological stress or both). Because psychological tension is so often associated with this syndrome, the name "tension headache" conveys many people's belief that the tension is psychological rather than muscular. However, in my experience, patients who suffer regularly from muscle tension headaches may best be treated by physical interventions.

For example, some years ago my dentist inquired if I had headaches. I did, with almost daily regularity, but had not really paid attention to them. (I had assumed them to be a function of the psychological tension I experienced while working at a pain clinic.) He evaluated my "bite" and concluded that the headaches were a result of chronic tension created by a very subtle malocclusion (Fricton, 1982, p. 25). A very brief and painless correction of the occlusion was accompanied by an abrupt cessation of the headaches.

More recently, I began to suffer frequent and severe muscle tension headaches and consulted a physical medicine specialist, who concluded that normal wear and tear on the cervical spine, in association with less than perfect spinal posture, resulting in pressure on cervical nerves, was precipitating these headaches. I was taught exercises to strengthen the appropriate muscles and others to correct my posture; gradually, these headaches improved. Occasionally, when I fail to keep up with the daily exercise regimen, I am presented with a headache to remind me to be more conscientious.

Although hypnosis can certainly be helpful with reducing the pain of muscle tension headache, it is only ameliorative, not curative. It is similar in its degree of amelioration to medication – aspirin, for example. However, some minutes or hours later, the pain will have returned, because the underlying cause for the pain has not been altered. Physical treatment, as discussed above, is essential for successful treatment. Although suggestions for relaxation might be adjunctively useful, it is my experience that physical treatments are the speediest and most effective means for reducing muscle tension.

Consequently, when patients seek treatment from me for this headache, I am most likely to refer them to a physical medicine specialist for treatment. I explained that this is far more likely to lead to a satisfactory outcome than hypnotic treatment; such corrective physical treatment is likely to cure, rather than palliate symptoms. There are exceptions, but as a rule such headaches can only be successfully treated by physical attention to the source of muscular tension.

Occasionally, but equally importantly, it is the case that the primary source of the muscle tension is emotional conflict, not poor posture. When this is so, it is appropriate to attend to the conflict's source and the patient's way of coping with it.

CASE EXAMPLE: DURKIN, 39, WITH MUSCLE TENSION HEADACHE

Durkin, a stenographer, had suffered from headaches since high school. His physician referred him to me after trying a variety of unsuccessful medical treatments.

As is always the case, I wanted to know about the source of Durkin's tension. A hypothesis occurred to me several minutes into the intake interview. Durkin was a very small man, only slightly over four feet tall. He lived alone. According to him, he had no friends, and was not close to his family. He enjoyed his work, though he complained that typewriters were too large, the keys spaced too far apart for comfort. He also complained, as an aside, that furniture was generally too large. He wondered why people tolerated such uncomfortably oversized furniture. He expressed these complaints with a perfectly straight face, with no apparent ironic intent.

It became clear, as our conversation continued, that Durkin found the world to be an intimidating place, fraught with physical discomfort and the risk of physical danger. My hypothesis was that much, if not all, of his tension (both emotional and physical) was a function of living with this constant sense of threat.

Durkin's physician had already told him that hypnotic treatment would be effective for him, so that is what Durkin expected from me. We arranged to begin such treatment the following day.

When we met the next day, Durkin reported that, as usual, he had a headache. He rated the intensity as 6 (out of 10), and rated it affectively as 8. Following hypnotic induction, I suggested to Durkin that his musculature would begin to relax very deeply, and that the pain would naturally reduce as his muscles relaxed. I spent some time repeating these suggestions and went to some effort to convey the deep level of relaxation I hoped he would experience. While hypnotized, he reported that he felt very relaxed, that he had no pain, and that he felt very well.

The problem, of course, involved extending the relief beyond the duration of the treatment appointment. How, I wondered, might I enable Durkin to feel safe enough in the world to maintain a reduced level of muscular tension? Unable to arrive at a satisfactory solution, I asked Durkin for his opinion:[1]

---

[1]The following suggestions for an "active and independent voice" are made to facilitate the patient's speaking while experiencing the relaxation and dissociation of the hypnotic state. I find these suggestions helpful for preventing the inadvertent ending of the hypnotic experience by a patient's attempt to speak without quite knowing how.

Durkin, as you continue to rest very deeply, and remain very comfortable, I'd like to ask that the muscles of your voice become independent and active, so that you can talk with me even though you remain very, very relaxed.

Allow the muscles of your voice to begin now to become independently active, so that the muscles of your breathing . . . and of your larynx . . . and your jaw . . . and your tongue . . . and your lips . . . all of the muscles of your voice can now become independent and active. And you can tell me, now, what are you aware of right now?

"I feel good."

"What number is the feeling in your head?"

"There is no feeling."

"None at all?"

"No. My head doesn't hurt."

"That's fine. Now, Durkin, I want you to imagine that you can speak from the very deepest, wisest part of you, and you can tell me: What do you need to feel this kind of comfort all of the time?"

"I don't know."

"That's fine, but let's just imagine that, deep within you, in that part of you that does sometimes surprise you with what you know . . . let's imagine that you can hear a voice from deep within you. Even if you think you don't know, just listen to that voice, and tell me what you hear."

After a long pause, "I need to be big."

"That's right, you need to feel big."

"No, I need to *be* big."

"How big do you need to be in order to feel comfortable?"

"I need to be big enough to beat up bullies."

"Do you know a bully?"

After a long pause, "People laugh at me."

"What do they laugh about?"

"They think I'm too small."

"Ahhh . . . they *think* you're too small. Is that right?"

"Yeah."

"And how do you feel about that?"

At this point, Durkin began to cry, very quietly. I remained in contact with him by making supportive, empathic statements, by expressing my interest in his feelings, and by expressing my gratitude for his willingness to talk with me about this painful subject. As I heard myself commenting aloud to Durkin about his courage, I began to formulate a plan for enabling him to feel less tense more of the time. After all, Durkin was being courageous by openly discussing with me a deeply painful topic (and one that I doubt he had ever spoken about before, with anyone).

I began gently to suggest to Durkin how important it was that he recognize his courage. I reminded him, too, that courage does not mean not being afraid. Because little time was left at this visit, I suggested to Durkin that he allow himself to think about his courage in the context of recognizing how frequently he was afraid but continued to function anyway. And I suggested that we could talk about this again. After giving him further suggestions for feeling less tense, for being less critical of himself, and for being curious about what we might accomplish at the next visit, we ended the hypnotic experience.

Three days later, Durkin arrived with what seemed to me a little less of the pugnacious quality in his demeanor than I had noticed previously. He said that he had a headache but that it was not "too bad." He rated it with an intensity of 4 and affectively as 1. Responding to a posthypnotic cue, Durkin developed a hypnotic state and began to relax.

We resumed the conversation of a few days previously. I asked Durkin if he had had an opportunity to think about courage. He said that he had not, really, but that he did like what I had said about it before, that is, about his being courageous. We continued to discuss courage, and fear, and threat, and the fact that courage depended upon both threat and fear, and so on.

For the next 16 weeks, Durkin and I met weekly for hypnotic conversations about courage. He continued to report general relief from his headaches, though he occasionally suffered from them. He also reported that he was more confident now and that I had been right in the first place about his courage. He had decided that he was, in fact, a very courageous person.

At one-month, three-month, and six-month follow-up meetings, Durkin's improvement seemed stable. He no longer complained of headaches, though he acknowledged that he sometimes had them.

Durkin's treatment illustrates the fact that sometimes pain can be a symptom of a more fundamental psychological problem. In Durkin's case, chronic anxiety seemed to result in chronic muscle tension, which resulted in headache pain. It was not possible, of course, to make Durkin taller. And it was not possible to change the way people responded to his short stature. It was possible, though, to facilitate a change in Durkin's attitude toward himself. Although Durkin's case demonstrates the dramatic improvement that can sometimes occur in otherwise intractable headaches, not every case has such satisfying results.

In summary, while most muscle tension problems are likely to be physically based, in some cases unresolved emotional conflict may need our attention. Artfulness may be required to orient the patient toward emotional aspects of the problem, especially if the patient tends to somaticize – and thereby to avoid awareness of emotional issues.

CLUSTER HEADACHE

Cluster headache, like migraine headache, can result in very severe, even disabling pain. Cluster headache is unilateral, intense, accompanied by autonomic phenomena (e.g., lacrimation, rhinitis, rhinorrhea)[2] and forehead sweating, all on the side of the head experiencing the pain. The pain usually comes without warning and lasts between 15 minutes and three hours. What constitutes the "cluster" is the frequency of the headaches – they tend to occur in clusters, separated by intervals free of headache (except for the variant called "chronic," which is not associated with headache-free intervals). The clusters vary from one attack within two days up to eight per day. In contrast to the case with migraine, most cluster headache sufferers are male. Again, unlike migraine sufferers, there seems to be no familial factor in the incidence of cluster headache. The etiology of this syndrome remains unknown (Oleson & Bonica, 1990, p. 717).

Pharmacological treatments have been reported to be effective. Ergotamine is commonly used to treat the acute attack, and a variety of medications has successfully been used to prevent attacks. I know of no literature reporting the use of hypnosis in treatment of this syndrome. However, I have treated four patients with cluster headache. In each case, I was struck by the patient's anxiety over the anticipated onset of the next painful attack, as well as associated anxiety that there would be no effective treatment. (All patients, of course, had already undergone medical evaluation, without finding effective treatment for their headaches.)

As with all recurrent pain syndromes, hypnotic treatment of cluster headache requires that the patient be able to utilize training in self-hypnosis and to respond to suggestions for analgesia during an attack. Two of the four patients in my practice actually experienced a reduction in frequency so that after three years the attacks did not recur. (It

[2]Lacrimation refers to tearing from the eye; rhinorrhea to running of the nose; rhinitis to inflammation of the epithelial mucosa that lines the nasal passages.

is possible that this reflects a natural course of the syndrome; it is unclear what, if any, role hypnosis may have played beyond facilitating analgesia during an attack.) The other two patients experienced variable success in diminishing the pain, but neither was free of attacks five years after treatment.

CASE EXAMPLE: MICK, 44, WITH CLUSTER HEADACHE

Mick, an engineer, had been referred to me by his neurologist after a lengthy and largely unsatisfactory trial of medications. His history was unremarkable, except that he had been troubled by severe headaches for nearly five years. His headaches tended to cluster in a one-to-three day period and recurred about every ten days. Significantly, he sometimes noticed a "bad" smell ("like burning rubber") in the minutes preceding the onset of a headache. Sometimes Mick benefitted from the medications and was able to continue working, and sometimes no medication could relieve the intense, debilitating pain on the right side of his head and face.

Mick agreed to see me out of desperation, with no real confidence or hope that I would be able to help. Understanding that the headaches were physical in origin, he was pessimistic about obtaining help from psychological treatments.[3] Consequently, much of the latter half of the intake appointment was taken up by my discussion of the treatment plan I thought would help. I confirmed for him that his headaches were physical in origin, and that, while psychological stress might conceivably contribute to the onset or intensity, it was probably not really a significant factor in his condition. I talked with him about the interface between mind and body and the psychological dimensions of the experience of pain. I suggested that his engineering education might facilitate the treatment I had in mind, since I expected to depend on the "executive control center" in his brain to exert influence on the "peripheral operations," including the receiving and processing of pain messages.

Mick seemed intrigued by this discussion and agreed to my recommendation that we plan to meet four times in the subsequent two weeks, using psychological methods to exert influence on his pain experience.

Still not using the word "hypnosis," at our next meeting I reminded

[3]His neurologist and I had previously agreed that she would not mention "hypnosis" when referring pain patients to me, since, in my view, this would create unhelpful expectations. She tended, instead, to tell patients that I was a psychologist with a great deal of experience in the treatment of physical pain.

Mick that our goal was to "re-engineer" the information about his head-ache pain, so that, even if the physical condition continued to exist, he would not have to suffer so severely with the pain. In the context of this discussion, I reminded him of mundane examples of mind-body interactions, including vasodilation of the subcutaneous facial vessels when he experienced embarrassment. He seemed interested and open to the possibilities I was suggesting.

I felt confident that Mick would be able to respond to my sugges-tions if he could be satisfied that they were reasonable. I continued:

So, Mick, I think we've accomplished enough by this discus-sion this morning, so let's now find a way to access the executive control center in your brain, so that the next time a headache comes you won't have to feel it so strongly. Is that OK with you?

Mick indicated his assent, adding that he'd be very grateful if we could just "turn down the volume by half" on his headache intensity.

As you continue to sit comfortably in that chair, why not just let your eyelids close so that you can hear me from deeper within yourself?

I continued the hypnotic induction, and within a few minutes Mick was resting quietly. After eliciting his responses to various sugges-tions, I was confident that he was experiencing a satisfactory level of hypnotic absorption. I then began to offer the following therapeutic suggestions:

You have now begun a process of altering your nervous system in ways that can make an important difference to your future health and comfort. I am now going to talk with you about some specific changes you can expect.

Although you may notice a general level of comfort and relax-ation throughout the remainder of the day, you may also notice a very subtle shift in your awareness of your body.

For some time now, you have learned that the terrible pain in your head and face can come at any time, without warning. Now, though, you can expect that this will change.

From now on, whenever you have the slightest inkling that pain may be on its way, you will notice a curious tingling that begins at the top of your head and very quickly spreads through-out your head and face, creating a sense of peculiar comfort.

Whenever you develop that odd sense of smell, for instance, that has signaled, in the past, that a headache was on the way, ... whenever you notice the smell ... you will also notice that curious tingling sensation, spreading from the top of your head, all over your head and face, leaving you with a very deep sense of comfort and well-being.

You can recreate the sense of comfort you feel right now, as well. Anytime you want to feel as you do right now ... quiet, restful, relaxed, comfortable ... all you have to do is to rest back, in a chair, or sofa, or bed ... and take a very deep, satisfying breath, and hold it ... hold it for a moment. And then, when you let it all the way out, you can let your eyelids close, and notice how quickly, and how automatically, these feelings of comfort and well-being wash over you ... just like water in a hot tub.

For reasons that may seem mysterious, at first, you will have the opportunity to discover that you are a man who used to have headaches, but now that has begun to change.

After repeating these suggestions and making other suggestions intended to increase his confidence in his ability to reduce his headaches, I suggested that he would soon awaken, feeling alert and refreshed. This he did. I then gave him an audiotape of the hypnotic treatment he had just experienced and asked him to listen to the tape twice a day, once in the morning and once in the evening, for the next several days. By providing such a tape I was giving Mick the opportunity to practice the development of his hypnotic skills, as well as to benefit from hearing the therapeutic suggestions repeatedly. By the time we next met, I assumed, he would have had an occasion to experience a headache and perhaps to experience a reduction of the pain.

Five days later, when Mick came for his next appointment, he announced that he had had one very intense headache the day after the treatment, but that the pain had lasted only a few minutes, which was far shorter than usual. He was very curious about this phenomenon and about the fact that he had had no other headaches since.

I suggested to Mick that perhaps he had already begun to experience the initial results of his effort to retrain his nervous system and that our work today would reinforce those results. We then did hypnotic work, which largely repeated the suggestions that I had given him previously, but also included suggestions intended to reinforce the therapeutic gains he had apparently already made.

We continued this work at two subsequent treatment appointments, one week apart. Mick reported a brief, very painful headache on two occasions – but again, the brevity of the headache was a new and, to him, very pleasing development.

At follow-up one month later, Mick told me much the same – that he would occasionally have brief, intense headaches, but they would not last long, and did not seem to come in clusters anymore.

Because he seemed to be so much improved, and because his improvement seemed stable, I recommended that we not meet again for six months, unless he needed to see me earlier. At six-month follow-up, Mick reported that he continued to listen to the audiotape, but only about once a week, "to keep it fresh." He also reported that he experienced headaches about once every ten days, as they had before, but that they lasted only a few minutes. The brevity of his headaches made them more tolerable, and he felt satisfied that he could continue to tolerate them at this level. He also expressed optimism that his increasing confidence in his hypnotic skills might provide even more substantial improvement over time. This did not prove to be the case, however, at least within the next year. I saw Mick twice, at six-month intervals, and his headaches remained stable, occurring about once every two weeks – but only once and for only a few minutes, without causing disability.

Although Mick's case demonstrates the dramatic improvement that can sometimes occur in otherwise intractable headaches, this is not always the case.

VASCULAR HEADACHE

Vascular headache differs from migraine headache in that, although the primary source of pain for both seems to be the dilation of vessels in the scalp and within the brain, vascular headaches are almost never as intense as migraine headaches and are not usually accompanied by the other migraine phenomena, such as photophobia, nausea, and so on. Unlike tension headache, vascular headache pain pulses with the heart beat and intensifies if the patient bends over (altering blood pressure within the head). Etiology of vascular headache is variable; three major sources are hormonal (associated with the menstrual cycle), food allergy or intolerance, and muscle tension. Evaluation of the etiology is important, obviously, to determine if relief may be found, for example, in avoiding certain foods, undertaking hormonal therapy, or pursuing physical therapy. Headache medications, such as aspirin, are normally quite effective. Hypnotic treatment can be valuable in those cases where analgesic medications are not effective. The patient may respond well to hypnotic suggestions not unlike those for migraine headache, namely, suggestions for reducing dilation of the vessels to a normal, comfortable level.

CASE EXAMPLE: CAROLYN, 14, VASCULAR HEADACHE

Carolyn was referred by her mother, a pediatrician colleague of mine. Carolyn had developed intensely painful vascular headaches about six months earlier. Like many migraine headaches, Carolyn's vascular headaches were associated with her menstrual cycle. Hormone treatment had been ruled out by Carolyn's physician. Carolyn's headache would develop gradually, over a period of about an hour, and was only partially responsive to aspirin. The headache would typically last throughout the day, rendering her fairly miserable and disabled.

I saw Carolyn in the company of her mother for the initial part of the intake interview. During this conversation, I saw that Carolyn and her mother seemed to agree about the nature and character of the headaches, and I did not see any evidence of psychological problems in either Carolyn or in her relationship with her mother. It seemed to me that, in this case, since physical remedies did not seem helpful, hypnosis would be a very good option.

A few days later, Carolyn arrived for her first treatment appointment. She had no questions about the treatment, although she seemed a bit anxious about it. After some preliminary conversation, in which I reminded her of the rationale I had described to her and her mother, we began a hypnotic induction. Carolyn had seemed to relax substantially during our conversation and was now able to respond readily to the suggestions for deep relaxation and dissociation that were a part of the induction.

Adolescents have an understandable enthusiasm for independence; as a consequence, I tend to use suggestions that are intended to be congruent with that enthusiasm. In this case, I also provided a number of suggestions and comments that were intended to draw Carolyn's attention to her ability to control her experience, to resist any suggestion that did not appeal to her, and to exert her own initiative whenever she wished to do so.

After establishing a secure context in which to create the treatment suggestions, I then reminded Carolyn that treatment would involve two goals:

1. Carolyn would use hypnosis to reduce the pain of headaches when they occurred.

2. Carolyn would use hypnosis to reduce the onset of future headaches by physiologically altering her body's response to the hormones that were now producing the headache response.

The following is an excerpt of what I told Carolyn as part of achieving the first goal:

> Carolyn, because you are learning a new way to use the power of your nervous system, you can change the way you feel your headaches. In the future, if you begin to feel the headache beginning to grow, all you have to do is to use your newfound power.
>
> Whenever you feel a headache beginning to grow, stop whatever you are doing, find a safe and comfortable place to sit or lie down, and let yourself imagine the blood vessels in your head as they automatically begin very slowly, very gently to reduce in size.
>
> As you watch your blood vessels very slowly, very gently begin to shrink ... ever so slightly ... you can also notice how deeply relaxed you begin to feel. You will begin to feel the same kind of deep absorption and deep comfort that you are feeling right now.
>
> Even though I will not be with you, even though you will be controlling this process all by yourself, you can remember the sound of my voice, you can remember that you have learned this process with me, and you can feel increasingly confident that you can do this all by yourself.

Here are some excerpts of the suggestions made to achieve the second goal:

> As you continue to experience the changes in your body ... as you continue to become older and more grown up ... you may sometimes be surprised at some of the changes you notice.
>
> You body will continue to change in healthy ways as you grow older, and your body will continue to accept the changes that are occurring in more comfortable ways. Just as you sometimes feel aches in joints, from the growth of your bones, so you have also felt headaches from the new hormones that your body is producing.
>
> But these headaches are like the growth pains of your joints. They are only temporary. Just as you have adjusted to the growth of your bones, so you are already beginning to adjust to

the new hormones. Even if you had not come to see me, you would have noticed, after a while, that your headaches became less and less frequent, and bothered you less and less.

In the weeks and months ahead, your body is adjusting to the hormones that you are producing, and your blood vessels will soon be more comfortable. Soon your blood vessels will respond in more and more comfortable ways to the hormones that flow through them. Soon there will be nothing to bother you. Soon you will have no more headaches of the kind you have been having.

We all have headaches, from time to time, and that's OK. You have had headaches before, and perhaps you will again, from time to time, for various reasons. But these headaches are almost at an end now.

I will be very surprised if you call me next week and say that you no longer have these headaches. I will be very surprised if you call me in, say, a month, to tell me that you are not having these headaches. But, Carolyn, I will not be surprised if you and I talk in, say, six months, and you tell me that you no longer have these headaches. I will not be surprised to learn, in a few months, that it is even difficult for you to remember what these headaches were like. Because they will soon be a part of your past . . . not your present, and not your future. Like so many of the changes you have experienced as you grow up, these headaches will just be a part of your past . . . of your growing up.

After the treatment, I recommended to Carolyn that we meet once a month for the next few months, to reinforce the treatment, and to monitor her progress.

One month later, Carolyn reported that she had had a headache the week before and that it had not been any different from previous headaches. She wondered if the treatment was working. I told Carolyn that it not was surprising that she had had another headache, because these changes do not usually occur so swiftly, but that we would know more in a few months. I also used hypnotic suggestions to reinforce the suggestions I had given her previously and made an audiotape of the suggestions, which I instructed Carolyn to listen to anytime that she felt the need to do so.

One month later, Carolyn reported that she had had her usual headache, except that she thought it was less intense than it had been before – a 3 instead of an 8. She reported the affective component was 1 (it had been 7 initially). She also reported that she had listened to the tape twice, in the evening, about a week before the headache. I again used hypnotic suggestions to reinforce the work we had already done, recommended that she continue to listen to the audiotape whenever she felt inclined to do so, and arranged a meeting a month later.

On the next visit, the fourth treatment visit, Carolyn reported that she had thought she was about to get a headache the previous week, but that it did not develop; except for that, she had not really thought about her headaches lately. I used hypnotic suggestions in the way I had done previously, reinforcing earlier suggestions.

At the fifth month, Carolyn again reported that she had thought she was about to get a headache on a couple of occasions, but that she did not. I told her that I thought it was unnecessary for me to use hypnotic treatment with her again, since it seemed that she had the situation well under control. I reminded her to listen to the tape anytime she wished to, if it seemed useful to keep a headache at bay, and recommended that she call me if she had any questions. Otherwise, I would meet with her in three months to hear how well she was doing.

I did not hear from Carolyn during the three-month interval, and she told me at the follow-up visit that she had forgotten about the tape, had forgotten about her headache – had even forgotten about the appointment until her mother reminded her a few days before. I asked Carolyn to telephone me anytime she had a question, and to be sure to call me in six months to let me know how well she was doing.

At one-year follow-up, Carolyn continued to be free of the vascular headaches, though she occasionally had what sounded like ordinary muscle contraction headaches.

One of the misconceptions about hypnotic treatment is that, once effective it will continue be effective. Unfortunately, this is not the case, which is why follow-up visits are essential to long-term therapeutic benefit. Follow-up contact with patients provides an opportunity to monitor their condition (they might not call if pain recurs); moreover, it provides ongoing reinforcement of the initial treatment.

Carolyn's case is instructive because it clearly reveals that, even in cases in which the presumed cause of the painful condition persists, hypnotic treatment can be of value. Her case also illustrates that the value may not be instantaneous. It is important that we persist in our treatment, if it seems reasonable to do so, even when relief does not occur quickly.

POSTTRAUMATIC HEADACHE

Following a concussion, some patients experience persistent headache. While there is no correlation between severity of the original injury and occurrence of posttraumatic headache, there is a relationship between severity of injury and duration of the symptoms (Oleson & Bonica, 1990, p. 720). The etiology of this headache is not yet understood.

This headache syndrome is also ordinarily responsive to medication. However, in some cases, medication has little or no effect. In such cases, hypnotic treatment may be helpful.

As in all pain syndromes, we must properly evaluate the patient, determining, among other things, the meaning of the pain to the patient. In my experience, posttraumatic headache seems more often fraught with meaning than are other headaches. In some cases, the patient has not yet had an opportunity to discuss the meaning of the original injury. Doing so often facilitates resolution of the syndrome. In cases where the injury raises the issue of blame or culpability in the patient's mind, discussion of this issue may result in substantial relief of anxiety or guilt, which may in turn result in reduced intensity and/or bothersomeness of the headache. In cases of persistent posttraumatic headache following mild injuries, issues of unresolved anger (at victimization), avoidant reactions, and/or need for compensation may play a significant role in the effectiveness of pain treatment, and should be evaluated (Pepping, personal communication, 1995).

In cases where there is amnesia as well as posttraumatic headache associated with the initial injury, patients sometimes seek hypnotherapeutic treatment to "find out what really happened" to cause the injury. Some practitioners then lead patients through reconstructive experiences, which they construe as a reliable memory of the events leading up to the initial injury. Sometimes patients feel pain relief subsequent to this procedure. However, one needs to bear in mind that this procedure is more likely to result in credible confabulation rather than reliable memory. This point may become crucial in any case in which legal action is likely to take place.

CASE EXAMPLE: TANYA, 26, WITH POSTTRAUMATIC HEADACHE

Tanya was referred to me by her neurologist one year after an auto accident in which she suffered a mild concussion. Since then she had suffered from constant, unremitting headache. Various medications and physical therapy had been tried, with no significant relief of the headache.

At her initial visit, Tanya rated the intensity of her pain at 7 and the affective component at 10, meaning that the pain was as bothersome as she could imagine a pain to be. Since such a rating is very unusual. I wondered how much of the pain and suffering was related to the accident and what that meant to Tanya and how much was related to actual noxious stimulation. When I asked what it was about her pain that was bothersome to her, Tanya was not very responsive. She said she did not know why it bothered her, it just did.

Tanya had already learned from her neurologist that the etiology of posttraumatic headache is unknown, although it is frequently associated with the kind of head injury she had sustained. However, usually such a headache resolves by one year after injury. In Tanya's case, of course, it had not.

Following the intake interview and review of her records, I decided that it was reasonable to use hypnotic treatment for Tanya's pain. If nothing else, such treatment might have diagnostic value, as long as there was a substantial psychological component to her pain and suffering. I explained the rationale for using hypnosis, and Tanya was eager to begin. We scheduled for four treatment appointments over the next two weeks.

Because the pain was constant and distracting, the hypnotic induction incorporated the experience of the headache:

> ... Imagine that you can feel yourself *inside* the pain ... let your mind focus very clearly, very steadily on the pain. And as you continue to hear the sound of my voice, notice that my voice seems to come almost from within the very center of the pain. ...
>
> ... Continue to hear the sound of my voice, coming from the very center of your head, of your mind, of your awareness. ...
>
> ... Allow yourself to become more and more absorbed by the comfort of my voice, by the gentle certainty that, for right now, everything is just fine ... knowing that there is nothing you have to do right now ... no obligations ... no commitments ... nothing you have to do right now, but hear the sound of my voice, and notice how easily it surrounds you, with a greater and greater sense of comfort and well-being. ...

Once Tanya responded to these suggestions, and once she verbally responded to questions about how she was feeling ("My head isn't hurting"), I offered suggestions for future headache relief. Among these suggestions were the following:

> ... You were seriously injured in the accident. Now, however, your injuries have healed. You no longer need to feel pain in your head, because the injury to your head has healed very well. ...

... You can enjoy discovering how easily you waken each morning, and notice how well you feel. You might even be surprised, sometimes, to notice that ... you feel well ... you feel comfortable. .... It's almost as though you've forgotten all about the headache. ...

When the treatment ended, Tanya reported that she was surprised how well she felt, that she had no headache at all. She seemed delighted by this result. I reminded her that we had three more appointments and said that we might know better what she needed in the future when we met again in a few days.

At the next treatment appointment, Tanya reported that the headache had returned within an hour or two of our previous appointment and that it remained unchanged, as though the treatment had never occurred. I used a posthypnotic suggestion to recreate the hypnotic experience, and Tanya responded well. Following suggestions for comfort and well-being, she reported feeling well again, with no headache. I reinforced the suggestions previously made and added further suggestions about continuing comfort and about there being no need for further headaches. I also instructed her in the use of self-hypnotic suggestions, in the event that the headache returned.

This pattern continued for the next two treatment appointments: Tanya felt well during the treatment but soon after the headache returned, remaining unabated until the next treatment.

At the fourth treatment appointment, I began to take more seriously my initial hypothesis that a significant component of Tanya's pain and suffering related to the auto accident, her injury, and what this might mean. Though we had discussed this issue in the initial intake interview, and though Tanya had expressed no particular concerns about this issue, I thought that further exploration might be productive.

I asked Tanya for her understanding of what was happening with respect to her headaches. Although Tanya was generally articulate, she responded quite minimally to these questions, as she had initially. She did not know why she had the headaches, and she did not know why the headaches did not respond better to the treatment. "But there must be a good reason," she said.

During the intake interview, Tanya had told me that her best friend had been driving the car at the time of the accident and had been killed. When pressed, Tanya had little to say about what she felt about this, except to say that she was sad about her friend's death.

Now, however, while hypnotized, Tanya responded more fully to questions about the accident. She felt enraged at her friend for having the accident. "If she weren't dead already, I could kill her, I'm so mad at her!" Tanya was angry that her friend's poor driving had resulted in this terrible loss to Tanya and in her almost being killed.

Using fantasy, I involved Tanya in a conversation with her friend about her feelings. Tanya took to this conversation very readily, engaging in animated conversation with her friend, expressing her anger about her friend's poor driving. Suddenly, Tanya stopped speaking and began to cry, at first very softly, then with greater and greater energy, until she was sobbing. She seemed to be experiencing, for the first time since the accident, a cathartic release of her feelings of grief and loss.

I supported Tanya in her emotional release and, when appropriate, attempted to facilitate a more peaceful resolution to her feelings toward her friend.

After several minutes, Tanya said, "I think my hateful feelings have been giving me these headaches."

I agreed that this might be true. If so, I said, "You have now found a healthy way to express your feelings, and you don't need to keep them inside your head anymore."

It is always difficult to know how to attribute symptomatic change. Maybe Tanya's headaches would have resolved anyway, given the time since the accident. Curiously, though, she left the office free of her headaches and remained so at one-, three-, and six-month follow-up visits.

Tanya's case demonstrates the sometimes complex nature of headache pain and the importance of remaining flexible in our treatment plan. Clearly, suggestions for direct reduction of the pain were not useful. As is often true in such cases, substantial, lasting pain relief came only when the emotional underpinnings of the pain were addressed.

8

DENTAL PAIN

Roseann Mulligan

MR. PLUM, a 62-year-old man, had been nursing a nagging jaw pain for some months before finally visiting his neighborhood dentist, who prescribed antibiotics and recommended a return visit in two weeks. There was no discussion about what options would be possible for Mr. Plum at the end of the antibiotic course of treatment, so he called me for a second opinion. When I saw Mr. Plum, he had only been on the antibiotics for four days. His pain had grown worse over the last few days and he was anxious to know the cause and to decide what should be done about it. When I examined him, I could see that one of his teeth was chronically infected and needed to be extracted. Typically, such infections are isolated from the rest of the body and their main effect is to destroy tissue, which, over time, can become extensive. Antibiotics will not cure the situation but are given initially, as they improve the effectiveness of local anesthetics when the tooth is subsequently extracted. For this reason, patients are frequently more comfortable during the extraction if it follows a full course of antibiotic therapy. I suggested that Mr. Plum continue taking antibiotics and return in a few days, when I would extract the tooth. However, Mr. Plum was exasperated by the pain and by the previous clinician's failure to relieve it. He did not want to wait. Given Mr. Plum's motivation, I agreed to extract the tooth that day.

Because Mr. Plum's blood pressure was elevated, I wanted to calm him before we commenced. I asked, "Mr. Plum, would you like me to help you become more relaxed, and more comfortable, so you will be ready to have your treatment?"

He did not hesitate. "No, I can do that myself."

I suggested, then, that he do what he needed to get ready, and I left him alone for a few minutes. Looking into the room, I watched him settling himself into the dental chair. His body language implied to me that he was focusing his attention inwardly to prepare himself for the procedure.

When I returned to his side, he indicated that he was ready. I injected local anesthetic into the tissues, checked for the onset of numbness, and, when it was evident, I began the process of extracting the tooth.

Initially, everything went well. My suggestions for reinterpretation of the sensations that he was likely to be feeling, along with whatever preparation Mr. Plum had done for himself, seemed effective. He appeared quite comfortable until the actual elevation of the tooth was begun, when he indicated, with a grimace, that he was hurting. Two supplemental local anesthetic doses were given, but were not effective.

It was clear to me that Mr. Plum could not remain comfortable while I extracted the tooth, and I was more concerned than I might have been otherwise because of his hypertension. I explained that I could not complete the procedure that day, as I had reached the limit of the local anesthetic appropriate for him and, moreover, that more local anesthetic would not help. Mr. Plum urged me to continue, assuring me that he would just "hang tight" through the pain. Mindful that such distress would further elevate his blood pressure, possibly creating an emergency, I declined his offer to be stoic and said that we would stop now and continue on another day. (Aside from Mr. Plum's hypertension, I would be unwilling to unnecessarily cause a patient pain. Dental treatment does not need to be painful.)

Mr. Plum reluctantly departed, armed with a prescription for an analgesic and my invitation to return at the end of the week. He was disappointed that he still carried the painful tooth but understood that I was acting in his best interests.

Three hours later, I received an urgent call from Mr. Plum. The anesthetic had worn off, he had not filled the analgesic prescription, he was in terrible pain, his bite was no longer comfortable, and he wanted the tooth removed!

Now, four hours after his previous visit, I again assessed Mr. Plum's vital signs and found that his blood pressure was further elevated. Though this was a concern to me, I nevertheless felt that the extraction could be safely accomplished. Moreover, this increasing blood pressure gave me even greater reason to relieve Mr. Plum's pain by successfully (and painlessly) extracting the tooth. If ever there was a time for "painless dentistry," this was it!

I explained to Mr. Plum that, since I had used a particular brand of local anesthetic in the morning, which we both knew was not that effective for him, this afternoon I was going to use an entirely different method I was confident would be successful, especially since we had already completed so much of the preliminary work that morning.

I then began the procedure by suggesting " . . . the anesthetic I am using penetrates to the nerves, entering the roots by the access we have already provided by our work this morning. . . . Now, I'm going to use an instrument to push the material all around the tooth . . . so you will probably feel pressure and, too, a pushing sensation . . . as I work the material around. But you will continue to feel comfortable and pleased at how well the process is working."

Actually, I was using only a topical anesthetic paste, which creates a numbing sensation at the surface of the gums, and a surgical instrument to manipulate the tissues, to create the pressure and "pushing sensation." Of course, this topical anesthetic cannot produce adequate anesthesia for an extraction. However, the sensations I was creating with the topical, in combination with the suggestions I continued to give for comfort and a sense of well-being, were intended to produce a hypnotic experience that would produce adequate anesthesia. Mr. Plum responded to these suggestions by closing his eyes and becoming very relaxed and quiet.

When I began to apply pressure to elevate the tooth – the point of the procedure that causes the greatest level of noxious stimulation – Mr. Plum remained quiet and relaxed, and he did not grimace. I completed the extraction quickly, and within a few minutes was performing the postoperative closure and clean-up. All the while, I continued to talk to Mr. Plum, offering suggestions for comfort and, as we finished, for rapid, uneventful healing.

If Mr. Plum was aware of any of these events, he did not show it. I specifically told him that we had finished, that the tooth was out, and that he could open his eyes and see it. He opened his eyes with a dazed look, and said, in a voice full of surprise, "You're already finished? I didn't feel anything at all!"

In dentistry, perhaps more than in other fields, it often happens that patients' expectation of pain and therefore their pain perception are not closely correlated with the severity of the actual physiological event. Quite often projected fears, anxieties, and phobias of the antici-pated procedure have a major impact on the pain experience. When the actual painful event occurs, the resulting suffering of the patient may seem totally out of proportion to the physical injury or treatment. The patient experiences distress. The dentist's typical response to such distress during routine dental appointments is to deny the pa-tient's experience either by actions (an unwillingness to stop and allow the patient time-out to regain composure) or by statements ("Oh, that can't hurt that much"). In the first case, the dentist may be perceived as sadistic; in the second, as unable to feel empathy. Neither percep-tion is likely to be accurate. What is usually occurring is that the dentist is responding to his or her knowledge of the actual physiologi-cal stimulation that he or she is inflicting.

Frequently, well-meaning dentists attempt to relieve patients' anxi-eties by employing a cognitive strategy of describing the care being provided and then rationalizing the magnitude of its impact. For a considerable number of patients, such an approach is not helpful and may even have the opposite effect. The dentist's description of what is occurring stimulates the patient's imagination about the extent of the procedure, and the patient becomes even more frightened. The patient may understand the logic of the explanation, but the fearful interpreta-tion of the impending hurt typically outweighs rationality.

All of us have experienced discomfort in our mouths, beginning with the eruption of teeth during infancy. It is unlikely that individu-als with highly charged negative feelings about oral health care would choose a career in dentistry. One might reasonably conclude, therefore, that dental care providers as a group are probably better responders (i.e., have less of the affective component of pain) to oral care treat-ment than the general population. This may partly explain why they do not always recognize or understand when a patient is experiencing anguish and suffering independent of the intensity of physiological stimulation.

It is unfortunate that dentists use their perceptions of how much physiological pain a procedure is likely to cause as the chief criterion by which to judge how a certain patient will react. It is common to hear a practitioner rationalize that he or she is performing "only" a particular treatment, the unspoken implication being that "only" means a routine, commonly practiced procedure – it may have negative sensations, but they are usually tolerated by most people. In fact, patients who don't fit into this typical pattern of accepting behavior are often labeled "problem patients" by clinicians.

MANAGEMENT OF PAIN
COMPONENTS IN DENTISTRY

The modern dentist is quite mindful of the sensory component of pain and has at his or her fingertips a variety of pain reduction modalities. These include anesthetics of a topical, regional, or systemic nature that can be utilized for diminishing sensation. Unfortunately, not every dentist is as well trained in managing the affective component of pain. And such management is not nearly as easy to accomplish. Blockage of the sensory component of pain is fairly predictable once the patient variables (weight, presence or absence of infection), drug variables (type, dosage, and modality), and delivery variables (site, technique) are considered. Of course, this is not the case with the affective component of pain.

For many years, a stress reduction protocol has been advocated for use in dental practices with medically or psychologically compromised patients (McCarthy, 1989, pp. 41–43). Typically, this protocol considers such factors as the time of day of the appointment (morning is when the patient is most rested) and length of appointments (shorter is better). Assessment of the need for pre- and postoperative anxiolytic agents is another component of this protocol. These management techniques focus on modifying the physiological milieu through manipulation of the physical environment or through medications that act on the central nervous system. No attention is given to any type of behavioral management of psychological stress, which can have a far greater and more immediate impact on the patient's well-being.

This is not to imply that psychological screening and patient management techniques are not employed by dentists or taught as part of dental school curricula in the United States. The reality, however, is that students are exposed to a limited number of psychological methods, and certainly not to the extent that they receive instruction in pharmacological techniques. Additionally, such training may be only didactic, rather than experiential, and may include interactions in "nonconfrontational" or simple situations with conventional patients, but not with patients in distress, unduly fearful patients, or patients for whom analgesia has been inadequate.

HYPNOTIC TECHNIQUES
IN DENTISTRY

The environment of the mouth and teeth is a very richly innervated part of the body. We need to fully appreciate that manipulations in that location can elicit a variety of responses both physiological and psychological. It is the rare patient who is as blasé about routine dental treatment as the typical dental practitioner. To the contrary, anticipatory anxiety is the most frequent reason that dentists are asked to provide pretreatment anxiolytic agents. Additional requests for postoperative analgesics may also result from the patient's expectation of postoperative pain.

Because most patients are anxious about dental care, they frequently respond readily to psychological interventions preparatory to treatment or during a procedure itself. Those individuals who are highly responsive to hypnotic methods may have little need for an actual hypnotic induction. In fact, the highly responsive patient may already be absorbed in a hypnotic state by the time he or she reaches the dental practice. An astute clinician can readily recognize such a state and use it by giving thoughtful suggestions to prevent discomfort during and after treatment. This process of psychological comfort and support should begin at the first contact between the patient and the clinician's office. Office staff can be trained to be supportive and involved in the therapeutic goals of the practitioner.

Hypnosis can be extremely effective when utilized in dentistry. Unlike most psychological management techniques, it can be introduced into the treatment forum by a variety of agents: the patient, the dental practitioner, or another health-care provider. Furthermore, it can be used to alleviate either the sensory and/or the affective components of pain as well as to fulfill a variety of other applications in dentistry (Auld, 1989; Eli, 1992; Erickson, Hershman, & Secter, 1990; Finkelstein, 1991).

Typically, my first appointment with a new patient involves minimal or no invasive procedures. It is an information-gathering, rapport-building opportunity, which for some highly phobic patients occurs in a less anxiety-provoking setting: my office rather than the treatment room. The next appointment takes place in the treatment room and often begins with a hypnotic induction that I record and give to the patient for daily practice at home. At subsequent visits, I hypnotize the patient, observing his or her ease or difficulty in developing a hypnotic experience and general facility with acquiring self-hypnotic skills. These observations guide my subsequent behavior with the patient.

The particular approach used to treat a dental patient is determined by the patient's need, motivation, and expectations, as well as the invasiveness of the particular procedure to be accomplished. For those patients who arrive anticipating a hypnotic induction, anything short of that may be unsuccessful. Other patients may arrive already experiencing a hypnotic state, in response to the anxiety or the pain they are suffering or to free-floating anxiety. In any case, the total medical and psychological context must be taken into account.

CASE EXAMPLE: MRS. WHITE, 82, NOT ROUTINE

Mrs. White presented for routine dental care at a clinic for quasi-independent elderly individuals. She was having no pain at the time she first presented for treatment, but confided to me that she had been negligent in caring for her mouth. Since the clinic was now so convenient, she decided it was time to seek care. During the initial consultation, Mrs. White demonstrated that she was quite aware and fully oriented.

Throughout the gathering of the diagnostic data and the review of our findings, Mrs. White was cooperative and pleasant. Reviewing her vital signs and medical history, I concluded that her placement in a residential facility related to her physical condition. She was a slightly built Caucasian woman, weighing less than 100 pounds, who had a history of nonspecific cardiac problems, chest pain, dizziness, and falls. My impression was that of a physically frail individual. Observation of her vital signs revealed her to be borderline hypertensive. Behaviorally, she appeared somewhat tentative and concerned about who would be providing her care. I called her primary physician, who confirmed the patient's cardiac problems as atherosclerosis, mild congestive heart failure, and stress-induced angina pectoris, for which he had prescribed nitroglycerin as needed.

Two appointments in the dental clinic were necessary in order to acquire and review all the diagnostic data and to develop and discuss a treatment approach with Mrs. White. At each appointment she appeared to be comfortable and cooperative with the process, and a treatment schedule was set up. We agreed that during her next appointment, treatment would begin, involving placement of her new fillings.

When Mrs. White arrived for her next visit, Spencer, the dental student who would be providing her care, confirmed that medical status had remained stable since we had previously reviewed her history, and that her vital signs remained similar to the baseline readings. After Spencer and I reviewed Mrs. White's case, I gave him permission to begin the treatment.

My attention was occupied with other patients for about 25 minutes, at which time I looked in on Mrs. White and Spencer. It was immediately evident to me that something was wrong. Spencer was engrossed in the procedure he was performing, focusing his attention on the oral environment, and seemed fully unaware of Mrs. White's difficulty. Her hands were grasped tightly across her chest. Remembering her cardiovascular disease history, including angina, I asked Spencer to advise me of her status.

Reflecting no concern, Spencer replied that he had asked Mrs. White what the problem was and she had responded that she was having chest pain. He had decided that the chest pain either was a figment of her imagination or was of a noncardiac nature – because the treatment he was performing was not stressful. In either case, he did not stop the dental treatment.

Clearly, Spencer's interpretation of the magnitude of his treatment and Mrs. White's experience of it were not the same. Unfortunately, Spencer believed his own interpretation and discounted her experience. I immediately stopped the dental treatment and assessed the patient's status, noting the presence of eyelid flutter. In response to my direct question about pain, Mrs. White briefly opened her eyes, but did not make eye contact, and whispered "Yes" before again closing her eyes. I understood that she was experiencing angina, so I quickly delivered a sublingual dose of nitroglycerin, while simultaneously having Spencer reassess her vital signs. Moving close to the patient's ear so she could hear me easily, I began speaking to her calmly but firmly:

Mrs. White, listen to me very carefully. You will probably be surprised at how quickly you notice the relief from discomfort spread across your chest, perhaps more quickly then you have ever felt before . . . and with every breath you take, being aware of an easing of the tightness and restraint previously experienced in your chest . . . just noticing the comfort taking its place. With each breath let that comfort grow and flow throughout every part of your chest, bringing relief and a wonderfully relaxed feeling. And isn't it interesting to note that this wonderfully comfortable and relaxed feeling can spread quite beyond your chest into other parts of your body . . . with every breath . . . into your arms and hands, neck and jaw, and, in fact, your entire head. Now isn't it surprising, but absolutely wonderful at the same time, the speed at which this remarkable, relaxing comfort can spread.

Within little over a minute Mrs. White indicated that she could feel the relief spreading and that the chest pain was almost gone. Since Mrs. White was reclined in a dental chair, I continued these suggestions, focusing upon relaxation, encouraging Mrs. White to feel "even more comfortable, perhaps more comfortable than you have ever felt before."

My goal in including suggestions for general comfort was to prevent the occurrence of a severe, rapid-onset headache, which can be a side-effect of sublingual nitroglycerin. After a short time, Mrs. White was quite comfortable, the chest pain was completely gone, no headache was present, the vital signs were established as stable and consistent with her history, and no other medical intervention was required. I then focused on the interrupted dental procedure.

It was important to redefine this episode. It had appeared that the dental procedure had precipitated the anginal attack. I first acknowledged that the difficult part of the procedure was over. (Spencer had interpreted the procedure correctly in that technically it was not difficult and was likely to have involved only a very small amount of noxious sensory stimulation; however, Mrs. White's perception was the critical factor governing the episode.)

I recognized Mrs. White's experience of difficulty (no matter what the technical level of treatment or sensory involvement may have been). She may or may not have heard Spencer's opinion of the relative ease of the procedure when I asked him for Mrs. White's status. Whether or not she heard this is really irrelevant – it was quite obvious to Mrs. White from Spencer's behavior (e.g., his disinterest in the chest pain and his continuation of the dental procedure), that he was denying her experience. Since I was the teacher of this student and, therefore, in Mrs. White's eyes a seasoned practitioner, she would give more weight to my interpretation of the event than to Spencer's interpretation. Therefore, my acknowledgment that the procedure had been difficult was important for the continuing rapport between us and my subsequent credibility.

I then made suggestions relating to Mrs. White's interest in caring for herself (an example of which was her coming to the dental clinic of her own accord to seek out care). I complimented her on her interest in taking care of her body and reminded her that she was the best authority on her body and therefore the one who could advise us if she would like to proceed with finishing the treatment we had already begun right then – or at the next clinic session the following week.

These new suggestions were intended to reinforce the following ideas:

1. I was concerned about her angina, but not unduly frightened by the fact that she had an episode of chest pain while undergoing dental care.
2. I felt capable of managing any future anginal attacks she might have during treatment.
3. I thought her teeth (and, by inference, her total health) were important and worth caring for.
4. I did not think that her cardiovascular condition was so serious that it would preclude her receiving dental care.
5. I gave control of the treatment situation back to her.

Since direct assertion of these ideas might have seemed paternalistic to Mrs. White, I embedded them in a general hypnotic discussion about comfort, laced with compliments to her for taking the initiative in caring for and about herself. By providing only two options concerning treatment, either continuing right then or the following week, I was purposely limiting Mrs. White's choices so that, no matter which option she chose, she would finish the procedure (which was a real dental necessity), even though it had precipitated the anginal attack. (It bears mentioning here that this experience was sufficiently traumatizing that she might have avoided further dental care.)

Before ending the hypnotic experience, I suggested to Mrs. White how comfortable she could feel at each successive appointment. "And I don't know when you might begin to feel as relaxed and comfortable as you do right now. . . . It may be each time you enter the doorway to the dental clinic, or when you sit in the dental chair and your head touches the headrest, or perhaps when the dental light is turned on. . . . It doesn't really matter when . . . just know that you can feel even more relaxed and comfortable than you do right now . . . and with every visit you can feel that relaxation growing even greater." I also suggested that, in the future, when I touched her on her shoulder, she could become deeply relaxed and comfortable. Using posthypnotic suggestions in this way greatly facilitates future hypnotic work.

Mrs. White decided to continue treatment that day. After that, she returned regularly to the clinic for her dental work. At each subsequent visit, as she was adjusting herself in the dental chair, and while we were exchanging pleasantries, I would touch her shoulder and suggest that she could do whatever she needed to become comfortable. Each time she responded by quickly becoming deeply relaxed and absorbed in the experience of comfort. There were no further episodes of angina while undergoing dental treatment. Thus, I was able to attract Mrs. White's attention, assess and avoid what might have become a medical emergency, and cement a rapport that stood us in good stead for future stressful procedures.

One might argue that Mrs. White was not hypnotized, since no formal induction was provided. Further, one might say that it was the nitroglycerin and not hypnosis that had the hoped-for effect on her symptoms. Remember, though, that individuals who are highly responsive to hypnotic suggestion may not need an actual induction in order to develop a hypnotic state (Hilgard & Hilgard, 1994, p. 15). In fact, Hilgard and Hilgard write that in such situations the formal induction is far less important than the therapeutic suggestions to reduce the pain. That Mrs. White was already in a hypnotic state was clear from the physical manifestations seen: the eyelid flutter; the quiet, abbreviated speech; the glazed look when she opened her eyes; the spontaneous eye closure, and the rapidity with which relief of her chest pain occurred.

Mrs. White's anginal attacks usually required her to take more than one sublingual nitroglycerin dose in order to lessen the chest pain. Commonly, the relief of her chest pain occurred only after 10 to 15 minutes of repeated nitroglycerin dosage, and the use of the nitroglycerin would be followed by a headache. Since this anginal episode did not follow that course, one could conclude that the hypnotic suggestions had a positive effect in modifying the extent and severity of the attack and in facilitating her future benign responses to the stress of receiving dental care.

Naturally occurring hypnotic phenomena should not be overlooked. In some cases, individuals may use the refuge of a hypnotic state as a coping mechanism. This spontaneous hypnotic state has been well-documented in the hypnotic literature (Barabasz & Barabasz, 1992; Spiegel & Spiegel, 1987). Given the generally fearful attitude toward dental care, the dental patient may already be experiencing a hypnotic condition by the time he or she reaches the dental practice or may lapse into this state during a dental procedure, particularly if difficulties arise. An astute clinician can readily recognize such a state and use it to the patient's advantage by providing appropriately worded suggestions regarding the reduction of discomfort, as well as positive suggestions for subsequent recovery and posttreatment course.

Some might dismiss the previous example as being an unusual occurrence, one that was solely the result of an inexperienced practitioner, a student still in the throes of learning. Experienced dental practitioners, they might claim, would not make such mistakes. Although there is some merit to that argument, it does happen that some practitioners may yield to the desire to complete treatment and ask a patient who is expressing discomfort to "Hang on, we're almost through!" In such a case, the patient may feel left alone without the anesthetic support and with no psychological supports to tolerate the pain or fear.

Facilitating the Natural Development
of the Patient's Altered State

In my experience, spontaneous hypnotic experiences occur in significant numbers of fearful and phobic dental patients, sometimes even when discussing their dental needs far from the dental office. Whenever this happens, the patient is likely to be receptive to therapeutic suggestions to help tolerate the stress that dentistry evokes. When a patient is actually sitting in the dental chair and difficulty occurs, obviously the patient's motivation to diminish the pain and increase comfort is particularly strong. As a result, an actual hypnotic induction may be unnecessary or quite brief, requiring only a few sentences to support and encourage the patient's natural inclinations. I might say:

> You really don't need to be here. Why don't you go somewhere else, where you would rather be, and can be relaxed and comfortable. While you are there, I will take care of everything here, and I will let you know when I am finished so that you can come back.

Other patients might need a further suggestion such as:

> Some people find it a lot easier to see where they are going if they just let their eyes close.

Observing the eyelid flutter, eye roll, and other physiologic manifestations of the patient's readiness to experience the hypnotic state will provide important clues about the patient's condition.

THE ORIGIN OF DENTAL FEARS
AND PHOBIAS

What happens to an adult patient who has a traumatic experience in a dental office? Does the patient brush off the experience as just another episode of life, or does it permanently affect his or her ability to manage any discomfort associated with dental care or to tolerate any future treatment, no matter how benign? Hilgard and Hilgard (1994, p. 145) posit that severe dental phobias are likely to have as their bases either an earlier traumatic episode in a dental office or a projection of someone else's experience onto themselves, with either situation most likely occurring during childhood. It is likely that the susceptible child is one who has yet to have his or her own positive experiences of dental treatment with which to compare exaggerated stories enthusiastically recited by others.

While it is true that dental fears and phobias are quite prevalent during childhood, in a substantial number of people such fears persist into adulthood (Dworkin, 1986). Studies show that from 8 to 16 percent of the population reports fear as the reason why they do not seek dental care (Gerschman, 1988). In a study surveying dentists, physicians, and psychologists about the origins of their patients' dental anxieties and phobias, single or multiple traumatic events were thought to be equal to childhood trauma as the most common cause of these conditions (Rodolfa, Kraft, & Reilley, 1990).

Some patients acknowledge that a previously frightening dental experience has resulted in a dental anxiety or phobia, while others do not have a clear understanding of why they now anguish over impending dental treatment. Still other individuals do not report fear of dental treatment but do not seek care because the dental experience constitutes a challenge to an unrelated phobia. For example, claustrophobic patients may find the dental treatment room and the prolonged proximity of the treatment team intolerably confining.

It has been my experience that women who report sexual or physical assault, as children or adults, are more likely to develop extreme phobias regarding their oral health. This phobia may be so intense that it even affects their ability to provide their own regular oral health care (e.g., tooth brushing). An exaggerated gag reflex may be a manifestation of such a history, as may the patient's grabbing of the hands of the dental practitioner to stop the treatment or a complete inability to tolerate any oral pain or treatment.

From early infancy, the mouth is the center of the sensory world, the medium for eating, play, vocalization, and exploration. A richly innervated structure, the mouth is the source of much stimulation for the person. Since the mouth is a highly charged emotional area, and since it is an "erotogenic zone" (Gerschman, 1988), we can readily understand the significance of events involving the oral cavity. It is not surprising that many patients approach dental care in a highly charged emotional state.

Fear of loss of control is a frequent concern of dental patients (Lightfoot, 1994). The actual positioning of the patient places him or her in a physically and emotionally vulnerable position. Lying supine in a modern dental chair requires one to place a great deal of trust in the practitioner, who sits in a superior position to the patient and wields sharp instruments in front of the patient's vigilant eyes. Allowing entry into the mouth and tolerating protracted treatment in an anatomical site that has life-prolonging functions (nutrition and respiration), as well as emotionally fulfilling ones (communication and sexual pleasure), can be overwhelming to some, thereby further heightening their fears.

As growing numbers of people recognize the need for a lifetime of preventive dental care, it is likely that more and more psychotherapists will be consulted by patients wishing to receive dental care but fearing to do so. Hypnotic treatment, of course, can be helpful in managing these patients. Various strategies that have been reported to be successful for patients with dental fears and phobias, ranging from relaxation to incorporating systematic desensitization with hypnotic methods, will be discussed later in this chapter (Rodolfa, Kraft, & Reilley, 1990).

HOW DO WE UNDERSTAND
CHRONIC OROFACIAL PAIN?

Recently a group of researchers at the University of Alabama found that among females with histories of sexual or physical abuse, a very high rate suffer from gastrointestinal conditions such as gastroesophageal reflux disease (92 percent) and irritable bowel syndrome (82 percent). They measured pain thresholds in the patients with abuse histories and found significantly lower thresholds than in a comparison group of patients who had not reported abuse (Scarinci, McDonald-Haile, Bradley, & Richter, 1994). In considering these results, one should remember that, in addition to its other functions, the oral cavity is the gateway to the gastrointestinal tract. Various muscles in the mouth provide chewing and swallowing functions; the temporomandibular joints are also actively involved in chewing of food for further action by the digestive tract. Therefore, all of these structures are considered part of the first functional unit of the gastrointestinal tract. It is important to appreciate that dysfunction of these joints results in oral or facial pain experienced by five to seven million people in the U.S.

Although chronic orofacial pain may be the result of conditions such as atypical odontalgia,[1] most commonly it involves the previously named anatomic structures and includes such nonodontogenic conditions as atypical facial pain, regional myofascial pain, and temporomandibular joint dysfunction (Van der Bijl, 1995). These afflictions, which cause debilitating pain and prolonged disability, are most often seen in women. Frequently, these patients require psychotherapy in addition to physical medicine modalities to achieve effective pain control (Van der Bijl, 1995).

Few controlled clinical studies have examined the efficacy of hypnotic treatment for psychiatric disorders (Brown, 1992); therefore, it is not surprising that little evidence can be found concerning the efficacy of hypnosis for the management of patients with chronic orofacial pain. A recent bibliographic review of the English language scientific literature on pain and anxiety control in dentistry identified 71 articles concerned with chronic oral facial pain, none of which referenced hypnosis (Hassett, 1994). Most descriptions of hypnotic treatment for orofacial pain deal with a reduction of the chronic physical tension held in the muscles of the face (Glazer, 1990; Neiburger, 1990). When orofacial pain is due to stress and anxiety, hypnotic techniques can be useful in managing stress responses. In the one abbreviated case report found, describing the use of hypnosis in the treatment of myofascial pain and temporomandibular joint clicking, relaxation and imagery were used and the patient reported some improvement. It is difficult to interpret this report, however, because it involves only one patient, the actual methods are not described in detail, and there was no follow-up (Simpson, Goepferd, Ogesen, & Zach, 1985).

Any discussion of orofacial pain must include the topic of bruxism. A condition involving the grinding of the teeth with a great deal of force, typically occurring during sleep, bruxism has been implicated as the etiologic precipitant in some types of chronic orofacial pain conditions. For years, it has been know that hypnotic treatment is effective in eliminating oral habits such as bruxism. Success was demonstrated by two different studies examining electromyographic evaluations of nighttime masseter muscle activity in bruxism patients recorded before and after hypnotic treatment intended to decrease muscle activity. These evaluations identified a significant decrease in masseter muscle activity levels, as well as decreases in subjective reports of facial discomfort (Clarke & Reynolds, 1991; Mulligan &

---

[1]Atypical odontalgia refers to pain that appears to be located in a tooth, but for which no clinical signs of disease, infection, or other pain source in that tooth can be found.

Clark, 1979). Various texts and manuals provide samples of inductions helpful for treating patients who demonstrate bruxism (Erickson, 1990; Golan, 1990; Neiburger, 1990; Reaney, 1990; Simpson, Goepferd, Ogesen, & Zach, 1985), as well as those patients needing help with stress and anxiety reduction (Field, 1990; Reaney, 1990; Wright, 1990).

PREPARATION OF
THE DENTAL PATIENT

A variety of approaches may be used to achieve the goal of preparing the patient to manage oral pain or to be comfortable during dental treatment. In some cases, the dentist may work directly with the patient; in other cases, the dentist and the psychotherapist might work together; if dental treatment has been concluded, the psychotherapist may work with the patient alone. The arrangement used, just like the treatment approach used, is tailored to the needs of the patient. The patient's point of entry into the health-care system will also affect the arrangement, as a result of the relationship and rapport established with the initial practitioner.

When the Dentist Treats the Patient's Anxiety

A patient who has acquired a dental phobia as a result of a previously difficult dental experience can frequently be managed quite easily by the dentist. When a dental phobia is only one aspect of complex psychological problems, a psychotherapist needs to be involved. A diagnosis of multiple phobias or other psychiatric disorders may not be initially obvious to the dentist. It may be only when the attempt to use hypnotic methods fails that the dentist realizes the complexity of the patient's underlying problem, and the need for a referral to a psychotherapist. It may be obvious that a psychotherapist should not attempt dental treatment. It may be less obvious, but just as important to recognize, that a dentist should not attempt to discover the nature of the underlying phobia. The hidden complexity may be a very unpleasant surprise.

For patients who come to me directly for help in dealing with their dental fears and phobias, my goal is to teach them to cope with their fears, not to uncover the source of their fear. Teaching the patient self-hypnosis can be an easy way to accomplish this. I begin by tape recording our hypnosis sessions. I then instruct the patient to take the tape home and use it to practice becoming deeply relaxed. I prescribe at least one practice session a day. My observation is that the more often the patient practices, the better he or she is able to become quickly absorbed in a hypnotic experience, at a deeper level, and with less intervention on my part. This is consistent with Hilgard and Hilgard's finding that practicing self-hypnosis allows an individual to acquire greater facility in using it (1994, p. 73). Following this protocol, the patient learns to accept much more rapidly the ownership of the hypnotic state, and thereby learns to produce it when needed, whether it be for comfort in the dental chair or at another time.

I adjust my hypnotic induction method at subsequent sessions by closely observing the patient. As he or she becomes more adept at the unassisted self-hypnosis skill, I modify the help I provide appropriately. In addition to the therapeutic suggestions regarding relaxation and comfort in dealing with all aspects of the dental environment, at each encounter I routinely include ego-strengthening suggestions in the hypnotic state to reinforce the fact that the patient can and will become master of herself, with the unspoken suggestion being that the patient can control her fears.

The Team: Psychotherapist and Dentist

Ideally, dentist and psychotherapist will cooperate. The therapist's consultation with the dentist about the general needs and concerns of the patient before the patient arrives in the dental office facilitates the dentist's successful management of that and subsequent dental visits. It is especially pleasing, to both dentist and psychotherapist, to have a collaboration that can carry them through the treatment of future patients. The source of a dental phobia may be unrelated to any previous dental care; instead, it may be related to some other perceived or real traumatic occurrence(s) in the patient's life. The symbolism as well as the reality of the role of the mouth in a person's life needs to be understood.

ANXIETY REDUCTION
VERSUS ANALGESIA

As we all know, dental patients do not anticipate visiting a dental office with pleasure. Commonly, dental patients are anxious and uncomfortable when they present for dental treatment. Some may even be irritable. In many cases, their pain perception is amplified by such a state of mind. Conveniently for dental practitioners, one of the most common feelings expressed by individuals who have been hypnotized is a sense of relaxation and banishment of tension, oftentimes unlike anything they have ever felt before (Hilgard & Hilgard, 1994, p. 17). Obviously, such a perception can help to ameliorate the aversive feelings people often have about dental treatment.

Frequently, in dentistry we target the reduction of anxiety, coupled with the achievement of comfort, as primary goals in the hypnotic induction. If the clinician links the two suggestions together, this allows the patient to do whatever he or she needs to do to maintain a comfortable state during the impending care. This is frequently achieved without direct suggestions, by using a permissive approach that allows the patient to do whatever is necessary to be comfortable during and after the course of therapy. This type of approach is also successful for those who are highly anxious about the implications of their pain (e.g., is the mouth ulcer some type of cancer?), whatever the level of pain being experienced.

Similarly, we can facilitate the reinterpretation of experiences. For example, what was formerly a feared experience (lying in the dental chair, feeling exposed and vulnerable) can be reframed as soothing and nonthreatening. I particularly like to use such imagery with children, suggesting, for example, that they imagine snuggling into their comfortable beds at home, or that the vibration of the handpiece feels like a tickle machine that makes them giggle, but not too much! Adults might be more amenable to the fantasy of swinging in a hammock on a deserted beach or floating on a fleecy, soft cloud.

The therapeutic goals of relaxation and hypnoanalgesia occur at a readily accessible level of hypnotic absorption, even in patients who are capable of achieving very profound hypnotic states (Hilgard & Hilgard, 1994, p. 80). At such a minimal depth, the patient stays involved, and helps to direct the pain reduction. This has two benefits for dental practitioners:

1. It minimizes the time needed to induce the hypnotic experience.
2. It significantly reduces those uncommon but untoward events, such as loss of contact with the dentist, that can occur with deepening the experience to a profound state.

Some patients may resist relaxing, feeling that they need to remain vigilant. A comment such as "you may now wish to watch your eyes close," frequently reduces vigilance by gently suggesting that the patient continue to "watch," at the same time that it facilitates eye closure and supports greater internal absorption, an important step toward developing a hypnotic experience.

I prefer that all of my patients close their eyes for safety reasons, since I am working in such close proximity to their eyes with materials that sometimes get splashed or splattered. If patients do not respond to my indirect suggestions to close their eyes, I may offer them a mirror (and safety glasses) to watch what is occurring in their mouths.

For vigilant patients, I frequently point out the areas of the mouth I am working in and engage their involvement in making certain areas numb so that the work can proceed. Using a direct reduction method, I draw parallels between the sensation of numbness of a local anesthetic used at some time during a prior dental experience and the current goal of numbness. As I move from one section of the mouth to another, I suggest that the patient move the numbness to the new area. Rarely do patients question how this is possible. Nor do I offer them further suggestions on how to accomplish this unless they ask. I never chat with the patient or my assistant when I am treating a patient who is hypnotized. All of my remarks are directed toward maintaining the patient's experience, providing therapeutic suggestions, and giving instructions to my assistant. Most commonly, the patient eventually puts the mirror down and closes his or her eyes, becoming fully involved in a hypnotic experience.

APPROACHES TO ANALGESIA

Approaches to modifying pain can be taught to the dental patient by the treating dentist, a psychologist, or another health-care provider with training in hypnosis. Some patients are quite capable of learning hypnotic phenomena that will help them during dental care at a site quite removed from the dental office (e.g., the psychologist's office). An independent self-hypnotic induction may then be accomplished by the patient in the dental office. For those who are not as comfortable with the self-hypnotic induction process, the psychotherapist might provide a tape recording of the hypnotic treatment, again recommending that the patient use the tape for daily practice. Such practice helps patients develop their self-hypnosis skills. Bringing the tape and a cassette player to the dental office and listening to it in the waiting room, as well as throughout the dental procedure, may be an effective way for the patient to develop an absorbing hypnotic experience.

With some patients, I use a formal induction. For instance, a modification of the glove anesthesia induction, and one which I believe is easier for a patient to accept, requires the patient to use his or her hands to remove the pain from the head and face. For further explanation of the glove anesthesia method see Bassman and Wester (1991) and Mulligan and Lindeman (1979).

CASE EXAMPLE: MRS. SCARLATTI, 88, WITH MULTIPLE COMPLAINTS

Mrs. Scarlatti's case illustrates this effective hypnotic approach. Mrs. Scarlatti was a very lonely woman; she told us that, although many of her family members lived within 50 miles of her, they rarely visited. However, her son characterized her as a complainer who exaggerated to get attention. Mrs. Scarlatti gave a history of chronic facial pain and temporomandibular joint involvement, although she had not sought care for those symptoms in the last several years, as she was essentially housebound.

Having neglected her oral health, she had developed a toothache, causing her to arrange a trip to see me at great inconvenience to her. I performed the appropriate treatment; when I was finished, she advised me that she had developed neck pain as a result of the dental appointment.

Because Mrs. Scarlatti's medical history included an extensive history of severe arthritis, I had provided a special neck roll for additional support to her neck during the treatment. In spite of this precaution, however, she complained quite vehemently about tremendous neck pain when the treatment was completed. Because of her significant arthritic condition, Mrs. Scarlatti was unable to hold her hands up to the back of her neck, the site of her pain. Therefore, I had her guide me to the exact location of her pain as I placed my hands on her neck. Then I asked Mrs. Scarlatti if she would be interested in my helping her to have relief from the pain. She responded quite positively. I asked her to focus on her breathing while I began talking to her.

> In a moment, but not yet, I'm going to ask you to take three very deep, very satisfying breaths, breathing in deeply and exhaling slowly . . . begin now with the first very deep, very satisfying breath, breathing in deeply and exhaling slowly . . . and as you exhale, noticing, just noticing how you can become more relaxed and comfortable . . . with each and every exhalation, feeling your back against the very comfortable dental chair . . . now take a second very deep, very satisfying breath . . . breathing in deeply and exhaling slowly . . . and noticing again how you can feel even more comfortable than you did just a moment ago . . . and isn't it

interesting how you already know, even though I haven't yet told
you, that at the end of the third very deep, very satisfying breath
you will feel more relaxed and more comfortable than you ever
thought possible . . . and why don't you go ahead and feel that
way now by taking that third very deep, very comfortable breath,
noticing the feeling of the comfortable dental chair against your
back . . . and you can continue to become more relaxed and comfortable with each subsequent breath even as I continue to talk
to you about other things. . . . And isn't it interesting that before
I mentioned the feeling of your back against the dental chair, you
had not even noticed that sensation . . . but once I mentioned it,
you became aware of the comfortable sensation of your back
against the chair. . . . At times we tune in to one part of the body
and ignore the rest . . . and sometimes when we ignore the rest of
the body a part of it may respond by causing pain . . . but now
that you are no longer ignoring your neck, the pain does not
need to bother you . . . so as you continue your nice, comfortable,
satisfying breaths, every time you exhale just let that pain go
from your neck into my hands, knowing that once the pain is all
gone from your neck, and into my hands, I will be able to shake it
loose from my hands and onto the floor . . . where it will be swept
up and discarded . . . with every breath let the pain flow out of
your neck and into my hands. [The patient can be encouraged to
have the pain flow faster if it seems to be taking awhile.]

I continued to encourage Mrs. Scarlatti to let the pain flow into my
hands. When this was accomplished, and before alerting her, I gave
her posthypnotic suggestions so that she could remove pain in a similar manner for herself, whenever she wanted to, just by imagining the
feeling of my hands on her neck. After becoming alert, Mrs. Scarlatti
remarked that she was pain-free. She was amazed at the rapidity of
the pain removal, particularly because previous pain episodes had been
severely debilitating, lasting all day, sometimes even several days.

It is easy to follow the progress of a patient when one is using this
type of induction, because the patient is instructed to hold his or her
hand over the painful site until the pain is gone from the site and
moved into the hand. When that occurs, the hand will fall away from
the site. This allows me to know when the hypnotic experience can be
comfortably brought to an end. Since, due to the location of her pain,
Mrs. Scarlatti wasn't able to use her own hands, I helped her learn the
amount of pain removal she could expect at a particular time. I did
this by suggesting to Mrs. Scarlatti (at what, through observation, I

perceived to be appropriate intervals) that one-quarter, one-half, two-thirds, and seven-eighths of the pain were gone, and commenting that she was probably eagerly looking forward to all of the pain being gone.

Once Mrs. Scarlatti acknowledged that all of the pain was gone and I had provided the appropriate concluding suggestions, I alerted her. At the same time, and within her view, I began shaking my hands with some vigor, clearly appearing as if I was "shaking off" something that was actually there. A staff member who walked by the door of the dental suite at the time brought towels to me, thinking that the treatment room must be without towels. When I waved her away, she was perplexed. However, Mrs. Scarlatti did not find my behavior strange. In fact, if I had not kept my part of the bargain, shaking off the pain that she sent from her neck to my hands, it is likely that trust would have been compromised, rendering similar hypnotic strategies in subsequent appointments less effective. Interestingly, Mrs. Scarlatti never commented on the unusual sight of her dentist standing in front of her, discussing posttreatment instructions and her future dental needs while "shaking off" her neck pain.

I used this induction technique on two additional visits with Mrs. Scarlatti. On the last occasion she arrived with neck pain, so I induced the hypnotic state prior to the treatment and provided suggestions that she could maintain her comfort not only during the entire procedure, but also throughout the day. Each time I performed this induction with Mrs. Scarlatti, her pain was successfully eliminated within approximately five minutes.

Although glove anesthesia and the induction used for Mrs. Scarlatti are both very effective, it is rare that I use such inductions. This is because I find that a generalized relaxation induction frequently accomplishes the dual goals of reducing anxiety and preparing the patient for the sensory stimulation of the dental procedure. Since relaxation facilitates my therapeutic goals, I find it beneficial to teach it to my patients by using it as a common induction technique.

I substitute other approaches when I believe the patient is uncomfortable experiencing relaxation. Typically, arthritic patients such as Mrs. Scarlatti say that they cannot find any comfortable position. Consequently, suggestions for progressive relaxation do not seem plausible (since these suggestions depend on such comfort). With Mrs. Scarlatti, I linked comfort to her breathing, which she obviously was accomplishing without difficulty. I also linked comfort to those inanimate objects with which her body was in contact, such as the dental chair.

Whether the patient is needle-phobic, has a hyperactive gag reflex, or is extremely sensitive to oral pain, relaxation techniques are generally quite effective. (Some typical relaxation inductions can be found in Erickson, Hershman, & Secter, 1990, and Wester & Smith, 1990.)

USING PATIENTS' ABILITIES

Individuals who readily develop a hypnotic state without assistance may do so as an automatic defense when they confront a stressful situation, though even these patients can profit from training in self-hypnosis. This may explain the diminished responsiveness to pain demonstrated by some patients. Quite often, patients with increased pain threshold will explain this phenomenon by suggesting that the procedure accomplished was simply not painful. These patients are not without any sensation in the treated area; rather, they describe feeling something, but they remark, tellingly, that the sensation was not troublesome. The sensory component remains, but the affective component is reduced.

CASE EXAMPLE: MRS. MARPLE, 67, ALLERGIC TO ANESTHETIC

Mrs. Marple had significant systemic diseases of the connective tissues, which required her to be on a wide variety of medications. Whether because of adverse interactions as a result of so many drugs, or her systemic disease, or a combination of both, Mrs. Marple insisted that she had an allergy to all local anesthetics and therefore needed to be treated using hypnosis. Mrs. Marple was well-oriented and very pleasant. She indicated she was seeing several different physicians for all her different ailments but no practitioners for her mental health. She carried a tripod cane, although she appeared not to rely on it. She said that her physical activity was quite reduced from what it had been previously, although she felt she had adapted well to the change. She did not appear to be depressed and frequently brought a puzzle book to pass the time while waiting for the transportation service to take her home.

Mrs. Marple's myriad physical problems were very real; anyone could notice several physical signs, including disseminated vascular lesions on her face, hands and arms, and deformity of her fingers, all of which were manifestations of her diseases. I determined that appropriate dental treatment for Mrs. Marple would require extraction of 18 teeth and extensive restorative and prosthetic care. Because of her systemic conditions, I elected to extract three and four teeth at each visit. At each appointment, I hypnotized Mrs. Marple using a relaxation induction. Each induction became shorter and shorter as she became more adept at the process. At her request, guided imagery was employed to help her develop a "getaway" place on the beach where she could go while her treatment was being accomplished. Everytime the student practitioner or I extracted her teeth, Mrs. Marple asked if she could have them so that during practice at home, she could focus on the teeth as part of her induction. All of her dental work was successfully accomplished, including the extractions, using hypnosis as the sole anesthetic agent. She was very relaxed, calm, and comfortable during each procedure.

Yet to this day (and we still see Mrs. Marple regularly for all her oral health needs), she claims that she was never hypnotized. I believe that this is because her perception of hypnosis was that she expected to feel nothing. This was not the case; she felt "something," although she reported that what she was feeling was not troublesome to her. She also had the impression that hypnosis would be more dramatic, similar to what she had seen on stage and television. Although I had initially described to her what hypnosis was and was not, she was not dissuaded. I did not attempt to change her beliefs, of course. The procedure was accomplished, the patient was comfortable, the therapeutic outcome was achieved — and that, of course, was the objective.

9

PAINFUL MEDICAL PROCEDURES

Christel J. Bejenke

MR. GALT, who had been exceedingly apprehensive for weeks preceding his upcoming surgery, arrived on the morning of surgery well rested, expressing a cheerful calm. The floor nurses who witnessed his anxiety prior to my preparatory visit with him found his calm demeanor very surprising. Even though on the day of surgery his operation was unexpectedly delayed for several hours, which is usually very distressing to patients unless they are heavily sedated, Mr. Galt required no sedation and arrived in the operating room light-hearted and relaxed. I helped him develop a hypnotic condition by using a posthypnotic cue (a deep breath), which facilitated a very gentle induction of general anesthesia.

Following the surgery, Mr. Galt was awake immediately after extubation. In fact, he told me later that, although I had explained to him that he would probably not remember what the surgeon would tell him in the recovery room, he did remember every complex detail. (Ironically, it was his unanesthetized wife, he said, "who got it all wrong.") Mr. Galt was free of pain in the recovery room, had a peaceful night, declined all offers of analgesic injections, but accepted two analgesic pills.

Mr. Galt had been expected to remain in the hospital for two days after surgery. However, when I went to visit him the next morning, he had already left the hospital (a little over twelve hours since discharge from the recovery room). That evening he felt so well that he went to the movies, and then jogged the following morning. Mr. Galt was deeply pleased by his experience and remarked that his friends and family were "amazed."

This chapter describes observations and conclusions from my own anesthesiology practice, as well as widely applicable clinical approaches that can make a medical procedure less traumatic than is usually expected. These approaches, including hypnosis and suggestion, can ameliorate or even prevent pain and suffering either directly or indirectly.

The goal of treating pain is to establish comfort. Those who deal with *chronic* pain conditions have long appreciated the fact that pain is a multidimensional condition, and that its opposite, comfort, does not necessarily equate with "freedom from pain" alone; rather, freedom from pain is only one component of comfort.

Acute pain, however, is still commonly viewed as reasonably unidimensional. If it were, we would be able to control acute pain with unidimensional approaches, for example, with appropriate doses of opioid medications. However, this is not always the case, which suggests that other factors may be at work. One factor with which we are quite familiar is anxiety. Treatment with anxiolytics sometimes does facilitate improved pain control, but this, too, is not always successful. In fact, we frequently see patients who are so heavily sedated that they are barely able to respond—yet their increased heart rate and blood pressure still reflect unacceptable levels of pain and/or anxiety.

In contrast, it is possible to achieve the goal of having patients arrive in the recovery room, even immediately following major surgery, smiling, with normal "stress-free" blood pressures and heart rates. Such patients report negligible or no discomfort, yet are very alert and cooperative. Since the focus of this book is hypnosis, the reader may assume that these patients have been hypnotized. This is true for some of these patients; others have been prepared with other techniques.

Egbert's (1986; Egbert, Battit, Turndorf, & Beecher, 1963; Egbert, Battit, Welch, & Bartlett, 1964) classic studies with surgical patients suggest at least some guidelines to preparing patients: He showed that an informational preoperative visit by the anesthesiologist rendered patients significantly calmer than many milligrams of potent sedatives; such patients also required lesser doses of pain medications postoperatively.

What factors need to be addressed to help patients achieve this degree of comfort? Let me mention a few, which can occur singly or in any combination. These include patients' sense of

- helplessness and dependence
- loss of control
- inability to comprehend the complexities of their illness and the recommended procedures
- seeing themselves as victims of either their illness or a "hostile system" or both
- being passive, voiceless recipients of incomprehensibly complex medical technology.

In my experience, the essential components for blocking the negative consequences of such perceptions are INFORMATION, INSTRUCTIONS, SUGGESTIONS (with or without hypnosis), and *the implicit message of commitment and caring* on the part of those who perform the procedure. For maximal effectiveness, these components must be in place before beginning the medical procedure.

Ideally, as in Egbert's study, the *physician* responsible for carrying out the medical procedure conveys information and suggestions, which are likely to include appropriate suggestions. However, with increasing frequency, an important part of patient preparation is managed by specialists skilled and trained in psychological approaches. The goals of either the physician or the psychologist are to:

- restore or maintain the patient's sense of competence
- increase the patient's sense of control
- foster self-mastery and independence
- enable the patient to retain dignity
- include the patient as an integral and active participant in his care instead of a passive recipient.

The approach used to accomplish these goals will depend upon the patient's needs and the clinical circumstances.

Because *physicians* are intimately familiar with the patient's medical condition, the planned procedure, and the technical components of the intervention they intend to perform, they can give detailed and explicit instructions and suggestions to the patient. In addition, since they are in charge of the medical procedure, they can make specific commitments to patients about the treatment and care they will receive.

Other practitioners, such as psychologists, must be more general and cautious regarding such details. As specialists, we each appreciate how much knowledge and experience are required to remain current in one's own specialty; no matter how up-to-date we may be in other fields, we will never be as knowledgeable as a specialist in that field. For example, patients often ask me, their anesthesiologist, surgical questions that I could easily answer, because, after all, I spend my days in operating rooms. But I make a point of deferring such questions to the surgeon and encouraging the patient to contact the surgeon for clarification. I can never know what a surgeon may have in mind for *this* particular patient at *this* particular time. I also know how difficult it becomes for me and the patient when a surgeon, internist, or someone else has made recommendations to a patient regarding anesthesia. It is not only unhelpful but counterproductive. Much unintended harm may need to be undone. Being even at slight variance with certain assumptions or details may confuse the patient and place the person who has made "the wrong assumptions" at risk of compromising his or her credibility with the patient. For the patient this creates a conflict around whom to trust – when he needs to trust both – and negates the intention of conveying a sense of security. Thus, the beneficial effect of the intervention may be lost. On the other hand, practitioners in psychological disciplines have an advantage over physicians: Not only do they have a keen perception of their patient's psychological needs, but they also have the skill and time to focus upon certain issues that physicians are less likely to understand or address.

Once information and instructions have been given, the clinician can utilize hypnotic techniques to increase the patient's receptivity to new possibilities. In a hypnotic state, helpful ideas can be explored less critically than in the fully conscious state, giving novel solutions a better chance of success.

APPLICATIONS OF HYPNOSIS AND SUGGESTION

Approaches using suggestion are appropriate to prepare patients for surgery, as well as for a variety of other interventions, including these diagnostic or therapeutic procedures:

- endoscopies (pulmonary or intestinal)
- chemotherapy
- radiation

- invasive radiology
- invasive cardiologic procedures such as angiography, pacemaker insertion, and angioplasties
- time in the intensive care unit
- anticipated prolonged artificial ventilation
- chronic renal dialysis
- preparation for organ or bone marrow transplantation
- obstetrics

In order to develop effective strategies, we need to understand certain characteristics of patients who are undergoing painful medical procedures. Let me summarize what I have learned by observing patients in a variety of such stressful situations:

1. Under conditions of stress and anxiety, patients become exquisitely susceptible to suggestions.
2. This state of heightened suggestibility extends from the moment a stressful intervention is contemplated until complete recovery.
3. Statements made during seemingly ordinary states of consciousness can function as suggestions that are as powerful as those given in a hypnotic circumstance (see case example below).
4. In this state, patients seem to follow certain hypnotic principles (e.g., "dominant effect" or "persons of superior authority") and to exhibit some signs of being hypnotized (e.g., focused attention, conscious amnesia, being very literal, suspending critical judgment).
5. Statements by persons of authority directly involved in their care are particularly powerful, while statements made by others may have little or no effect.
6. There appears to be a hierarchy to the patient's perception of authority (e.g., the person carrying out the procedure is likely to have the highest authority).

Let me illustrate these observations with a case from my own practice.

CASE EXAMPLE: MS. ROARK, RECEIVING
AN UNINTENDED SUGGESTION

Ms. Roark, for whom I had used hypnoanesthesia for a Marshall-Marchetti operation (a major abdomino-vaginal procedure) had been alert and pain-free during the operation but experienced excruciating pain upon arrival in the recovery room. (The fact that I had used hypnoanesthesia is not the relevant point here.) This pain could not be controlled by the hypnotic techniques that had kept her completely comfortable during the more than two-hour operation. I asked Ms. Roark, in the awake state, whether she knew why she had such severe pain *now*, after she had undergone the much more painful operation itself without any discomfort. I reminded her that she certainly knew how to control pain, since she had successfully done so in the operating room, to the surprise of her doctors and nurses. She was as puzzled and frustrated as I was, but she had no explanation. I induced a hypnotic state once again and asked the same question. The answer was prompt and without hesitation: "When I saw Dr. X [her surgeon] for the first time in his office [many weeks earlier], and we discussed the operation, he said, *"You will hurt like hell when you wake up in the recovery room."*

This surgeon certainly had not hypnotized the patient in his office — he knew nothing about hypnotic methods. Nor, of course, did he intend to produce an untoward effect by conscientiously giving information for a valid "informed consent." In retrospect, however, one may assume that this "information" functioned as a suggestion, to which Ms. Roark was exceptionally receptive. Neither was Ms. Roark herself aware that she had been particularly suggestible. One may, however, assume that she was in a hypnosis-related state, for she exhibited a quality typical of such a state, conscious amnesia for the conversation, yet she recounted it apparently verbatim while hypnotized. (I say "verbatim," because the words she used were not idioms she herself would normally use, but sounded quite characteristic of this particular surgeon.) It became clear to me at that point that *she was unwittingly carrying out her surgeon's unintentional suggestion.*

But why, one wonders, would she carry out *this* suggestion, which was expressed only in a casual conversation, and why was it not canceled by the hypnotic work done later, which had enabled her to create her own analgesia for the extensive operation, and which had specifically addressed postoperative pain control?

One might speculate that she believed that the hoped-for good results were contingent upon *all* the surgeon's statements becoming true. Suffering, as her surgeon had described — or, better, "prescribed" — seemed a necessary component to the eventual successful outcome of her operation. It is particularly noteworthy that the surgeon's statement to Ms. Roark was apparently more powerful than my suggestion given to her during a hypnotic state. This further demonstrates that *a formal hypnotic state is not required in order for sugges-*

tions to be powerfully effective. Under circumstances of stress and anxiety, simple statements may be experienced as compelling suggestions.

Once we attend to this issue, many of us may remember examples from our own practices where similar, though perhaps less dramatic, events have occurred: Most anesthesiologists, for example, have had patients with technically adequate spinal or regional anesthetics – yet some were, inexplicably, uncomfortable. We have seen the opposite as well: Patients with technically marginal or even poor anesthetic blocks can be very comfortable, often with nothing more than a little reassurance and possibly minimal supplementation by analgesics. As is characteristic of the often disparaged "placebo effect," these results cannot always be equated with purely physiological or pharmacological effects. We are obligated to take such examples seriously and to be mindful of the unusually powerful effect of our statements to patients. We might consider the following:

1. Seemingly innocent, casual conversations or comments can function as powerful suggestions.
2. Words carelessly used can have powerful *detrimental* effects.
3. Comments from persons of authority function as particularly effective suggestions.
4. Words with *negative connotations* may elicit untoward responses.
5. The reverse is also true: Words with *positive connotations* can elicit facilitating responses and result in beneficial effects.
6. Body language, sighs, "pregnant pauses," and other nonverbal communications contain suggestions as effectively as do words.
7. Suggestibility can be used therapeutically to the patient's benefit.

Table 9.1 gives examples of phrases with negative connotations to which patients are commonly exposed (left column) and their implicit message (in *italics*). These are juxtaposed with suggested modifications that include positive suggestions (right column, with comments in *italics*).

In stressful situations patients regress to primary process thinking (Bonke, 1990), becoming literal and concrete in their thinking and tending to think in absolute categories. This condition can be utilized to the patient's benefit: When language appropriate to that condition is employed and thoughtful suggestions are given, the following beneficial effects can be observed:

Table 9.1

Phrases with Unintended Negative Connotations or Even Suggestions (*left*) and Alternatives That Either Are Neutral or Contain Positive Suggestions (*right*)

Patient's Interpretation	*Possible Alternatives*
"You will be **put to sleep**" (*to many a euphemism for death, especially children who have lost a beloved pet or grandparent*) "You'll **go under** . . . " (*dying, drowning*)	"An anesthesiologist will administer your anesthetic. Anesthesia has to do with **comfort**. And the anesthesiologist will be there with you and watch that everything is **safe** while you are very relaxed. . . . "
At end of the operation as the patient is just waking up	
"It's **all over**." ("*I am dead*") "**You're finished**." ("*dead*")	"Good morning!" or "Hello" (*cheerfully*), "Dr. **just finished your operation** and you are **safe**. . . . " "Pretty soon you will be very clear-headed and maybe very **surprised** how much **easier** everything has been for you . . . and how much **better** you can **feel** than you thought."
In the recovery room or later	
"Let me know **when you have pain**." (*there will be pain*) "Tell me **when you start hurting**." (*same*) "Do you have pain?"	"Let me know how I can make you **more comfortable**. There are so many ways we can do that: Would you like . . . (a pillow under your knees/another warm blanket)? Can I put your head up a bit more? Would you like the light out of your eyes? Would you like to rinse your mouth? And you can also let me know if you would like a little medicine. . . . " (*By offering the above maneuvers first, "pain" is not only not mentioned, but it is* **deemphasized** *as a sine qua non or something to dwell on*) "Can I make you more comfortable?"
"I'll put this here so you can have it when you get sick (or: when you need it)" (as the nurse places the emesis basin by the patient's face). (*I am expected to and will get sick and vomit*)	(*First, one does not need to put an emesis basin at the patient's face when he arrives in the recovery room — it's an old and common habit. If it should be necessary, a basin can be reached very quickly. If one absolutely cannot do without, then it should be accompanied by a less noxious comment, like:*) " . . . sometimes people like to clear their throat or rinse their mouth after an operation. . . . "

(*Continued*)

Table 9.1
Continued

"Tell me when you get sick." (*same*)	(*If patients do vomit it can be **utilized** positively:*) "**GOOD**! You're rid of **THAT**! Your stomach just was not in the mood to digest that stale stuff. Now you can feel so much better and you can already look forward to quenching your hunger and your thirst just as soon as Dr. X says it's good for you. . . . "

- Extremely apprehensive patients become calm, relaxed, and cooperative, and express having a sense of control.
- Preprocedure sedation is rarely required.
- Requirement for anesthetic agents is decreased.
- Patients awaken postoperatively calm, comfortable, and characteristically "smiling," a most unusual sight in a recovery room.
- Postoperative requirement for narcotics is significantly reduced.[1]
- Nausea and vomiting are markedly decreased. (With today's anesthetic agents and techniques vomiting is no longer usual, but it was common postoperatively until about five years ago.)
- Patients are mobilized earlier, discharged earlier, and resume full activity sooner.
- Generally, patients are very cooperative and proactive and, therefore, easier to handle.

CASE EXAMPLE: MRS. REARDEN, 45, ADVANCED
BREAST CANCER, BILATERAL MASTECTOMIES

Mrs. Rearden, with advanced breast cancer, was scheduled for right modified radical and left simple mastectomy. She was extremely apprehensive about the surgery. She had been referred to me several months prior to surgery for anxiety reduction while she was undergoing chemotherapy in order to reduce the size of her tumor in preparation for surgery. She had experienced relief of her anxiety following just one hypnotic treatment. Because of severe anxiety regarding the operation and her disease, she requested preoperative hypnotic prepa-

[1]After major operations, patients who have been prepared with hypnosis frequently require even less medication for pain control than those prepared with suggestions but without hypnosis.

ration. This was carried out during my routine pre-anesthesia visit a few days preceding her operation.

The "favorite place" induction was used, followed by two fractionations[2] using breath and shoulder pressure, followed by rehearsal of the procedure from the perspective of full recovery (see Demonstration 9.1 at the end of this chapter). This included suggestions for calmness, restful sleep before the operation, comfort before, during and after the operation, minimal intraoperative bleeding, rapid recovery with minimal edema formation and minimal accumulation of serum and lymph postoperatively. Appreciation of and mourning for the organs she would lose were included in the hypnotic work.

Because of her extreme apprehension, her oncologist had prescribed sedatives and sleeping pills. Her parents had traveled from a distant city to offer emotional support to her. After the hypnotic treatment, Mrs. Rearden required none of the medications; to everyone's surprise, she was completely calm, rational, and cheerful, and she slept well. She declined to be entertained or kept busy by family and friends, and instead took long walks on the beach by herself.

On the day of surgery, Mrs. Rearden remained very calm ("less nervous than going on a trip," she said), despite the fact that she had to wait several hours before being taken to the operating room. She later recounted feeling somewhat irritated by well-meaning persons who tried to distract her in an effort to calm and comfort her, as she felt no need for it. She remembers that I came to her room to escort her to the operating room, but remembers nothing beyond that until she awoke after surgery. She assumed someone "had slipped me something," though no sedation was given. I had reinduced a hypnotic state by using posthypnotic cues, and continued giving Mrs. Rearden suggestions during transport to the operating room.

During this time she exhibited none of the signs commonly associated with or expected during a hypnotic state, such as lethargy or catalepsy. In fact, she remained conversant and fully cooperative throughout, moved herself to the operating table, and participated appropriately in whatever was required of her. (This is a very common occurrence and negates the concerns that a hypnotic condition may hamper patient cooperation and delay the necessary rapid and smooth process in the operating room.) Interestingly, she did have amnesia for these events, one of the signs of a hypnotic condition.

[2]A fractionation is a "deepening" procedure, involving rapidly rearousing the patient to full wakefulness, then immediately reinducing the hypnotic state, resulting in a more absorbed hypnotic experience.

I continued to give her suggestions throughout anesthetic induction, intubation, surgery, emergence from anesthesia, and on her way to the recovery room. She required minimal amounts of anesthesia during the surgery and awoke immediately after extubation, smiling. When told in the recovery room that blood loss had been extremely minimal, she was elated but not surprised. She had no pain. She later told me that, because the floor nurses had great compassion for her, they insisted on giving her opioid injections (Demerol) that evening and during the night. She said she did not need this (but she acquiesced, she said, on their behalf). The medication caused her to feel nausea. By morning, she refused any further opioids and remained comfortable. The surgical resident visited her that day and told her he had "never seen anyone with this disposition." Recounting this, she said, chuckling, "We know it had nothing to do with "disposition.'"

The remainder of Mrs. Rearden's recovery was easier than anticipated. She had been told she would not be able to drive for two weeks, but did so (after receiving permission from her surgeon) without pain on the fourth day after surgery.

An expected consequence of modified radical mastectomy is often prolonged serum accumulation, which may extend for many weeks and require repeated aspiration of that fluid. Mrs. Rearden's drains were removed four days after discharge from the hospital, and she never required a single aspiration, which is somewhat better than average.

KEY ELEMENTS IN PREPARING
A PATIENT FOR
STRESSFUL PROCEDURES

The preprocedure preparation determines to a large extent whether the patient's entire medical experience will be a pleasant or an unpleasant one. Clearly, then, it is important that we use this opportunity well.

In the clinical situation, the three elements of *information, instructions*, and *suggestions* (with and without hypnosis) cannot be separated, as they are in the illustrations below. Maximal effect and benefit to the patient require constant imaginative interweaving of all three.

Information

Most patients are bewildered, overwhelmed, and intimidated by the seeming complexity of what they are expected to absorb and for which they often lack reference points. By their own description, their response frequently is to "shut down," meaning that they no longer hear, register, absorb, or process anything they are being told. It is, in fact, common that many patients have no recollection of what was discussed at a particular visit in a surgeon's or oncologist's office, especially if the content had features that the patient perceived as "threatening."

(In recognition of this fact, a neurosurgeon in our community had made it a habit to record his preoperative conversations with his patients. When patients denied having been told certain facts, he replayed the tape for them. Patients were often in utter disbelief, especially when they heard their own questions or comments, of which they had no recollection whatsoever.)

Before inundating the patient with information, we must learn how he understands the procedure, his perception of his role vis-à-vis the procedure, his fears and potential coping skills. Often, simple reframing can be beneficial: If the patient says, "I'm here because I haven't any choice," one might respond, "It seems to me that you have given a lot of thought to it and decided that (having that problem of bleeding taken care of/that lump removed/that hernia fixed) will make your life a whole lot easier." Or, if the patient says, "I already know I will feel awful after the operation. I always get terribly sick and throw up for days. And the pain is horrible," the clinician, without giving guarantees or making false promises, can help greatly with a simple aside like, "Would you mind if it would be quite different for you this time?" In addition, reasons should be given why the experience *can* be different (that we no longer believe that severe pain or protracted nausea is ever justified; that there now are many safe options and that methods of pain and nausea control are significantly more effective than they used to be. Those options need to be described so that the patient can choose which he prefers). As a corollary to "reading between the lines," one must often "listen between the patient's words" to hear his or her concerns and then address them most effectively.

In order for the patient to benefit from our interactions, and to be truly informed (instead of simply satisfying the letter of the law regarding informed consent), we need to use language that the patient can understand. Further, we need to give the patient sufficient time to digest this information. As we observe the patient closely during such an interaction we can notice when we "begin to lose him." If we observe the patient's growing confusion, we need to slow down and, if necessary, change strategy. The information we provide to the patient must be factual, specific, honest, direct, and as explicit and detailed as necessary. Information, even with potentially difficult content, will not necessarily increase the patient's apprehension. On the contrary, even initially highly apprehensive patients tend to be much more relaxed after reviewing and discussing the options, procedures, sequence of events, expected sensations, possible complications and risks. A surprisingly small percentage of patients would rather not know. Yet, even those patients may become engaged and interested in learning what to expect once they discover that the information does not have to be incomprehensible to them. One such patient said, after I had finished our discussion, "Understanding gives power and makes you free." The effectiveness of this approach to informing a patient is made clear when patients comment postoperatively, "It was exactly as you had said." (When patients realize this, they are calmer, highly cooperative, and experience increased confidence in the medical system, which "has kept its promise." All of this will impact beneficially on any future procedure and is particularly important in cancer patients, for whom this operation may be only the first of a multitude of fear-inducing interventions.)

An additional benefit of an effective informational visit is for the patient to come away with the feeling of having *choices*. Even if such options and choices appear minuscule on the surface, they nevertheless greatly enhance the patient's sense of *control*, which effectively counters the ubiquitous sense of helplessness, infantilization, and victimization by the medical "system." Choices can be crucial to increasing trust, lessening anxiety, and rendering aversive stimuli more tolerable. Such choices might include, for example, whether or when he wishes to take a sedative at night or, on the morning of surgery, what type of anesthetic approach will be used, what mode of postoperative pain control he or she prefers (intramuscular injection, patient controlled analgesia, epidural, etc.) after having been given reasons as to their benefits.

Choices are of particular importance to adolescents, and even to children: what flavor he or she prefers be applied to the anesthesia mask; which toe or finger for the pulse oximeter; which arm for the blood pressure cuff; whether he or she prefers induction by breathing from a mask or by injection; whether he or she likes to sit or lie down during induction of anesthesia.

Both adults and children derive a particular sense of *control* when they are shown that they can influence, physiologic functions which they have no idea they can possibly influence, for example, heart rate, oxygenation, or end-tidal carbon dioxide concentration. For this purpose, their attention is drawn to the displays of the electrocardiograph, pulse oximeter, or capnograph. By observing their numeric or graphic displays, patients can witness how they can affect the numerical readout or the frequency or amplitude of the excursions of the graphic display. When, for example, their attention is drawn to the *pulse oximeter*, which reflects heart rate and degree of oxygenation numerically (at times graphically as well), or the *EKG*, patients can be informed that they *can* change their heart rate. This usually occurs gradually with progressive relaxation or sedation, but can be particularly impressive when patients "hold a long, deep breath" (i.e., perform a Valsalva's maneuver). When attention is drawn to the *capnograph* (which displays a numerical and graphic readout of the exhaled carbon dioxide) patients can observe how longer and slower breaths can, for example, extend the graphic line horizontally (explained to children as "long, flat mountains"), while rapid shallow breaths result in narrow peaked lines (for children: "many thin, high peaks"). Children enjoy being given the choice of making either "many thin, high peaks" or "long, flat mountains."

None of this is simply a time-consuming exercise but actually allows improved spontaneous ventilation, oxygenation, and consequently smooth induction of anesthesia via mask in the case of the capnograph. In the case of the pulse oximeter or EKG it facilitates gentler and smoother induction by utilizing progressive relaxation and improved oxygenation. These are examples of transforming potentially traumatic experiences into positive ones and beneficially affecting physiologic functions. All methods described above can also be utilized to induce a hypnotic state, which not infrequently occurs spontaneously under these conditions.

As mentioned earlier, the physician's approach will, of necessity, vary from that of the psychologist's, but the effect on the patient can be very similar. While only the physician can supply certain information, the psychologist can make it possible for the patient to have the skill, composure, and persistence to obtain adequate information from the appropriate sources without feeling overwhelmed, intimidated, or guilty—and then to retain it, assimilate it, and deal with it. Once obtained, this information can be incorporated into the remainder of the psychologist's work with the patient. However, rather than attempting to repeat to the patient what the psychologist understands the physician to have told the patient, the psychologist should use more general suggestions, " . . . and as time goes on . . . you may be surprised to discover that everything your doctor has explained to you will become easier and easier to understand and will make more and more sense to you. And if there is anything you still need to have clarified, it will be very easy and natural for you to ask. . . . "

In order to minimize repeat visits to physicians' offices and repetitive telephone conversations and inquiries, a helpful and cost-effective option is for the patient to bring a tape recorder to all physician office visits. (It must, of course, be recognized and respected that not all physicians are comfortable with this approach and they *must always be asked in advance.*) When he is more composed the patient can review the taped information and hear what he had not heard before; residual questions can then be asked more efficiently. I have found this particularly helpful for cancer patients.

Often patients have entirely incorrect and peculiar perceptions about physiologic processes or medical interventions. Thus, an integral part of providing information includes explaining physiologic functions, as well as the purpose and rationale of expected procedures. Especially when accompanied by supportive and reassuring suggestions, this allows the patient to tolerate otherwise uncomfortable and frightening sensations with equanimity.

Instructions

Well-intended admonitions from nurses or physicians to "just relax" are *not* helpful, instead confirming to the patient his or her inability to do so. This only further amplifies a sense of helplessness. It can, however, be very helpful to show a patient *how* to relax.

Effective instructions teach patients what *they* can do to beneficially influence the course of their medical condition. Even more importantly, as they discover that they have the understanding, skill, and ability to do certain things for themselves, the potential sense of victimization or passivity decreases and the experience of being an active member of the treatment team is enhanced. Patients experience this approach as greatly empowering.

Patients commonly lack trust in their own ability to assertively gather the information they need to have, as well as to communicate their questions and concerns. They need to know that if they fail in one attempt to gain information, they can pursue others. For example, patients often assume that if they do not speak with the anesthesiologist prior to the procedure, they will be too sedated to make their concerns known when they are being wheeled into the operating room. To make sure the anesthesiologist is made aware of the patient's concerns and requests, the patient can, for example, tape a note to the front of this chart, which the anesthesiologist is bound to see because he or she must review the chart. (Such a note might read: "To my anesthesiologist: After my last operation I [was terribly sick for a long time/had terrible pain in the recovery room/was very cold]. Is there anything you can do so that this does not happen this time?") Such a request can usually be accommodated, especially if the anesthesiologist is aware of the problem. It is calming to the patient to know that he has succeeded in communicating his concerns.

To further counteract patients' sense of helplessness, they can be informed and instructed that, before and after an operation, they can accomplish a few simple tasks that are beneficial to pain control and to overall recovery from the operation. Even when certain specific information about the operation is not known to the person preparing the patient, the following principles apply almost universally.

Maintaining normal nutrition and activity before the operation is important, as is getting adequate rest. Many patients believe that it does not matter whether they get a good night's sleep before the operation, because they "will be asleep anyway." To correct this misconception, I might say, "Your day of surgery goes much better and you recover more easily when you have a good night's rest and pleasant, relaxed days before your surgery."

Relaxing the muscles surrounding the incision reduces postoperative pain. To facilitate this effect, I might say, "You know that, when you have a cut or bruise on your hand, it feels a whole lot better when you let that hand go limp and relaxed than when you make a tight fist. It's the same after your operation. You can already start thinking about and practicing to let the muscles in that area go limp – like a rag doll. That also helps bring healing nutrients to those tissues so you can heal better."

The patient can be instructed and encouraged to practice relaxing the appropriate structures (e.g., abdomen, shoulders, neck and extremities). A pillow "under the knees" and elevating the head of the bed will relax abdominal muscles, as will "chest-breathing." Both will be beneficial in the case of abdominal incisions. And the patient can request the pillow from nurses, further enhancing the patient's sense of control. (If a pillow is contraindicated, this will be explained by the staff.)

For thoracic incisions, abdominal breathing should be encouraged, and it is something the patient can learn to do effectively well in advance. (This exercise is usually more difficult for women to accomplish than for men.) Operated extremities feel better when elevated – which is routinely done by nurses. However, the arm on the side of a modified radical mastectomy is not always supported, though it would be beneficial. The patient can be instructed to request such support and to "allow that arm to go completely limp and let the nurse lift it onto the pillow." Exercises such as taking deep breaths frequently, moving arms and legs, fingers and toes, tensing and relaxing leg muscles, are usually beneficial. In addition, the patient can be encouraged to ask the physician in advance what other exercises would be beneficial considering the particular condition and procedure.

Information and instructions go hand in hand, and are intended to counteract patients' perceptions of their incompetence, helplessness, and the dread of giving up control. Knowing what is happening and having things to do tend to greatly lessen the fear of loss of control. As a result, such patients tend to be calmer, more cooperative, more comfortable, more active, and are easier to care for. And they often recover more rapidly.

Suggestions

The degree to which suggestions are general or specific is determined by the needs of patient and the situation. I have found that *indirect, open-ended, permissive* suggestions are often more effective than direct authoritarian ones because they utilize the patient's innate skills, imagination, creativity, and life experiences. Moreover, such suggestions are less likely to elicit resistance.

When creating a suggestion, it is useful to involve all of the patient's senses. However, since sound is the most persistent mode of perception, even under profound sedation and anesthesia, it is very important to focus upon the patient's experience of sound.

As always, the goal is to support the patient's independence and self-sufficiency, for the reasons already described, and because there will be occasions when no one is available to induce, reinforce, or deepen the hypnotic state. Independence and self-sufficiency can be supported by reinforcing the patient's characteristic skills and by designing suggestions to be self-perpetuating. *Self-perpetuation* is achieved by linking suggestions to cues that can be expected to recur automatically or repeatedly for extended periods of time. Examples of automatically recurring cues include breathing, rhythmic beeping of monitors, the sounds of ventilators, the squeeze of the blood pressure cuff, ringing of telephones, nurses or visitors walking into the room, toilets flushing, etc.

When suggestions without hypnotic induction, also known as *"waking suggestions,"* are part of an instructional and informational visit, they are part of an ongoing dialogue, and therefore spoken in an ordinary, conversational tone. To anyone not experienced with hypnotic methods these remarks are probably not recognizable as suggestions. It is obvious that direct, authoritarian suggestions (e.g., "You will feel no pain," or "You will not be nauseated, and you will relish everything presented to you with a ravenous appetite") would be inappropriate. This is not how we normally speak. On the other hand, indirect, permissive, open-ended suggestions are experienced by the patient as a part of normal conversation. Such suggestions allow the patient options and choices, convey respect for individuality and freedom, and encourage or challenge only the patient's creativity to develop even better solutions.

In addition to examples given in earlier paragraphs, Demonstration 9.2 illustrates how commonly expressed patient concerns might be effectively addressed. (See appendix section to this chapter, page 262 ff.)

EXAMPLES OF PREOPERATIVE WAKING SUGGESTIONS

Many patients are very surprised when they hear that their operation is already finished. And I don't know whether you will be more surprised that everything might seem to have gone so quickly, or more surprised that you can wake up so easily, or even more surprised that you can feel a whole lot better than you might have expected.

Often, patients have told me that they felt such a sense of relief as they become aware of that pressure underneath the bandages (defuses the fear of pain) as they were waking up in the recovery room. Because then they knew that the operation was safely finished, and that healing had already begun.

You might be very surprised, when you look back a few days after your operation, how much easier everything may seem to have gone for you.

When you look back after your operation you might discover that the hard part was not the operation at all, but those things that are already behind you now: Going to the doctor, getting all that information, making the decision, and so on.

Further examples can be found in Demonstration 9.2 in the chapter appendix. In addition, many of the suggestions found in the verbalizations of "preparation with hypnosis" can be employed here as well. See Table 9.2, page 237 ff.

Besides helping to relieve preoperative anxiety, reduce the need for pre-, intra-, and postoperative medications, and enhance recovery, suggestions can simultaneously counteract the terror patients might otherwise experience should unexpected intraprocedural awareness occur. Adequately prepared, the patient may not be overwhelmed by otherwise unexpected and not understood experiences.

Notice how frequently I have been focusing on sound throughout the patient preparation. It is easy to remind the patient:

> As you already know, there are ever so many sounds and conversations in the operating room, and you might find it very *reassuring* to hear the hustle and bustle that goes on, which lets you know that everything that is happening in that room happens only for *your* benefit. Everyone in that room is working only on *your behalf*, to achieve the very best for you and to make everything safe. It all might sound to you like just a babbling brook . . . or gentle raindrops . . . with no meaning other than that you can feel peaceful, comfortable, and relaxed. . . . And you don't even need to bother to pay attention to any of them, unless you are addressed by name.

Thus, the patient is given information that there is noise in the room, but is encouraged to experience it as a basis for security instead of fear. In addition, drawing attention to sounds that are guaranteed to recur can cue the patient's response to the occurrence of those sounds (even postoperatively). For example:

> So, when you hear the beeping . . . of the many monitors and machines . . . it, too, lets you know that you are very safe . . . because everything is being watched so closely. . . . And when you hear that huffing and puffing of the breathing machine . . . and when you feel your chest rise and fall . . . with those long *easy* breaths that the machine helps you take . . . [Thus, the machine *helps*, it does not overpower, or force.] . . . it lets you know that you can relax even more . . . because the machine is doing even the work of breathing for you. . . . And all these sounds let you know . . . that there is someone watching these sounds . . . and watching *you* to make sure that everything works as perfectly as possible . . . and that you are safe. . . . [This counters common fears that no-one will be watching. *"You are safe"* is one of the most important statements a patient can hear pre-, intra-, and postoperatively.]

Because it is likely that patients *will* be exposed to negative suggestions, it is important to prepare them in such a way that they can
disregard or reject them. Negative suggestions are sometimes not easily erased, canceled, or modified, as my patient, Ms. Roark, demonstrated (see p. 213). On the other hand, a positive approach can serve
as an effective stress reduction method. Thus we can make the surgical
experience less traumatic for our patients and, at the same time, make
the job of the care providers easier as well.

It is very useful to invite the patient's family to participate in the
preoperative visit, if the patient agrees – and usually both patient and
family members are delighted. Not only can relatives provide important additional information, which the patient often forgets to mention, but they can be very supportive throughout the patient's ordeal.
They, too, can benefit from this approach. They feel equally calmed by
information and suggestions, some of which can even be directed at
them:

> Many families don't know that when a patient is taken to the
> operating area, sometimes quite a long time can pass before the
> operation actually begins. During this time he/she will be very
> well taken care of, and, of course, in the operating room as well.
> You might imagine that much needs to be taken care of before
> the surgeon can actually begin. So, for you, the time may seem
> much longer than [the patient] will actually spend in the operat-
> ing room. And you know that the surgeon will report to you
> shortly after the operation – it is always such a relief to see him.
> After the operation, and for several more hours, [the patient] will
> be in the recovery room. That does not mean that she will be
> asleep the whole time – in fact, most patients are very awake. But
> it is a wonderful place to be, because there she has the best kind
> of care, including her very own nurse, who can look after all her
> needs and make her very comfortable.

When family members participate, the patient has not only important allies, but also informed coaches who will often continue the suggestions that have been used. Since the family members have also
been calmed and informed, they are less likely to affect the patient
with their understandable concerns and anxiety.

EXAMPLES OF SUGGESTIONS LINKED TO EVENTS

Immediately postoperatively, the blood pressure is checked at five-
minute to hourly intervals, often by automatic devices. One can utilize

this by defining it as a cue and linking it with a therapeutic response: "Whenever you feel that tight squeeze of the blood pressure cuff, it will remind you of the comfort you are feeling right now."

There are a number of other highly probable events that you can also utilize:

> When you hear the *beeping of the monitors . . .*
> When you become aware of the *pressure underneath the bandages . . .*
> When the *nurse* comes into the room . . .
> Whenever you feel the *breathing* machine give you an extra big breath . . .

(See Demonstration 9.2 in the chapter's appendix for more examples.)

EXAMPLES OF SUGGESTIONS LINKED TO PATIENTS' REMARKS

Any communication, remark, or query from the patient can be used as a cue for a therapeutic response. It is important, of course, that accurate information, including normal physiologic functions, be linked to the suggestion.

Patients who are frightened because they had previous bad experiences, such as severe pain, protracted nausea, and vomiting, tend to become perceptibly more comfortable if told, "Wouldn't it be nice if it could be a whole lot easier (or quite different) for you this time? There is a good chance that it will be." But, whenever possible, patients also should be given *reasons* to substantiate our claim.

> [*Regarding nausea*] Modern anesthetics no longer make patients sick, as the old ones did. Besides, we now have very good ways of preventing nausea. And we have powerful new medicines to take care of it *if* it should happen.

> [*Regarding pain*] Today we have very different ideas about pain than we did in the old days. We have better ways of making patients comfortable, and we no longer believe that they have to suffer a lot of pain. I think you will be very surprised that you can be a whole lot more comfortable than you had thought. And, if you need to be any *more* comfortable, all you need to do is ask.

A patient, as she is waking up on the way from the operating room to the recovery room, says, "That was easy," or "That was a piece of cake." I might respond, "If the hard part was this easy, just imagine how easy the rest is going to be for you."

Immediately postoperatively, a patient says in surprise, "It doesn't hurt!" or "I'm not sick." I might respond, "That was the plan, and you already know that this comfort can stay and stay and stay."

When pain medication is given, it should be accompanied with a comment like: "I am giving you this very powerful medicine, which will make you much more comfortable in just a little bit. [It is wise not to give a precise time frame, for often the "placebo effect" precedes and outlasts the pharmacologic effect.] If you need to be any more comfortable [instead of "when you have pain again"], you can just let me know."

Some suggestions regarding physiologic functions need to be specific. Both patients and physicians are generally unaware that even autonomic functions can be affected by imagery or suggestions. Disbrow, Bennett, and Owings (1993) showed that postoperative ileus resolved earlier in patients who received suggestions to that effect. Intraoperative blood loss can be decreased by preoperative instructions as well: Bennett, Benson, and Kuiken (1986) reported that a group of patients lost significantly less blood than expected when they had been instructed preoperatively that "it is very important that the blood move away from (the surgical site) and to other parts of the body during the operation." Similar results were achieved by Enquist, von Konow, and Bystedt (1995) at the Karolinska Institute in Stockholm, in major oral surgery cases, for which blood loss is ordinarily significant. Enquist's instructions and suggestions were given in the context of a hypnotic experience; Bennett's instructions and suggestions during ordinary conversation.

EXAMPLES OF COMMON DISTRESSING DEVICES

Below are some examples of how *information, instructions*, and *suggestions* can be used to ameliorate the distress and discomfort that result from unpleasant, uncomfortable, painful, and sometimes frightening medical devices, and how their tolerance can be greatly improved.

Chest tubes can be very painful with every breath the patient takes, but modern anesthetic techniques (e.g., thoracic epidurals) are extremely effective and permit patients to be very comfortable, especially if analgesia is created preemptively:

These tubes help drain away fluid and air that accumulates and allows your lungs to work in a healthier way as they are healing. ... Each time you hear that gurgling sound in the suction apparatus into which the tubes drain, you can know that it protects you from breathlessness (a major concern of patients regarding thoracic surgery) and brings you closer to complete healing.

Bladder catheters are commonly perceived as exceedingly irritating, especially after vaginal repairs. Patients complain more about the discomfort catheters cause (an irresistible urge to void), than about surgical pain.

As you awaken after your operation and become aware of that little tube—they call it a catheter—which drains your bladder, it lets you know that your operation is safely taken care of, and that your recovery has already begun. [*This suggestion replaces awareness of an unpleasant sensation, which is not even mentioned, with a truism to which one assigns a pleasant connotation, thus shifting focus from something physically irritating to something emotionally appealing.*] And you can be so relieved . . . [*This open-ended suggestion points to: Relieved of what? Urine? Worry? The patient will fill in whatever is appropriate for him or her at that moment.*] . . . because it means that you don't even have to think about finding a bathroom [*This suggestion has multiple meanings: Right after surgery no patient would want to have to rush to the bathroom—so this is a benefit. But you also suggest, "You don't even have to think about . . . ," thus also indirectly suggesting disregard for the sensation of the catheter*] because your bladder is being emptied automatically and continuously. In fact, you can let all those muscles down there know that they can just relax, and let go, and go limp, because for right now, there is nothing that you or they need to hold back. It also helps that area heal more perfectly.

Another important physiologic concern can be addressed at the same time: A problem common to vaginal repair is the inability to *resume* voiding naturally for many days, even weeks occasionally, after removal of the catheter. A salutary suggestion can be as follows:

And, as you feel the healing taking place in that area—and your body knows just how to carry away the debris so that there is no undue swelling [*edema is very common and a significant cause for inability to void*], and how to bring healing nutrients to the tissues, you can already begin to look forward to the day when Dr. X [surgeon] removes that catheter. Already looking forward to having your bladder work quickly, easily and naturally, so that, as soon as there is just the right amount of urine in the bladder . . . not too much and not too little . . . just right, you will be able to empty it naturally and completely. [*This addresses the problems that occur after catheter removal—inability to void and urinary retention. But, if the suggestion is not made properly, the patient may be running to the bathroom every few minutes—"... not too much and not too little . . . just right . . . "prevents that.*]

Naso-gastric tubes remain in place after a number of gastrointestinal operations to drain the naturally produced gastric secretions which would endanger the patient if not removed. Such tubes can be quite irritating, especially to the nose and throat, occasionally causing gagging. A helpful suggestion to prevent this irritation is:

As you awaken after your operation and become aware of that little tube in your nose, it lets you know that your operation is safely finished. And you can be so relieved. It means that your [part of the body that has been repaired] is being given the best chance to rest and heal quickly, easily and comfortably, because the stomach juices that might be irritating to the healing tissues are being siphoned away.

The tube can be removed only after ileus has resolved and a number of suggestions may hasten this. Disbrow et al. (1993) demonstrated that ileus after gastrointestinal surgery resolved twice as rapidly in patients who had been given physiologically precise suggestions (without hypnosis): "Your stomach will churn and growl, your intestines pump and gurgle, and you will feel hungry soon . . . " and "get back to eating your favorite food as soon as possible."

Mechanical ventilation via endotracheal or tracheostomy tubes is mandatory after certain major operations and for certain serious medical conditions. It is commonly assumed that the sensation of the endotracheal tube and the "forced" ventilation are so irritating and distressing that patients are routinely heavily sedated, paralyzed, or both, often for extended periods of time. Otherwise patients experience violent coughing (called "bucking") and/or "fight the ventilator" (resist the breaths given by the machine, and/or breathe "against" it). This leads not only to additional discomfort, but also to poor ventilation, exertion, and even exhaustion, all of which may have serious ventilatory and cardiovascular consequences.

It has been my experience that patients who are well prepared (with information, instructions and suggestions) can tolerate mechanical ventilation easily: They can remain alert, yet very calm and cooperative. Patients need to be given very explicit and precise information and instructions first, so that they have a good understanding of the physiology, expected sensations, and reasons for this intervention. Suggestions can then follow:

As you begin to awaken after your operation, and become aware of the breathing tube in your (nose/mouth/throat), you can know that your operation is safely completed, and that healing has already begun. And you can be so relieved. It means that your [area of surgery] is being given the best chance to rest, and to heal quickly and easily. As you know, this sophisticated machine *helps* you, so that you don't even need to do the work of breathing for yourself for right then. [*This suggestion transforms something which might otherwise be experienced as an overpowering assault into something beneficial.*] This machine knows exactly how to give you the right kind of breath, and how often. So, when you hear that huffing and puffing of the machine, and feel your chest rise and fall . . . [*If this suggestion is given while the patient is in a hypnotic state, the word "rise" is timed to coincide with inhalation, and "fall" to exhalation. In addition, exhalation is accompanied by downward shoulder pressure and the word "down."*] . . . you can just settle back and relax and let that machine do the work for you. [*This suggestion is self-perpetuating, since the breaths recur over and over. Each new breath automatically repeats the suggestion and triggers further relaxation.*] And you don't even need to pay attention to the sounds of the machine, or to the many other noises, beeps, squeals, conversations, telephones, beepers, and whatever else. Because there are very conscientious and competent people who know what it all means. *They* are watching everything and watching *you*, to make sure that all works well. [*This is an important suggestion, because patients are frightened by the cacophony of sounds, and may become hypervigilant to the sounds of "their" ventilator and "their" monitors, which for now are their "lifeline."*] In fact, all those sounds might begin to just blend together into this gentle, soothing kind of hum. It might sound to you like the murmuring of a brook, or waves in the ocean that gently come and go, or like a waterfall, or soft rain, or wind – I really don't know. You might become so comfortably lazy – because all that work is being done for you – that you can just settle back comfortably into a long, good rest so that the healing can go on in the most perfect way.

Paralysis (euphemistically called "muscle relaxation"). The sensation of paralysis is unimaginable to patients, because most of us have never experienced it, and it can be a terribly frightening experience.

Usually physicians believe that patients will not register the experience of paralysis when sedated, but studies of intraoperative awareness have shown that this is not entirely correct. Therefore, it is reasonable to assume that the same holds true for profound sedation – maybe even for unconsciousness. And that would include such current favorite tranquilizers as Midazolam and Triazolam, which are selected for their supposed "amnestic" properties.

The experience of paralysis may evoke terror, unless it is explained effectively in advance. The following is an example of such an explanation:

Sometimes, it helps a breathing machine to work even more efficiently if patients are given a medicine that makes all their muscles go completely limp. This feeling is very different from any feeling you may have ever had, *but you can know that you will be completely safe.* Every muscle in your body becomes limp and relaxed. . . . [*It is wise to avoid the word "paralyzed."*] . . . your fingers, your feet, your chest. Some people find this a very interesting experience . . . [*thus deflecting attention away from fear to novelty, curiosity, "scientific experiment and observation"*] and just like to watch what it feels like when they think of moving a finger, but it won't. [*It's best not to say, "You can't."*] [*This describes what paralysis does and what it feels like.*] After a while, a finger or eyelid might move just a little bit . . . and then again not. [*As paralysis begins to wear off, patients regain some ability to move, but then are given another dose of paralyzing drug, preventing further movement again.*]

The above examples illustrate both how inseparably intertwined and interdependent information, instructions, and suggestions are and how every medical situation lends itself to providing helpful interventions. On the surface, these verbalizations may look like routine conversations, but in reality they are therapeutic tools.

These examples further illustrate how important it is that the *per-*

son preparing the patient has a good understanding of the details of the impending medical procedure. When *patients* understand "their" procedure by having as much information as is appropriate, and when this information is, in addition, coupled with the other two components (instruction and suggestions), they generally tolerate otherwise distressing experiences with equanimity and cooperation.

PREPROCEDURE PREPARATION WITH FORMAL HYPNOTIC INDUCTION

When preprocedure preparation is done *without* formal hypnotic methods, all interactions (including information and instructions) should be liberally interspersed with suggestions. In contrast, when formal hypnotic methods are to be used, it is essential to make a distinct separation between the informational and instructional work, on the one hand, and the hypnotic work, on the other.

Information and instructions should always precede hypnotic work, for two reasons:

1. An informed consent based on information presented during an "induced altered state of consciousness" would most certainly be legally invalid.
2. The patient must never be placed in a position where he or she might wonder whether there might be amnesia for any pertinent information or discussion.[3]

Here are some general principles to follow in using hypnotic methods to prepare patients for procedures:

1. As induction techniques for patients who are unfamiliar with hypnosis (and the vast majority of my patients are), I personally favor progressive relaxation or a "favorite place," as well as indirect, permissive, open-ended suggestions. These approaches feel very natural and conversational, are unlikely to generate a sense of being under someone else's control, feel nonthreatening, and are therefore more likely to be appealing to the patient.

---

[3]This may appear paradoxical in view of earlier statements that spontaneous amnesia has been observed in patients under stress. However, such amnesia has not been intentionally induced by the clinician and does not lead to the patient to wonder about the possibility of coercion.

2. Deepening can be achieved rapidly with several brief fractionations.
3. At the same time, cues (e.g., deep breaths, shoulder pressure, or combinations of both) can be included, which can not only function as rapid inductions or deepening techniques but later promote comfort throughout an otherwise painful experience even when no one experienced with hypnotic methods is available. Such cues are exceptionally helpful during procedures done under local anesthesia or sedation. Recovery room nurses can be instructed to remind the patient to take a deep breath or to place their hand on the patient's shoulder. (In my experience, nurses in recovery rooms appreciate having this opportunity to promote a patient's comfort so easily.)
4. Next, the experience of the anticipated procedure is "rehearsed" (in the hypnotic state); that is, it is reviewed from the perspective of its future successful completion (see Demonstration 9.1). Suggestions for comfort, effective control of bleeding, disregard for overheard comments in the operating room while under anesthesia, lack of unpleasant side-effects, rapid healing, return of physiologic functions postoperatively, and increased sense of control are interspersed throughout the intervention (see Demonstration 9.2).
5. By means of time distortion, experiences of comfort can be expanded, while experiences of discomfort contracted.
6. If clarification or resolution of issues was achieved during the informational session, this will be reinforced in a nondirective way.
7. Since it is impossible to anticipate everything that could possibly happen, it is essential to include the suggestion that the patient has the ability to easily adjust to unanticipated events while remaining calm, comfortable, and relaxed. (One could say, "And you might already be very curious what else there will be that we haven't even talked about, and how pleased you will be to discover after your operation how easily and naturally that, too, had gone for you.")
8. If appropriate, the patient's ability to make choices for himself is addressed, and ego-strengthening suggestions are offered.

For further details regarding verbalizations or wording of specific suggestions during patient preparation with *formal* hypnotic techniques, see Table 9.2. All statements contained in that table can be used during formal hypnotic interventions. Detailed statements rec-

Table 9.2

Examples of Suggestions during Formal Hypnotic Interventions for
Pre-procedure Patient Preparation*

Verbalizations	Comments

Time progression to beyond discharge from hospital.

"As you look back some time after your recovery . . . (and I don't know when that might be) – it could be a week later, or a month, or some time in between, or may be earlier – as you look back and discover . . . how **much easier** everything has been for you than you might have expected. . . . "

Suggestion that the entire experience **could be easier** than the patient may think at this time. The following is a **"retrospective review"** of things or events yet to come, including numerous positive options.

Meeting the anesthesiologist

" . . . how, as you met your anesthesiologist . . . you had **known just what you needed** to ask . . . so that you could feel very reassured."

Suggestion to be clearheaded and not experience **"white coat intimidation."**

Sleep night preoperatively

" . . . how **refreshed** you had awakened the morning of your (procedure) . . . with the **good feeling** . . . that you had done all you needed to do . . . and that you were in good hands."

Suggestion for sleep, peace of mind, confirming that the patient has been **in control** all along.

Arrival in hospital

" . . . how, . . . as you settled into your bed, . . . you felt yourself taking one of those long **relaxing breaths** . . . and feeling yourself sinking . . . into that **delicious comfort** . . . that you are feeling right now . . . that could stay and stay . . . and stay . . . and only get **more profound** with everything that happened . . . even though . . . when it had been necessary for you to communicate with anyone . . . or answer questions . . . you had been able to do so . . . **easily, naturally, clearly,** . . . knowing everything you needed to be aware of . . . and being able to ask any questions that might still have needed settling. . . . "

Indirect suggestion for **automatic hypnotic experience** once in hospital: In this case the patient had been taught self-hypnotic induction by "taking a big breath"; therefore, the breath is used over and over again to induce or deepen the hypnotic state.

This suggestion keeps the patient from developing somnolence, which might make communication with him difficult and be of grave concern to doctors and others (unless they really understood hypnosis, which they cannot be expected to understand). At this stage necessary information may still need to be obtained from the patient by the caregivers.

*For introduction to the basic concept of "rehearsal from the perspective of time progression," please see Demonstration 9.1.

(Continued)

Table 9.2
Continued

Verbalizations	Comments
Being transported to the operating room	
" . . . and as you had moved . . . to the bed on which you would be rolled to the operating room, . . . you had again taken one of those wonderfully deep relaxing breaths, . . . and **instantly felt yourself sinking into even deeper comfort** . . . and everything that had happened . . . like every wiggle and jiggle of the wheels of that bed, or any squealing of the wheels . . . or the motion of the elevator . . . or conversations around you . . . had been another signal . . . just like the feel of your breath . . . or the pressure of my hand on your shoulder right now . . . to allow you to become even more comfortable. . . . "	Suggestion that everything that happens will function as a **cue for deepening**; numerous examples are given so that the patient will assume that everything else will serve the same function. Again, these are **self-perpetuating suggestions** because these cues are bound to recur over and over again.
Arrival in the operating room	
" . . . and, when you had arrived in the operating room . . . and met your anesthesiologist who would be in charge of looking after you . . . as soon as you had moved yourself to that operating table . . . you had felt yourself take an **extra deep breath** . . . which had allowed you to sink **even deeper into this wonderful comfort** you had created for yourself over and over again . . . which was made even deeper by every **sound, each word, touch, beep, conversation, or the squeeze of the blood pressure cuff on your arm.**"	Suggestion to **reinduce or deepen the hypnotic state.** Feeling **safe** in the care of the anesthesiologist. Each possible sensation being used as a **cue for deepening.** This suggestion also contains the **implicit message** that conversations do not necessarily need to have meaning other than being messages for comfort.
Distraction through use of own creativity	
" . . . By now . . . you may already have decided or discovered . . . what wonderful things you would be dreaming about . . . and you might have already slipped into this **safe dreamy state** . . . while others were doing their job . . . of **looking after you** . . . so gently, . . . so **efficiently,** . . . and so **caringly.**"	Suggestion to resort to one's own inner resources. Reassured that he is being looked after while not able to do so himself.

Table 9.2
Continued

Verbalizations	*Comments*
Induction of anesthesia	
" . . . and when you had noticed that the anesthetic medicine began to take effect . . . you could really **welcome** it for the **good things** it was going to do for you . . . by **augmenting that comfort** that you already had created for yourself . . . so that your own comfort could work for you **in complete harmony** . . . with the comfort the anesthetic was helping you achieve. . . . "	Patients in a hypnotic state **always notice** "that there is something different" (usually they say "there is something wrong") when the anesthetic is begun. If not prepared, patients will become frightened, often terminate the hypnotic state spontaneously, and actually will require larger doses of medication for induction. This is averted with such a suggestion, in which case the induction dose is frequently reduced.

ommended for rehearsal of the surgical experience are contained in the Demonstration 9.2 in the chapter appendix. Remember also that nearly all suggestions included in the sections dealing with use of suggestions *without* formal hypnosis can be used equally well *with* formal hypnotic approaches.

Suggestions on the Day of Surgery

Nurses and physicians often attempt to lessen a patient's anxiety by distracting her with jokes, glib remarks, friendly bantering, and so on. At other times a patient is treated impersonally, like an object, while the staff carry on their own conversations. Such practices are not calming or reassuring, but have the opposite effect. They convince the patient that having the responsibility for his well-being—maybe even for his life—is nothing but mundane routine for us and that we do not appreciate the seriousness of the situation.

Recognition of such perceptions may lead to more helpful approaches: For example, in the case of patients who have had a preoperative hypnotic experience, a hypnotic state can be reinduced on the way to the operating room. For other patients, even patients not previously prepared with any of the measures discussed in this chapter, suggestions are given while they are being rolled down the hall on the gurney. Here, too, one can draw attention to a patient's "favorite place" by saying, "I imagine that if I were to give you a magic wand right now, you could probably think of a wonderful place you could take yourself to. Where would that be?" Almost every patient responds, without hesitation, by naming a special place.

After the patient has given very rudimentary information about his "favorite place," he is gently guided by means of queries which direct his attention to details of "his place," to engage all the senses.

> what the sky looks like, how the soil feels underfoot . . . whether there are clouds in the sky, and if so, whether they are big billowy ones, or little wispy ones, whether they are very still, or moving . . . and if they are moving, whether they are all moving in the same direction . . . or some this way, and others in another . . . which direction the sun is coming from . . . whether they can feel the warmth of the sun . . . and what it feels like on the other side. . . .

This style of inquiry very quickly facilitates a patient's absorption into his or her imagination. If the patient does not answer my question directly, this may indicate that he may be very absorbed and may be already dissociated from the hospital environment.

Appropriate suggestions are then interspersed (verbalizations in Demonstration 9.2 can be modified as appropriate).

It is important not to impose "my" idea of such a place, or to describe the "patient's place" *for* him. This often happens when physicians or nurses try to "get in on the conversation," assuming that I am just "chatting," not realizing that it involves control and restraint and is guided by technical skill. In doing so, they sometimes tend to suggest their own experiences to the patient, which more likely than not conflict with the patient's images and are therefore much less effective. This, of course, is not usually helpful, for it distracts the patient from her own experience.

The preceding was an example of *distracting* the patient from the operating room environment. The opposite approach, namely of *utilizing* it by directing the patient's attention to it, is equally effective: Operating room sounds – usually distressing and menacing – can be reinterpreted and transformed into conveying a sense of protection, comfort, and security, devoid of any other meaning:

> All these sounds . . . can let you know . . . that you are very safe: . . . each beep of the monitors . . . the huffing and puffing of the machines . . . the squealing . . . all of it is just another signal for you . . . that you can allow yourself to drift into even deeper com-

fort . . . whether it is metal sounds . . . or a funny buzzing or hiss-
ing over there . . . or people talking . . . it all only means that everything is being readied for your benefit . . . to take very good
care of you . . . to watch over you . . . and you don't even need to
pay attention to any of these sounds in particular . . . they only
let you know that you are safe . . . and that everything is going
well for you . . . so that you can relax even more. . . .

As the patient's attention is drawn to the monitors, while they are
being placed, the rhythmic sounds of the electrocardiogram or the
pulse oximeter, for instance, can be not only utilized as reassurance of
close monitoring but also linked to progressive relaxation and a pleasant hypnotic experience. [4]
Often, within moments, the patient will be deeply absorbed in internal imagination. If this occurs, I immediately begin to shift my suggestions to focus upon freedom from pain and side-effects, easy recovery and healing, and whatever else applies to this particular patient.
It is important to stress that none of these interactions with the
patient take additional time for me as the anesthesiologist beyond the
time normally allotted for such routine tasks as applying and calibrat-
ing monitors, placing lines, ventilating, intubating, etc. This approach
does, however, require considerably more intellectual focus in order to
use the time well and to create thoughtful, helpful suggestions.

Suggestions to Prepare Children

As LeBaron and Zeltzer describe in Chapter 11, and as we see in
Cindy's case below, pediatric patients benefit greatly from these approaches. These methods are especially effective to avoid the psychological trauma of a frightening and painful environment by facilitating
the development of the hypnotic state *before* entering the operating
room.
Children can be easily distracted by such techniques as visiting a
favorite place, playing a favorite game, watching an imaginary television program, being in a swing or carousel, playing with favorite pets
or playmates, going on a space flight. The same utilization of operating
room equipment and activity that I described above can be used to
great advantage with children. We can use video screen monitors,

---

[4]See Bejenke (1990) for a more complete description of ways to use a
variety of other operating room equipment as hypnotic induction aids in anesthesiology for adult and pediatric patients.

operating rooms lights, and other operating room furnishings as hypnotic induction aids. The EKG monitor, in particular, can serve as a very effective tool for distraction or even hypnotic induction in children. The irregularly moving lines on an EKG screen can be interpreted as fluttering birds, the EKG's signal as chirping, which can create rhymes in rhythm with the EKG signal ("beep . . . beep . . . beep . . . Lisa wants to sleep. . . . ").

CASE EXAMPLE: CINDY, 4, FINGER REIMPLANTATION

On the way from the emergency room to the operating room (a distance of about 150 yards), I talked to Cindy about her favorite TV program ("Woody the Woodpecker"). Because of a "full stomach" (which increases anesthetic risk significantly and must be handled according to strict rules), an intravenous line was mandatory. By the time we arrived in the operating room, she was in a deep hypnotic state and showed no response to placement of an intravenous cannula, even though she could not tolerate being touched a few minutes earlier.

   Rapid sequence induction of anesthesia, intubation, and the three-hour surgery were uneventful. During the operation, I offered suggestions for freedom from pain and for an easy and comfortable recovery. To prevent aspiration of gastric contents, patients with full stomachs are not extubated until fully awake. This process is unpleasant, and usually results in severe coughing and struggling. To protect Cindy from this experience, I said to her, while she was still deeply anesthetized toward the end of the operation, that she would soon begin to become aware of "that little straw in your mouth" (the reframed description of the endotracheal tube). I told her that, when "you are ready for me to take it out, you can just give me a big smile." To the amazement of the nurses (who know the unpleasantness an extubation process usually involves), Cindy sat straight up on the operating table with a wide grin on her face. A peculiar and most unusual sight: a smiling child with an endotracheal tube protruding from her mouth! She did not cough, struggle, or cry, was extubated uneventfully, and made an excellent recovery.

Suggestions during Induction of Anesthesia

During induction of general anesthesia, I continue speaking to the patient, offering supportive suggestions beyond the point where the patient is assumed to be asleep. Every action that is taken for the patient, by me or someone else, is accompanied by my explanatory and reassuring comments and suggestions. For example, as I am placing the endotracheal tube down the sleeping patient's throat, I may say, " . . . and now you can feel the breathing tube being placed gently into your throat, to make breathing safe for you." This is followed by suggestions for comfort during and after the operation, other appropriate suggestions, and reinforcement of suggestions that address this patient's particular concerns.

Suggestions during the Operation

I continue to make suggestions to the patient, even after he or she is anesthetized. Since the habits of the operating room have not yet incorporated the fact that, at some level, the patient continues to hear, someone in the room may make an unfortunate remark (e.g., poor prognosis, pathology reports, or negative comments about the patient). If it is not possible for me to prevent such a remark or to make it physically impossible for the patient to hear it (e.g., by blocking the patient's ear canals with cotton balls, or creating noise by rubbing the patient's ears, or speaking to the patient), I address the patient by name and make corrective statements, which must, however, *never* be untrue or deceptive (Bejenke, 1990, 1993, 1995b; Bonke, 1990; Moerman, Bonke, & Oosting, 1993).

Suggestions during Emergence from Anesthesia

It is important to resume speaking to the patient prior to emergence. I tailor the suggestions, of course, so they are appropriate to the circumstances. For example, I find it helpful to remind the patient of the presence of the endotracheal tube, which is there "to make breathing safe for you," of catheters, and of other sensations the patient may notice that have developed since he or she went to sleep. If I had anticipated postoperative ventilation, then I would have already prepared the patient with positive suggestions for that eventuality preoperatively; those are now reinforced. It is interesting to observe how calmly such patients tolerate extended artificial ventilation postoperatively, in contrast to the struggling that one otherwise witnesses. (If the patient has *not* been prepared for this intervention preoperatively, appropriate suggestions are given now.)

CASE EXAMPLE: MS. FRANCON, COMFORTABLE DURING PARALYSIS

Ms. Francon was a hysterectomy patient whose profound muscle paralysis, created for the operation, could not be immediately reversed at the end of the operation, and who, therefore, required mechanical ventilation via endotracheal tube for hours in the recovery room. Because she was so profoundly paralyzed, it was impossible to assess her level of awareness, but I spoke to her as if she were awake, reminding her of the safety of the endotracheal tube, of the function of the ventilator, and of my ongoing care for her. I instructed the nurses to treat her in the same way. Her vital signs never indicated any distress. She remained completely calm and cooperative even when muscle paralysis began to wane. (This is when patients usually begin to struggle and are frightened and agitated.) After the paralysis had been reversed and I extubated her, she reported that she had been fully awake upon arrival in the recovery room (that is, for many hours). She remembered every detail of her experience but never felt any anxiety whatsoever because of the explanations given to her and the continued personal contact with the nurses. In fact, she said, she found the experience quite interesting. In this case, I had not made a hypnotic induction at any time, because it had not been indicated initially. The patient had only received the usual information, instructions, and positive suggestions in preparation for surgery, including waking suggestions to which she responded well. During the period of paralysis, suggestions were offered along with information.

Suggestions in the Recovery Room

Nurses report that patients who have received adequate preoperative preparation and intraoperative suggestions are exceptionally easy to take care of. They arouse readily, often arrive in the recovery room awake and smiling, are calm, rational, and cooperative, require very little if any pain medication, and are less distressed than usual by tubes and catheters. It is worth mentioning that even nurses who do not know that these patients have received special care remark that there is something unusual about them. In the recovery room, by using posthypnotic cues, I can easily reinduce or deepen the hypnotic state, and nurses can be instructed in simple deepening techniques by using cues that I have already established with the patient.

Patient comments in the recovery room, such as, "This was easy!" "Nothing to it," "I can't believe it," "When do I get to go dancing?" "Amazing," and "You must be kidding," give us an opportunity to immediately respond to their delight and to support their pleasant experience with an additional positive suggestion like, "That was the plan . . ." or " . . . and if the hard part was this easy, just imagine how easy the rest is going to be for you."

Preoperative preparation is essential for such results, however. It is much less satisfying to attempt hypnotic techniques in the recovery room for patients who have not been previously prepared in this manner. Such patients have already been traumatized, physically and psychologically, without having developed skills for coping. Consequently, these patients are tense, frightened, usually in severe pain, and frequently angry. They are often confused and unable to listen, because they are groggy from the heavy medications. Yet, as I discussed at the beginning of the chapter, pain and "suffering" are sometimes not adequately treated by medication alone. Such unprepared patients, for example, often require large doses of medications to achieve only moderate comfort.

The postoperative course of well-prepared patients is usually less distressing than that of unprepared patients, even in those cases where severe complications arise. These patients rarely complain of pain and must often be encouraged to accept small amounts of analgesics. Also, they are more active and are frequently discharged earlier than unprepared patients. The following case illustrates the course of a patient prepared with information, instructions, and hypnosis.

CASE EXAMPLE: MR. GALT, 55, FEARFUL OF DEATH

Mr. Galt, introduced at the beginning of the chapter, was experiencing severe preoperative apprehension prior to his parathyroidectomy. A self-described "control freak," he considered submitting to anesthesia to be the ultimate loss of control. Though he had numerous concerns about his operation, he was especially preoccupied with the fear of death under anesthesia. Mr. Galt had sought numerous consultations and second opinions regarding his surgery and had spent many hours researching the medical literature. For some time he had been suffering sleep deprivation as a result of his growing apprehension.

The preanesthesia visit with me, several days before surgery, included a thorough discussion of his anesthetic options, instructions, and hypnotic rehearsal (similar to the one described at the end of the chapter). After the hypnotic experience, Mr. Galt commented spontaneously, "I tapped into a wellspring of my own power." Because of his newfound calm, he used none of the sedatives he had previously requested; he was relaxed and slept very well in the remaining days before surgery.

Mr. Galt arrived on the morning of surgery well rested, expressing a cheerful calm. The floor nurses who had seen him prior to the intervention found his calm demeanor very surprising. He had to wait many hours before being taken to the operating room. Although this prolonged wait is usually very distressing to patients, unless they are sedated, Mr. Galt required no sedation, and arrived in the operating room very alert, yet calm and cooperative. I helped him develop a hypnotic condition by using a posthypnotic cue (a deep breath), which facilitated a very gentle induction of general anesthesia.

Following the surgery, Mr. Galt was awake immediately after extubation. He was free of pain in the recovery room, had a peaceful night, declined all offers of analgesic injections, but accepted two analgesic pills. He left the hospital a little over twelve hours after discharge from the recovery room. That evening, he felt so well that he went to the movies, and then he jogged the following morning. As might be expected, Mr. Galt was deeply pleased by his experience.

Special Considerations

It is not safe to suggest the removal of all unpleasant sensations postoperatively at all times, because this may interfere with the appropriate evaluation of the patient. Suggestions should therefore include a comment such as:

> ... even though you can be very comfortable after your (operation, procedure), whenever your doctor comes to check you, you can allow yourself to have all the normal feelings that patients have who don't know what you know about making yourself comfortable. This is important, so your doctor can know exactly how well you are healing. The moment he finishes the examination you can go right back into your own special comfort.

It is neither appropriate nor necessary to give the patient the impression that analgesia achieved with hypnotic techniques must be complete at all times (except in case of hypnoanesthesia). The purpose is to establish multidimensional comfort, which is rarely achievable solely by pharmacological means. But we should not give the patient the impression that accepting analgesic medication constitutes failure on his or her part.

It takes effort for the patient to maintain and continue a hypnotic state. Although posthypnotic suggestions are very helpful, they also may need to be reinforced from time to time. If the patient is sedated, or if the person who has trained the patient is not readily available for reinforcement, the patient may not always be able to induce a self-hypnotic state. I encourage patients to ask for medications "whenever you feel you could use a little rest" from the work that he or she has been doing so well. This holds true particularly for the nights, when sleep is needed.

Because self-hypnosis is work, I have designed self-perpetuating suggestions; these are very helpful, though not quite identical to reinforcement by a trained person. Therefore, I explain or demonstrate to nurses and family members very simple cues that I have used with the patient. This supports the family members' wish to be helpful to the patient and establishes stronger bonds between the patient and family members.

It does not serve the patient's best interest to be so zealous about positive suggestions that we misinform or deceive the patient. It is of paramount importance to be honest with the patient and to present medical facts accurately without exaggerating or minimizing. Even risks must be presented honestly – always with compassion and respect.

We are all frequently exposed to noise, sounds, beeps, telephones, toilets flushing, ad infinitum almost everywhere. Certain sounds that have been suggested as cues for induction or deepening could inadvertently create a hypnotic experience when it is not appropriate, and thus cause unexpected difficulties. To obviate this possibility, I usually include the proviso – just as I do when teaching hypnoanalgesia which could be misguidedly used, say, by a young skier who has sustained an injury and wants to have just one more run – that: " . . . It will work only when it is in your best interest, at the right time, in the right place; all it will do otherwise is to make you comfortable and alert to anything you need." Or, "Whenever it is appropriate for you to experience comfort, this can happen for you, even though you will remain fully attentive, alert and competent to whatever you need to do, to your activities and responsibilities."

Patients need to be warned not to overdo:

> Because you can feel so very much better after your operation than you might expect, some people have a tendency to demand more of themselves than is good for them. And it is good for you to know that your body deserves the same time to heal, in the weeks and months to come, as everybody else's who had such an operation. The difference is that you can enjoy it so much more because you can feel so well while you take good care of yourself and watch your body complete the healing.

HYPNOANESTHESIA

The single most dramatic use of hypnosis for acute medical situations is for burn patients, as David Patterson discusses in Chapter 10. Hypnotic intervention can dramatically improve the patient's experience of his injury, treatments, and recovery, and is very useful for pain control and improving nutrition and activity. Hypnoanesthesia eases the numerous necessary painful treatment procedures. Ideally, hypnotic treatment begins as early as the patient's arrival in the emergency room and extends throughout his hospital stay and into eventual reconstructive surgery and rehabilitation.

Burn patients who have experienced the benefit of hypnotic anesthesia can then use this skill for any other intervention as well. Frequently, for example, burn contractures render patients at exceedingly high anesthetic risk for reconstructive surgery, due to the compromise of their breathing passage. Using hypnosis, awake intubations or tracheostomies can be accomplished without causing significant pain or distress to such patients, who cannot otherwise be safely anesthetized until the airway is secured.

The use of hypnoanesthesia for other interventions is too vast a topic to be addressed here. To describe the necessary steps requires a chapter in itself. Several important considerations must, however, be kept in mind: Only clinicians with extensive training and experience with hypnotic methods should attempt hypnoanesthesia. If such a clinician is not also an anesthesiologist, it is mandatory that an anesthesiologist be present during the procedure, because providing analgesia is only *one* of many essential responsibilities an anesthesiologist has for the patient's well-being and safety. These cannot be provided by anyone else, not even a physician-specialist in another field (just as cardiac surgery would not be done by a general or orthopedic surgeon, though both are skilled in surgical techniques). If patients themselves are highly skilled and experienced in self-hypnosis, it is reasonable for them to apply those skills to the extent they choose. But it is always wise to have good communication among and understanding on the part of the physicians participating in the procedure.

Claims that hypnoanesthesia is safer than conventional anesthesia are today untenable and reflect outdated information. Hypnoanesthesia has, for example, been advocated for patients who are "allergic to all anesthetics," but such a condition is not actually known to exist. While it is true that patients usually recover exceptionally easily after hypnoanesthesia, nearly identical results are achieved by preoperative preparation with formal hypnotic methods (in conjunction with information and instructions as described earlier), but followed by well-conducted conventional anesthesia.

USE OF HYPNOTIC TECHNIQUES FOR OTHER INTERVENTIONS

Endoscopies

Progressive relaxation induction (by using tightening versus relaxing the hand both for the original induction as for fractionations and rapid inductions) is particularly useful. This can then be utilized as a cue to relax the oral, esophageal, rectal sphincters, etc.

> Just before Dr. X begins to get ready to insert the instrument in your (mouth, rectum, etc.) . . . you can make that tight fist . . . and when you let that go . . . just as we have practiced here . . . all those muscles in the area . . . where the doctor needs to work . . . get as limp as your hand, after you let that fist go . . . limp, and lazy, and comfortable and relaxed . . . so that the instrument can pass smoothly, gently and easily . . . and whatever pressure you feel . . . can be just another signal . . . like the pressure of my hand on your shoulder . . . to allow you to go into even deeper and more relaxed comfort. . . .

Cancer Patients

Karen Syrjala and Sari Roth-Roemer have explored the benefit of hypnotic interventions in the medical treatment of cancer patients. Let me merely emphasize that a thorough preparation (as outlined in this chapter) can allow cancer patients to experience an operation as much easier than anticipated. This often modifies the patient's perception of the illness as an unalterably frightening, horrible experience and can be an invaluable therapeutic tool for the patient's future medical course (Bejenke, 1993, 1995a).

As mentioned earlier, another very helpful preparatory intervention is to address appreciation of, leave-taking from, and mourning for the organ to be lost through surgery. This can take many forms and result not only in great relief, but also frequently in loss of sensation for that organ even before its surgical removal, which can have important analgesic implications both pre- and postoperatively (Bejenke, 1995a). In addition, we can support the patient's capacity for hopefulness and for regaining a sense of choice and control. This can be an invaluable therapeutic tool for the patient's future medical course.

Obstetrics

Although childbirth does not ordinarily involve painful medical procedures, preparation for childbirth is a useful and significant application of hypnotic methods, and I have included its exploration in this chapter.

In *Anesthesia for Obstetrics*, Hughes and DeVore write: "The experience of childbirth ranges from agony to ecstasy. However, a comparison of pain scores revealed that the degree of pain accompanying labor ranged, on average, between that of cancer pain and amputation of a digit" (1993, p. 103).

As for surgery, anesthesia for obstetrics has become much safer and more flexible, with a greater number of choices. Yet, many women desire "natural childbirth" because they do not view childbirth as a medical event; they want to experience the birth as a family event, and perhaps they believe that natural childbirth is safer for their baby.

Obviously, psychological factors play a paramount role in the pain experienced by obstetric patients. This has been recognized in the development of psychological approaches to analgesia for childbirth. Methods such as "natural childbirth" (Dick-Read, 1959), "psychoprophylaxis" (Lamaze, 1958), and the LeBoyer (1975) technique of "Birth without Violence" make use of a variety of psychological approaches and should be known to anyone preparing women for delivery with any psychological technique, including hypnosis.

Moya and James (1960) demonstrated that the acid-base ratio of the newborn's blood (an important measure of its health) was significantly better (immediately at birth, and one hour later) after childbirth with hypnoanesthesia than with general anesthesia, and Flowers claimed that hypnosis shortened labor (Flowers, Littlejohn, & Wells, 1960). Since these early studies, much research has been carried out regarding the detrimental effect of maternal stress on fetal outcome, which has led to very safe and effective anesthetic techniques for childbirth, including intrathecal and epidural local anesthetics with or without minute doses of narcotics (Morishima, Pederson, & Finster, 1978; Myers, 1975; Shnider et al., 1979). Such modern anesthetic techniques have made childbirth not only more comfortable for the mother but also safer for the baby. Considering the beneficial effect of reducing maternal stress places added importance on inclusion of hypnotic preparation of the mother-to-be.

Is there an ideal time to begin hypnotic training for delivery? It should be late enough so that the mother has passed those gestational stages during which fetal losses are most common, but not so late that the patient is not fully prepared in the event that labor should occur prematurely. A reasonable time is six to ten weeks before the expected date of delivery.

The patient's goals and her response to training will determine the approach and the number of sessions required. Obviously, there is not the degree of urgency felt as in many of the previously discussed medical conditions. Thus, sessions can be scheduled over a period of time, and the patient has an opportunity to practice and become self-sufficient.

It is important that both the patient and the person training her have an understanding of the anatomy and physiology of childbirth, and that the trainer use terminology that the patient readily understands. It is therefore helpful to familiarize oneself with the instructional booklet a patient will have received from her obstetrician and to review her understanding of labor prior to beginning hypnotic work. Since many patients attend classes in pyschoprophylaxis (Lamaze), it is important for the hypnosis practitioner to have a good understanding of what his or her patient learns in her Lamaze classes and to blend the two approaches.

Since the goal is to avoid words that may involve negative associations, I avoid the term labor "pain" and instead use the word "contraction." However, "labor" can be used to advantage by reminding the mother that labor is hard work and that she deserves to rest as much and as profoundly as possible, especially between contractions. For this reason, during training, I emphasize teaching her rapid deepening methods that are associated with automatically recurring cues (e.g., the squeezing of the blood pressure cuff, which I discussed earlier).

However, the most persistent and compelling recurring stimuli are, of course, the contractions, which also lend themselves to utilization. I might say, for example:

> Whenever you feel a contraction fading away, you can allow yourself to go totally limp, and sink back into the comfort of your pillows, drifting into this wonderfully deep comfort which you already know so well, and which can last and last and last. In fact, you might discover that the rest between contractions may seem to last so very much longer than you had thought . . . so that you can really get a wonderfully profound rest . . . and feel so refreshed, strengthened and energized when it is time for the next contraction. . . . And you might not even need to pay attention when the next contraction begins – because there are experts watching, and counting, and timing, and they will let you know

when they need your help . . . so that you can just enjoy that comfortable, peaceful feeling. . . . And it might even feel as if the contraction passes more quickly and more easily. . . . " (I say " . . . it might feel as if . . . " in order to avoid affecting the actual duration of the contractions.)

It is important to prepare patients in such a way that they are able to adjust rapidly and cope appropriately with the unexpected and with potential problems. In this medical domain, more than in any other, conditions can change suddenly and critically. If I were to prepare the patient for only a certain sequence of events, any other occurrence could provoke anxiety and lead to unpleasant consequences. Thus, as always, it is important to be thoughtful when creating suggestions, for example:

As you progress through the different experiences of labor and giving birth, you may be very curious about which of them will seem very familiar and which quite different from what you might have expected. And you may already begin to look forward to the opportunity to discover how you can use your own creativity again and again to find ways to use your skills. At the appropriate time, creating just the right kind of comfort or relaxation. At another, strength and endurance. At another, calm concentration. And at yet another, something else. So that you can achieve your goal for your baby and yourself in the best possible way, being very pleased with your ability to use your own skills so creatively.

So that, when you look back some time after the delivery, you might just marvel at how easily you adjusted to whatever had been required at the time. And you already know that much can change very quickly during a birth. So it is for your benefit and your baby's, to be ready and flexible to adjust to whatever is best and safest. And it is so good to know that there are professionals who know exactly what needs to be done when. All you need to do is your best in helping them do their best for you.

(This suggestion includes the eventuality of an emergency Cesarean section and any other emergency intervention without specifically naming them.) It is also important, of course, to encourage cooperation with doctors', midwives' and nurses' instructions and recommendations.

The patient needs to be encouraged to feel free to utilize medications for a number of reasons: She needs to understand that taking medications does not mean her failure at natural childbirth, but, rather, enhances her own ability to do the work required of her (" . . . so that you can rest up for the important part"). In addition, analgesia provided by medication, if used according to up-to-date medical information, not only is safe but also improves fetal outcome.

Patients can be taught rapid inductions and deepening elicited by and linked to certain cues which are present when you are not. Two types of cues are useful:

1. Those cues that happen automatically (such as the squeeze of the blood pressure cuff, contractions, conversations, examinations, etc.), which have been discussed earlier. I do not include the beeping of the fetal monitor, since it can be a source of anxiety for the mother. In general, I de-emphasize the sounds of the fetal monitor and assign it a minor role. For example, I might say:

> You already know that there are so many sounds in those labor rooms and you really don't need to bother with them, because there are professionals who are trained to know what they mean. So you can just relax and leave to others what is their job. Your only job is to use every opportunity to rest up, so you will be ready for the next step. And all those sounds can just lull you into deeper comfort – like a gentle wave, or a gentle breeze.

2. Those created by the practitioner and patient. I find pressure on a shoulder most useful, especially when coupled with exhalation; squeezing of a hand, putting thumb and forefinger together, etc., are also effective. Such cues can then be used by the patient herself or reinforced by her coach.

If the patient agrees, hypnoanesthesia can be created, which can resemble the characteristics of spinal anesthesia, in that there is no sensation from about the waist on down. Today, women often prefer to have a rather acute awareness of the birth, even if some discomfort should be associated with it, and some even feel deprived of the major portion of the experience if all sensation is removed. It is therefore necessary to understand the patient's wishes, expectations, and needs clearly.

By means of hypnotic approaches, another form of analgesia can be established, which allows the patient to experience the *sensations* of the delivery *without* pain.

> As you remain aware of your comfort, which you have created by (mention whatever skills she has been taught), you can at the

same time appreciate how well and easily your labor is progressing. Each time you begin to feel a new contraction arising, you can take one of those refreshing breaths, and, as you inhale, feel yourself replenishing your comfort, and as you exhale, expel whatever you don't need right then. And feeling so pleased with how well you are doing, and how every contraction is bringing you closer to holding your baby in your arms. Feeling your birth canal relaxing, and opening up ever so gently, and ever so persistently, and ever so easily . . . and responding so naturally, in just the right way, to the waves of relaxation that the contractions are sending into that area . . . on and on and on. . . .

Analgesia suggestions need to take into account the varying degree and progression of intensity of the contractions. Suggestions can be for the mother "to sleep through" the contractions, until her participation becomes necessary, "so that you can be especially strong for the important part." (Note that I do not say "the hard part.")
Toward the end of labor, the mother will be asked to push. She can be prepared with suggestions regarding "pushing."

. . . and when the midwife or doctor tells you that it is time to push, you will be so rested and will have gathered so much energy . . . that you will find it very easy to push in just the right way, at just the right time, for just the right length of time . . . feeling so in tune with your body . . . your baby . . . and your team . . . and once the contraction wanes, you can again plunge back into that relaxed state to gather even more strength for the next contraction, which may seem still so far away.

Labor coaches serve a number of important functions. In addition to offering emotional support, they can also enhance comfort by massaging, distracting, encouraging, and pacing the mother. The practitioner will need to decide when to involve the coach. An initial joint session may be helpful, but I allow the couple to make that decision. I have found that I make progress much faster when the coach is not present during the initial training. Once the patient has adequate self-hypnotic skills (usually by the second session), the coach should attend one or several training sessions, in order to become familiar with using the cues and to practice under the trainer's supervision until he or she is competent. Some couples enjoy designing their own cues. I find it very hard to predict, however, how rapidly a person will become adept at coaching. Persons who have attended Lamaze classes are sometimes more attuned to observing; on the other hand, a mother's preconceptions may either facilitate or inhibit learning. Childbirth can be a rewarding and enriching experience for a prepared mother, and this experience can be enhanced by the welcome and useful participation of the father.

Although hypnosis is assumed to be useful mainly for delivery, its use during early stages of pregnancy may benefit a number of patients. Certain patients may benefit from receiving assistance with psychological problems, such as anxiety regarding the pregnancy, or medical problems, such as hyperemesis, diet difficulties, insomnia, fatigue, and so on.

Hyperemesis (in its mild form referred to as "morning sickness"), the severe, persistent nausea and vomiting of early pregnancy, is not only extremely unpleasant and debilitating but can become a serious medical condition, occasionally even continuing until delivery and requiring intensive care admission. Hypnotic treatment can substantially improve or resolve this problem, often avoiding hospitalization. Psychological practitioners may be asked to treat these symptoms in pregnant women.

CONCLUSIONS

We often underestimate the degree of distress patients experience in the period surrounding a medical procedure. Patients need to be able to use strategies that can alter negative perceptions and experiences of their condition, of the planned treatment, and of their own role within that context. This can result in significant postprocedural benefits, including reduction of pain. Recognizing that patients are in a state of unusually high suggestibility, we can utilize this condition for their benefit: to develop a sense of competence and control, to become active participants in their treatment process, and to discover or develop new skills for coping, and for proactively influencing their recovery.

This chapter has explored a variety of hypnotic techniques which can be employed during the period surrounding medical procedures. Using surgery and anesthesia as a prototype, I have described ways by which clinicians of varying disciplines can achieve significant benefits for their patients with rather simple interventions, which are more easily accessible than is commonly assumed. Very little time is required to achieve substantial benefits for patients undergoing traumatic medical procedures. This fact is of particular importance to physicians, who can simply incorporate the majority of the approaches I have described into routine interactions with their patients.

APPENDIX

Demonstration 9.1
Rehearsal of the Surgical Experience: Demonstration

In this example, the surgery is viewed from the perspective of a point in the future when recovery will have already occurred. Sensations that would normally be frightening, disturbing, or distracting are utilized to enhance the patient's state of comfort and sense of control.

And I wonder how surprised you will be – and I really don't know when, *after* your operation – it might be a month later, or a week, or a few days, or somewhere in between – when you look back and discover . . . how much easier everything had been for you . . . than you might have expected. [*Note: No specific predictions or promises are made. It is most important NOT to suggest anything that could turn out very differently: We can't anticipate or predict medical events, but we can give the patient the option of viewing whatever does happen in a more positive light, and we can support his ability to deal with it to his best advantage.*]
I wonder if you'll remember, especially, as you had left this place today, how this relaxed, peaceful comfort stayed with you, even though you had been very awake and energetic, and how pleased you had felt with yourself for having learned new skills so quickly and easily . . . and how you had felt that wonderful sense of confidence and achievement . . . that you knew what you needed to know in order to go about what you needed to do for yourself, comfortably and confidently.
In fact, you might have even felt a sense of joyful anticipation of the *good* things in store for you . . . all the caring and pampering that was awaiting you. And, on that day after your operation . . . and I still don't know when that might have been . . . you had marveled at how quickly the time between now and the operation seemed to have gone for you.
How well you had slept those nights, whether or not you had taken some medicine [*leaving the option to the patient*]. How refreshed you had awakened in the mornings, especially the morning of your operation. And how quickly the time seemed to have gone for you, from the moment of getting up that morning, getting yourself to the hospital, changing into hospital clothes and on and on.
In fact, how, with every step that had brought you closer to

your operation, you had felt yourself becoming more comfortably relaxed – just like now. And the moment you were settling into that hospital bed, you had felt yourself taking one of those big, deep breaths [*cue*] – just like that – and you had instantly felt yourself drifting into this very kind of delicious comfort that you are feeling right now . . . even though you had been able to respond entirely appropriately to anyone who needed to communicate with you – perfectly naturally, logically, and easily. [*It is important that the patient is alert and responsive at the time just prior to the procedure, in order to be able to communicate with his caregivers.*] You had known just what to ask for . . . or about . . . and understood everything exactly the way you usually do . . . with a very clear, calm head.

And on that day after your operation – and I still don't quite know when that might have been – you looked back and marveled at how quickly and comfortably the waiting time had passed. [*This can be a very supportive suggestion, as the waiting time is often extended hours beyond the planned time, and patients can get very anxious.*] And once you were being picked up with that rolling bed to be taken to the operating room, you had again found yourself taking another one of those *deep* breaths, [*cue*] . . . the moment you had felt yourself settling on that bed, and every wiggle and jiggle of those wheels, and every bump in the road, the opening and closing of doors, and the conversations around you . . . had been just another signal [*cue*] like the feel of your breath right now, or the pressure of my hand on your shoulder [*more cues*] . . . another signal to allow you to drift into ever more peaceful comfort.

The same had happened as you settled yourself on the operating table, even though you had been able to speak to your doctors and nurses so clearly and calmly. In fact, you had become even more relaxed with every sound that your vocal chords made, and with every word your lips and tongue had formed. [*Usually, the need to communicate and speak would alert the patient. However, this suggestion supports communicating as a cue for deepening the experience.*]

And you had felt reassured when you became aware of those bright lights, all the many monitors that were being applied and attached, and that oxygen . . . how the squeeze of the blood pressure cuff and the beeping and all the other sounds were letting you know that you were very safe; knowing that all that hustle and bustle, and all the many people around you were there only to work on *your* behalf, in your best interest, to make things safe and comfortable for *you*, so that you could just relax into your very own comfort, with nothing to bother, and nothing to disturb.

These suggestions are so "generic" that they are applicable to practically all interventional situations for which a patient might be prepared. Beyond this point it is difficult to continue in such a general way because, as the anesthetic approach varies, situations will also vary.

For patients undergoing general anesthesia I would now move into a description of the anesthetic induction, intubation, intraoperative sensations, termination of anesthesia, and extubation. For those receiving other types of anesthesia, I would rehearse those experiences. Though this is possible for someone who is not the anesthesiologist to do, it is not easy. It requires a good deal of personal preparation to create plausible, meaningful suggestions. One more generic approach (still using a future perspective) might be:

As you look back on that day and marvel at how good it had felt settling yourself comfortably on that operating table; feeling so pleased that you had taken the opportunity to discuss with your doctors everything that you had needed to know about this particular time, that you had discussed with the anesthesiologist whatever questions you might have had. So that, when you felt the anesthetic medicine taking effect [*Because this suggestion is so generic it can include any type of anesthesia: block, conduction, intravenous or general.*] you could welcome it for the good things it would do for you, to augment the comfort which you had already created for yourself and to work in conjunction with your own skills.

[*The suggestion of welcoming the medicine is a very important one for the following reason: I have observed that patients in a hypnotic state immediately recognize when medication is given. Because it creates a feeling very different from the hypnotic state, patients perceive it as something foreign or strange, and may become startled. If not prepared for this experience, patients may spontaneously alert from the hypnotic experience, to explore what is happening. Similarly, they may resist the sedating effect of the medication, requiring larger doses to be used. This is, of course, counterproductive. Consequently, I usually let patients know when I begin to inject medication.*]

And you could stay in this safe anesthetic state throughout the operation . . . already looking forward to waking up, feeling refreshed. You know, of course, that the noises and sounds will continue, just as before.

[*The following suggestions are intended to protect the patient from the possibly detrimental effects of intraoperative awareness.*]

In fact, there may even be some sounds that you had never heard before. But they, too, can be just another signal for even more comfort, just like the feel of your breath, or the sound of my voice, or the pressure of my hand on your shoulder. But you don't need to pay attention to anything in particular, unless you are addressed by name. Everything else can just blend together like a gentle soothing hum, like the sound of ocean waves, or gentle rain, or beautiful music . . . the words of which are so soothing.

As you know, there will be a time when the area to be operated on will be washed with a cleansing solution, and rubbed a bit. I wonder how *very comfortable* that will feel to you [*analgesia suggestions*] . . . whether it will seem like a very soothing liquid is poured over you, that can soak into the whole area to be operated on so it makes everything pleasantly without feeling . . . or *slightly numb.*

[*Unless patients have a dental phobia, they can be reminded of the feeling of local anesthetic taking effect, so that there may be "sensation for touch, but nothing bothersome."*]

(If the patient had developed loss of sensation:)

. . . or maybe it will feel kind of wooden-like, or maybe like your hands – there, but not there . . . feeling, but not feeling or comfortable in a very different way. . . . I really don't know . . . but *you* already know that there are many different ways of being comfortable. You already know that your body knows how to do a lot of things. It knows how to breathe and how to heal, because it has a lot of experience doing that . . . and a whole lot else that you may not ever have thought about . . . and you can be very glad for that. . . .

Suggestions to Decrease
Intraoperative Blood Loss

It knows how to have just the right amount of blood supply to the tissues. So, during the operation, the blood might drain away from (the area operated on) just enough so that there is not too much bleeding, so that Dr. X (the surgeon) can see very well, but just enough to form a solid, healthy clot. And then, after the operation, there will be enough blood to bring nutrients to let the healing take place quickly, easily, naturally, and comfortably, and without swelling, or seeping, or oozing, . . . and then carry away the debris most efficiently.

Preparing Patient for Easy
Postoperative Course

And I wonder – on that day after your operation – what you will remember as the biggest surprise when you heard the doctor tell you that your operation was *already* finished. Whether it was that everything seemed to have gone so much more quickly than you had expected . . . or that you felt so much more comfortable . . . with nothing to bother, and nothing to disturb . . . or that you felt so well rested, and so pleasantly alert . . . or that you felt so glad and reassured when you became aware of the pressure underneath those bandages, because it allowed you to know that everything was safely taken care of, and the healing had already begun.

Suggestions for Anti-Nausea and
Resumption of Peristalsis

Or that you were already looking forward to quenching your hunger and your thirst just as soon as your doctor would allow it . . . or that you could already feel your stomach and intestines beginning to work gently in just the right way, in just the right direction.

How you had found yourself – automatically – taking one of those big, deep breaths . . . and instantly feeling this very wonderful comfort that you are feeling right now, spreading through your whole being – body and mind. And how everything that happened – every sound, every touch, every sensation – had been just another signal, like the feel of your breath or the pressure of my hand – to allow you to feel even better.

And, as you look back and remember . . . how you had enjoyed the pampering and gentle care in the recovery room, and later, too . . . and the surprise on the faces of your nurses and doctors that you were doing so *very well.*

Encouragement to Feel Free to Ask for or Accept Medications

And how you had known just when to ask for a little bit of medicine to make your comfort even more perfect, and how quickly it had worked, how long its effect lasted . . . and how easy it was to heal. . . .

Caveat Not to Overdo

But even though you had felt so much better than most patients do after such an operation, you had appreciated the fact that you deserved the same length of time to mend fully—but that you could enjoy having that special time to yourself. [*This is an important point, because patients might overdo since they feel so well.*]

Demonstration 9.2
Examples of Verbalizations during Pre-procedure Patient Preparation

Pre-procedure Verbalizations*	*Comment*
Fear of operating room environment	
" . . . as you know, there are many sounds in the operating room . . . and you might find it very reassuring . . . to hear the hustle and bustle that goes on, . . . which lets you know that everything that is happening in that room . . . happens only for your benefit. Everyone in that room . . . is working only on your behalf . . . and to achieve the very best for you . . . and to make everything safe. . . . "	1. The patient is given **information** that there is noise in the room. But instead of allowing it to become the usual frightening experience, or telling him to disregard it (which is difficult), it is **utilized**: he is encouraged to register it, but offered the option of **interpreting** it as a basis for security. 2. Drawing attention to sounds that are guaranteed to recur, is used as a **hypnotic cue** that elicits the suggested response whenever the sounds occur/recur (even postoperatively: in PACU or ICU, on the wards) and is a **deepening strategy**. 3. Repetitions phrased slightly differently are very effective. 4. The phrase "you are safe" is the single most important statement a patient can hear.
Regarding induction of anesthesia	
" . . . when you begin to notice (feel) the anesthetic medicine (flow into your vein) . . . you can welcome it for the good things it will do for you . . . to deepen the comfort even further which you have already begun to create for yourself. . . . "	Defuses fear of the anesthetic. While placing monitors one can accomplish a relaxation exercise to which I am referring. This wording gives the patient a measure of control by "already having created his own comfort." (As induction and/or sedation is begun, this is repeated, "I am now beginning to . . . etc.")
Intubation	
" . . . once you are quite relaxed – as part of **modern, safe** anesthesia . . . and to make breathing extra safe during the operation – . . . the anesthesiologist will place a breathing tube through your mouth or nose into your windpipe. . . . It is very easy and safe to breathe this way. . . . "	Recent evidence of intra-anesthetic awareness identifies the induction period as being one of the most likely ones for awareness. Understanding intubation as **normal** and an **important safety feature** prevents the fright and psychological trauma of assuming that "something went terribly wrong" (see separate paragraph).

*These verbalizations can be used with or without hypnosis.

Demonstration 9.2
Continued

Pre-procedure Verbalizations	Comment

Ventilation

" . . . And when you hear that huffing and puffing of the breathing machine, . . . and when you feel your chest rise and fall . . . with those long easy (!) breaths, that the machine helps you take. . . . "

(timed to ventilation when used intra-operatively)
The breaths are "easy" and the machine "helps"; it does not force or overpower. (When . . . then: see later.)

Paralysis

" . . . it lets you know that you can relax even more . . . because the machine is doing even the work of breathing for you. . . . And all these sounds let you know . . . that there is someone watching these sounds . . . and **watching you** . . . to make sure that everything works as perfectly as possible . . . and that you are safe. . . . "

double meaning:
1. Indirect suggestion to relax all along.
2. The patient will have been informed of muscle "relaxation" (euphemism for paralysis), which can be an extremely frightening experience when awareness occurs, because patients may assume that something was wrong and no-one has noticed. This sentence defuses such an assumption and prevents potentially serious consequences.

Reduction of anxiety: future orientation

" . . . I don't know whether you will be more **surprised** . . . when you hear someone tell you that your operation is **already completed** . . . that everything will seem to have gone so much **more quickly** than you might have expected . . . or more surprised that you can wake up so **easily** . . . or even more surprised that you can feel so much **more comfortable** than you might have thought. . . . "

1. Unexpectedly "good" things **can** happen.
2. **Double (or multiple) binds.**
3. No promises are made, but **possibilities are offered** which the patient may chose to take – and most patients do.
4. **Time progression** beyond the feared operation: "She expects me to survive this and wake up." Without having to bring up the possibility of dying under anesthesia – a common unverbalized fear – this sentence counters that concern.

Pain control

" . . . and when you feel that **pressure** underneath those bandages . . . as you are waking up . . . you can be so **relieved** . . . because it lets you know that your operation is completed . . . and that **healing** has already begun . . . and that you are **safe** . . . "

1. **When . . . then statements** are very useful: They tie a fact to a positive suggestion.
2. Reinterpret something noxious as something less so: **pain as pressure.**

(Continued)

Demonstration 9.2
Continued

Pre-procedure Verbalizations	*Comments*
" . . . It also lets you know that this is a **good time** to let all those muscles go limp and **relax** . . . because, as you know, when you have a bruise or little cut on your hand it **feels a whole lot better** when you let that hand go limp . . . than when you make a tight fist. . . . "	3. Gives the patient something **he can do** for himself; i.e. removes him from a passive victim status to that of an **active participant**. 4. **Analogy** to something **very familiar**, but **much less noxious** (bruised hand vs. surgical incision), and offers simple, logical remedy.

Prevention of nausea; return of peristalsis and bowel function

" . . . and I wonder what it will be that you will **look forward to MOST** . . . to help quench your hunger and your thirst after surgery . . . so that you can hardly wait for Dr. X to allow you to take that first delicious sip. I wonder whether you will be thinking about your **favorite food** as you go into the operating room and waking up in the recovery room; that you can **already taste** how you will relish every sip that trickles down your throat so deliciously . . . and the flavor and texture of every bite you eat . . . so you can already hear those pleasant gurgling sounds in your stomach and intestines. . . . How you will enjoy eating just the right amount that is good for you—not too much, and not too little—and how your stomach and intestines will digest them in the most perfect and efficient way . . . and pass it on in the right direction . . . and how good it feels to feel the food being passed along gently. . . . "	Hunger, thirst, and peristalsis are excellent **anti-nausea suggestions**, because hunger and nausea cannot co-exist. (Note: Nausea and vomiting are accompanied by retrograde peristalsis; hunger and thirst by antegrade peristalsis.) I add the **caveat** "as soon as your doctor permits it," since there have been cases of consuming food earlier than appropriate after such a suggestion and of overeating after suggestions of being ravenously hungry right away. Both can be followed by serious consequences. "Right direction" (vomiting is reverse peristalsis!)

Catheter discomfort

" . . . When you become aware of the catheter in your bladder . . . you can be so **relieved** . . . knowing that your operation is **safely taken care of** . . . and your **recovery has already begun** . . . and it is good to know . . . that your bladder is being **emptied automatically** . . . without you having to find a bathroom. . . . In fact, you can just let all of those muscles down	"When . . . then . . . ": Catheters are often more distressing than operative pain but can be surprisingly well tolerated when pre- and intra-procedural suggestions have been given. "Relieved" is **open-ended**: Relieved of what? (of having to go to the bathroom? of urine? worries? of pain?) The patient will interpret it in a way most suitable to his or her needs and situa-

Demonstration 9.2
Continued

Pre-procedure Verbalizations	Comment

there, know ... that they, too, can **just relax and let go and go limp** ... for now ... because there is nothing you need to hold back right then. ... "

tion. "For now" and "right then" address the fact that patients may have inadequate control of urine after the catheter is removed because of continuing inappropriately to keep "those muscles too relaxed."

Return of bladder function

" ... but you can already **look forward** to the moment – only a few days after the operation – when your doctor decides it is time for the catheter to be removed ... By then everything down there will have **healed** (enough) ... that your bladder will be able to **work just right** ... so that it will let you know when there is **just the right amount** of urine in your bladder to empty it ... easily and naturally ... **not too much and not too little urine in it** ... **just right.**"

Following certain pelvic operations, it can take some time for the bladder to resume normal function. Need for re-catheterization is common and often a problem.

This suggestion is very effective and many patients never need to be re-catheterized after removal of the original catheter.

Prevention of pulmonary complications

" ... That pressure underneath those bandages can also be a reminder ... that this is a good time to take a **deep healthy breath** every once in a while ... to fill your lungs with oxygen ... so you can **heal even more quickly** ... And, after you have held that breath for a while ... you can let it out with a **sigh of relief.** ... "
(*It is a good idea to practice this just once preoperatively*)
" ... And I wonder ... how many things will remind you to take such a nice breath ... whether it will be someone's TV ... or the sunshine ... or the telephone ... or some nice flowers ... I really don't know. ... "

Deep breathing is important postoperatively but often hard to achieve. A Valsalva's maneuver (holding a big breath) is most effective to expand atalectatic lungs and is identical to exercises usually ordered by means of equipment (such as incentive spirometers). This statement contains an **instruction and incentive**, puts the patient in **control**, gives him/her an **active role**, and includes **self-perpetuating** suggestions for relaxation and comfort ("sigh of relief"). It is self-perpetuating because the patient will, of course, become aware of "the pressure underneath the bandages" over and over again, which is the posthypnotic cue for a deep breath, etc. (plus some of the other cues mentioned).
(*Can be reiterated in the recovery room during any stage of awareness.*)
(*Continued*)

Demonstration 9.2
Continued

Pre-procedure Verbalizations	*Comment*
Reduce helplessness/increase control	
" ... To help you relax even more, you can ask the nurses to put a pillow under your (knees/arm, etc.) or to help you change position, or turn ... "	Gives patient even **additional control** (control over nurses!); further reduces helplessness. *(Reiterate in recovery room)*
Future orientation	
" ... You might be **very surprised** when you look back a few days after the operation ... how much **easier** everything may seem to have gone for you ... than you might have expected ... and so **pleased** all along with how **surprised and pleased your doctors** and nurses had been ... with your **quick and easy recovery** ... so that you could really **enjoy** the good care and **getting well** ... that pampering ... and looking forward to taking very good care of yourself ... when you got home ... knowing just how much was **good for you** to do ... and when it was time for a rest ... and feeling so **pleased with yourself and your success** ... and getting stronger and **stronger** ... and **better** and better ... in all kinds of ways ... every day ... and every hour of every day ... and every minute of every hour ... and on and on like that. ... "	**No promises** are made that there will not be anything unpleasant, but the patient is given a number of choices and **opportunities to reinterpret** sensations and experiences positively if he so chooses and to **focus away from the negative.** *(Reiterate in recovery room)* A **caveat** is included in these suggestions without allowing it to have a negative connotations: Often patients do so well that they have a tendency to overdo. Should this be the case, they are reminded that their body **deserves** the same care and time to heal that other people are given, except that they **can enjoy** it so much more because they can be so much more comfortable. Ego-strengthening suggestions are included.

10

BURN PAIN

David R. Patterson

I WAS RELATIVELY new to the staff of the burn center when I was paged for the consult. Chuck, an elderly man with a huge burn, was refusing to cooperate with dressing changes. Even though his surgeons had administered high doses of morphine and Valium to him, Chuck still experienced the dressing changes as excruciatingly painful.

More analgesic medication would be unsafe for him. Also, if Chuck did not allow his wounds to be treated soon, he would likely deteriorate; untreated wounds in such instances often become lethal. When I explained this to Chuck, as had other staff members, he pleaded that we "just let me die." He said that the pain was too terrible for him ever to go into "that room" again. Privately, I doubted that anything could help Chuck control his pain, even as I tried to think of how best to help Chuck with this difficult dilemma.

As Chuck's experience illustrates, if there is a pain more excruciating than a severe burn injury, it is the pain that results from the treatment of the burn. Debridement of the wound involves scrubbing away the burned tissue to give the new, very raw tissue a chance to grow and heal the wound. As you might imagine, the scrubbing of this tissue is extremely painful. Similarly, the frequent dressing changes also stimulate damaged tissue, resulting in excruciating pain.

Not so long ago, most severely burned patients died of their injuries, and the pain of burn treatment was not much of an issue. Now, however, because the quality of burn care is improving, increasing numbers of people are surviving their burns, leaving them with the challenge of enduring the prolonged treatment that often follows (Currerie, Braun, & Shires, 1980). People who would have died from their burns a few years ago now face months of hospital care, including almost daily painful procedures. Unfortunately, the enthusiasm in the field of burn care that has been directed towards decreasing mortality has not been extended toward reducing suffering in burn survivors.

Burn injuries are a fairly common form of trauma, and are often accompanied by dire social problems. In the United States alone, an estimated 70,000 emergency room visits and 60,000 hospitalizations result from burn injuries annually (Patterson, Everett, Bombardier et al., 1993). Efforts to reduce pain and suffering in survivors are complicated by the social ills that so often accompany their injuries. People hospitalized for burn injuries are more likely to have diagnoses of personality disorders and histories of psychiatric illness, substance abuse, homelessness, and unemployment than the general population. All too often, burn injuries result from physical assault or abuse. Once hospitalized, patients may experience a number of psychiatric symptoms that can exacerbate pain or complicate its treatment. Our review of the literature (Patterson, Everett, Bombardier et al., 1993) indicated that estimates of delirium among burn patients range between 19 and 57 percent, moderate depression from 23 to 61 percent, general anxiety from 13 to 47 percent, and post-traumatic stress disorder 30 percent. The presence of subclinical anxiety is likely universal for those undergoing burn treatment. Since all of these psychological variables interact powerfully with pain, it is useful for the clinician to be aware of their presence.

Optimal pain control for patients with burns requires at least a rudimentary understanding of the care of this type of trauma. Patients with large burns undergo dramatic metabolic changes, requiring fluid resuscitation and often massive caloric intake. A burn of any substantial size has the potential to become a large, infected open wound. Left untreated, such wounds can result in substantial disfigurement, amputation, or death. Many burn centers aggressively treat deep burn injuries through the use of early surgical excision and grafting (Burke, Quinby, & Bondoc, 1976; Engrav, Heimbach, Reus, Harnar, & Marvin, 1983). Such care strategies typically involve frequent wound cleanings (i.e., once or twice a day), as well as multiple surgeries.

Patients with burns in their joints will likely show dramatic con-tractures without the use of splints and frequent, aggressive range of motion exercises. The least painful experience for burn patients is to remain undisturbed until their wounds are no longer sensitive. How-ever, such passive approaches to burn care will result in poor long-term outcomes, if not higher mortality rates. Consequently, most burn cen-ters typically perform multiple intrusive procedures on a patient every day. Although general anesthesia can be used for major burn surger-ies, providing such interventions for every medical procedure would be too dangerous and costly. Finally, optimal burn care typically requires that patients undergo multiple, invasive daily procedures without gen-eral anesthesia, a pattern that can last from a period of a few days up to several months.

A patient with a severe burn is unique in several ways, even when compared to patients who have suffered other forms of physical trauma. Every trauma patient will experience pain. But a burn injury is different, in that its care requires repeated procedures which usually stimulate intense noxious feelings. As such, patients with severe burns often experience excruciating pain every day, sometimes for many months.

When large areas of skin are burned, the body undergoes massive defensive metabolic changes. For example, the caloric needs of a per-son with large area burns are equivalent to those of one who is continu-ously running in place for 24 hours. Fluid requirements are similarly unusually demanding. The physiology of a severe burn, as well as the need for aggressive medical care, often causes substantial and prolonged changes in a patient's sensorium. When a burn patient awakens, he or she must begin to cope with the life-threatening nature of the injury, as well as the potential loss of others' life and of property that may have accompanied a fire.

The unique elements of burn injury continue to affect patients well after they are discharged from the hospital. Visible disfigurement may create social stigmatization, sexual problems, and a tendency to be-come socially isolated. Burned joints may contract, thereby impairing the patient's movement. No other physical trauma consistently results in the intensity and quality of pain with which burn patients must contend over such long periods of time. Moreover, such trauma often is accompanied by fears of dying, delirium, posttraumatic stress disor-der and depression. Consequently, burn injuries result in an array of physical and emotional complications, the extent of which is unrivaled by most other forms of trauma.

Effective pain control requires an understanding of the stages of burn care as well as a basic knowledge of care strategies. Patients with very severe burn injuries go through three phases of care: *intensive care, acute care*, and *rehabilitation*. Those with less severe burns may require only the latter two phases.

Intensive care is typically oriented towards patients whose injuries are life-threatening. During this phase patients are undergoing a variety of aggressive procedures and often show changes in their sensorium. During the acute phase of care, patients are no longer in a life-threatening situation and are more alert. However, they are still undergoing multiple procedures and, given their improved alertness, are more capable of being emotionally threatened by the impact of their injuries. The rehabilitation phase occurs once patients are discharged; although patients in this stage of care may not be experiencing acute noxious stimulation, chronic pain and emotional stress are still potential problems. The optimal application of hypnotic treatment to burn care varies substantially with the phase of care.

THE NATURE OF BURN PAIN

Understanding the nature of burn pain is prerequisite to using hypnotic treatment. Of particular importance is the difference between *procedural pain* and *background pain*. Procedural pain refers to what patients experience as they undergo the range of medical and therapeutic interventions described above. Such pain is typically acute, intense and of limited duration. The onset of procedural pain is almost always predictable, thus making a psychological tool such as hypnosis an ideal adjunct for its control. Background pain refers to that pain experienced by patients while they are relatively immobile and are between procedures. In contrast to procedural pain, background pain is of lower intensity, longer duration, and is less predictable.

The literature is surprisingly scarce when it comes to defining qualitative and quantitative aspects of burn pain. Patients rate their pain as being severe or excruciating in spite of receiving opioid drugs (Perry, Heidrich & Ramos, 1981). Pain ratings vary widely not only from patient to patient, but also over the course of treatment for a given patient (Choiniere, Melzack, Rondeau, Girard, & Paquin, 1989). Additionally, burn pain is often linked with psychological symptoms such as posttraumatic stress disorder or depression (Klein & Charlton, 1980; Perry, Cella, Falkenberg, Heidrich, & Goodwin, 1987). Our own work has demonstrated that burn pain is not correlated with the size or the depth of a burn (Patterson, Marvin, Campbell, Everett, & Heimbach, 1993). Thus, a patient with a superficial burn may experience more pain than another patient with a deeper wound. Further, patients with a small burn area sometimes report more pain than those with large surface area burns. The distress of burn pain cannot be predicted by the nature and extent of burn injury.

In spite of the exciting potential applications of hypnotic treatment, opioid-based medications justifiably remain the cornerstone of treatment for burn pain. Opioid drugs are typically tailored to the characteristics of burn pain described above (Patterson & Sharar, in press). For background pain, patients ideally receive long-acting opioids, such as time-release morphine or methadone, or self-administered morphine through a patient controlled analgesia machine. For procedural pain, a good treatment plan will involve shorter-acting, more potent opioids such as hydromorphone or a stronger form of synthetic morphine. The latter types of drugs produce a powerful analgesic effect, but they are metabolized quickly and will not cause prolonged lethargy. Opioids are often accompanied by tranquilizers, which can reduce anxiety that usually accompanies a burn injury (Patterson & Sharar, in press).

In any case, it is important that those responsible for pain control in a burn center do not defer the appropriate use of pain medication. It is well documented that patients with acute pain, both from burn and other forms of injury, are undermedicated (Angell, 1982; Melzack, 1990). Clinicians who are enthusiastic advocates of hypnotic treatment must be careful not to contribute to this problem by suggesting that the beneficial effects of hypnotic treatment negate the utility of opioid drugs.

Our experimental investigations lead me to conclude that, despite the importance of opioid drugs, they do not offer a fully satisfying treatment for burn pain. People vary in their degree of analgesic responsiveness to opioids, and many will experience aversive reactions. As mentioned, moreover, patients report high levels of pain in spite of receiving morphine. State-of-the-art burn care involves a variety of approaches to pain, one of which is hypnotic treatment.

The importance of treating burn pain (as well as the burn itself) is becoming increasingly apparent. Over the past few decades there have been a number of studies indicating that aggressive treatment of acute pain can prevent a number of deleterious physiological effects and improve health outcome (Patterson & Sharar, in press). Our own research has demonstrated that, in patients hospitalized for burn care, better pain control is associated with more favorable adjustment after leaving the hospital (Ptacek, Patterson, Montgomery, & Heimbach, 1995). Both practical and humanitarian reasons point to the importance of effective control of burn pain.

COGNITIONS AND SUGGESTIONS

My colleagues and I have discussed cognitive-behavioral approaches to burn pain elsewhere (Everett, Patterson, & Chen, 1990; Patterson, 1992). Exploring these approaches can be useful in formulating suggestions for reducing burn pain via hypnotic treatment. In previous discussion, we have divided psychological approaches to burn pain into the areas of *cognitive, preparatory*, and *behavioral* interventions.

The prolific literature on cognitive-behavioral approaches to psychotherapy has been extended to the area of pain control as well (Fordyce, 1976; Holzman & Turk, 1986). Patients undergoing burn treatment will certainly have thoughts about their experience, many of which can be altered in a way that positively affects their level of comfort. As a first step to using hypnotic treatment, it is useful to discern what thoughts patients have about their care and what general cognitive styles they use when faced with aversive procedures.

As a general rule, patients approach aversive medical procedures with one of two cognitive styles. Either they are *repressors* and wish to know as little as possible about what awaits them or they are *sensitizers* and cope by gaining as much information as they can (Everett et al., 1990). The cognitive styles of patients can be assessed by asking them how they approach medical procedures (e.g., "If you have to go through a new procedure with the doctor or the dentist, how much information do you like to have beforehand?" "When the nurses are working on you, do you pay attention to what they do or would you just as soon let your mind wander?"). Patients who are repressors will likely respond better to distraction techniques. Examples might include pleasant imagery (e.g., "during your dressing change you will find yourself relaxing at the beach"), dissociation ("at the time your wounds are scrubbed you will discover that you are able to float away from the experience, to be as far removed as you would like"), time distortion, or amnesia.

Patients who are sensitizers may respond poorly to such dissociative suggestions, demonstrating instead a hypervigilant approach to the procedure. Rather than ignoring these patients' cognitive style, we tailor suggestions to the style and facilitate their focus on physical sensations, thereby allowing them to gain more control over their experiences. For example, the patient may be told:

As the nurse continues to clean your wound, notice what you are experiencing. Your first thought may be that the sensation you feel is pain. That is a reasonable first impression. But pay attention to the sensation, and see if you can notice other sensations besides, or in addition to, your pain. For instance, maybe what you feel is a burning sensation that is not necessarily pain. Just because you feel a burning sensation does not mean that you have to feel pain. In fact, the more you pay attention to your wound, the more you realize that you are experiencing a variety of sensations, many of which are actually not unpleasant at all. And the more you pay attention, the more you realize that you can change the sensation you are experiencing. Just as you cannot hold a single thought in your head forever, you cannot be aware of merely a single sensation . . . eventually your experience has to change.

Through such suggestions, patients are allowed to remain focused on the procedure while being given suggestions for analgesia within the context of their confronting approach.

There is a substantial body of research indicating that providing patients with preparatory information about impending medical procedures can reduce their pain and anxiety. Everett et al. (1990) divide preparatory information used in burn care into two categories, *procedural information* and *sensory information*. Procedural information refers to what will happen to patients as they undergo a procedure, while sensory information refers to what they may feel at various stages of the intervention. Principles of hypnotic treatment can be useful in insuring that this information is given to the patient in the most beneficial way. For example, a patient may be told that he or she will "experience a stinging sensation when the antiseptic solution is applied to the burn wound." Since people interpret information quite literally, both while experiencing hypnosis or when under stress, adding the statement, " . . . that will last for a brief period of time . . . " might facilitate the patient's comfort. Using hypnotic suggestion to maximize comfort would take this statement a step further. For example, the patient could be told,

. . . You might experience a stinging sensation when the antiseptic solution is applied that will last for a brief period of time. When you feel this sensation, it will mean that your dressing change is over except for having the nurses wrap you up in comfortable bandages. Perhaps you will be so happy to know that you have gotten through your dressing change that you won't even feel the stinging sensation.

The third area of cognitive-behavioral approaches to burn pain involves behavioral techniques. Behavioral techniques can be divided into stimulus (classical) and reinforcement (operant) conditioning. An understanding of classical conditioning is helpful for understanding the use of hypnotic treatment with burn pain. Considering the application of operant conditioning, on the other hand, can help identify circumstances when hypnotic treatment will be less useful.

The principles of classical conditioning help us predict behavior if we are able to identify the stimulus that elicits the response. In the case of burn pain, patients undergo a series of highly aversive procedures that can be paired with identifiable stimuli. The sights, sounds and smells of a treatment room can elicit anxiety and suffering, if not actual pain, in patients awaiting wound care. This is particularly evident with children, who have been known to cry hysterically when catching sight of a nurse wearing green scrubs. Behavior therapies often treat phobias by pairing conditioned stimuli with a relaxation response. With hypnosis, stimuli that become associated with anxiety and burn pain can become tied to suggestions for comfort and analgesia. Thus, a patient who is being prepared for a painful dressing change can be told that:

> ... When you find yourself lying in the metal tub and the nurse begins to pull at your dressings, all of the comfort you are feeling now will come rushing back.... All of the sights, sounds and smells of the room for dressing changes will become reminders that you can be absolutely relaxed during your wound care.

Thus, stimuli that would have ordinarily elicited anxiety instead become cues for analgesia.

Operant reinforcement principles provide less guidance for structuring suggestions but are useful in predicting situations where hypnotic treatment will be of little benefit. For example, some patients repeatedly complain of pain between procedures, despite heavy doses of medication. This pattern of behavior often becomes more evident in the case of background rather than procedural pain. Since background pain can almost always be controlled with regular, sufficient doses of opioid drugs, in patients who persistently complain of such pain there are often factors in addition to noxious input contributing to their pain behaviors. The relief from opioid or other comfort-inducing drugs, the satisfaction of dependency needs, or the gratification from solicitous behavior from family members may all be more potent in evoking suffering (to gain these rewards) than noxious stimulation from the actual burn injury itself. Hypnotic treatment focused on analgesia may have little to contribute in these circumstances, since it is focused on reduction of pain awareness, rather than on what may be the patient's actual needs. In these cases, providing time-contingent medication regimens or addressing the patient's emotional needs may be more effective approaches to relieving the patient's suffering.

GENERAL CONSIDERATIONS FOR THE USE OF HYPNOSIS WITH BURN PAIN

Review of the Literature on Hypnosis in Burn Treatment

There has been a surprising number of reports published on the use of hypnotic treatment with burn patients. The earliest, and likely most influential, was a report by Crasilneck and his colleagues in 1955. The authors reported that they were able not only to reduce pain in six out of eight patients studied, but also to increase appetite and mobility in some patients. Further, the clinician's work only required an average of one and a half hours; subsequent inductions could be reinforced by the medical staff.

At least 14 reports on the use of hypnosis with burn pain have been published since Crasilneck, Stirman, Wilson et al.'s (1955) original report. All of the findings of these reports have been positive. When my colleagues and I (Patterson et al., 1987) reviewed these studies we found that six of the twelve reports indicated 100 percent success rates, three reported rates between 62.5 and 75 percent and the remaining three reported statistically significant results. Unfortunately, all but two of the studies were case reports with no form of objective measurement. There are two notable exceptions: Wakeman and Kaplan (1978) conducted a well-designed study revealing that patients who used hypnosis required less pain medication than a control group; and Hammond, Heye, and Grant (1983) reported a significant analgesic effect when a sun lamp was used to induce sunburn and patients served as their own controls. The other reports, while inadequately designed, yielded some interesting clinical information. For example, Finer and Nylen (1961) reported that one patient was able to undergo five major burn surgeries with hypnosis as the sole anesthetic. Schafer (1975) found that anxious children and adolescents were the least likely to respond well to this technique. This finding mirrors our own clinical experience indicating that if children are exposed to a number of painful procedures without adequate analgesia, their anxiety level reaches a point where almost any intervention, including hypnotic treatment, fails to control their pain or calm them down. On the other hand, a series of studies has also reported that children, when reached early enough, have a good response to hypnosis in the burn unit (Patterson et al., 1987). (Sam LeBaron and Lonnie Zeltzer discuss the treatment of children's pain in Chapter 11.)

Our own projects have attempted to build upon this wealth of clinical information and to remedy some of the deficiencies we have observed in the study designs. In addition to the typical absence of a control group, the concerns we had with most of these studies included: (1) the lack of any objective measurement, (2) the lack of a description of the hypnotic interventions clear enough to replicate, (3) no report of the duration of treatments and number of procedures patients have undergone, and (4) no description of the type of pain experienced by patients. With respect to the latter point, it is unclear from these studies if the focus of interventions was on procedural or background pain.

In the first of a series of studies, we addressed some of these problems by investigating whether Rapid Induction Analgesia (RIA) (Barber, 1977) would result in a decrease in visual analogue scale (VAS) (Gift, 1989) ratings of pain for burn patients undergoing multiple wound care procedures (Patterson, Questad, & deLateur, 1989). We reported that a group of eight patients with burn injuries showed a significant drop in pain ratings after hypnotic treatment, a decrease that was not seen in a group of fourteen control patients. Unfortunately, the study design did not include a randomly assigned control group. Consequently, we conducted an experiment in which patients with burns were randomly assigned to groups that received either hypnotic treatment, pain medication alone, or an attention-control visit from a psychologist (Patterson, Everett, Burns, & Marvin, 1992).

Consistent with our predictions, patients receiving hypnotic treatment in addition to their pain medication demonstrated greater drops in their VAS scores than did either of the control groups. In these two studies, patients were entered into the protocol because they had high initial pain scores (i.e., VAS > 5). However, when we attempted to replicate these findings with all patients admitted for burn care rather than simply those with high pain scores, the pain scores of patients who had been hypnotized were no different from those of controls (Everett, Patterson, Burns, Montgomery, & Heimbach, 1993). We concluded that hypnotic treatment might be more effective for burn patients who have high levels of pain. Understandably, patients may be more receptive to a new technique such as hypnotic treatment when faced with extreme discomfort.

In summary, there have been a number of very compelling case reports suggesting the analgesic effects hypnotic treatment can have on burn pain. Unfortunately, these reports are seriously limited in what one might conclude from them. While more controlled studies still indicate that hypnotic treatment can be effective, the results are not nearly as dramatic as those reported in the early clinical literature.

Response to Hypnotic Suggestions

One of the most replicated findings in the experimental hypnosis literature is that people vary in the degree to which they are responsive to hypnosis (Hilgard, 1967b). Recent summaries suggest that most people fall into the moderate range of responsivity to hypnotic suggestion (Bates, 1993). The degree to which people respond on tests of responsivity has been found to be an important variable in the experimental pain control literature. As would be expected, subjects scoring higher in responsivity show the greatest reduction of experimentally induced pain (Bowers & LeBaron, 1986; Hilgard, 1980). However, this relationship has not been found to be as straightforward when clinical pain reduction has been the dependent variable (Gillett & Coe, 1984; Tenenbaum, Kurtz, & Bienias, 1990). In fact, the evidence suggests that, overall, subjects scoring low on responsivity might still be candidates for hypnotic treatment. The usefulness of the variable in predicting clinical effect remains unclear (Patterson, Goldberg, & Ehde, in press).

Responsivity is a difficult variable to study on the burn unit. A surprising number of patients lack the arm mobility to carry out suggestions required by these scales, such as the Hypnotic Induction Profile (Spiegel & Spiegel, 1987); further, medications, fatigue, and physiological changes can hinder the administration of longer scales such as the Stanford Scale of Hypnotic Susceptibility (Weitzenhoffer & Hilgard, 1959). Even though such variables also likely affect the clinical use of hypnotic treatment on the burn unit, clinical interventions can often provide the flexibility necessary to work around them. In any case, the variable of responsivity has received only a modicum of investigation as it relates to burn pain. While it does play some role in determining which patients have an analgesic response, other variables, such as the willingness to demonstrate new modes of behavior in response to excruciating pain, are likely to be more powerful in the clinical context.

Burn Wound Healing

The possibility that hypnotic treatment can attenuate the progression of a burn injury or facilitate wound healing has been enthusiastically discussed. There is a precedent for this notion in the dermatological literature: DuBrueuil and Spanos (1993) concluded that there is support for the effectiveness of hypnotic treatment for warts. Ewin (1986) has argued that hypnotic treatment can have a similarly dramatic effect on burn injuries. He contends that by intervening early enough (typically in the emergency room), the clinician can prevent a first degree (superficial) burn from progressing to a second degree (partial thickness) burn, or a second degree burn from progressing to a third degree (full thickness) burn. One rationale is that the inflammatory process is mediated by the central nervous system and, therefore, it can be influenced by processes such as hypnosis, which may involve such mediation (Chapman, Goodell, & Woff, 1959).

Ewin has reported a number of case studies to support his contention that the progression of burn injuries can be slowed or stopped by the early application of hypnotic treatment (Ewin, 1979, 1986). He supports his argument by citing studies which suggest that blister formation can be stimulated through hypnotic suggestion. However, empirical support for blister formation through hypnosis is questionable at best (Spanos, McNeil, & Henderikus, 1982). Furthermore, others have argued that skin inflammation and blister formation are separate processes; one cannot be used as evidence for the existence of the other (Van der Does & Van Dyck, 1989).

In his hypnotic interventions, Ewin instructs patients to "cool" the affected area. In a controlled study, Moore and Kaplan (1983) instructed patients with bilateral thigh burns to warm one leg in order to stimulate blood flow. Four out of the five subjects demonstrated accelerated healing in the limb upon which suggestions were focused. Thus, their isolated but promising findings were associated with vasodilation rather than vasoconstriction. Although some of the published case reports have showed promising results, Van der Does and Van Dyck (1989) were skeptical in their review of the effects of hypnotic treatment and wound healing. They argue that the findings are based on a very limited number of patients and that a body of experimental studies in support of these clinical results does not exist. The research in this area is admittedly inadequate, with exaggerated claims for the success of hypnotic interventions. In order to adequately test the efficacy of hypnotic treatment, we need controlled investigations of the effects of such interventions on wound healing, with sufficiently large samples of subjects with both high and low responsivity.

Contraindications for Hypnotic Treatment

There are at least two types of patients that appear consistently to have a poor response on the burn unit. One group includes those patients who, as a result of religious beliefs, find the concept of hypnotic treatment to be unacceptable or threatening. I have encountered several patients who literally regard hypnosis as the "devil's work." Attempts to convince patients otherwise usually result only in increased hostility. Unless hypnotic treatment can be encouraged by a trusted representative of the patient's religion, pursuing this treatment with such patients will be counterproductive. The other patients who rarely respond to burn unit hypnotic treatment are those who are demonstrating drug-seeking behavior. Such patients have typically lost touch with the sensory aspect of their pain, and their behavior is driven by a quest for the emotional comfort of opioid medication. Since the issue with these patients is more the emotionally comforting effects of drugs than the need for analgesia, hypnotic treatment will often be a wasted effort. Such patients will typically show little interest in hypnotic treatment and, if they do, will not cooperate well with the procedure.

Another potentially problematic group consists of patients whose pain behavior on the burn unit is driven by dependency needs in addition to noxious sensory stimulation. For such patients, it is the attention of the staff and family members that motivates much of their pain behavior. Eliminating pain may represent the loss of an important and real – and probably rare – source of nurturing for these individuals. Such patients may enthusiastically welcome the presence of the clinician because of the attention he or she will provide. However, the success of the procedure will be thwarted by the dynamics described above. With such patients, efforts to address dependency needs directly are more likely to be effective than hypnosis focused on analgesia. In this respect, the visit of a clinician who acknowledges the patient's current emotional state may satisfy the patient's needs better than one who focuses on reducing pain. Further, scheduling the visits regularly, rather than in response to patient distress, can prevent the patient from generating symptoms that will insure a visit from the staff.

There are other burn unit patients for whom hypnotic treatment simply is not effective; why such treatment fails may not always be apparent. An important principle to keep in mind is that no pain intervention, including hypnotic treatment, works for all patients. Even the most powerful opioid drugs do not work with all patients on the burn unit. I stress this point because I have occasionally encountered clinicians who argue that hypnotic treatment works for all burn patients and should be the treatment of choice in this setting. Claims of this nature are likely to engender justified skepticism among burn unit team members. A clinician who understands the limitations of hypnotic treatment and the need for multiple pain treatment modalities will be more likely to generate the trust of both patients and staff.

APPLICATIONS OF HYPNOSIS
TO BURN CARE

Preparing the Patient

Patients who are hospitalized for the care of severe burn injuries are among the most receptive to hypnotic treatment a clinician will ever encounter. They are faced with the prospect of enduring a number of extremely unpleasant procedures that can cause severe pain and anxiety in the most stoic of individuals. On the burn unit, offers to perform hypnotic treatment are often met with the comment, "I'll try anything to get rid of this pain." My work with hypnotic treatment has primarily been done in the Pacific Northwest region where independence and hardiness are especially regarded as virtues. Nevertheless, such stalwarts as loggers, farmers, and salmon fishermen have almost always greeted the idea of hypnotic treatment in an open manner, if not with enthusiasm.

A number of steps can be taken to minimize resistance and enhance the effects of analgesia with burn patients. First, people on a burn unit, while more likely to have personality disorders, are less likely to have neurotic characteristics and are not seeking psychological or psychiatric treatment. Clinicians practicing hypnotic treatment should emphasize that their presence is for the control of pain and that they try to see as many patients as possible. In this way, patients won't perceive that they have been singled out for having mental health problems. Second, hypnotic treatment should be presented in a manner that discourages patients from believing that they are weak or character-flawed if they are unable to participate in the process. I often use comparisons to the experience of being lost in the absorption of sports activities, hard work, art or music to explain how the process of hypnosis works.

It is useful to gain a sense of how patients have experienced their previous procedures before beginning. I ask patients what thoughts they had during their dressing change. Of particular interest is whether patients can differentiate between "hurt" and "harm." If a patient states that the procedure "hurts like hell but I know what was happening was good for me," then he is ready for hypnotic treatment. On the other hand, if patients fear that what the staff is doing to them will make them worse, they often take a hypervigilant stance towards wound care and monitor the nurse's every move. In these cases, some education is necessary; if patients are unable to trust the staff, then hypnotic treatment is less likely to be effective.

Even when patients are unwilling to give up their need to monitor what occurs during dressing change, hypnotic treatment can still be used, as described in the section on patients who tend to cope with threatening situations by becoming sensitized to stimuli. However, the basis of the hypnotic intervention should be the attenuation procedures discussed in the cognitive-behavioral techniques section. Specifically, such patients can be encouraged to focus intently on the procedure, and accordingly, to experience changes in their sensations. Although this approach can occasionally be effective, interventions that allow patients to dissociate are easier to apply and more likely to be effective.

Some patients on the burn unit may fear that a successful hypnotic experience will result in an intolerable loss of control. Concerns of this nature can usually be addressed by framing the intervention as self-hypnosis. Self-hypnosis has other advantages in this type of setting. In particular, since patients undergo frequent procedures, it is difficult, if not impossible, for a clinician to be present for all of them. Teaching patients to induce their own hypnotic experiences not only decreases resistance but also proves useful in overcoming such logistical barriers.

The Emergency Room

Patients will almost always end up in an emergency room as the first stage of their hospital burn care. In the overall picture of care for a severe burn, this typically represents only a small fraction of the total treatment time. An emergency room visit will generally not last longer than a few hours, which will be followed by months of care. At the same time, however, the time in the emergency room may be the last period of lucidity patients experience before entering the confusion and somnolence that often accompany intensive burn care. As such, this brief period of time may represent a valuable window in which hypnotic treatment and other psychological interventions can be applied.

Burn patients in the emergency room may be alert and awake for a number of reasons. First, the medical team has usually not had a chance to provide the analgesic and sedative agents that induce somnolence and confusion. Second, such patients are typically still under the influence of physiological changes their bodies have initiated to survive the trauma. Adrenaline secreted in response to a burn injury can result in the patient's being surprisingly alert with minimal pain. For example, one patient, prior to being admitted to our burn unit, pulled two survivors out of a plane wreck and then walked seven miles for help on a broken leg, with 40 percent of his body burned (full thickness). Patients have related to me that they felt the need to stay awake until they believed they were taken care of (i.e., admitted to a hospital), at which point they lapsed into a prolonged state of delirium. In any case, many patients in the emergency room will have the level of consciousness necessary for at least a brief hypnotic intervention.

Although patients in the emergency room may be lucid and relatively pain free, they are also likely to be highly anxious, traumatized, emotionally regressed and suggestible. This suggests that patients at this stage are ideal candidates for hypnotic treatment. However, they are also particularly vulnerable to harmful suggestions. Clinicians as well as emergency team members must be careful to communicate in a way that takes into account the extreme anxiety and vulnerability that the patient is experiencing.

For practical purposes, hypnotic treatment practiced in the emergency room usually must be administered by a member of the medical staff who is frequently present in this setting. Few emergency room physicians and nurses are well trained in hypnotic treatment, which perhaps explains the paucity of literature in this area. Ewin (1979) has written the most about this area, at least with respect to burn care. He argues that the variables of belief, necessity, and motivation provide the framework for successful hypnotic treatment in this setting. His reports about slowing or reversing the progression of a burn in the emergency room have, as mentioned earlier, been met with skepticism because they are based on anecdotes and have not been subjected to empirical scrutiny; nevertheless, he has offered clinicians examples of inductions that will promote analgesia and coping in some patients.

Ewin's (1984) inductions capitalize on the suggestibility, anxiety, and emotional regression that might be expected in emergency room patients. Patients are encouraged to put their faith in the medical team, for example, by being told, "The first thing I want you to do is turn the care of the burn over to us, so you don't have to worry about it at all" (p. 222). He then helps patients go to a safe, peaceful place of their choice. Once patients have found this place they are given suggestions to promote healing and comfort, "Now while you are off at your peaceful place I want you to also notice that all of the injured areas are cool and comfortable. Notice how cool and comfortable they actually are, and when you can really feel this, you'll let me know because this finger will slowly rise . . . " (p. 224). This initial induction is reportedly easily induced on subsequent days by having the patients "return to their peaceful place."

The types of inductions that will most likely be effective in the emergency room are those which are brief, direct, and put relatively more control in the hands of the therapist. Patients in such settings are typically in crisis and in need of direction. Making decisions will often be taxing and frightening to them. The more that the clinician demonstrates competence and mastery over the environment, the more effective he or she will be in this setting.

The Intensive Care Unit

When patients hospitalized for burn injuries are in an intensive care unit (ICU), their trauma is usually regarded as life-threatening. Burn centers often adopt criteria for placing patients at this level of care, such as adults demonstrating greater than 20 percent of their body surface as open, unhealed wounds. Among children and elderly adults, this criterion may lower to 10 percent of their body burned. Any life-threatening complications of the burn injury (e.g., inhalation injuries, renal failure) will also typically result in intensive care. Patients may remain in burn unit ICUs anywhere from one day to several months.

Understanding the nature of the ICU environment and care at this stage is important to designing interventions for emotional distress and pain. Patients in any ICU typically undergo repeated forms of intrusive, potentially painful, medical procedures. They are often heavily medicated with agents that can induce lethargy, amnesia, and confusion. Sustained sleep is rare in this environment, since patients are awakened regularly to check vital signs and to participate in procedures. ICUs are increasingly characterized by the presence of highly technical equipment, one effect of which is to make a sterile environment an even less humane one. Masks, gowns, and gloves serve to dehumanize a staff that might already lack the time to provide much nurturance to patients.

With the cumulative effects of such circumstances, it is not surprising that patients on the burn ICU are often lethargic and confused. Delirium is a frequently reported complication in this setting. The patient's ability to converse, sustain concentration. and remember day-to-day events is compromised. It is common for such patients to alternate between sleep and partial wakefulness, so that any semblance of diurnal cycles is lost. Patients on burn unit ICU wards will typically receive high doses of opioid drugs. Consequently, the possibility of hallucinations must be added to the gamut of cognitive reactions experienced by patients in this setting.

Those patients who are able to retain some level of alertness through this experience are at risk for experiencing high levels of anxiety. Many patients have narrowly escaped death, and others face the possibility that their wounds may still prove to be mortal. Patients may also be anxious about the bizarre, technological environment that surrounds them. Patients live in fear of impending burn debridements, which may constitute hours of excruciating pain. Patients' ability to control their environment, often a primary buffer against anxiety, is limited or nonexistent. Regression to dependency is often the easiest route a patient can take. Reliance on more primitive defense mechanisms, such as denial, is to be expected and even encouraged.

When considering hypnotic treatment in the burn unit ICU, we must first ask whether the patient is cognitively capable of benefiting from this type of intervention. A significant proportion of patients will be unable to recognize their family members, much less undergo a process that requires attention and concentration. Other patients who appear lucid may quickly drift off during a normal conversation. However, there are a few ICU patients who can be helped substantially by hypnotic treatment.

The typical physical and emotional condition of patients on the ICU provides an important guide for administering hypnotic treatment. First, patients who are able to attend adequately for hypnotic treatment will often not be able to do so for long. Consequently, the clinician will have a limited window in which to work, necessitating the use of brief inductions. Second, patients in the ICU are often overwhelmed by stimuli, emotionally vulnerable, and highly suggestible. As such, they will be far less resistant to hypnotic treatment than under other circumstances and more likely to respond to suggestion. This typical emotional state of patients has a number of implications for how hypnotic treatment is applied. Instructions should be given with a maximum of clarity. Since patients are unlikely to be resistant, direct simple suggestions for facilitating a hypnotic experience will usually be of most benefit. The use of indirect statements or confusion will typically be of little value and may serve only to disrupt the patient's concentration.

In respecting the patient's fragile emotional state, it is important

Table 10.1
Induction for the ICU

Statement to Patient	Comment
You have been through quite a trauma and I'm part of the team that focuses on getting you out of the hospital and back to work as soon as possible. I am also interested in making you as comfortable as possible as you go through the remainder of your care.	The implicit message is that with regard to survival, the patient is over the worst. The possibility of the patient's not surviving is not raised.
As a way to make our patients more comfortable, we often offer hypnotic treatment in addition to their pain medication. I wanted to see if you would be interested in this type of approach. Would you like to begin right now?	The statement that many patients on the burn unit go through hypnotic treatment normalizes this approach. Patients often fear that we will reduce their pain medication but may be afraid to admit this; therefore, hypnotic treatment is offered as an addition to analgesic drugs. It is rare for patients to refuse hypnotic treatment on the ICU, as long as they are aware that their pain medication will not be reduced. Often this offer is met with statements such as "I'll try anything to get rid of this pain."
Now, will it be OK if, as a result of our talk, you find yourself going into a comfortable sleep-like state from which you can awake at any time?	Some patients will need to be hypervigilant about their care or may not respond to a dissociative suggestion, for whatever reason. This question is designed to assess for this in laymen's terms. Note that the patient's choice regarding waking up is offered to counteract the patient's perceiving sleep as a metaphor for death.
Good, now where do you like to go to relax?	A description of the patient's favorite place to relax is elicited, including descriptors that will later be used to stimulate imagery from a variety of sensory modalities.

(Continued)

Table 10.1
Continued

Statement to Patient	Comment
Fine. Now close your eyes, take a deep breath and let it out very slowly. (*As the patient lets his breath out, I put my hand on his forehead and gently turn his head to one side.*) . . . That's fine. . . .	The instructions are brief, straightforward, and simple. Moving the patient's head is designed to surprise him, capture his attention, communicate my willingness to actively intervene and facilitate the induction. If the patient's forehead is burned, another area of the body can be selected, such as the shoulder.
Now I am going to count from one to ten. With each number I count allow yourself to become deeper and deeper relaxed. When I reach 10 you will find yourself in a very deep, very comfortable state of relaxation. Are you ready to begin? One, two, three . . . that's right, find yourself becoming more and more relaxed as the numbers grow larger. Notice how slow your breathing is . . . four, five, six . . . good . . . just letting yourself sink deeper into the bed . . . just listening to the sounds of my voice . . . getting more and more relaxed . . . really slowing down your breathing now . . . seven . . . your head and neck are so deeply relaxed now . . . your arms and legs . . . your whole body just heavy and relaxed . . . eight . . . the only thing you can hear is my voice . . . the only thing you can notice is how comfortable you are . . . we are almost there . . . nine . . . really noticing that deep feeling of relaxation, heaviness, and comfort . . . really feeling your breathing slowing down . . . deeper and deeper . . . and now ten . . . (*at the count of ten I put my palm on the patient's forehead and move it gently to one side again*).	The counting begins at a relatively quick pace. As the induction progresses, the counting slows and the pauses between statements lengthen.

Table 10.1
Continued

Statement to Patient	Comment
That's right, deeply, deeply relaxed. . . . It's as if you are asleep but you can still hear my voice. . . . And as I continue talking you find that you are at your relaxing place (*the patient's identified relaxation scenario is specifically identified*). Notice what you see there . . . what does it smell like? . . . You are absolutely comfortable when you go to your place. Now, as you remain in your comfortable place I would like you to notice how comfortable it feels to be this way . . . and how you can become more and more relaxed and you continue breathing slowly . . . now, I would like you to go to a level where you are absolutely comfortable . . . a state of mind where your body will know just what you need to do to get yourself better.	
As you continue to move closer and closer to the special state of mind, I would like you to know that when you get there, the back part of your mind will give us a signal . . . specifically, when you are at a place where your mind will really help you feel comfortable, safe and knowing what you need to know to heal your wounds quickly it will signal us by allowing this finger to rise seemingly on its own power.	The notion of the "back part of the mind" can be substituted for the "unconscious," or whatever metaphor is comfortable to the clinician and patient.
(*Upon seeing the finger rise*) Good. Now as you remain at this very special place, notice how good it feels to know that deep inside you know what it will take to move through your burn care comfortably and safely . . .	This finger signaling allows the patient to be the judge of what constitutes his optimal level of comfort and to quicken the pace of the overall induction. The patient almost always provides this signal. However, if no finger signal occurs, the therapist can work around this by assuring patients that they can benefit no matter what their current level is or that they may actually reach their optimal level some time in the future.

(Continued)

Table 10.1
Continued

Statement to Patient	Comment
... that your wounds will heal quickly and that you will move through care with only those sensations that you need to have ... in fact, it will be perfectly okay if the only thing that you feel during your wound care is a sense of well-being and relaxation.	Some patients may need to have some experience of pain, so I attempt to give them control over the amount of analgesia they will experience.
You are doing very well. Now just continue to stay in the state of mind where you find out that there are things you can do to recover from your burn in a rapid and comfortable fashion. You may stay in this comfortable state for as long as you would like. . . .	At this point any other suggestions that the patient may need can be implemented, such as suggestions for performance in therapy or eating.
In fact, at the time you are ready to return to a wakeful state we will allow your finger to signal us once again by slowly rising up again.	The patient is left to decide when to return from the induction via this signaling. Patients often need these instructions repeated, particularly if they are in a deep state of relaxation.

That's very good. In a moment I will begin counting back so you can return to a temporary state of alertness. Before I do, however, I want you to remember a couple of things. First, whenever I touch you on the forehead like this, whenever the nurse touches you on the forehead like this, or whenever your [spouse] touches you on the forehead like this, you will become as relaxed as you are right now. . . . Even more comfortable than you feel right now. . . . (*This sequence can be repeated for emphasis.*) I also want to remind you that you can return to your comfortable place whenever you want. . . . As a matter of fact, you will find yourself counting from one to ten and going to your place before all of your future dressing changes. Now, I am going to count from ten back to one. When I	The presence of the signal is reinforced by the response, "That's very good." This is a very important reassurance and encouragement to the patient.
	
	    On the ICU I usually have close family members observe the induction and participate in the posthypnotic suggestion.
	
	    With hypnotic treatment on the ICU, states of wakefulness are regarded as being as transient as hypnotic states. The patient is given the message that he will be alert until the next painful procedure. Occasionally, I leave patients in the hypnotic state with the instructions that they will return to an awake state when they are fully rested and ready to continue their care in a comfortable manner.

(Continued)

reach the number one you will find
yourself alert, awake and comfortable. However, you will also know
that you can return to a deeply relaxed state from now on, whenever it
will benefit you (*the patient is counted back up with suggestions for
wakefulness*).

---

to protect the defenses that are activated for the patient's survival.
Focusing on the cosmetic impact of the burn injury, for example, will
be less effective than moment-to-moment coping, since the latter is far
more likely to be the source of the patient's concern. Wording that can
exacerbate anxiety about death (e.g., "you will feel nothing") should be
avoided. Finally, the clinician should be aware that ICU patients often
have difficulty discriminating dreams from conscious cognition and
reality from hallucinations. Hypnotic suggestions can remain with a
patient in a dream-like state for days. Although the phenomenon
might work to the patient's advantage with benign suggestions, poorly
worded interventions may have a harmful emotional impact on the
patient's ICU experience.

In summary, effective techniques on the ICU will be brief, rely on
direct suggestions and focus on limited agendas typically including
survival and immediate comfort. Table 10.1 illustrates an induction
that might be used on the ICU, along with rationale for the comments
made.

Acute Care

During the acute care stage of burn treatment, the injury is no longer
life-threatening but is still severe enough to require inpatient hospitalization. The patient may have a burn area that is open but is less than
20 percent of the body surface area. Acute burn care typically involves
frequent care procedures, such as daily wound cleanings, as well as
more intensive rehabilitation efforts (e.g., walking, range of motion
exercises). Patients are more stable physiologically than in the ICU.
As a result they are more alert, talkative, and better able to comprehend the impact of their injury. Nevertheless, they are still in substantial pain. In fact, since they are no longer intubated or on intravenous
lines, they are likely to be receiving less medication. This, in combination with their increased wakefulness, may lead to some patients' expe-

riencing even higher levels of pain than they did in the intensive care unit.

The improved cognitive status of patients in acute care can contribute to their level of suffering. Patients are better able to evaluate the ramifications of their injury on their future. Some patients may be forced to contend with disfigurement. Physical impairment will force many patients to change or lose their jobs. Patients often must cope with the loss of human lives, pets, or property that occurred when they sustained their burns. Finally, many burn injuries are the result of an assault, a life-threatening event that would present a challenge to anyone's ability to cope.

The pain experience of a patient in acute burn care typically involves a constant level of background pain, over which are superimposed brief periods of procedural pain. The pain can be exacerbated by anxiety over procedures. Anxiety and depression may also be associated with the cause or long-term impact of the fire and burn injury.

The nature of burn pain facilitates the use of hypnotic treatment in some respects but hinders it in other ways. In favor of hypnotic treatment is the predictable and time-limited nature of procedural pain. A clinician who knows when and how long a patient will be in pain can do a great deal using hypnotic treatment as a preemptive intervention. The large number of procedures that patients must go through in burn care, however, presents a challenge to the use of hypnotic treatment. Although this intervention may be useful for a few dressing changes, it is unclear how much the patient may benefit after a dozen wound care procedures. Further, in most settings it will be prohibitive in terms of time and cost for the clinician to be present at all wound care procedures.

To address the various challenges described, an ideal protocol for hypnotic treatment should:

1. initially occur before the patient is actually undergoing a procedure and experiencing high levels of pain;
2. take place when the patient is on dosages of medication that will not interfere with attention, learning, and memory;
3. not require the continued presence of the clinician;
4. involve the participation and reinforcement of the staff, while not requiring too much of their time;
5. minimize what psychological resistance patients might offer while they are in this phase of care.

To meet these criteria I have adapted Barber's (1977) Rapid Induction Analgesia (RIA), which had initially been developed for use with dental pain. This protocol can easily be modified for the procedures that patients undergo in burn care. Further, it is brief, does not require the clinician's participation during dressing changes, includes the staff, and is structured in a manner that avoids engendering patient resistance.

Our protocol involves working with patients one to two hours prior to their dressing change. Patients undergo RIA with specific posthypnotic suggestions geared toward their wound care or physical therapy. Nurses are then provided with a standard set of instructions that highlight the induction and provide posthypnotic cues for analgesia. The interested reader can find RIA printed in its entirety elsewhere (Barber, 1977; Barber & Adrian, 1982). The procedure involves the subject's visualizing and walking down a staircase with 20 steps. The count to 20 is interspersed with instructions for attention, relaxation, deepening of the relaxed state, and cooperation. At the base of the staircase, the subject is given suggestions for confusion and amnesia, the latter theoretically serving to strengthen posthypnotic suggestions. Subjects are then provided with posthypnotic suggestions tied to procedures that will occur in the future and to facilitate greater control of the process, a touch on the shoulder by a health-care provider.

To understand how we apply RIA to patients in the burn unit it is important to read this induction as it is written in its original form. Obviously, we exchange the references to dental care for ones pertaining to burn care. Thus, a burn patient relaxes, counts down 20 steps, and is told that "you may be surprised that the room in which you have your dressing changes is the place for the memory [of comfort and relaxation] to surface." Further, the patient is reminded that feelings of analgesia and comfort "will come rushing back whenever the nurse begins to take off your bandages." The patient is cued to experience comfort by several of the environmental characteristics of the wound care room, such as a metal hydrotank, curtains, and the busy activities of nurses and doctors. In this way, cues that ordinarily would have been stimulus-bound to anxiety become posthypnotic cues for analgesia. Patients are also given tactile cues that are reinforced by nursing, such as, "whenever you are touched on the shoulder like this, you will experience a feeling. . . . " (Naturally, a nonburned body part is selected for the touching cue.)

When RIA is not effective in producing analgesia, as described, it becomes important to accompany patients to their dressing change to help them through the procedure. In this respect, the clinician's participation often involves coaching as much as hypnotic treatment. Patients who are in pain during dressing change should be encouraged to focus on their breathing. They can also be instructed to focus all their sensation on a body part other than the one that the nurse is cleaning. We have learned that the pain behavior evidenced during dressing change should not necessarily be interpreted as a sign that the hypnotic treatment has failed. Often patients will show physical indicators of pain during procedures, only to report later that their pain was well controlled. Such observations are consistent with the experimental work of Hilgard (Hilgard & Hilgard, 1994), who reports that physiological indicators of pain may be accompanied by apparent lack of awareness of pain. It is also important to realize that as a function of hypnotic treatment or pharmacologic agents, patients may have amnesia for what occurs during wound care.

CASE EXAMPLE: JOHN, 25, SUFFERED AN ELECTRICAL BURN

Background. John was hospitalized at a regional burn unit after sustaining a massive electrical burn. While driving with a friend, he stopped to remove a high voltage wire that had fallen onto a wet road. When he picked up the wire, it conducted a bolt of high voltage, badly burning both his arms and both his legs.

John was air-evacuated to the trauma unit center and admitted to the burns/plastics intensive care unit. He remained on the ICU for several months before being transferred to the burns/plastics acute care floor, where he remained several additional months. He was then transferred to the rehabilitation medicine unit, approximately eight months after his injury. He was on the rehabilitation unit for an additional six months before being discharged, making his total hospitalization time since his injury one year and two months.

John was admitted to the hospital with all four of his limbs present, though they were severely burned. The medical staff monitored the status of each of his wounds, with the hope that amputation would not be necessary. However, over time, it became necessary for him first to undergo a below-the-elbow amputation of his right arm. Two months later, he received a left above-the-knee amputation. His right leg was amputated above-the-knee four months later. The surgeons worked extensively to salvage his left hand, and future surgeries are likely to be done to improve its function.

Additional complications of John's injury included severely impaired bowel and bladder function, which necessitated surgical remedies, including a colostomy. In addition to these procedures, John has had multiple skin grafts and flaps to the various burned areas. John's rehabilitation course was impeded by skin breakdowns, which pro-

longed his immobilization. When John was finally discharged from the
hospital, he had endured 32 major surgeries.

John left the hospital in an electric wheelchair, and was using a
right upper-extremity hook prosthesis. He had recently undergone
urologic surgery to restore urinary tract function, although the success of this procedure remained uncertain. He was able to urinate only
sporadically, and only with significant pain. His bowel function was
maintained through his colostomy. Sexual functioning was compromised by erectile failure and a lack of penile sensation. His urologist
had advocated insertion of a penile prosthesis. It appeared that John
was still producing retrievable sperm but, in the absence of a romantic
relationship, this fact was not a very satisfying one.

Hospital course. Extreme pain and suffering became routine for
John, particularly during the first eight months of his hospitalization.
The effects of the trauma itself were sufficient to cause severe pain for
the first several weeks of his hospitalization. He then was forced to
cope with additional pain from multiple surgeries, as well as the pain
of daily wound debridement.

While on the ICU, John showed sustained periods of lethargy and
confusion. He appeared to have a paradoxical reaction to a tranquilizer
(lorazepam), although it was unclear to what degree his reaction (primarily increased confusion) was also the result of the natural social
isolation and sensory deprivation of the ICU.

With time, John became more alert, though he continued to experience significant pain. He began to develop a pattern of nausea in the
days before and after surgeries, which seemed to be at least partially
stress related. His pain was controlled primarily through opioid medication (hydromorphone for dressing changes and methadone for background pain). John remained on a methadone-based pain cocktail for
over a year, at which time he requested gradual withdrawal from this
medication.

When he was not feeling sick or in pain, John usually demonstrated
a good-natured, positive attitude. While he often showed signs of grief
and anxiety, particularly with his family, he did not demonstrate a
pervasive depression. The dignity he demonstrated in the face of his
injury was remarkable, and seemed to reflect a well-developed personality, as well as the support of his caring, emotionally healthy family.

Psychological interventions. While he was on the ICU, John went
through periods of lucidity and intense pain. He also endured periods
of time when he began to believe that a limb would be salvaged, only

to have his hope dashed by yet another amputation. He endured three amputations, and on each occasion he had to quickly adjust to the fact that he would be facing life with one less limb. As the psychologist on the team, I visited John on an almost daily basis, with the primary goals of reducing his pain and facilitating adjustment to his difficult future.

I found it particularly difficult to inspire hope in this patient while he was in the ICU facing multiple amputations. Conventional cognitive-behavioral strategies (e.g., decatastrophizing, reinterpreting thoughts) seemed pallid in contrast to the enormity of his loss. Hypnotic intervention became an opportunity for me to discover things that might be usefully said to John. Specifically, I would suggest that John relax and offer suggestions for deepening his absorption in the experience; then, based on my experience of him at that moment, I would offer statements that might be of use to him. Thus, I made statements such as: "You may find as you breathe deeply that you are able to access internal resources that you were not aware were there," or "Isn't it interesting that even when matters might have appeared hopeless, you are able to turn inside and find different pathways to take." Such statements might appear superficial or nonsensical in a normal conversation. However, when put to the patient in the hypnotic context, on the ICU, they seemed quite helpful. In response to hypnotic intervention, John became less depressed and suffered less from pain. This intervention offered something equally important to me. Using hypnosis in this way gave me the opportunity to say something I hoped was helpful to John, even though, in the context of his terrible pain and loss, I felt inadequate to the task. Part of me insisted that it was impossible, really, to find the right thing to say; nonetheless, John seemed comforted by my words.

The other application of hypnosis was to directly initiate pain control. John underwent wound cleanings, almost daily, for nearly a year. Actually, if John were not going through daily wound care, it would be only because he was undergoing major surgery. Hypnotic treatment was useful in decreasing the intense pain of wound care, as well as helping John prepare for each surgery.

Nonhypnotic psychological interventions were also important to John's care. His parents spent the majority of time at the hospital. As is often the case with parents who find it hard to witness the suffering of their child, John's mother was sometimes overbearing in her attempts to be helpful to him. I intervened frequently to facilitate her relationship with John and with the clinical staff. John also had two sisters and an older brother. His brother took on the role of expressing grief for the family, eventually requiring referral to another psychologist to help him work through his anguish.

Most of my visits with John were focused on providing supportive psychotherapy. The primary focus of psychological treatment was to enable John to cope with the vigorous demands of treatment, rather than to facilitate any in-depth exploration of the impact of his injury. John never showed any prolonged symptoms of anxiety, depression, or poor interpersonal relationships, despite the gravity of his injury. As is the case with many people who acquire disabilities, it was important not to assume that he would require psychotherapy in order to make a good long-term adjustment. Even so, John was referred to a psychotherapist close to his home community after discharge. As was anticipated, he was not interested in pursuing this mode of treatment. Several years later, John reported that he was reasonably content with life. He was living independently on his parents' farm and working full-time, driving a combine machine with his remaining hand. He did lack a romantic partner in his life, which I realized was a source of loneliness for him. His family and a small, tight-knit community were important to him as a means of maintaining good functioning.

Working with John demonstrated some of the more wearing and rewarding aspects of working on a burn unit. On many occasions, the staff and I felt helpless in our ability to diminish the emotional and physical suffering experienced by both John and his family. On the other hand, the satisfaction of seeing his degree of recovery was very great, and the gratitude that John and his family showed toward the staff was deeply rewarding to us.

Hypnosis provided a useful means to provide support during moments of despair and to reduce John's pain. However, as is so often the case, hypnosis was only one of a variety of psychological interventions used with John and his family. Once we were able to successfully move him through the rigors of burn care and rehabilitation, his healthy personality and strong social support seemed sufficient to enable him to adjust to his extensive disability.

CASE EXAMPLE: CHUCK, 62, WOULD RATHER DIE

Chuck required daily dressing changes for the care of a 30 percent total body surface area (TBSA) burn. As his complaints about pain grew, Chuck was given increasing doses of hydromorphone (Dilaudid) as well as diazepam (Valium). The burn unit staff determined that he was at maximal dosages of both types of medication, yet the patient said that his pain was so severe that he would not undergo another dressing change. In fact, Chuck indicated that he would "rather die than go through another dressing change."

In our initial conversation Chuck agreed that, if there were some way to avoid the agony of the dressing changes, he would be willing to cooperate. I explained to him that hypnotic interventions often made a real difference to the comfort of these procedures. Although skeptical, Chuck was sufficiently interested to pursue this possibility. He underwent one hypnotic treatment using the protocol described earlier.

I suggested that Chuck imagine stepping down a staircase as a way of inducing the internal absorption necessary to develop a hypnotic experience. His legs moved with each step I counted, indicating that he was responding literally and motorically to my instructions – which suggested a high degree of absorption in the experience. Following suggestions for comfort, Chuck was left with a posthypnotic suggestion that when his nurse touched him on the shoulder, he would return to a state of comfort.

I did not attend his dressing change; later, however, when I returned to his ward, I found several staff members who were excited about the outcome of the hypnotic intervention, particularly the posthypnotic suggestion. Chuck had been touched once by the nurse during wound care, at which point he became quiescent – even asleep, apparently – for two hours. During the dressing change, Chuck exhibited no pain behaviors, nor did he show any indication that he was aware his nurses were working on him. This single hypnotic intervention was sufficient to support him through his several remaining dressing changes with no complaints of pain. When I saw Chuck two months after hospital discharge for a follow-up clinic appointment, I was pleased to learn that he continued to benefit from this hypnotic treatment. Chuck's case shows the dramatic potential of hypnotic intervention, particularly with someone so responsive.

CASE EXAMPLE: JOE, AN ANGRY YOUNG MAN

After lecturing to a burn center staff as a visiting scholar, I asked if any audience member would be willing to volunteer for a demonstration. The attendees requested instead that I hypnotize one of the patients on the ward, one whose case had been difficult to manage. Joe was an angry man in his twenties with a 40 percent burn. Although he agreed to hypnotic treatment, he rejected all of my attempts to gain rapport with him. Joe answered my questions with curt, one-word responses, and made no effort to cooperate. When I asked him if he would like to feel more relaxed as a result of hypnotic treatment, his reply was an emphatic "no."

At this point, it appeared to my colleagues in the audience that I was not succeeding with this patient. I then employed the Ericksonian principle (Erickson, 1980) of utilization in response to his resistance. Specifically, I said, in response to his lack of enthusiasm, "Good . . . I want you to remain as tense as you can while I talk with you." Within a minute after I said this, Joe was so deeply relaxed he was snoring. His response to questions, however, indicated that he was not sleeping but experiencing a profoundly relaxing hypnotic state. Wishing to be of some benefit to him, I offered Joe suggestions for analgesia.

I left Joe in this state, with suggestions that he would experience substantial comfort when he awoke. When I left, the burn unit staff was somewhat confused but seemed less skeptical than before about hypnosis. Although this induction was primarily designed to be a clinical demonstration, Joe experienced substantial pain control, at least for the duration of my visit. Although I never found out how long his analgesia lasted, the burn unit staff did contact me with requests for more information, wanting to learn how these interventions could be used with other patients.

CASE EXAMPLE: MOE, BURNED BY JEALOUSY

Moe was an ex-football player in his twenties, hospitalized with a 12 percent burn after his petite girlfriend, Gina, threw scalding water on his back as a punishment for his infidelity. Moe was finding his dressing changes intolerable despite receiving high doses of hydromorphone. When I talked with Moe about hypnotic treatment for pain relief, Gina was sitting in his hospital room. Apparently, the conflict that provoked the burn had been resolved.

Moe was both hostile and skeptical about the prospect of hypnotic treatment. Gina, however, appeared quite intrigued by this offer, as well as eager to help. I noticed that she was very focused on my questions and comments, and demonstrated friendliness and unusual interpersonal grace in her willingness to help Moe.

It was my hope that if Moe observed an induction experienced by someone he knew and trusted, he would be able to see that it was a benign procedure and would be less frightened by it. Also, Gina's willingness to participate would be the strongest endorsement of this treatment that she could possibly make. I asked Gina if she would be willing to demonstrate an induction. She enthusiastically agreed, and following Moe's admonition ("Don't you hurt her!"), I began a hypnotic induction with Gina. I suggested relaxation and comfort to her, followed by a suggestion for the posthypnotic experience of alertness and clarity. My intention was to demonstrate to Moe the simplicity and safety of the hypnotic experience.

Moe was attentive to all of this. In fact, he seemed fascinated by the procedure and afterward agreed to participate in a hypnotic experience himself. The subsequent hypnotic treatment was so successful in relieving his pain that Moe requested that no more drugs be administered during his dressing changes. The nurses were so intrigued by his response that they called the physicians in to observe his wound cleaning. Moe would lay wide awake and grinning, while the nurses scrubbed his wound as vigorously as they needed. Ordinarily, of course, this would create excruciating pain.

Interestingly, Moe never requested medication during procedures, but did request drugs for the period after his dressing change when he emerged from the hypnotic state.

How might we understand this paradoxical response? Moe had a dramatic analgesic effect while he was hypnotized. When he perceived that the hypnotic state was over, he experienced a return of baseline level pain. Although this baseline pain was successfully controlled with medication, Moe might also have responded well to a posthypnotic suggestion for continued comfort. For example, I might have said, "When you emerge from your state of hypnosis you will continue to feel very comfortable."

The fact that I did not use hypnosis in this way is an interesting example of clinical bias. It was likely my that own bias – that hypnosis works much better for acute episodes rather than ongoing pain – prevented me from even attempting to treat Moe's baseline pain hypnotically. This illustrates how both the patient and the clinician's beliefs and expectations about how hypnosis works have a substantial impact on the therapeutic outcome.

In any case, Moe was able to undergo all of his future dressing changes painlessly, with that single experience of hypnosis providing the sole anesthetic during procedures.

OTHER LESSONS LEARNED

Other patients have also taught me about using hypnotic treatment on a burn unit. I learned about amnesia, for example, when one woman denied that hypnotic treatment was effective for her dressing changes until her nurse showed her how much skin had been removed during her debridement. She had no recall of the worst part of her wound care, indicating how hypnotic treatment can have unexpected amnesic effects.

I learned that there can be important unexpected benefits to hypnotic analgesia. For instance, a particularly delightful outcome of hypnotic treatment has been that of patients who, because of the pain of their burned legs, refused to walk. On several occasions, hypnotic treatment resulted in analgesic response and dramatic increase in mobility with these patients. Such mobility is, of course, essential to successful healing and rehabilitation to good function.

Burn unit environments are noisy, fast-paced, and often not conducive to the quiet atmospheres favored by most clinicians who use hypnotic treatment. Successful inductions on burn units most often integrate the noises surrounding the patient. At times, hypnotic inductions also must be performed with other patients in the room. I was taught that caution must be exercised with regard to this latter circumstance. Once while hypnotizing a burn patient in the presence of his roommate, I suggested that tapping a fork on a coffee cup would immediately reinstate the hypnotic experience. When I gave the post-hypnotic suggestion to the patient, he demonstrated no response. However, the nurse behind his curtain later reported that his roommate immediately dropped into a somnolent state.

This incident taught me that it is important to be mindful of the impact that an induction inadvertently may have on people within hearing of the conversation. It also illustrated that a posthypnotic suggestion should convey a context. Thus, patients might be told that they will respond to a suggestion "this time and this time only" or "for as long as you are in this hospital." The fact that patients can take hypnotic suggestions quite literally is a lesson that any clinician working with hypnosis should keep in mind.

Long-term Rehabilitation

The rehabilitation phase of burn care generally coincides with discharge from acute hospitalization, even though rehabilitation efforts should be initiated during earlier stages of burn care (Avni, 1980; Patterson et al., 1987). Patients in the rehabilitation phase typically have most, if not all, of their burn injury healed. Consequently, acute procedural pain is generally not a problem. At the same time, since most burn centers discourage the use of opioid drugs after discharge, because of increasing side-effects of long-term use, patients may need alternative procedures to cope with pain that remains. Intense, usually painful rehabilitative efforts now become a central feature of the patient's life. Patients, who have been largely immobile for days or even weeks in the hospital, are likely to suffer from the disuse of muscles and tendons and ligaments. A severe burn or grafted area will show some degree of scarring. Scarring in a joint area contracts the affected area (e.g., arms, legs, fingers, toes, neck). Burned joints are a particularly vexing problem. A burn patient who is not adequately rehabilitated will develop severely contracted limbs to the degree that mobility eventually becomes impossible. When this occurs, function can only be restored with surgical release procedures, in which a large piece of scarred area is removed to mitigate the effects of contractures. Consequently, rehabilitation is essential for optimal healing and future functioning. Hypnotic interventions can promote needed comfort for patients undergoing the pain of rehabilitation.

Once out of the hospital, patients experience the full psychological ramifications of their injury. Fortunately, most patients show improved psychological status as time passes (Patterson, Everett, Bombardier et al., 1993). However, many still experience a number of complications such as nightmares, phobic reactions, and generalized anxiety. Pruritis (itching) can be particularly troublesome. Patients with cosmetic disfigurement have a potentially deeper, more enduring layer of psychological problems with which they must contend. Social isolation, decreased self-esteem, and sexual problems may all accompany scarring (Cash & Pruzinsky, 1990).

In evaluating the long-term psychological impact of burn injuries, clinicians must be particularly sensitive to social and financial variables. Persistent psychological distress in the face of healing injuries is often held in place by environmental factors. Pending litigation regarding the cause of the burn is one of the more powerful detriments to psychological recovery. The process of litigation is a frequent reminder to patients that they have experienced a trauma. (See Chapters 1, 2, and 3 for further discussion of the potential harm of litigation.) Further, full emotional recovery may reduce the size of a monetary settlement.

Between 39 and 60 percent of burn injuries are estimated to occur in the work setting (Patterson, Marvin, Campbell et al., 1993). Patients burned at work are often angry at their employer, a feeling that might have predated their injury. Psychological symptoms may reflect patients' ambivalence toward their employer and toward the prospect of returning to work. Other sources of social and financial disincentives to psychological improvement might be the solicitous behavior of a spouse or family member. Effective rehabilitation requires our thoughtful attention to these issues.

Hypnotic treatment can benefit patients during the rehabilitation phase of burn care, but its application is less obvious and straightforward. Since patients are no longer suffering excruciating pain, their motivation for engaging in novel interventions has decreased and their defenses have typically returned to preinjury levels. Further, many of the complications evidenced by patients are kept in place by the environmental forces discussed above. Nevertheless, clinicians who are sensitive to these factors can still apply hypnotic treatment effectively with many patients, primarily by suggesti ng physical comfort and increased confidence and optimism.

Patients who suffer from psychological problems associated with the trauma of the burn or of subsequent treatment can benefit from brief sessions of hypnotic treatment. Nightmares, simple phobias, and pruritis all respond well to brief hypnotic interventions. For some of the more chronic problems, the clinician may have to address complicating factors before attempting hypnotic treatment. In our burn unit we rely on vocational counselors to address the systems issues that are associated with employers and insurance companies. When working with patients during the rehabilitation phase, the focus of interventions will often be on increasing the patient's physical activity rather than on decreasing pain.

SUMMARY

Burn injuries provide a tremendous challenge to the people who sustain them, as well as to the clinicians who provide treatment. For many people, a burn injury represents the predictable culmination of a series of unfortunate life events. Such patients' preinjury history often includes substance abuse, poor socioeconomic circumstances, interpersonal violence, and unusual risk-taking. For other patients, the burn was not predictable and represents ill fortune.

In either case, burn injuries are a traumatic event that takes the patient to the extreme limits of life experience. This trauma can result in a variety of psychological reactions, as well as the most intense, horrifying pain imaginable. Despite the stress inherent in treating burn injuries, providing care for this group of patients can be extremely rewarding. Most patients with burns who make it to the hospital ultimately survive and, with good care, show remarkable improvement in their appearance and function. They are often very appreciative of the burn team's efforts.

With respect to hypnosis, people with acute burn injuries are unusually receptive. Because of their recent trauma, they are often psychologically regressed and highly suggestible. Further, the extreme intensity of pain suffered by these patients motivates them to accept a treatment approach that in other circumstances may well have been rejected. When working with these patients, it is important that we attend to both the nature of pain and to the phase of burn care. Patients can be treated with hypnosis and suggestion in the emergency room, intensive care units, acute care units, or during postdischarge rehabilitation. During each phase of care, interventions must be tailored to the patient's emotional needs and to the complicating factors that can accompany care.

Section III

POPULATIONS OF
SPECIAL INTEREST

11

CHILDREN IN PAIN

Samuel LeBaron
Lonnie K. Zeltzer

WENDY IS AN appealing 13-year-old girl who probably has leukemia. A bone marrow aspiration is essential to make the diagnosis that will guide her treatment. The physician has informed Wendy and her parents that the procedure involves inserting a needle into one of her large bones, usually the iliac crest of the pelvic bone. After insertion, a syringe is attached to the needle, and a small amount of marrow is aspirated. The physician emphasizes that, although it sounds frightening, the procedure will be very quick. Wendy understands "needle" and "bone," but she notices a change in the physician's voice and that he looks away when he tells her not to worry. Wendy clutches her mother's hand and begins to cry.

The physician knows Wendy is frightened, but he is at a loss for comforting words. Since general anesthesia will not be used in this procedure, how can he reassure her? He imagines her lying on the treatment table with her hip exposed. He imagines her crying as the local anesthetic numbs the skin over her hip. When she sees the bone marrow needle, almost as thick as a pencil, he knows she will lose control. She will pull away, and the nurse will come to restrain her.

The physician knows that insertion of the needle through the skin is not painful, thanks to the local anesthetic. He also knows, though, that the pressure required to force the needle through the tough outer layer of bone will be more than any pressure or any pain Wendy has ever felt. She will think that her hip is surely being crushed. Once the needle has penetrated the bone, there will be a moment of rest as the syringe is attached. Then, as suction begins to draw the marrow from its place deep in the hollow of the bone, there will be a sudden, electric, stabbing pain, felt throughout her leg and hip. The physician knows that Wendy's body and mind will be squeezed by a fist of pain for a few seconds. He is grateful that it will then be over.

Afterward, the physician knows that Wendy will turn away from him, from the nurse, and from her parents. She will cover her eyes, wet with tears, and remain quiet and still for a long time.

Pain in children has been generally ignored by clinicians until recently (Barber, 1989; Schechter, Berde, & Yaster, 1993). This has been due in part to a lack of both knowledge and skills—but only in part. Our own attitudes toward pain and toward children, as well as clinical restraints introduced by managed care, also contribute substantially to the way we deal with painful procedures and painful conditions in children (Barber, 1989). With no better alternatives available, many clinics and hospitals continue to perform painful medical procedures in children using the "hold 'em down" method. This is a source of stress not only for the children and their parents, but for clinicians as well.

Children with chronic and recurrent pain due to conditions such as arthritis, sickle cell anemia, headaches, hemophilia, and abdominal pain are not ordinarily provided with sufficient analgesic medication or other effective remedies, and are often left to suffer in silence. Referral to a mental health professional for psychological intervention is often a measure of last resort, made only after extensive medical testing and attempted medical treatments have failed to relieve or lessen the child's pain. Often the referring physician has been trained to think that if there is no identifiable physical finding, then the child's distress must be attributable to a psychological cause. It is hoped that the psychologist or psychiatrist will identify and treat that cause. Often, though, by the time the problem has reached the mental health professional's office, it has become a substantial one, much more difficult to treat than it would have been initially.

Our goals in this chapter are to discuss some of the underlying reasons for the persistent undertreatment of pain in children, and then to guide you through an introduction to psychological interventions for chronic and acute pain in children.

THE UNDERTREATMENT OF PAIN IN CHILDREN

There are many reasons why pain and its treatment in children have not been adequately considered in the past. Throughout history – and still in some cultures – children have been viewed as parental possessions, to be handled and used or discarded as parents saw fit. Corporal punishment of children has always been tolerated, because parents have always been regarded as final arbiters of their children's fate. This acceptance of substantial pain and suffering in children has cultural roots in traditions – extant in virtually every culture around the globe – that viewed the ability to tolerate pain either as a virtue or as a fate to be accepted gracefully.

It has been only since the late 1960s, in North America, that the concept of "child abuse" has been viewed as within the scope of pediatrics, with physical findings first described by Kempe and Helfer (1980). Now a physician is required by law to report suspected abuse, often on the basis of some physical evidence. The irony is that the medical establishment itself continues to abuse children, with the justification that inflicting pain is a necessary part of medical care.

What are the consequences of the undertreatment of pain in children? We now know that repeated painful experiences tend to lead to feelings of helplessness and the development of anticipatory fear of future medical care. Clinicians see children in whom chronic pain has led to anxiety or depression. There is evidence that early, prolonged, intense, and/or repeated pain experiences can disrupt not only psychological growth but also normal neural development and may actually lead to increased pain sensitivity (lowered threshold for pain stimuli, overlapping somatic dermatomes, and possibly the development of visceral hyperalgesia). There is reason to speculate that significant childhood pain may lead to adult chronic pain (Zeltzer, Arnoult, Hamilton, & DeLaura, 1994).

With modern availability of analgesic medication and of psychological techniques, it is not usually necessary to inflict pain with medical procedures. However, misconceptions about pediatric pain, difficulties in pediatric pain assessment, and lack of knowledge regarding how best to reduce children's suffering have led to the continuing association of pain and medical care. This is true in adults, but especially in children.

Thus, often physicians inflict or do not adequately treat pain in children because they have been trained to believe that there is no alternative, that "all that can be done is being done in the child's best interests," or that "the benefits outweigh the risks." We continue in our painful ways not out of malice but because we lack the skills and knowledge necessary to change. Our hope is that the awareness of our limitations may help us to become less grim, dry, and inattentive to the cries of children who remind us how much we hurt them even as we try to help.

Let us evaluate each of these issues, since they hold critical relevance for treatment of pain – including psychological treatment – and for facilitating a team approach to treating children's pain.

MISCONCEPTIONS ABOUT PAIN IN CHILDREN

There are a number of misconceptions about pain in infants and children that have fostered a delay in the adequate treatment of pediatric pain.

Myth: Children Do Not Feel Pain

This belief was the justification for performing major operations on children without anesthesia. It seems unbelievable that, in America, neonatal surgery was customarily performed with little or no anesthesia until the last decade (Anand, Sipple, Schofield et al., 1988). The belief was that newborns, especially premature infants, do not have a nervous system sufficiently developed to feel pain, because of insufficient myelinization. What was not considered was the relatively shorter distances that nociceptive impulses had to travel from the periphery to the spinal cord and brain compared to adults. How physicians could observe obvious signs of pain and hold to the belief that the child was not suffering requires a psychological analysis beyond the scope of this chapter; however, the theme is explored by Perry (1984). But this fact should alert all of us to the power of our own personal limitations in the context of apparently providing patient care.

As if it were necessary to do so, it has recently been demonstrated that afferent sensory pathways are sufficiently developed in newborns for them to feel pain. However, the pain inhibitory system is not well developed. Thus, newborns, infants, and perhaps children (to what age is unknown) may actually feel more pain with the same amount of stimulation, compared to an adult. In 1987, the American Academy of Pediatrics published a statement indicating that it was not ethical to perform painful procedures on newborns without appropriate anesthesia.

Myth: Children Will Not Remember Pain

Another misconception is that, even if infants and young children feel pain, they will not remember it. Some physicians believe that even in older children and adolescents it is unnecessary to treat acute pain, since pain of relatively short duration will have no long-lasting effects. Thus, children in any hospital setting, and in emergency departments in particular, are heard screaming variations of "Stop it! You're hurting me!" or "No more owie!" Often, the smaller the child, the more likely the child is to be held down during a medical procedure (circumcision is the prime example), while shame is the method often used to restrain adolescents ("You should be able to take it like a man!").

When children cry in the emergency room or in hospitals, it is typically believed that the underlying reason is fear rather than pain. Thus, children are expected to be fearful. What amounts to torture is justified by statements such as, "Can't do much about that!" and "The child will get over it." Since we know that most clinicians do not wish to torture children, how do we understand this behavior?

Myth: Pain Is a Necessary Part of Care

Until the advent, in the nineteenth century, of modern anesthetic techniques, this belief was unfortunately accurate; in the context of contemporary analgesia, however, it is without foundation. Nonetheless, it still exerts powerful influences: Unaided by adequate analgesics, children are typically restrained to get through any painful procedures as fast as possible. Unfortunately, clinicians who understand how to treat pain in children and who can help them to cope with pain are not ordinarily available in clinics to provide intervention for children undergoing painful medical procedures. Unless such a professional is part of the treating team and integral to the child's care, referral to a mental health professional for acute pain management is typically made only in those circumstances where either the parent insists or the child is so uncooperative that the procedure cannot be performed.

Myth: Pain Treatment Is Too Expensive

Concern about added cost is typically given as the reason for delayed referral in cases where problems were apparent long before the referral. However, with the development of pain management services carried out by departments of anesthesiology, such children are now often referred to anesthesiologists, who provide general anesthesia for painful procedures. Anesthesia costs far exceed those of psychological intervention and may not be the best mode of pain treatment for every distressed child.

Myth: Pain Medication Leads to Addiction

Another misconception related to the undertreatment of pain is that if children, especially adolescents, receive opiates, they will become addicted. This view promotes a treatment strategy that revolves around trying to use as little narcotic analgesic medication as possible. This approach is based on ill-conceived fear of medications, rather than evidence.

Many clinicians confuse the physiological, psychological, and social phenomena associated with drug tolerance, addiction, and drug-seeking behavior. Tolerance is an increasing need for higher doses to obtain the same effect. This is a purely physiological phenomenon. Addiction, a more complex phenomenon, is the experience of craving a substance. Drug-seeking behavior may result from tolerance, addiction, or of inadequate treatment of pain.

All of us, when we are in pain, manifest drug-seeking behavior, searching for a bottle of analgesics in our medicine cabinet. One may generally expect a relationship between intensity of pain and intensity of drug-seeking behavior, but this is not always the case. It is easy for us to become confused when our judgment is impaired by a suspicion that a patient's requests for pain medication are not a reflection of the patient's pain. At these times, we infer that the drug-seeking behavior is not motivated by pain but by a wish to enjoy the pleasurable qualities of opioids. This issue is full of emotional, ethical, and legal questions that cause us to have passionate, though not always rational, opinions. The topic deserves a fuller exploration than we are presently devoting to it.

There is no evidence that providing opiods to children for adequate pain relief results in addiction. On the contrary, there is evidence that pain, if left untreated, may result in a significant psychological and physiological burden.

HOW ARE CHILDREN DIFFERENT FROM ADULTS?

In many respects, the differences between treating children and adults are quite obvious. Yet, it may be helpful to review some of these differences briefly in order to be mindful of children's special needs.

As Erik Erikson (1968) has pointed out, children and their adult caregivers pass through a lifelong series of developmental challenges. Young children need to feel secure in their world. They need to depend on and trust their caregivers. By doing so, children learn that their physical and social environment is safe and secure enough to permit exploration. Without this basis, children have difficulty moving on to subsequent challenges that involve the development of competence and a greater maturity in relationships and action.

Pain or a major painful illness or trauma can pose a major threat to a successful passage through these early developmental stages, impeding the development of self-esteem, intimacy, and self-efficacy. Fortunately, close support from parents and clinicians can safeguard the child, so pain, if treated appropriately, may become ultimately a source of strength rather than a handicap.

Adolescents, ironically, often need this close support, even while they may reject it in their struggle to develop independence and mastery over life challenges. Indeed, adolescents in pain are particularly notorious for expressing anger and confusion. Helping an adolescent in pain is not difficult if the clinician respects the naturalness of the adolescent's behavior – and the inevitable conflict between needs for autonomy and for dependence on reassuring adults. Adolescents often frustrate us because they seem unpredictable regarding their needs from one day to another – and because they confront us with our own unresolved conflicts. Yet, these apparently contradictory needs are not, after all, very different from what we need as adults. In an acute crisis, we need and hope for a style of care that is relatively directive and parental; when the clinical problem becomes more chronic, we want to be more in charge of our destiny. We prefer in this case a clinician who encourages our autonomy, a clinician who acts more as a consultant, who helps us identify a series of alternatives from which we will choose. This shift in paradigm from "acute pain/directive, comforting treatment"– to "chronic pain/consultant clinician" is one that generally works as well with adults as it does with children and adolescents (LeBaron, Reyher, & Stack, 1985).

Clinicians can generally assume that the model described above is a good place to start. But we need to remember that adolescents, whether in acute or chronic pain, may momentarily resist. The physical threat at a given moment may mobilize a strong counterreaction in the adolescent. The attempt to maintain autonomy may take the form of withdrawal, sarcasm, rage, tears, or rejection of all help, including any medical treatment. The clinician who feels frustrated or at a loss in this situation needs to remember that no clinical situation is fixed and static. The clinical dilemma is more like a dance: one step back, one to the side, two forward, pause, and begin again. It is our challenge to find ways to offer both comfort and gentle reassurance to that part of the adolescent that is a frightened four-year-old and respect the adolescent's need to step back before moving closer again.

Effective pain intervention occurs within a context of recognizing varying developmental, emotional, and cognitive needs. Imagery techniques singularly utilize the child's developmental level. Images are often invoked to assist with systematic desensitization, relaxation, or hypnosis. Although hypnotic techniques for children often make use of imagery, the two are not at all the same. If one looks at the hypnotic experience as a sort of intense involvement in thoughts, ideas, images, or actions that results in a dissociative state, this helps to explain the great diversity of "hypnotic" phenomena in children. Whether we are physically playing with a child, asking her to imagine a scene, or telling a story that blends action and fantasy, we are implicitly inviting (and assisting) the child to dissociate from a "reality" orientation.

Thus, "hypnosis" with children two or three years old is more likely to utilize an object such as a stuffed animal or soap bubbles floating in the air (Kuttner, Bowman, & Teasdale, 1988), whereas children four to six years old have a greater capacity for active "make believe," without props. Older children are more likely to enjoy internal images and dramas. This transition from involvement with external objects, to make-believe play, to the internal elaboration of diverse images depends on increasing cognitive and social maturity (Hilgard & LeBaron, 1984; LeBaron, Zeltzer & Fanurik, 1989). Our choice of intervention, then, must accommodate these natural variations, described more specifically below.

A DEVELOPMENTAL VIEW
OF FANTASY

Ages One to Three: Action Play with Objects

Between the ages of one to about two or three years old, children can be observed spending hours imitating parents, each other, and characters from stories and TV programs. At times, the two-year-old may repeat the same scene over and over, every detail and nuance present in each repetition. This slavish insistence on repetition both amuses and frustrates the parent who reads the same bedtime story to his two-year-old for the hundredth time, while the child seems as entranced as if it were the first time. When the parent attempts an ad lib variation on the story, hoping to make it more interesting, the child insists indignantly, "But that's not the way the story goes!" Clearly, the child obtains satisfaction and pleasure from the faithful repetition of details, some of which will probably be replicated in play the next day. The child this age typically has little interest in elaboration and embellishment of familiar storylines, since he does not yet have the ability to focus attention on internalized images or to develop these images into a storyline or a fantasy.

Favorite and familiar objects become important props for this imitative play. Children want to imitate a parent sweeping a floor, hammering a nail or washing dishes. So they seek a broom, a hammer, some dishes, or objects that are a close facsimile.

Psychological interventions designed to reduce pain or anxiety of a child this age make use of objects such as picture books, toys, stuffed animals, soap bubbles – all designed to involve the child in a more pleasant experience. A suggestion that this child imagine (rather than play with) an object or a scene is much more difficult and less engaging for the child.

Ages Four to Six: Sociodramatic Play

Gradually, pretend play becomes less dependent on objects and begins to include concepts and roles. This play is also characterized by its social qualities. Whereas the younger child is the producer, director, and star of her own show, the five-year-old wants to include playmates. There is discussion and negotiation about the roles and lines that each character will speak. These are often rehearsed and elaborated and may evolve as the play continues. Props are still an important part of this play, but there is clearly an ability to include sustained imaginative sequences, with little or no external props. Sociodramatic play represents a transition from the earlier form of play with its total dependence on external objects to the complete representation of images and events in one's imagination – the development of a rich and varied fantasy life.

In contrast to younger children, who have much greater difficulty projecting an idea of their behavior into the future, children four to five years old can benefit from play therapy to help rehearse new ways of coping with difficult situations. Unlike older children, the four-year-old child may be unable (or is only beginning) to describe conceptually the relation between rehearsing a behavior and its application to a future situation, but the learning of new behavior and development of enhanced confidence can occur nevertheless.

Ages Seven and Older:
Internalized Imagination

In both the early action play with objects and the subsequent sociodramatic play, the imagined events are acted out overtly. As children pass through the early years of school, they learn to restrict and control their overt behavior. Understandably, an adaptive way of coping with these physical restrictions is to imagine "What if . . . ?" At the same time, there is a rapid growth in the ability to hold concepts and images in the child's mind. These abilities are readily observed in the child's ability to consider past events, to develop hypotheses about future events, or even to consider events that are improbable – all completely on a cognitive level.

At this stage of maturity, children (as well as adolescents and adults) can benefit from physically rehearsing events, but they have the additional benefit of complex imaginary rehearsal – fantasizing – that may include imagined overt behavior, imagined emotions, and alternate behaviors of both self and others. You will find a more complete discussion of the developmental view of fantasy in Singer (1973) and J. Hilgard and LeBaron (1984).

Play, Imagination, and Hypnotic Ability

Traditionally, hypnotic phenomena have been thought to include relaxation, focused attention, suggestion, and responses that are subjectively perceived by the patient as some combination of somatic, cognitive, and emotional experience. These are characteristic of the immediate associations that most of us have to the idea of hypnosis, in the same way that many of us associate the idea of meditation with sitting motionless, breathing deeply, and remaining very quiet. However, just as there are active forms of meditation that teach the student to meditate while going on with activities of daily life, so, too, there are forms of hypnotic experience that involve hetero- or self-suggestion while remaining alert and active.

When working with children, it is particularly important to understand that, while the concept of giving suggestions and guiding the patient's attention appears to be useful regardless of age, the techniques for accomplishing that goal differ in important ways depending on age.

We adults are proud of our critical abilities. We value independent thinking. These are among the qualities that seem to help us achieve success in adult life. Thus, it is often difficult to suspend those treasured qualities and experience what (initially at least) feels like a passive, dependent mode of behavior, with another person directing our attention and physical behavior.

It is difficult, when in a critical frame of mind, to so intensely imagine having a bag of ice on a sore joint that both the idea and the image become real and compelling. But if we are first invited to sit quietly in a soft chair, to breathe deeply, to relax, to let go of our cares and concerns, to pay attention to the therapist's voice, etc., then we may be able – temporarily – to suspend our usual level of critical evaluation. Then, the ice bag has a chance to become more real to us.

It is clear to us, as we enter into this interaction with the clinician, that our suspension of critical evaluation is not only temporary but also conditional. The implication is, "I will agree to not be critical of what you say as long as it doesn't violate our social contract." In other words, we understand that the interaction is intended to be safe, respectful, interesting, and helpful in some way. Paradoxically, then, we are not really agreeing to suspend our critical faculties entirely. Rather, we are agreeing that our critical faculties will be sent off to "patrol the perimeter" – to keep us safe – while letting us have a good (and/or therapeutic) time.

In most instances, all of this appears to happen easily; yet, it's so complicated! It's no wonder that we adults have a more compelling and interesting reaction to suggestion when we undergo a settling in period of a few minutes referred to in hypnosis jargon as an "induction." During this time, the instructions to relax, close our eyes, focus on the clinician's voice, and so on, provide just the transition many of us need. This process also provides a psychological transition for us as clinicians as we move from an everyday conversational tone of voice to one that is more dramatic, intense, or in various other ways more compelling to ourselves and to our patients.

What about children? Do they need an "induction" to make a transition from a critical mode of thinking to a more make-believe orientation? As any observer of children knows, they're already there, ready for fantasy, much of the time. As any parent and teacher knows, the more common challenge is how to get children from the land of make-believe back to our adult version of reality. With this in mind, the idea of an adult-style "induction" as a prelude to using imagery and suggestion in children seems redundant.

Observation of children at play and in conversation gives some clues about what's needed:

Four-year-old Kevin, sitting on his mother's lap: "I don't want a shot! It's going to hurt!"

Mother: "Would you like a story? Let's read a story."

Kevin picks up a book: "I want this one. But I don't want a shot."

Mother: "Oh, look! This story is about a baby elephant! What do you think he does when he bumps his nose on a tree?"

Kevin: "Did he cry?"

Mother: "He thought he was going to cry, but instead the mommy elephant gave the baby elephant a kiss on the nose, and he felt all better."

Kevin: "Are you going to give me a kiss?"

Mother: "I sure will, sweetie. And a big hug, too."

Kevin: "Then I'll feel better?"

Mother: "That's right. And then we'll go home and play."

Children at play consciously establish necessary rules for their drama in somewhat the same way that some movies begin with a spoken or printed introduction, to "set the stage." Once the dramatic flow begins, however, the action can acquire a sense of reality, and the distinction between reality and make-believe may become blurred. The following example illustrates this transition:

Allison, six years old to her friends: "Let's play school. I'll be the teacher, and you be the students. . . ."

Later, Mom comes in the room and observes their play: "Are you pretending to be their teacher, dear?"

Allison: "I'm not pretending! I *am* the teacher."

Mario, nine years old, walks slowly, with a limp: "Hey, wait for me, Steve! My ankle hurts."

Steve, also nine: "What's the matter with it?"

Mario: "My dad said I sprained it last week when we were up in the mountains."

Steve: "Hey, I know! Let's say we're in the army. You got your foot shot!"

Mario: "OK. Quick! They're shooting at us! Run for cover!"

(Both boys run at full speed to hide in some bushes.)

From observation of children, we can notice that the need for an induction (that is, for a process that assists the transition to an easy involvement in fantasy) develops as the child's critical reasoning abilities become stronger. This usually occurs somewhere between nine to twelve years of age. Prior to that time, children at play do not stop to "induce a trance." They just begin to play. To be more precise, they just begin to play after a brief explanation to themselves or others of what the premise of the drama will be: "Let's play house." "Let's play

with our dolls." "Let's be cops and robbers. I'll shoot you and just
before you die, you'll shoot me." And so on.

PROBLEMS IN THE ASSESSMENT
OF PAIN IN CHILDREN

In addition to appreciating the child's developmental stage of imagination and hypnotic ability, in order to treat children in pain it is crucial
to assess their degree of suffering. This assessment helps us to determine a baseline of behavior and experience, as well as to predict the
eventual effectiveness of treatment. It is often difficult to obtain a
report of pain directly from the child. For example, self-reports of pain
are impossible for the infant and preverbal young child. For young
children, therefore, assessment is based on observation of behavior,
such as whimpering, crying, and so on. Even for older children, the
evaluation can be difficult, since the same word to describe pain may
have a different meaning for the child than for the adult. For example,
during one intervention, the image and sensation of cold air from an
air conditioner were used to help 11-year-old Lloyd with a bone marrow
aspiration. It was suggested that the sensation of cold air would make
the skin on the hip feel numb. When Lloyd was asked how the imagined air conditioner had helped him, he replied that it "nauseated his
hip" so that he was not bothered by the needle. When asked whether
Lloyd meant that the air conditioner anesthetized or numbed his hip,
he replied "Yeah!" Typically, when children are asked to describe their
pain, they reply, "It just hurts!" Further differentiation between a
"little hurt" and a "big hurt" often presents a challenge.

It is much easier to obtain a useful assessment of pain if the clinician practices careful observation. In situations where a child is unlikely to provide a rating or description of his or her own pain, we must
rely entirely on observation. This presents some interesting challenges. For example, how can we differentiate between behaviors that
represent anxiety and those signaling pain? During acute pain, the
child's behavior often represents a combination of anxiety and pain,
commonly labeled as "distress." Withdrawn behavior in the child with
long-standing pain may represent a combination of pain and depression, with either factor predominating.

Additionally, there are individual, developmental, familial, and cultural differences in pain expression. Some children tend to be very
expressive when in pain, while others tend to suffer in silence. Older
children and adolescents, who have learned more cognitive coping
strategies, tend to be less vocally demonstrative when in pain. How-

ever, we still look for age-appropriate body language, such as muscle rigidity, sweating, or clenching of fist or jaw, which may represent attempts to cope with anxiety and/or pain.

Families tend to create implicit and explicit rules for their children of what constitutes appropriate behaviors to display in public, including pain-related behavior. A common example is the father or mother who admonishes the 10-year-old boy, "Stop crying! You're not a girl!"

Some medical conditions present particular challenges for the assessment of associated pain. For example, with recurring or long-lasting pain related to illnesses such as arthritis or bone cancer, caregivers often require "proof" that a child's continued pain complaints are justified. Unfortunately, one still hears caregivers ask, "Is this child's pain real?" The ability of a child momentarily to divert attention to a game, movie, or television but then complain of pain as a caregiver enters the room is sometimes mistakenly interpreted as evidence that the pain is either bogus or exaggerated. This behavior is typically labeled as "attention-getting" (for the younger child), "drug-seeking behavior" (for the adolescent), or simply "manipulative." In any case, since this behavior is seen as an unpleasant characteristic of the child, "limit-setting" is often the clinical response, rather than a thoughtful reevaluation of the meaning behind the child's behavior.

PSYCHOLOGICAL APPROACHES TO PAIN MANAGEMENT

Utilizing the Power of the Medical Establishment

Pain specialists are often made to feel "ancillary" and therefore somewhat unimportant. This is unfortunate, because many pain problems are treated more effectively with a psychological intervention than with a medical one. It is essential for physicians, psychologists, social workers, nurses, psychiatrists – all who treat the child – to communicate and collaborate as part of the team. It is equally important for the child to recognize that these caregivers function effectively as members of a team, all with equal status, but with different roles.

In the case of an acute pain situation such as a medical procedure, the concept of a team is more difficult to achieve, because the physician is rightly perceived as having the greatest power by virtue of the ability to inflict pain (e.g., by using a needle) or to relieve pain (e.g., by administering a medication). Therefore, in the acute pain situation the patient will typically focus more attention on the physician. This focus of attention may be a source of anxiety (if the physician is perceived as one who is about to inflict pain, for example) or of relief and comfort, or an ambivalent mixture of both.

Therefore, it is very helpful if the treating physician and the pain specialist, as well as the nurse and other providers, can discuss their preferred styles of handling various challenges that arise in the acute pain situation. While working with the child, each can give information and instructions to the child, and refer to each other by name, as a way of demonstrating equal status and authority as they work in partnership to help the child. This will instill confidence in the child that it is OK to shift the focus of attention from the physician to the colleague who is interacting with the child.

Involving the Parents

Attitudes and practices in the medical environment often minimize the importance of parents. Often, they seem to be tolerated, as if they were present only because of their biological or legal status with the child. This is unfortunate, because parents are usually welcome and helpful allies in understanding and treating their children. Parents spontaneously treat their children's pain in ways that are well-known across many cultures: with a kiss, a hug, a song, a distracting joke or story, and with reassurance. Yet, in the presence of physicians, nurses, and other clinicians in the medical setting, they frequently stand back, both literally and figuratively, out of deference to what they may perceive as a greater power. Through our words and our behavior, we need to invite the parents to act as members of a team that will create a circle of concern and knowledge around the child.

Discovering Children's
Self-Directed Coping Skills

The primary goal of psychological intervention for pain control is to decrease suffering and enhance the child's feeling of security and comfort. In addition, clinicians and parents need to help the child develop successful coping strategies.[1] Coping is a self-regulatory process serv-

---

[1]It is important for us to be clear about the distinction between providing comfort and facilitating coping skills. Providing comfort creates a primarily receptive or dependent role for the child; facilitating coping skills promotes independence and self-efficacy. The former is of primary importance in the treatment of acute pain, whereas the latter is essential for management of long-term pain. There is some overlap, of course, between these distinctions.

ing the basic motive of control over oneself and one's world. "Successful coping" occurs when children's appraisal in anticipation of an event (anticipatory coping) and during the event (encounter coping) results in an experience of mastery or accomplishment. Obviously, children facing the same pain event will differ in their coping abilities, as well as in their perception of the situation, for a number of reasons, including past experiences, age, and temperament.

Hilgard and LeBaron (1984) described a variety of self-directed coping techniques developed by children and adolescents who underwent repeated painful medical procedures. These techniques included physical as well as cognitive behaviors.

CASE EXAMPLE: MARTIN, SIX YEARS OLD, FOUND A RELIGIOUS SOLUTION[2]

Martin was a sociable, bright boy who initially experienced a great deal of pain during bone marrow aspirations. Like many children, he soon developed a great anticipatory anxiety to these repeated traumas.

Martin complained to his father about the anxiety and the pain. His was a family with a strong Christian tradition, so the father suggested that Martin try to relax by reciting Psalm 23 to himself. In fact, his father told him that if he would do this, the bone marrow aspiration would not hurt. Fortunately, this suggestion was very effective.

Following his father's suggestion, Martin was able to remain relaxed and calm throughout subsequent procedures. His description of the pain suggested it was now greatly diminished. He was quite enthusiastic about the improvement. He said that as long as he kept his mind on Psalm 23, there was no pain. When asked to describe his experience, he said, "It's like going to sleep, but you don't close your eyes."

CASE EXAMPLE: DAN, TEN YEARS OLD, SWAM WITH HIS GRANDPA

Dan surprised his nurses and physicians by the unusually low level of anxiety and pain that he seemed to experience during most of his bone marrow aspirations. He appeared relaxed and good-humored during these procedures. He often engaged in an active banter with the

[2]The following three cases were taken from Hilgard and LeBaron, 1984, pp. 117–120.

nurses. Apparently, he had independently learned these very effective ways of managing his distress.

When asked to describe what helped him cope, he replied that conversations (with the staff) as well as deep breathing kept his mind busy. He added that, when the nurse and doctor did not talk, he kept his mind busy by imagining he was back in Idaho, swimming with his grandpa.

CASE EXAMPLE: EDWARD, 14, USED IRONY

Edward was a large, husky boy. He had been diagnosed with leukemia three years previously. He was observed to be completely relaxed and calm during preparations for a bone marrow aspiration. His feet dangled off one end of the table because he was so tall. As the female physician (who was rather small) was about to insert the bone marrow needle, Edward said in an ironic tone, "Dig in." Later, as she was pushing hard to get through the bone, he continued to tease her: "You're getting some exercise!"

During an interview afterwards, Edward described some of the techniques he had learned: "On [the television show] 'Emergency' they rescue people, take people to hospitals, and they've got some comedy there. I think about the comedy of it . . . I'm related to the movie. I'm actually a part of it. Today I was thinking about the old man who is always complaining of something. The doctors know it's a fake. First day it's his back, the next day it's his leg. Next day he thinks he's having a heart attack. I seemed to be really there. I was a part of it."

The first few bone marrow aspirations had been very painful for Edward, but when he discovered that becoming a part of the TV program diminished his pain, he continued with that technique. In an interview focused on how Edward's past experiences may have predisposed him to his self-directed intervention, he described some prior encounters with pain. At age eight, he had cut his hand on a plate glass window and required 20 stitches. He had enjoyed playing Monopoly with his mother and found that, during suturing, playing the game in his mind took him away from the pain. Later, when a toenail was removed, Edward made the pain "disappear" by concentrating on an image and sensation of ice around the toe and telling himself that the toe was too cold to feel anything.

These children's capacity for self-directed coping is impressive. We can learn much from them in our efforts to help other children develop coping strategies.

Tailoring Interventions to Coping Style

Some attention has been paid to tailoring interventions to children's individual coping styles. For example, in a laboratory investigation of pain in children (LeBaron, Zeltzer, & Fanurik, 1989; Fanurik, Zeltzer, Roberts, & Blount, 1993), children whose natural coping style was to focus their attention away from the acute pain ("distractors") developed significantly higher pain tolerance than other children when provided with a brief hypnotic intervention. Conversely, pain tolerance in these same children was dramatically reduced when a sensory monitoring intervention was administered in which they were helped to focus their attention on the nonpainful aspects of the sensory experience. However, neither type of intervention significantly improved pain control for children who naturally focused their attention on the sensory stimulus ("attenders"). Interestingly, though, those children who were exposed to the hypnotic intervention, regardless of coping style, were more likely to use distraction when exposed to the same laboratory pain paradigm two years later (Fanurik, Mizell, & Zeltzer, unpublished manuscript).

This concept of goodness-of-fit between the child's coping style and psychological intervention becomes more complicated when considering parental coping style and needs as well (Blount, Corbin, Sturges, et al., 1989). Providing psychological intervention for children in pain must take into account qualities of the child's family, especially of the parents. For example, Schechter, Bernstein, Beck, et al. (1991) found that parents' predictions of their child's distress during a medical procedure were significantly correlated with the actual distress of their children. This suggests to us that parents play a significant role in teaching children not only how to *behave* but also how to *experience* pain. Understanding the parents' perceptions, then, often helps us to better understand the child's perceptions.

There are other considerations when providing interventions for children in pain. The amount of adequate sleep can play a key role in the efficacy of the intervention. Children with sleep deprivation tend to become more irritable and are less able to cope with daily hassles. They are certainly less able to cope with a significant pain event. When children have somatic symptoms, such as pain, itching, nausea, or vomiting, their sleep may be disrupted.

Hospitalization can disrupt children's sleep because of unfamiliarity of surroundings, repetitive sleep disruption related to medical monitoring or nearby noise from other children, or fear. If they have been exposed to multiple pain experiences, these children tend to be hypervigilant, fearfully anticipating the next pain event. Such sleep disruption can substantially attenuate a child's ability to cope with pain and anxiety.

Also, most sedating agents, such as benzodiazepines (e.g., lorazepam), reduce amounts of both REM and stage III-IV sleep (deeper, restorative sleep). Thus, by making the child appear more "sleepy" (but not providing restorative sleep), such agents may serve to falsely reassure the care-provider or parent of the child's good sleep, while doing little to benefit the child. Psychological interventions, especially for the hospitalized child or for the child with long-standing pain, may be most effective if they are also aimed at facilitating restorative sleep.

Previous unpleasant experiences with pain can lead to anticipatory anxiety in future similar situations (e.g., medical procedures). Unsuccessful coping attempts can lead to decreased self-confidence, poor perception of coping abilities, and negative expectations for coping with future procedures. Conversely, successful use of coping skills can contribute to feelings of mastery and confidence. For these reasons, the Consensus Conference on the Treatment of Cancer Pain in Children (Zeltzer, Altman, Kohen et al., 1990) has recommended adequate pharmacologic intervention for the first invasive medical procedure for the newly diagnosed child with cancer and psychological interventions for all other procedures after the staff has more time to get to know the child and family. Pharmacologic pain control strategies for later procedures can be used more selectively.

Efficacy of interventions should be assessed frequently with behavioral and self-report data and, in the medical setting, with psychological measures as well. In the hospital, optimal communication with the child's medical team can be facilitated if the pain specialist makes a note in the patient's medical record regarding the decision leading to a particular type of intervention and the results of that intervention. Interventions should be flexible in approach, based on changing situations and children's needs and abilities.

The mental health professional who is called to a treatment room to "Do something!" to calm a screaming, flailing child must have realistic expectations. Although the staff may expect the therapist to "hypnotize" the child, who would then be expected (unrealistically) to act as if he or she had just received a general anesthetic, the clinician often can do no more than assess the child and situation (which may, in fact, be sufficient). Actually, this calm, objective observation may be quite useful in designing subsequent practice, desensitization, and support.

Ultimately, the goal of intervention is to offer comfort, during a procedure, and to help the child cope, rather than to get the child to "behave" while suffering silently (Bush & Harkins, 1991; McGrath, 1990).

SPECIFIC THERAPEUTIC TECHNIQUES

The treatment of pain with techniques such as sensory-cognitive preparation, distraction, relaxation, and hypnosis have been described elsewhere (J. Hilgard & LeBaron, 1982, 1984; Katz, Kellerman, & Ellenberg, 1987; Kellerman, Zeltzer, Ellenberg, & Dash, 1983; Kuttner et al., 1988; Olness, 1981; Siegel & Peterson, 1981; Zeltzer & LeBaron, 1982).

Psychological intervention "packages," which include a combination of breathing, imagery, rehearsal, and modeling, have demonstrated efficacy (Jay, Elliott, Ozolins et al., 1985). Distraction techniques that involve competitive sensory input (e.g., music, video games) may be sufficient for some children to help them to cope with medical procedures. However, if a child is extremely anxious, or the procedure is very painful or invasive, then the child may require intensive pharmacologic intervention. Of course, psychological and pharmacological interventions are not mutually exclusive. Such children should be offered psychological therapies for their pain experiences as well, especially if they are highly anxious.

There are a number of common psychological interventions for pain control, which are outlined here. The reader interested in greater detail is referred to Berde, Ablin, Glazer, Miser, et al. (1990); Hilgard and LeBaron (1984); Olness and Gardner (1988); Kuttner, Bowman, and Teasdale (1988); Zeltzer (1994); Zeltzer, Anderson, and Schechter (1990); Zeltzer, Jay, and Fisher (1989); Zeltzer and LeBaron (1986).

Preparation typically involves providing mechanical and sensory information. Information can shape cognitive expectations, thus increasing a sense of control over the pain event (Ludwick-Rosenthal & Neufeld, 1988; Routh & Sanfilippo, 1991). How much information to provide depends especially on the child's developmental status, level of anxiety, perceived control, and coping style.

Desensitization is particularly helpful for children experiencing anticipatory distress. The child may be gradually exposed to the impending stimulus with imagery and/or doll play and may practice with a mock procedure. *Modeling* and *rehearsal* through use of videos, dolls, or other techniques can help children visualize the procedure they will undergo. *Videotapes* for parents can teach them coping skills that they can demonstrate to their children or use themselves. *Positive self-statements* (e.g., "I know what to do," "I've done this before") can be combined with thought-stopping and positive reinforcement to encourage feelings of self-efficacy.

Distraction techniques, such as counting or blowing bubbles, are particularly helpful for children who have difficulty focusing on imagery. Hypnosis, imagery, and other forms of imaginative involvement enable dissociation from an unpleasant experience, while maintaining continued attention on a pleasant one. *Suggestion* is also often used to help "reframe" or redefine the sensory experience, to render it more tolerable.

The following examples demonstrate the use of various psychological interventions, including hypnotic treatment. For further reading on child hypnotic treatment, readers are referred to Barber and Adrian (1982); Olness and Gardner (1988); J. Hilgard and LeBaron (1982); Zeltzer and LeBaron (1986). We emphasize that hypnotic treatment is not merely a technique to be applied to all children in pain; nor is a child who has received one type of intervention destined to continue to receive that same intervention indefinitely. Children's individual needs and the particular type of pain situation guide both initial interventions and later shifts in approach.

CASE EXAMPLE: JOHNNY, THREE, TERRIFIED OF A BONE MARROW ASPIRATION

Johnny was brought to the treatment room in the hospital to undergo a bone marrow biopsy as part of his evaluation for a suspected diagnosis of leukemia. His nurse carried him with his connected IV line, crying and struggling, to the treatment room, with his parents following. Once in the treatment room, he was allowed to sit on his father's lap while the staff awaited both the physician and the pain specialist, who was to provide sedation. During the next ten minutes, Johnny screamed and struggled, while his tearful father held him. When I (LZ) entered the room, the nurse appeared stressed, Johnny was screaming, and his father was crying.

The first thing I did was to acknowledge the father, approach Johnny, and exclaim, "Johnny! One of your noses just landed on your dad's arm! Look!" Johnny (as well as his father) seemed bewildered and immediately stopped crying, looking intently at his father's arm. Crouching down at the boy's level, I then said, "Oh, look! There's another nose on your knee!" Johnny, still confused, looked at his knee. After I pointed to another "nose" on dad's other arm, Johnny began to smile. I began pointing out and counting still more "noses," as Johnny chuckled. During this time, I directed the nurse to begin administering midazolam (a short-acting sedative) into Johnny's intravenous line. As the play behavior continued, monitoring leads for EKG and pulse oximeter were placed and Johnny was then administered propofol, an intravenous anesthetic. As he became unconscious, he was gently laid on the table. The father was offered the option of waiting outside the treatment room, where he would be informed when the procedure was completed, so that he could reenter the room before Johnny awoke.

The above case might have begun less traumatically for all if a mental health specialist had initiated some general approaches for nursing when confronted with Johnny's first medical procedure. For example, the play intervention could have been initiated in Johnny's hospital room, and the father, rather than the nurse, could have carried Johnny to the treatment room. There was an underlying assumption that since Johnny was to receive sedation/anesthesia for the procedure, he did not require any prior "psychological" intervention. Everyone simply waited for the pain specialist to bring the "magic drugs," rather than engaging Johnny in play behavior intended to capture his attention by appealing to his curiosity – and preventing the trauma.

Bewilderment can be a benign "attention-grabber," because a child's natural curiosity can often override extreme anxiety and help focus the child's attention on something other than the impending expected pain. If the bewilderment is maintained, the child's attention focuses on trying to understand what is happening, rather than catastrophizing. With a young child, soap bubbles unexpectedly blown by the child as he exhales can also serve to maintain focus of attention, especially if these become incorporated into the fantasy.

Johnny's case illustrates the efficacy of combining psychological and pharmacologic interventions, and demonstrates that even the use of anesthesia does not obviate the need for a psychological approach to pain management.

CASE EXAMPLE: SALLY, NINE, FEARFUL OF REPEATED
BONE MARROW ASPIRATIONS

Sally had been fearful of the repeated bone marrow aspirations that she must undergo as part of her cancer treatment. Her previous experiences involved being physically restrained while she screamed and struggled. After each procedure, she remained silent and withdrawn. Her mother described her increasingly difficult experiences of bringing Sally to the clinic on procedure days, including one day in which Sally ran out of the clinic and into the hospital parking lot, refusing to reenter the clinic. After that episode, her mother avoided informing Sally in advance of a procedure.

However, after the first "unexpected" procedure, Sally refused to come to the clinic at any time. After Sally's mother reported that she had great difficulty getting Sally to come to the clinic for any more treatments, I (LZ) was asked to see Sally. I met with Sally and her mother on a non-procedure day and learned that Sally had an excellent imagination. She described in detail how the "bone arrow" crunched through her bones and how she could feel it "sucking out her marrow." She said she felt helpless and could not stop thinking about the pain of the procedure and "how awful it will be."

I then learned that Sally loved to swim in the ocean and "ride the waves." When I asked her to describe riding the waves, she was able to do so in great detail (with helpful prompting), as if she were there experiencing it. Questions about the feel of the water, the taste of the salt, and the wind on her face helped her to become increasingly involved in this imaginary experience.

Because of Sally's extreme conditioned anticipatory anxiety related to procedures, I arranged two more sessions, during which we went on an imaginary trip to the beach. While this occurred, I also asked her simultaneously to imagine undergoing the bone marrow aspiration. The next step was to imagine being at the beach again while I simulated some of the fearful steps of the procedure, such as washing her skin with alcohol, creating a pinching sensation and a pressure sensation to simulate the pressure of the needle against her bone. After each practice session, I complimented Sally about her coping abilities and her excellent imagination.

I also repeatedly mentioned that when people use the part of their brain where imagination exists, the sensations (feelings) in their body tend to feel "different," and that it would be interesting to notice in what way her next procedure would feel "different" to Sally. I encouraged Sally to use her imagination at home in ways that felt pleasant, so "that part of her brain would get stronger." Eventually, she might notice that "pokes" and other "medical things" that used to bother her would begin to feel different and not bother her in the same way anymore. Sally's mother was present for all sessions and was encouraged to practice with her if Sally wanted her mother's help.

The day of the next planned procedure, Sally and I met early to practice in the treatment room itself, with her mother's help. With Sally's direction, we rehearsed a bone marrow aspiration. Later, when the time for the actual procedure was announced, Sally became tearful. I reminded her that her brain had learned some new ways to change feelings in her body. Just like riding a bicycle, once she learned these new skills, they were there to help her. She was encouraged to take some slow deep breaths and picture herself blowing up a big balloon filled with helium, which she allowed to help lift her forward to the treatment room.

Once in the treatment room, Sally again began to cry, and again her mother and I helped her to become involved in an imaginary adventure involving the beach and riding the waves. As her mother worked alongside me, she became increasingly active in helping Sally to maintain imaginative involvement, while I increasingly took the role of encouraging mom to continue to help Sally in this way. Sally screamed briefly during the needle stick but immediately became involved again in her imaginary adventure, as mom introduced new surprises that helped recapture Sally's attention during the adventure. After the procedure, everyone in the treatment room praised Sally for being so brave as she rode the ocean waves so well. Sally appeared pleased with herself and said that the procedure "wasn't so bad."

Sally's case illustrates the development of anticipatory anxiety related to unsuccessful coping and the child's understandable expectations that the pain event (the painful aspiration procedure) would necessarily overwhelm her abilities to cope with future procedures.

Earlier referral to a pain specialist might have facilitated Sally's abilities to cope and reduced staff time by helping her to be much easier to manage. Because learned helplessness impeded effective coping, Sally required desensitization before she could practice effective coping during mock procedures, culminating in a practice session in the treatment room itself. I not only learned about her interests but helped her to utilize her own imagination to alter her situational experience. I helped Sally to have a variety of sensory experiences (touch, smell, visual, auditory) during the imaginary event and appealed to her curiosity by including surprises in the adventure. During this time, I was also modeling behavior for her mother that would help her to enhance Sally's coping efforts. It is important to note that, although Sally cried at various points before and during the procedure, I did not respond as if we had failed. Moreover, Sally was reinforced after the procedure for her effective coping excellence and learned that she really did have substantial control over the comfort of her experience during the procedure.

It should be noted that not all children have the degree of success that Sally did. When a child continues to experience a high degree of pain and anxiety, the possibility of pharmacologic treatment should be seriously considered. In this event, it is also important to reassure the patient and the parent that this does not represent a failure on their part. It is essential that medication not be seen as a solution to problem patients, but as an important part of any child's effective care.

CASE EXAMPLE: ERIK, 15, WITH CHRONIC RECURRING HEADACHES

Erik, the son of a prominent physician and a noted psychologist, was referred by his parents to the pain clinic after they attended a lecture by the director of the clinic about nonpharmacologic approaches to pain management. An honor student and star athlete, Erik had been evaluated and treated unsuccessfully by three different neurologists for headaches for the past three years. Radiographic studies and other tests failed to identify the cause of the headaches, and a variety of drugs had been tried.

In our first meeting, I (LZ) inquired about Erik's pain (location, duration, timing, palliative and aggravating factors, his own view of etiology and treatment), his family, school, hobbies, friends, and personal ambitions. Erik seemed to be a well-adjusted young man, who was basically quite happy. However, he seemed to feel very pressured toward high achievement in all spheres of his life and found it difficult to relax physically, mentally, and emotionally. Therefore, the emphasis of treatment was to teach Erik techniques for relaxation.

He was guided in progressive relaxation, focusing his attention first on his toes and then slowly moving up toward his head. I then encouraged Erik to imagine being in a place where he knew "how to feel good." I asked him to signal with his finger when he was "there," which he did. After a few minutes to allow him to do something "fun" and "enjoyable" there, I suggested that part of his brain could listen and learn something new, while the "rest" of him could continue to enjoy his experience of feeling good. I suggested that he "find" that part of his brain that was the "central relay station" for sensations and feelings. Various examples were provided (e.g., "like a pilot would see . . . different knobs and switches, and colored lights").

I continued:

Please let me know by lifting an index finger when you locate this part of your brain. . . . Good. . . . Now find the switches that control the areas of your head where your headaches are located. . . . Can you see them? . . . Good. . . . Now you can begin to gradually turn the knobs or move those switches to decrease the amount of signals . . . or electricity . . . or sensations that get to the brain. It might be like a traffic light changing color to keep all the traffic you don't want from coming into the city. . . . As you observe this part of your brain, you can notice your brain doesn't have to be asleep. In fact, it may feel quite active, and you may notice, perhaps ever so slightly at first, some differences in the sensations in your head. . . . Gradually, you can notice these new pleasant feelings replacing your headaches.

Five more weekly sessions followed, with Erik indicating that his headaches were significantly relieved. One more follow-up session took place a month after the fifth session, during which Erik reported that his headaches were gone. His parents, who came to that session with Erik, confirmed that report. A Christmas card a year later indicated that the headaches had not returned.

Erik was clearly a healthy, energetic, achievement-oriented adolescent from a high-achieving family. The pressure to achieve may have been the major cause of Erik's headaches; no other problems emerged during the initial evaluation. Thus, a symptom-focused approach was used, with considerable success. This approach involved progressive relaxation to help Erik narrow the focus of his attention, pleasant imagery to promote a sense of enjoyment, and a suggestion to change the headaches, using "a brain central sensation station" imagery. Suggestions giving Erik permission to have time to relax and engage in enjoyable imagery – just to have fun – probably contributed to the relief of his symptoms.

CASE EXAMPLE: KERRIE, EIGHT, WHO HAD A FACIAL LACERATION

While she was playing soccer, Kerrie's chin collided with another player's head. She was brought to my [SL] office for sutures of her split chin. When the physician entered the room, Kerrie was holding a piece of bloody gauze to her chin. As her mother described how the accident had happened, Kerrie's eyes filled with tears.

"Do I have to get stitches?" she asked in a trembling voice.

"I hope you can get some of my special magic stitches," I answered with a cheerful voice. "Let me take a look, and I can tell you how much fun we'll have. Oh, that's a beauty! This is your lucky day! You can get some of my special stitches. They're blue! When your friends see your chin, they're going to want stitches too."

Kerrie seemed quite thoughtful, and she looked a little less afraid. "Will it hurt?" she asked in a fearful whisper.

I continued reframing her experience by gently whispering in Kerrie's ear: "Ever felt what fairies feet are like? Sometimes tingle, sometimes prickle, sometimes tickle. That's what it will be like. Hurt? Naw . . . I don't think so – but if it does, you let me know, and I'll stop."

"OK," she said, smiling a little now.

Kerrie had a deep, jagged laceration on her chin, which would require three small sutures. I signaled to the nurse to bring in a tray with the lidocaine syringe and suturing equipment, all covered with a towel, of course, to avoid frightening Kerrie.

"First, I'll wash your chin with some magic soap – It feels so good, so cool, that maybe you'll feel some tingling. Let me know if you do."

Kerrie laid back on the treatment table with her mom at her side. I washed her chin with enthusiasm and a flourish, as if creating a work of art. "Aha! Look, Mom, what a beautiful chin!"

At the same time, I asked Kerrie if she believed in fairies. Of course she did, although she had never seen any.

"I'm going to put this magic tent over your face so you can feel fairies dance on your chin," I said, while opening a paper sheet with a hole in the middle to create a sterile field for the suturing. "By the way, you and your mom can peek at each other under the edge of the tent."

This way of communicating with Kerrie allowed me to continue the technical medical procedure while simultaneously attending to Kerrie's (and Mom's) needs for comfort and security.

With one hand, I lightly pinched the chin. "Now you can feel the fairy toes dancing across your chin." At the same time a small amount of lidocaine was dribbled from a syringe and infused into the surrounding tissue (thus, I was not depending solely on psychological pain management, since medical management was so readily available).

All the while, Kerrie, her mother, and I chatted cheerfully about fairies, tiny giraffes, and a pet kitten, all of whom were having a picnic on Kerrie's chin. Three sutures were then easily placed, with no discomfort to Kerrie. As she sat up afterward, Kerrie grinned. She blinked her eyes the way people do when they come out of a darkened movie theater into the sunlight. "Are we done? Do I have stitches?"

Unlike Johnny, Kerrie had no previous horrible experiences to convince her that this one would also be horrible. But she had enough information to suspect that needles (and, therefore, pain) would inevitably be part of her experience. Yet, she was willing to trust that I could help her without causing pain. She was receptive to my suggestion of "special," "magic" stitches. Further, a tone of voice that conveyed excitement and pleasure, rather than regret, helped support the expectation of magic and wonder, rather than pain and fear.

The involvement of the child's interest in fantasy and in comforting attention to her chin served two purposes: It provided a more pleasant focus than worrying about pain (which already existed because of the injury); and it offered a way for the child to reinterpret the sensations that she did feel. For example, if the momentary stinging that occurs as the anesthetic is injected is interpreted as "fairies' feet dancing" or a "kitten licking my chin," the child can perceive it as tolerable, sometimes even pleasurable. Without this reinterpretation, children are very likely to worry that the stinging is a harbinger of greater pain yet to come, and their fear and vigilance escalate quickly.

It is important to note that, although Kerrie's case demonstrates a physician providing psychological intervention while suturing her chin, the intervention could have also been provided by a psychologist, social worker, nurse, or other professional. In that case, it is helpful for the physician and pain specialist to work together, communicating shared expectations and intentions, so that the child knows they are working in collaboration.

CASE EXAMPLE: ALEJANDRO, 13, SURE HE HAD A BRAIN TUMOR

Alejandro came to the clinic with his older sister because he had experienced nagging headaches for several months. He was sure he had a brain tumor. He had received a thorough evaluation from a neurologist, including a CT scan. But in spite of the neurologist's insistence that the headaches were most likely due to muscle tension, and not a tumor, the boy was not convinced. Consequently, Alejandro was referred to me for further exploration of this issue.

I [SL] reviewed the boy's medical history and symptoms. Then I obtained a developmental and psychosocial history, including current family functioning, school performance, peer relations, and use of drugs and alcohol. My physical examination further confirmed the neurologist's conclusion that there was no evidence of a brain lesion.

Alejandro's family had split up about a year earlier. The father had returned to Mexico because he was unable to find steady work in the United States. The mother moved to another city 200 miles away for a better job, and Alejandro and his younger sister were to stay with an older sister, 23, who had obtained a secure and well-paying job.

The mother had promised that within a few months she would come for Alejandro and his younger sister, but as the year passed she changed her mind. She said that by the following summer she would be able to move to a larger apartment and provide better for Alejandro and his younger sister. This was a great disappointment to Alejandro. He often felt sad, and his academic performance gradually slipped from A's and B's to D's and F's. He became withdrawn and angry.

During the past Christmas, the entire family was reunited at the older sister's apartment, including the father, who traveled from Mexico for a few days. Alejandro seemed to be his former cheerful self during the holidays. But as January and February passed, he began to complain of headaches. When June arrived, his anticipated move to be with his mother was crushed when she announced that she could not afford the larger apartment. So they would have to wait yet one more year. By the end of September, when he was seen in clinic, Alejandro was complaining of daily severe headaches.

I asked Alejandro if he could get a picture in his mind of what the tumor looked like. With little hesitation, he answered: "It's dark red. It looks really ugly."

"Does the tumor feel like anything? Does it have feelings in it, like happy or sad, weak or strong, angry or pleasant?"

"It feels sad and lonely."

The headaches appeared to be emotionally based, related to the disintegration of the family structure – particularly to the loss of parental contact – and to feelings of having been betrayed. After consideration of this, I said "I'm glad you came to see me. I think your headaches are serious. In fact, I agree with you. I think you do have a brain tumor, but of a different kind. The kind you have comes from feeling lonely, sad, and disappointed. I think I can help you to feel better."

Alejandro's eyes widened and he sat up straight in his chair. He appeared to be very, very interested. "You think you can cure my brain tumor?" he asked, with no little amazement.

"Yes. But this isn't the kind of brain tumor that comes from cancer, so you don't need surgery or medicine. It comes from hurt feelings, so what you need is for all of us to talk about how to help the family."

Alejandro sat quietly, staring at me. "Now I want you to look at your tumor again, one last time," I said. "Does it need anything else?"

Alejandro sat for a moment, eyes wide open, staring into space. He appeared to be intensely involved with the mental image of his tumor. After a while, he said, in a soft voice, "No. It doesn't need anything more."

There was no further visualization used. From this point on, what occurred was a series of planning sessions with Alejandro and his older sister, who was initially astounded by my approach but quite supportive nonetheless. The older sister contacted the mother by phone, and they discussed how to have more contact with the children and how to rearrange the family finances so as to support their living together again. As these discussions were occurring, Alejandro received some extra academic help from a tutor at school. His mother came to visit more often. His school work steadily improved. By Christmas, Alejandro and his younger sister were able to rejoin their mother. After the initial visit, he did not complain of another headache.

This case illustrates the importance of the clinician's knowledge that pain symptoms do not necessarily require a medical solution. (Alejandro did not require surgery or chemotherapy to treat his "tumor.") Alejandro's case also illustrates that, once the clinician hypothesizes the nature of the problem, imagery and suggestion can be used in a brief, focused intervention. In this case, implicit messages were given to the patient that his tumor was the projection of his emotions. These messages eventually proved to be quite helpful.

Often, children (and adolescents even more so) find it very difficult to say "I'm afraid" or "I'm lonely." You may ask in five different ways how the adolescent feels, and the response will be a variation of "I dunno" or "OK, I guess." Attribution of feelings to a tumor or, in other instances, to a sore joint or to a drawing the patient might create, helps the patient project emotional feelings somatically, and thereby to express them safely. In this case, I invited Alejandro to look at his "'tumor' one last time" – an implicit suggestion that the "tumor" would soon disappear.

The effectiveness of this kind of intervention depends on the patient's confidence that the clinician will truly be helpful. Fundamental to this trust was the clinician's respectful acknowledgment of the patient's point of view – but with the inclusion of the clinician's own judgment. Therefore, it was crucial that I communicate my judgment (that this was an example of somatizing) in a kind and respectful way.

It is important to note that the crucial intervention in most psychological problems is not a clever or subtle suggestion or image, but, rather, respectful, competent counseling. Indeed, it is likely that a well-trained family therapist would have been successful in "curing" this boy's "tumor" by providing appropriate family intervention and support, without using imagery at all. The use of imagery and suggestion in this case was an efficient and useful way of harnessing the energy and anxiety attached to the idea of a tumor to facilitate the basic therapeutic work that needed to occur in the family. While not a clinical necessity, it appeared to be greatly facilitative of rapid change.

CASE EXAMPLE: TOM, 18, WITH PHANTOM LIMB PAIN

J. Hilgard and LeBaron (1984) described an 18-year-old adolescent who was disabled by phantom limb pain. Tom's left leg had been amputated following a diagnosis of a malignant bone tumor (osteosarcoma). During the year since surgery, he had been plagued by a variety of unpleasant sensations in his absent leg and foot. The least annoying of these were mild sensations of tingling and itching. More troublesome were recurrent aching sensations and painful jerking. These were severe enough to disrupt sleep as well as Tom's activities during the day. The most bothersome sensations were severe stabbing pains—"like a thousand pins"—in the sole of his phantom foot.

Because of the frequent disruption of sleep, Tom said that he often felt tired and irritable; yet, he was very pleasant and enthusiastic about receiving some help with this problem. In fact, Tom described himself as the sort of person who loved challenges and did not like to give in to adversity. He had been a member of his high school varsity wrestling team at the time of his surgery. Since then, he had been working assiduously to get back in shape and rejoin the team. As he talked enthusiastically about returning to the team and driving his car (modified to accommodate his amputation), it seemed clear that he loved tackling difficult problems. He appeared to meet challenges in a critical, logical manner.

Clearly, Tom liked being in control. He had achieved success through effort, rather than relaxation, so he was more likely to develop confidence in our work together if we practiced muscle tension first, rather than relaxation. So I [SL] asked him to tighten all the muscles in his scalp, then his face, neck, arms, and so on, in a progressive fashion, letting each muscle group relax as we moved on to the next group . . . but without really emphasizing the relaxation component.

When we came to the leg muscles, Tom seemed quite intrigued with the idea of tensing the muscles of both legs. For a moment, he stared at me with a grin, as if he thought maybe I was joking. I suggested it might be easier if he first leaned back in his chair and got a picture of his left leg in his mind . . . imagine it reattached to his body . . . try to feel it reattached, moving, responsive to his brain, so he could tighten both legs, together. Once he understood what I had suggested, he sat back in his chair and closed his eyes. I waited in silence for only a few seconds.

"That was easy!" he said suddenly, opening his eyes. He grinned, like a kid who has just learned to ride his bike.

"I'm glad it was so easy," I said. "What was it like, feeling your left leg do what you asked it to do?"

"Kinda weird! But it was great! First I wiggled my toes, then I moved my leg a little, then I tightened the muscles, then all of a sudden, both my legs felt more relaxed."

Then I asked Tom to repeat the entire process again, but this time we would take a little longer, following the tensing of each muscle group by focusing on relaxation of those muscles before moving to the next group.

After Tom completed this process he reported that he felt very, very relaxed. Even better, he said that some annoying sensations like tingling and mild cramps in his phantom leg, which had bothered him at the beginning of the procedure, had now resolved. I suggested that, because we had reached the end of our allotted time together, we would meet again in a few days. Tom readily agreed. He said he would continue to practice the muscle exercises, because he felt they would be quite helpful.

At the beginning of the next treatment, I mentioned to Tom that mental alertness is compatible with muscle relaxation, because I wanted to reassure him that he could maintain all of the control and autonomy he needed while still practicing this relaxed state. I then asked him to pay attention to sensations in the back of his left hand. I wanted to begin exploring how well he could focus his attention on various sensations. If he could gain some control over the sensations in his hand, this skill and confidence might be applied to treating the sensations in his phantom limb.

> Now pay close attention to whether you feel more warmth or coolness in your hand . . . or whether there is more heaviness or lightness . . . or perhaps you may notice some slight twitching or tingling. Whatever you notice is okay. Whatever you notice, you can experiment with it if you wish. . . . Try increasing or decreasing one sensation or another. . . . Or, if you prefer, just continue to notice what's happening, without needing to do anything about it at all. . . .

After a few minutes of silence, I added the following thought, accentuated with a bit of a dramatic whisper, hoping to emphasize the importance of the message:

> If you pay very, very close attention, it's possible that you may notice something else in the middle of the tingling and all of the other feelings. . . . Somewhere among all those other sensations, you may notice some little empty spaces, where there are no sensations at all — *little spots of numbness*.

My hope was not only to emphasize the importance of this idea, but also to convey a feeling of "magic" about it — an impression given through the tone of my voice (or my whisper, in this case) — that there was an experience here that was out of the ordinary. We all enjoy drama and intrigue and readily associate them with out-of-the-ordinary, even magical experiences. My hope was that Tom would find the thought as intriguing as I did, and that he would consider it very carefully . . . and imaginatively.

Tom sat very still in his chair and, without my suggesting it, closed his eyes as if he were absorbed in deep concentration.

I then continued expressing some thoughts that were intended to serve two purposes: First, I wanted to emphasize the idea that he could experience some numbness in his hand; second, I wanted to put the suggestion in a context that would be relevant to his own experience:

> While wrestling, you might well have suffered a bruise or a strain that you really didn't notice until the match was over. In order to win the match, you somehow kept the pain out of your mind, so it was numb. . . . You enjoy adventures and interesting experiences. . . . What an interesting experience it could be to discover how much of the same numbness you can notice right now in the back of your hand. Why don't you test any numbness in your hand, by pinching the back of both hands?

After Tom noticed the numbness, I encouraged him to continue to explore and practice whatever he was learning about his sensations. He continued to do all of this with his eyes closed, apparently still deeply focused on his inner experience. I suggested that he now open his eyes and refocus his attention on the surrounding environment. He promptly opened his eyes, although he looked a little dazed for a few seconds.

"Wow, that was interesting!" he said.

I asked him what the experience had been like. He described how he had allowed himself to slip easily into an extremely relaxed state, just like when he had done the muscle exercises. This had made it easier for him to concentrate on the task I had given him. He had been surprised by how relaxed, yet how alert he had felt. He found himself very attentive to each word I had said, because each word had become "very real and true" to him.

Tom reported that the numbness in the back of his hand had spread quickly from a few isolated spots to include, finally, his entire hand. He then mentioned, with great enthusiasm, that a numbness in his phantom limb had occurred without any conscious thought or effort on his part. It seemed to me that he recognized an implicit suggestion that the experience of numbness of his hand could transfer to his left leg.

During the next session, I gave Tom similar suggestions and added further that the same numbness could occur in his leg, any time he wished. This portion of the treatment was audiotaped. I then gave Tom the tape to listen to at home, to practice with if he felt the need.

At the next meeting about two weeks later, Tom described considerable reduction in all of the unpleasant sensations in his phantom leg, ranging from 50 percent to 100 percent relief. He usually experienced a complete remission of symptoms after listening to the tape recording at home. At other times, he achieved variable but very satisfactory success, just using his own suggestions.

"At times," Tom said, "The pain doesn't go away the way I want it to, but I've learned to just go with the pain now, and it doesn't bother me as much as it used to." An additional change was that, since Tom was no longer awakened from sleep by pain, his sleep pattern returned to normal.

CHILDREN WHO APPEAR TO HAVE LITTLE INTEREST IN IMAGERY

An appreciation of the variation in children's needs and preferences is essential to effective treatment. Some children appear to be inherently very interested and responsive to the use of suggestion, imagery, and fantasy to help relieve their pain. Others, although seemingly very motivated to feel comfort, simply do not respond well to these approaches.

A significant amount of this variability seems to be related to early childhood involvement in make-believe fantasies and experiences of story telling with their parents (LeBaron, Zeltzer, & Fanurik, 1989). However, other situational variables also play a very significant role in determining the child's receptiveness. These include the child's level of anxiety, alertness, and general feeling of well-being.

Some children present a very interesting challenge to the clinician who invites their involvement in imagery and fantasy:

Clinician: "Would you like to feel some little fairies dancing across your chin?"
Child: "I don't believe in fairies."
Clinician: "How would you like to have Fluffy, that little kitten you were telling me about, curled up right here on you lap while we do this?
Child (incredulous): "We can't have Fluffy here in the office!"

Such interactions are not infrequent, even with children who are at an age and of a predisposition to enjoy stories and fantasies about fairies, kittens, and other sympathetic creatures. Whatever the reason – because of underlying predisposition or temporary anxiety – these children simply do not find the images and make-believe offered by the kindly clinician to be at all helpful.

Here is one of many ways that you might respond to such a child (the physician is preparing to suture a laceration over the eyebrow):

Clinician: "You're right, we can have a great time without any fairies or kittens. While Dr. Jones is fixing your eyebrow, would you prefer to know everything she's doing, or do you want to tell me about the camping trip you just finished?"

Child: "I don't want her to stick me with a needle! That's going to hurt!"

Clinician: "OK, then. So let's let Dr. Jones cover both of our faces with this sheet. I'll put my face down here too, so we can see each other. Like a tent. Like camping."

Physician: "Oh, you two are so lucky to go camping! Have fun! I'll give you a phone call if there's anything I need to tell you."

Clinician: "Thanks, Dr. Jones! Now, Dr. Jones is just washing your eyebrow with soap. That will help it. So you went camping up in the mountains?"

Child: "Uh-huh."

Clinician: "Under a tent?"

Child: "Uh-huh."

Clinician: "Like this one. Like this tent that you and I are under. Except bigger." (The clinician notices that Dr. Jones is about to infuse a local anesthetic into the eyebrow.) "When you were camping, you could have woke up in the morning . . . and there's the sun coming up, shining right in your face! Kind of warm. Not hot, really . . . more warm, warm sun, so that you think of wearing a hat to keep it out of your eyes, then you begin to wonder if somebody's going to do some pancakes over the campfire. . . . Did you have any?"

Child: "No."

Clinician: "Would you like some pancakes for breakfast while you're camping?"

Child: "Oh, yes! Of course! I love pancakes! But we didn't bring any pancake mix. What are you doing? Are you going to stick me with a needle?"

Clinician: "Dr. Jones put the special medicine in your eyebrow so it would feel good while we're camping. Right now, she's just pressing on it with her finger. Just like when you put your hat on to keep the sun out of your eyes while you're camping. So what would you like for breakfast?"

Child: "I would love pancakes!"

Clinician: "What if I had a bag of magic pancake mix right here in my pocket? Mmmm . . . tastes great. With maple syrup. Let's stir it up and put some in a pan. If you have a glove to protect your hand, you could hold the frying pan. Be careful when you bend close to the fire. The heat can feel good and warm on your face in the early morning. . . . "

Child: "I tasted one of the pancakes! It's sweet. . . . "

But what if, in spite of our most compassionate and creative intervention possible, the child still seems uninterested or does not benefit from our efforts? We are understandably more personally invested in our behavioral interventions than we are in the pills or ointments we recommend. This investment is an important support for the challenges of our work. This great personal investment springs from the compassion and commitment we feel toward the patient.

Yet we will inevitably have the experience, repeated again and again, of children who do not benefit from our intervention as much as we hope. We may feel inadequate, and even angry at these children for frustrating our good intentions. Or, rather than blaming the children, we might blame the parents, the physician, or ourselves. But what we imagine to be a "failure" may be, in a larger context, more successfully comforting to the patient than we realize. Whatever else is the case, our calm and compassionate presence is a value to our patients. Our challenge is to balance our enthusiastic need to help with a calm and intelligent detachment, so that even in the greatest physical and emotional turmoil the patient and parents know they have not been abandoned: We are there, doing our best. Even as the patient tries to reject adult help, there is also a lonely hope that the adult will never leave.

CONCLUSION

There is much to learn when we help children and adolescents with pain. Sometimes we have been most helpful when we have made little use of the standard techniques. Specific techniques may be either quite powerful or quite inadequate, depending on our skill and sense of timing, as well as the child's acceptance of those skills. When we feel the most uncertain regarding what specific techniques to use, it is often helpful to become less active, less clever – and to become quieter, calmer, and more observant. This often inspires children to bring their own clever creativity to life, knowing that we are still there, ready to receive and value them.

12

ELDERS IN PAIN

Samuel LeBaron
William C. Fowkes

MRS. TAKAKI is 89 years old, but she still walks every day around the block with her dog. Both of them are old, and this year they are both walking slower with each passing month. Although Mrs. Takaki doesn't speak much English, and I know only five words of Japanese, I still look forward to our morning encounter as I return from jogging. She is in a perpetual bowing position as she walks. When I bow to her, she laughs and nods her head. Then she says several rapid phrases that I can only hope is a blessing on me and my family. She takes my hand this morning and slowly uncurls her fingers, gnarled with rheumatoid arthritis. A smooth pebble slides from her hand into mine.

She laughs as she sees the pleasure her gift has brought me. I know where I'll put it: In the pot with the Bonzai tree she gave me last year. Her body is as twisted as the Bonzai, but she has a genius for simple beauty. Once a month, she invites me for a tea ceremony. During the tea ceremony, she always rubs her painfully arthritic hands together for a long time over the hot charcoal. Once a week, I take fifteen seconds to wheel her garbage can out to the curb alongside my own. Every morning, when I see her shuffling toward me at the end of my jog, I thank her silently.

The management of pain in elders is neglected in the training of physicians, psychologists, and providers of social services (Ferrell, 1991). Yet, the prevalence of pain has been estimated to be 100 percent greater in those over the age of 60 compared to those under 60 (Crook, Rideout, & Browne, 1984). There is some evidence, for example, that at least 80 percent of elderly people have some form of arthritic pain (Davis, 1988). As our population of elders increases, and as we all grow toward older age, the importance of understanding how to treat pain in this age group becomes more apparent. When we care for the elderly, we are caring for our grandparents, our parents . . . and our future selves.

In this chapter we illustrate and discuss nonpharmacologic treatment of problems related to pain. We assume that analgesics and other classes of medication will be used as needed for all patients in pain. Discussions of medication for pain for elders may be found in Kepes (1983).

What we wish to address here is how our relationship with and response to an elderly man or woman who is our patient create a context within which suffering is understood. Recall now the discussion from Chapters 1, 4, and 5 that the experience of pain and suffering is powerfully determined by the meaning of pain to the patient and by the influences of culture, family, and past experience. The patient's needs for empathy, dependence, or autonomy affect how and when the individual experiences pain and suffering. Expressions of pain ("I feel so much pain!" or "I don't get around much anymore") may generate either support or avoidance by a caregiver. Often, there are attendant emotional consequences, mostly discouragement, pessimism, and depression.

THE MEANING OF PAIN

To understand the experience of pain in elders more clearly, let us consider the various meanings that pain may have for those in the later years of life. Some elders fear and resent pain because it heralds a decline toward increasing loss of function and, ultimately, death. Such an elder may respond to pain with denial or with much complaining and anger, sometimes turned toward a physician or family members. Elders who deny pain because of fear may try to push themselves toward greater activity, or they may retreat physically and emotionally into a dark hut of depression.

CASE EXAMPLE: MR. WILLIS, 82, WITH PROSTATE CANCER

Mr. Willis stopped taking his medication. This occurred after one of his cancer specialists complained that another specialist had been wrong to change one of the medications. This was extremely upsetting to Mr. Willis. He felt that somehow it was his fault that there was a disagreement between his physicians.

Many clinicians are so awkward around pain and death that they retreat from human contact with the patient to technology or "facts" to try to maintain a sense of control. Often, patients such as Mr. Willis with a terminal or chronic illness feel guilty or angry when problems arise in their treatment. Understandably, due to the physicians' retreat, the patient is likely to feel abandoned.

Mr. Willis returned to see me (WF), his family physician, because he didn't know what to do. He appeared sad. He often felt like crying, he was fatigued, his sleep was disturbed, and his appetite gone. He also said that he and his wife, to whom he had been devoted for 48 years, had never had marital problems – until recently. As he became more depressed, Mr. Willis ruminated more and more about his illness and pain.

I invited Mrs. Willis into the examining room, and said to her, "Your husband says that you're just not getting along very well for the past couple of months. Is that your feeling about it?" She agreed. I asked, "Well, what is it? What's the problem as you see it?"

Mrs. Willis admitted that she was fed up with his complaints of pain. "I just hate him being sick all the time and moaning and groaning and lying around and complaining. I'm tired of it." Mrs. Willis felt that her husband was depressed. She had said this over and over again to some of the doctors who were taking care of him. The only response either of them received was a suggestion to see a psychiatrist. This was not helpful. Mr. and Mrs. Willis did not need to see a psychiatrist or any additional doctor. They needed to discuss these problems in detail with the doctors already treating Mr. Willis.

This dilemma is common for patients who receive fragmented care. The cardiologist deals with heart and lungs and the urologist with the prostate but nobody treats Mr. Willis as a whole person with feelings about his present predicament. The alternative, of course, to such "partialist care" is comprehensive care, which includes consideration of physical, emotional, and familial influences on the patient. (This care requires more than technical knowledge, of course; it also carries the additional, sometimes onerous requirement that the clinician be willing to compassionately attend to the patient's feelings – and to tolerate the clinician's own feelings that are naturally evoked in the process.)

I told Mr. Willis that I would resolve the dispute between the other physicians about his medication. Then I said, "There is nothing in your history or exam that would suggest that you're at death's door. On the contrary, there's every indication that you could feel a lot better if your depression were treated."

Mr. Willis seemed interested. He appeared pleased that his wife had been invited into the session and that they had began to discuss what was happening between the two of them. They had not talked about that before. She hadn't really issued a specific complaint; she had just been angry. So now the problem was out in the open: She was just tired of the complaining.

Mr. Willis was given a prescription for antidepressants and was encouraged to return for more discussion of his fears and needs, which, subsequently, he did. As the weeks passed, he changed from a sad, morose person to somebody who was hopeful and could smile readily. As this change occurred, his complaints of pain decreased significantly.

For Mr. Willis, pain was a recurring reminder of loss that seemed to drive him deeper into depression. Other elders appear to experience pain not so much as a threat but as a nuisance—and perhaps a severe one. They do not seem, however, to suffer fear or anguish in relation to the pain. Instead, some elders laugh at their pains or remark that the pain is a valuable part of their present existence. Some have been heard to make comments such as: "When I wake up in the morning and feel my joints ache, I know I'm still alive." Why do some elders feel this way about pain while others experience pain as a severe threat?

Part of the answer lies in the meaning of the pain. Like everyone else, an elder's interpretation of a pain sensation is affected by the location, severity, frequency, and duration of the pain, all of which are clues to both the patient and clinician about the possible morbidity of the condition represented by the pain. In addition, factors such as environmental contingencies, a desire to be stoic, and the elder's degree of equanimity versus anxiety in everyday life will all affect the experience and the expression of pain.

Understanding the role of pain in the human condition is a lifelong challenge. Symptoms are often attributed to life events that may or may not truly be causal factors. Such explanations are useful for both the patient and physician to understand and discuss, particularly with regard to self-limiting types of pain problems. Although the practical value of such explanatory models decreases when more serious, aggressive biological disease is present, even then an appreciation of the patient's understanding of his or her pain may provide an opportunity to relieve anxiety and suffering to some degree.

Elderly patients, in particular, often present unusual combinations of symptoms. Sometimes they have pain for reasons that are unclear; other times they may have no discomfort associated with an illness or trauma that would ordinarily cause pain. For example, an elder with pneumonia may have no cough or fever; the only symptom may be falling down.

Although some elders tend to embellish their symptoms, our clinical experience suggests that elders more frequently downplay the severity of their symptoms. Perhaps some elders simply do not experience their symptoms as dramatically as a younger person. This blunting may reflect actual age-related changes in the nervous system that result in slowing and reduction of afferent stimulation, thereby assisting in the process of coping with pain. Or perhaps blunting of symptoms occurs because elders develop another psychological way of coping with discomfort. They may notice aching joints but, having become accustomed to many aches and pains, think them unworthy of mention. In summary, we see that reporting of symptoms is affected by (1) sensory-perceptual changes, and (2) coping strategies that may include denial, self-distraction, or reinterpretation of the symptoms as a natural part of growing older.

Involvement in Meaningful Activities and Goals: Effects on Function

One of the most salient themes of old age is the tension between dependency, on the one hand, and separation and isolation, on the other.

CASE EXAMPLE: RAUL AND JULIA SALCIDO, IN THEIR EARLY EIGHTIES, MAKING NEW LIVES

Raul and Julia had lived in a quiet suburban neighborhood for 30 years. For many years, they had no reason to move. However, with advancing years, they began to feel isolated from their children. Though they had several children, they all lived some distance away. The Salcidos didn't belong to any church or social group. They had a large number of close friends, but those friends had their own families and activities, and there was nobody whom they felt they could call on for an extended period of assistance if one of them became critically ill.

They were increasingly aware of the possibility that one of them could have a stroke or fall and break a hip or have some other major problem. They had both already experienced a taste of disability: Julia had moderately severe arthritic degeneration in her hips and spine. Sometimes she had difficulty getting out of bed for days at a time.

Raul had chronic muscle pain from fibromyalgia, and he also suffered from moderate emphysema and recurrent bronchitis. They both agreed that they would rather die than become so debilitated that they would have to be cared for by strangers.

Raul and Julia discussed their concerns with their children, whose response was unanimous: "We would like to be involved in your care if you have any problems. Is there any way that you would consider moving closer to where we live? If you wouldn't mind moving to our rural area and buying some property right next door, we would love nothing better than to be involved in your care for whatever time it takes. It would be an honor, a pleasure."

Some of the other Salcido children also considered moving to the same small town, because they had visited there and loved it. So it happened that, over the following couple of years, a few other siblings did move to that town. Still Mr. and Mrs. Salcido debated. Because it was so remote, there was no doctor in the town, and so, although they would have family close by, getting medical care would be quite an ordeal.

As they were considering all of this, a doctor moved to that small town and set up her office a stone's throw from where one of their children lived. The Salcidos now felt that a change was feasible. They bought an old house on a lot next to one of their son's homes. It required extensive renovation to make it habitable; in fact, when they moved in, late in the fall, there was no running water or electricity installed yet. They spent the entire winter in that house without electricity or running water, working on the renovation.

Mrs. Salcido, who was fairly frail and continued to have daily back pain, did much of the interior repainting in the huge house. The following summer, a friend asked her where she found the strength to do this. She said, "It was strange. Every night as I went to bed in a sleeping bag on the floor I felt so tired I wondered if I would die during the night. But as I fell asleep I thought of how much fun it would be to get up the following morning and finish painting the next wall. It was such a joy to see each ugly, dirty wall covered over with beautiful, fresh paint. I haven't felt that much energy for years. I haven't seen my husband have such energy for years. I don't know where it comes from. He works 15-hour days and he's 80 years old! He groans with fatigue and he can hardly walk at the end of the day, and yet he's up at 5 or 6 the next morning already working!"

The Salcidos' story illustrates the potential advantages of living with challenges that the elder finds manageable and familiar. These challenges may include cleaning the house or yard or walking a mile each day to pick up mail or groceries. People do not have to live like pioneers to experience these physical challenges. There are everyday physical challenges such as gardening, cleaning, and volunteer work that are healthful, both physically and spiritually. The purpose of these familiar challenges is to add meaning, purpose, and value to life. When life has lost its meaning and purpose, symptoms are often experienced with overwhelming severity.

There were times when Mr. Salcido felt his muscles and joints aching so badly that he could hardly get out of bed. His physician suggested some anti-inflammatory medication. Mr. Salcido declined, saying, "I respect your opinion, but first I want to find other ways." He preferred alternate medical treatment whenever possible. He heard from a friend about bee pollen, a nontraditional alternative that suited his rebellious style. He took some bee pollen, drank some herbal tea, and within two hours felt much better. Over the following days, as he became more active in his garden, his aches and pains continued to improve markedly. Was it the pain that changed, or his suffering from his pain? Or was it both? His answer was: "Oh sure, I still ache. Almost all the time. But the aching isn't as bad, and it doesn't bother me as much, because I enjoy what I'm doing."

When physicians hear stories of dramatic improvement due to herbs or bee pollen, a part of them wants to say, "Oh come on!" But this reaction serves only to maintain a particular view of how people function, rather than fostering understanding of the patient's viewpoint. It's critical to start with the patient's point of view.

That was what Mr. Salcido's physician did. She encouraged whatever worked well for him, accepting his language, experience and values, as long as he was not harming himself. How often do clinicians and family honor elders who take such initiative? Often they are ridiculed or patronized instead.

Many individuals interacting with health-care professionals use alternative methods of care that are quite effective for them. They may avoid mentioning these to their clinicians because of fear that they would be ridiculed, and that their confidence in their treatment would be compromised.

The Salcidos have lived in their beautiful, comfortable house for about four years now. The raw forest and rocky fields around it have been transformed into beautiful gardens. Each year they set a new goal: an extension of the garden or a new fence.

Once, Mrs. Salcido went to visit friends in a city that was a three-hour car ride away. For some reason, possibly because of sitting in a very sagging seat and moving very little during the long ride, she developed severe back pain. By the time she returned from the trip two days later, she could not get out of the car without assistance.

She went to her physician and asked what to do. The physician examined her, then asked, "What do you feel that you need to do? Do you feel you need to move or that you need to stay in bed?"

Mrs. Salcido said, "Well, I feel like I need to move but I'm worried about hurting myself."

The physician answered, "If you feel you need to move, then do anything it takes to move."

During the next week, Mrs. Salcido moved around her house on her hands and knees. She couldn't stand up. Each morning she slid out of bed onto the floor and crawled to the bathroom, where she pulled herself up on the toilet. Then she crawled down the stairs, still on hands and knees, to the kitchen, where she prepared some breakfast with her husband's help.

Of course, her husband and family helped her frequently. They encouraged her to do what she could, but they also said, "Let us know if you need something." This seemed to be just the right balance for her. Within a week she was up on her feet, bent over, walking with assistance. For the next three months she walked around, bent over, hanging on to the wall. She forced herself to get out and walk every day. She forced herself to clean the house. Now, a year later, she walks upright. She makes sure that she walks a half-mile every day to pick up the mail.

This illustrates the importance of having family support that encourages autonomy rather than dependency and helplessness, support that encourages independence while acknowledging increasing limitations in strength, memory, and physical stamina as the years pass. This case also illustrates the importance of relating recommendations to the personal style and belief system of the patient. In this case, the patient felt that movement was important, and this was fully supported.[1]

Pain as a Messenger

Patients are often unaware that problems of life may be disguised by symptoms such as pain; yet this is often the case. Discussing this as a possibility requires sensitivity and a solid relationship of trust and confidence with the patient.

[1]Perhaps it is worth noting that clinical approval and support of a patient's preferences depend on the clinician's judgment that this will be in the patient's interest and well-being.

The clinician needs to be ready to hear a variety of messages that are communicated by pain complaints. These messages may speak of loss, conflict, difficult changes in life circumstances, stress, isolation, failure, or of lifelong personality problems. These messages may also speak of the patient's determination and perseverance. Acknowledgment of these messages is essential to appropriate treatment, of course. But more, this acknowledgment can be profoundly nourishing to the patient, because it expresses deep understanding and honors a life and a soul.

However, such communication is not easy. The patient, preferring to focus merely on the pain, may resist the clinician's attempt to attend to other issues. However, it is essential that the clinician be clear about his or her judgment of the problem, while listening patiently and observing, gradually helping the patient refocus on nonmedical issues. Doing so may not only reveal unresolved life problems but also facilitate the patient's awareness of his or her strengths. This awareness, in turn, helps remind the elder of the importance of his or her place in the scheme of things, which may be important to keeping a person alive.

There are two important types of nutrition: One is the food we eat, and the other is the knowledge of our meaning, life purpose, and value. When the awareness of meaning and purpose is lost, we tend to feel that there is no longer a place in the world for us. In this condition, sometimes people lose the will to live – but they may be aware only of pain, for which they seek treatment.

Reconnecting to the Meaning of Life

In some cases, the clinician's primary task is to help reconnect the person to his or her place in the scheme of things. That may happen partly through just valuing a patient so clearly he or she is reminded: "You have a value. You're still important."

Honoring a patient's values often requires flexibility and patience on the clinician's part. We need to know and honor the person's way of dealing with the world. Is this an individual who really wants to control her destiny, in terms of large and small decisions? Or does she prefer a much more passive response to her own care? It will not help to say to the latter person over and over again, "Well, what do you think you need?" She will answer, "What do *you* think I should do, doctor?"

Elders may exercise control by asking questions, expressing wishes, or insisting on the continuation of a long tradition of doing things in a certain way, whether the pain is major or minor. If they have many other disabilities or if their voice and power are taken away in a number of ways, then to insist on a particular medication or on a certain method of treatment is not a helpful strategy. Having a firm opinion may enable the person to maintain a sense of self; it is a way of controlling his or her destiny. If the treatment threatens or removes that sense of self, then elders feel that they have no rudder, no sense of direction, energy, or autonomy. Paradoxically, we sometimes try to remove pain in people who feel they have nothing left to hold onto but the pain. Flexibility is the first step in treatment.

CASE EXAMPLE: MRS. YEE, 60, WITH KNEE PAIN

As a part of her active life, Mrs. Yee loved to go dancing with her husband, and she loved to travel. She developed pain in her knee while she was dancing. It had started to improve a little, until a few days later when she went dancing again; then it hurt even more. The knee was swollen and she could hardly walk. After the pain continued unabated for a week, she became very worried about it, so she came to see me.

On examination of her knee, I (SL) found no indication of any severe ligament damage or other serious injury. It appeared to be a combination of mild "wear and tear" in her joint and mild muscle strain. She was reassured that, if she would abstain from dancing for a while, do some exercises, put ice on it, and just take care of it, it would get better in six to eight weeks. She was satisfied with this recommendation.

Returning to my office about a month later, she said that she was feeling much, much better. After pulling and pressing and hammering her knee, I agreed with her that she was doing much better. Mrs. Yee said, apologetically, "I guess I should tell you that I went to see a Chinese doctor." She studied my face very closely as she said that, waiting for my reaction.

I replied, "Oh, that's fine."

Mrs. Yee seemed relieved. "You're not angry with me?"

I replied, "No, I'm happy for you to get any kind of help that seems useful to you. Did you feel it was helpful?"

She said, "Yes, I think it was helpful. They wrapped some medicine, some kind of herbs, around my knee and put an ace bandage around that and made it feel better. Every day I would put that on and they told me to continue to do the things that you told me to do like the exercises. But the herbs would help also, so I felt both together were really helpful. But I was afraid that you would be angry with me for going to somebody else."

I remarked that I thought she was very fortunate to be able to draw expertise from more than one world, and to bring both of those worlds together to work on her problem.

She said, "I'm so relieved that you're not angry. Do you think I should continue to see that Chinese doctor?"

I replied, "As long as it seems helpful to you, then that's fine."

About two weeks later, she came back for another visit. She had started very carefully dancing again, and reported that she had very few problems with her knee. She said, "You know, I've been thinking a lot about going to see the Chinese doctor. I don't think there was anything in that medicine that helped me, but I think it was really important for me to go see him because when I was a little girl that was the kind of doctor we saw in China."

Mrs. Yee had considerable insight into her own needs. She recognized that she could obtain needed extra reassurance from her own culture and background. She found reassurance in the familiar.

RESPONDING TO ANXIETY: CREATING A DIFFERENT KIND OF COMFORT

Effective patient education and reassurance require the clinician's time and willingness to learn about the patient's worst fears. These fears are lurking in the dark until a clinician who is willing to listen calls them forth.

Allen Barbour (1995) describes the process of learning how to listen to the psychological meaning of a patient's pain complaint in *Caring for Patients: A Critique of the Medical Model*. He stresses the importance of recognizing that many somatic complaints are a socially acceptable way of saying: "I'm afraid. I'm lonely. I'm suffering from loss." Barbour's observations suggest that an isolated focus on somatic complaints can accentuate the patient's experience of loss. It is as if the clinician is saying to the patient, "Your sense of loss isn't even important to me." The goal, Barbour suggests, is to search for implicit messages and then respond to those messages, as well as to the explicit somatic complaint: "I understand that you feel lonely. I'm glad you came to see me!" This response may be expressed in words, in the clinician's behavior, and in tone of voice. The patient needs to know that the clinician finds value in the encounter.

RESPECTFUL REFOCUSING
ON STRENGTHS

While listening with concern to the patient's complaints about pain, we also focus on strengths. Acknowledging the patient's strengths in an enthusiastic, affectionate way can be part of a process of helping him to revive the vital, healthy part of himself. Acknowledgment of a patient's appearance and of her interests also enhances the strength of the therapeutic relationship and helps to diffuse the focus on somatic complaints.

CASE EXAMPLE: MR. BILLINGS, 82, WHO HURT ALL OVER

Mr. Billings, strong, independent, and self-sufficient, could pass for 70. At the moment, however, everything was hurting – his back, shoulders, hands, knees, feet, and so on. I (WF) said, "George, you're 82 years old and you really are in excellent shape. Look at you – running the community garden, working hard. What's wrong with you? You're just really in good shape." The next two visits he came in and said with a smile, "Gosh, you know I've been really feeling good. I'm really in pretty good shape."

There is a danger that, while reminding elderly patients of their strengths and good functioning, we may seem patronizing or merely dismissive. It is essential to genuinely respect the patient, to be sincere when communicating honor and value toward the elder. There needs to be a marriage between the two forces: On the one hand, we listen seriously to the specific complaint; on the other, we respond both directly and (when appropriate) indirectly to any underlying concerns. Finding the right balance is a challenge requiring the mind of a strategist and the heart of an artist. We need to be active and attentive, but at the same time quiet and observant. And we need to be mindful of our own needs and motivations when dealing with a patient; otherwise, we will inevitably discover, too late, that we have not been listening, that we have been patronizing.

COMBINING INTELLECT
AND INTUITION

A few years ago, Siegel (1990) proclaimed that, in case after case, loving one's patients was an essential, powerful tool missing from North American medicine. We share his concerns about the sterility and weakness of high-tech medicine. But narrowly developed ideas often hold a paradox, simultaneously representing both strength and weakness. For us, what was missing from his book was the rich complexity and puzzling uncertainty of most of human life. The author's view seemed to be that if we are sufficiently sweet, intuitive, and loving, our patients will recover their health – independent of the particular problem. Such a reaction is understandable, given the opposite view, which is that health and illness are unrelated to human emotions and to the consequences of life events. However, one can hope for an approach to human experience that synthesizes such limited points of reference and includes the broad and deep complexity of human life.

One day we discussed these issues with an elderly patient, who was quite eloquent. He said, "Personally, I'd like to go to a doctor who is kind, loving, and sensitive, but who also looks at my ear, or examines my abdomen and thinks about it and orders some tests when appropriate. If I see a therapist, I'm not looking for a sweet goody-two-shoes. I want somebody who's sensitive, sure – but I also hope he's tough and honest. I want people taking care of me who are thinking, real human beings. Those kinds of people get tired, impatient, or bored at times. If I want somebody who does nothing but love me, I'll go see my mother. She's not critical. She'll sit there and hold my hand and say, 'You're so wonderful.' She'll pat my head and say, 'I'm so glad to see you.' But she's not going to be a good physician or therapist for me."

We need to struggle with this idea. Many patients want help from clinicians who are sharp intellectually, and who don't mind thinking, analyzing, being critical; they also value clinicians who are willing to risk the possibility of "causing trouble" in a kind way, by being thoughtful and bringing up disturbing possibilities. We all need that. It is in that context that love becomes alive and compassionate. It becomes real. And we need to remember that this alive quality does not exclude irritation, confusion, and impatience.

Sometimes, we tell our elderly pain patients that we are confused about the best treatment. For example, "Right now I feel like a blind man. I feel confused and uncertain about how things are going with you. I need more information. Until I get that, I'm not sure how to proceed with relieving this pain." Often, we don't really feel what we'd call an "affectionate" concern; instead, it may feel like a *commitment* that is that is alternately bitter, passionate, and sweet in its fierce determination. The clinician may say to herself, "Even though I don't feel an affectionate concern for this patient, I'm struggling with this because I do care for her as a patient and I want to help her."

FRUSTRATION AND ANGER
TOWARD PATIENTS

When we're dealing with a patient who has any kind of medical problem, whether pain or something else, if we genuinely like the person, that affection seems to have its own therapeutic value. But it is not always elicited within us in the same way or to the same degree. If you really don't resonate with or like someone, how can you do as good a job? Some long-term pain patients are very frustrating. Because of the chronicity of their pain, and the reluctance of many care-providers to become committed to a long-term professional relationship, many of these patients become dishonest as they try to cope with their pain and the reaction of their surroundings. Such patients may view the care provider as an obstruction to obtaining what they need. Manipulative behavior develops when suffering is not relieved, and/or when drug dependence occurs. This is difficult to deal with.

One of the most effective things we can do with such difficult patients is to lay all of our cards out on the table, including the fact that we feel frustrated and that we're not sure where we're going. This may have a very therapeutic effect. Paradoxically, such frank communication, if free from blame (no easy task!), may help the clinician and patient feel like a team again, just when they were beginning to feel like they were adversaries. At the very least, clear communication promotes honesty and helps to diminish the patient's manipulative behavior and the caregiver's avoidance.

THE ROLE OF IMAGINATION
AND SUGGESTION

Elders are as able as younger patients to benefit from therapeutic interventions based on imagination and suggestion, although the themes that occupy the imagination vary with the patient's age. The imagination of youth is often filled with the same images that are found in popular books and films: cute animals, action and adventure, or romance. Elders, on the other hand, often use imagination as a tool to help put events of the past and the future into a perspective, in order to find, or deepen, the meaning of their present circumstances. When one simplifies these two extremes as a search for physical experience and mastery among the young versus a search for meaning among the elderly, this contrast brings to mind Erik Erikson's views of human development and reminds us of the importance of a developmental perspective.

CASE EXAMPLE: MR. KAY, 67, SUFFERING FROM
TRIGEMINAL NEURALGIA

Mr. Kay had suffered from trigeminal neuralgia for nearly four years. The side-effects of the several medications he had tried were worse than the pain itself. He had also tried acupuncture, herbal medicine, biofeedback, and meditation without any resolution of his symptoms. He experienced a severe attack about every two weeks, with frequent, aching pain in between. In fact, at our first meeting, he rated the present intensity of the aching pain as 4 out of 10.

Mr. Kay had restricted his activities severely in the past six months. An accomplished amateur violinist, he participated in local concerts and sat on the board of directors of a large metropolitan opera company. Aside from his family, including his eight grandchildren, music was the passion of his life. He also enjoyed cooking gourmet meals for friends and family. As his pain increased in intensity and frequency, he had become more withdrawn, and he felt his usual rich and varied life slipping away.

Born in Poland, Mr. Kay was sent, at 14, together with his mother and sister, to the concentration camp at Auschwitz. His father was taken prisoner by the Nazis and was never seen or heard from again. Miraculously, Mr. Kay, his mother and sister all survived Auschwitz. After liberation and several months of rehabilitation, they recovered their physical health, and subsequently emigrated to the United States. Mr. Kay met his wife in America, where they raised a family and developed very successful professional careers.

When I (SL) first met Mr. Kay, I was struck by his warmth and good humor. He expressed great hope that hypnotic treatment would be helpful in relieving his dreadful pain. After we had talked for a while, I asked him if he would like to have an experience that he might find both pleasant and interesting. He eagerly agreed and asked what he should do. I invited him to sit back in his chair and to close his eyes in order to more easily notice some pleasant scenes. He smiled and commented that he often did this on his own, when listening to music. I suggested that he allow his mind to float freely until he noticed some pictures, images, or thoughts that seemed particularly pleasant to him. At the same time I also suggested slow, deep breathing, and I made comments about the deep relaxation that he could experience from his face and head all the way down to his toes.

After three or four minutes of relaxation, Mr. Kay mentioned that he had a picture of the San Francisco Symphony Orchestra in his mind. He could see it clearly and described it in detail. With some encouragement he began to hear the music more clearly. It was one of his favorite pieces: the "Moonlight Music" from the opera *Capriccio*, by Richard Strauss. With deep feeling, he described the music as sensual, sweet, and slightly melancholy. After several minutes, he sighed, and said with a little smile, "The music has finished." I invited him to gradually return to my office and open his eyes. When his eyes opened, he blinked, then slowly smiled.

"What a pleasant experience," he said. I asked him whether the aching pain he had been experiencing had changed "in any way." He stopped for a moment to think, and then said, with some surprise, "Yes, actually it's completely gone. Now that I think of it, I don't notice any pain."

We had several subsequent treatments, each one lasting at least 45 minutes. He particularly enjoyed spending time listening to music during these sessions, and he reported that the music felt like a deep, healing fluid that washed away his pain and suffering.

What was additionally meaningful to him about these experiences was that they were an affirmation of the decision he had made when he came to the United States to devote himself to living life to its fullest. Enjoyment of the arts, including poetry, literature, and music, was a fulfilling way of enjoying life with friends and loved ones. All of these experiences seemed to act as an antidote to the horrors he had experienced in the Nazi concentration camp. He also commented that whenever he recalled a memory of the years he spent in the Nazi camp, the intensity of his pain would suddenly increase. Therefore, he felt very cautious about recalling any memories at all from his childhood, for fear that unwanted memories would return, causing him great pain. Rather, he preferred to devote himself entirely to his family, music, and all the beauty in life that he could capture and experience.

It was very tempting for me to assume that somehow his pain was connected to a denial of feelings or recollections that needed to be expressed or reexperienced. On various occasions when the topic arose, I wondered out loud whether it would be helpful for him to go deeper into some of those feelings and experiences. Each time he listened thoughtfully and agreed to consider that question. He never seemed irritated or impatient that I had posed the question. Finally, he said that, although he had understood the logic of what I had wondered, he trusted his judgment in leaving all of those bad memories behind.

A new question arose in my mind: Were there any *pleasant* memories and experiences from the past that might have been discarded along with the horrible ones? I asked him if he would like to journey back to times in his childhood that were pleasant. He seemed surprised and at first a little wary, but then agreed that he would be willing to find out.

I asked him then, as I had each time before, to allow his mind to clear, to close his eyes, to take several deep breaths, then to experience himself traveling to whatever place and time he would like. For a few minutes, he appeared as deeply relaxed as usual during our sessions. Then the expression on his face seemed somehow more intense than usual. He began to speak slowly, softly, as if recounting a dream, while in the midst of it. He saw his old family home back in Poland. He described in detail the fresh green grass and the trees that grew around the house. He saw the front door, the deeply textured wood and the polished brass handle. He opened the door and went inside. He found himself in the bedroom where he slept as a child.

After some long moments of silence, he smiled and spoke of the wallpaper and the texture of the paint on the ceiling. Then there followed a long silence as he appeared deeply involved in some scene. After about 20 minutes I invited him to gradually return to the present whenever he was ready. After three or four minutes, his breathing seemed to indicate a gradual arousal from a deep concentration and a shift in his consciousness back to this room.

Finally, he opened his eyes and smiled. His eyes filled with tears as he described the texture and color of the wallpaper in his bedroom. He had even noticed a spot on the wall where he had once scratched away the wallpaper down to the paint as he lay in bed and listened to the birds in the trees outside. Nobody but him knew about this spot because it was right next to the mattress. Now when he saw that familiar, long forgotten wallpaper, a series of pleasant memories began to return.

Next, he had felt himself outside, in winter. He was walking through the snow with his sister. They were holding hands with their mittens, coats, and scarves wrapped around them. He felt warm and secure. The sharp freshness of the cold, winter air brought back the exhilaration of being outside playing. He felt again how the two of them gradually became tired and hungry and went back inside for a warm dinner around the family table. He remembered all this with tears in his eyes, which I imagined was going to lead to an expression of grief, perhaps over the loss of this golden period of his life.

To the contrary, Mr. Kay was glad to discover that he still had such strong memories and images. He said, "I haven't had those vivid memories for years and years, and I'm so grateful to have them back. I feel like they'll never leave me now."

Since he had fewer and fewer pain attacks and was less bothered by the aching in his face, we agreed that we could postpone any further meetings. We did not meet for several months, at which time he came back, saying that he had had a series of pain attacks in his face during the past three weeks. He attributed these to an increase in fatigue and stress related to an illness his wife had recently experienced.

We had one session, during which he spent about 20 minutes deeply relaxed, listening again to the "Moonlight Music" from *Capriccio* in his mind. As he opened his eyes after listening to this music he sighed and said with a smile, "This is just like taking medicine, except better. I feel so lucky to be able to have the pain stop so easily and pleasantly."

He called me about a week later to say that everytime he felt he was going to have some pain, he would sit quietly for a while with eyes closed. Sometimes he played one of his favorite musical recordings; at other times he would listen to the music in his head, accompanied by an image of the orchestra. He was happy to report that in every case it helped him to feel relief from the pain. His pain continued to diminish, and follow-up after one year revealed that he had had only a few pain attacks since that time.

Mr. Kay's case illustrates ways in which this kind of imaginal approach can, with very few explicit suggestions, help patients to discover a path that proves to be helpful. Although I was tempted to explore what must have been a deep well of emotional pain, I was, fortunately, able to resist. Instead, I respected Mr. Kay's wishes to leave those memories buried. Doing so freed me to then think of the potential value of reexperiencing pleasant memories, which Mr. Kay was able to do, with evident benefit. This case helps me to remember the importance of not being too closely wedded to my psychological hypotheses and personal wishes for a patient, but to hold them in my mind while I explore other, perhaps less obvious avenues.

Although Mr. Kay improved substantially, other patients with quite similar symptoms have not. We need to be ready to consider with the patient a variety of treatment options, ranging from psychological to medical and surgical.

CASE EXAMPLE: MRS. BIRCH, 65, WITH MULTIPLE RECURRING PAINS

Although Mrs. Birch loved to tell funny stories and to make jokes, her humor always seemed to have a bitter edge. She had seen family physicians, internists, cardiologists, gastroenterologists, neurologists, rheumatologists, psychologists, and psychiatrists for complaints that included blurred vision, weakness, dizziness, nausea, fatigue, chronic headache, pain in her jaw, her throat, her chest, and her abdomen.

The most constant of these complaints were headache and chest pain. She had complained of many of these symptoms on and off for years, but they seemed to have increased in severity and frequency within the past few months. A number of the physicians and mental health professionals who had evaluated her thought that she appeared a little depressed at times. Yet neither antidepressants nor individual psychotherapy had been helpful in relieving the depression.

Her physicians told Mrs. Birch several times that they had no idea why she continued to suffer so many problems, despite EKGs, EEGs, chest x-rays, treadmill tests, endoscopy, barium enema, CT scans, psychotherapy and counseling. Various treatments had been tried, often with initial enthusiasm and determination on Mrs. Birch's part to feel better; inevitably, within a few weeks she reported feeling no better— sometimes even worse—and terminated whatever the current treatment regimen happened to be.

Because I (SL) was known by my colleagues to have effectively used imagery and suggestion in some difficult cases, Mrs. Birch was referred to me. She seemed quite cooperative and enthusiastic about whatever I could offer; however, nothing I suggested or attempted, over a period of several meetings, seemed to help her in any way.

Mrs. Birch was surprisingly active for a woman with so many physical ailments. She had been married for more than forty years, and she and her husband seemed to have quite a congenial, even affectionate relationship. Both had recently retired, Mr. Birch from his position as a bank executive, Mrs. Birch as a director of purchasing for a large department store chain. Both had been, and still were, involved in a variety of charities and community projects. Their three children and several grandchildren all lived within a hundred miles, and they enjoyed frequent family gatherings.

What was most immediately striking to me about Mrs. Birch was her very attractive appearance. Her hair still had much of the same honey blonde color of her youth, although now liberally mixed with gray. Her fair skin was slightly tanned and only slightly wrinkled, mostly around her mouth and eyes. If I had not known better, I would have guessed her age to be at least 15 years younger than it was. About 5'6", she had almost the same weight and figure as she had 30 years previously. I knew this from seeing photographs in an album that she brought one day, to show me pictures of her children when they were babies. On the first page of the album was a wedding photograph of herself and Mr. Birch. She was so strikingly beautiful that I felt my heart stop for a second. She was scornful of dieting, but she was careful to eat and exercise in a way that maintained her slender and athletic appearance. She and her husband played tennis, usually with friends, everyday.

Unlike other "impossible patients" I had seen, I actually enjoyed seeing Mrs. Birch in my office since, in spite of her complaints, she was usually very pleasant, often quite funny. I told her a number of times I could imagine her having a successful career as a nightclub comic, because of her ability to see humor in almost every experience. However, her humor often took the form of a bitter satire, suggesting seething anger beneath the humor.

Finally, I told her frankly that if I expected to understand and solve her problems, I probably would have resented her coming to see me again and again. She would have only reminded me of my shortcomings as a clinician.

"But I have to admit," I told her, "I don't know how to help you. That thought makes me feel quite sad, because you are such a sweet, good person."

To my amazement, Mrs. Birch just smiled at me for a moment, and then said softly, "Thank you."

She said these two words with such feeling that it seemed as if she felt I had offered her more than a simple compliment in the context of announcing my own limitations. She asked if she could come back again in a few weeks.

I was about to reply, "If it helps you . . . ," but I remembered that nothing seemed to help and, perhaps intuitively, I realized that wasn't really the point. So I simply said, "Yes, please, come anytime you like."

So our meetings continued like this, for several weeks more. Mrs. Birch reported to me about her ongoing panoply of symptoms, often appearing truly miserable and ill. But she also never failed to report about more happy topics, such as her grandchildren or an upcoming trip with her husband. These topics seemed to lift her out of the gloom a little, yet she always finished with a look of such unhappiness! She remained an enigma to me, no matter what questions I asked her or what possibilities I considered. I inevitably apologized for having nothing helpful to offer her, and she always smiled sweetly in response and thanked me with far more expression of gratitude than I imagined I deserved.

One day she left an urgent message at my office, asking me to call her immediately. When she answered the phone, her voice sounded very strained. Her chest pain had returned, this time more severely than ever before. The pain radiated up to her jaw and down into her left arm. She felt as if she could hardly breathe. Briefly, I considered telling her to go to the emergency room.

Then she said softly, "It was horrible." Her voice sounded as if she were crying.

"What was horrible?" I asked.

There was a long silence, unbroken except for her uneven breathing. Finally, she whispered, "The dream."

"What was the dream?" There was no answer. "When did you have the dream?" Still no answer. I looked at my watch. I had patients waiting for me. I wondered if, in spite of all the tests, Mrs. Birch was having a heart attack. I felt exasperated and worried. Then, finally, she said, "Last night. It woke me up. I couldn't go back to sleep." Her voice was full of tears.

Again, I felt torn between my curiosity about the dream and my worry that she was having a heart attack while telling me about the dream. "Can I just ask you a few more questions about the chest pain you're having? When did the pain start?"

"During the night. When I had the dream."

Okay, I thought. Maybe she is having a heart attack, but we apparently have to find out what this dream is about! "Mrs. Birch, can you tell me a little about the dream?"

"No, I can't remember it."

"You can't remember the dream? You said it was horrible. Can you remember any part of it?"

"No. Well, I mean, I don't want to remember it."

"If it's too much to think about right now, we don't have to talk about it. I do want to check out what's causing the chest pain, though."

"The dream."

"What do you mean?" I asked, in spite of myself, because I believed she needed emergency medical evaluation, yet, at the same time, I did feel that this dream might be an important key to understanding her chest pain. But, like Mrs. Birch, I didn't want to think about it just at this moment.

"The dream was so frightening. I was in a car. That's all I remember. I wish I could make it go away. I feel like I'm dying."

Again, I thought of treatment options. Refer her to somebody? The psychiatrist or psychologist she had seen previously? Have her come see me at the end of the day? Go the emergency room immediately? I was very confused and uncertain. Maybe just a few more questions would help me to feel clear.

"Mrs. Birch, do you think it would be helpful for you to find out more about the dream?"

"Yes, I do." Her voice sounded more calm now, with even a hint of authority to it.

"Then, would you mind closing your eyes for a few moments? See if you can let the scene that you remember – the one with the car – come back into your mind." Again, there was silence, unbroken only by her uneven breathing. I felt like I was beginning to get chest pain, myself, from a growing anxious thought that I was being a complete fool.

"Okay," she said finally. "I'm sitting in a car."

"Good. Describe everything you can see." As foolish as I felt, this exploration of her dream seemed deeply important, not only to resolving her immediate chest pain but also to the resolution of her chronic complaints.

"The car is a convertible. I'm driving it. My mother is sitting in the front seat, beside me. I feel like I'm young . . . maybe 15 or 16. I'm wearing a real pretty dress I had at that age. That's all."

"Can you see the road? Can you see where it goes?"

"We're out in the country somewhere. There's a policeman standing in the middle of the road." Now her voice sounded afraid and tearful again.

"As long as you feel that you can, keep telling me everything that's happening."

"He's holding out a hand, signaling me to stop the car. He's walking over to the car. . . . " At this point, Mrs. Birch began to sob audibly.

"Is there anything else?" I continued to feel compelled, somehow, by the belief that our exploration of this dream was very important.

"He's smiling. He bends over, and . . . he bends over and puts his hand inside my dress, over my breast. He just keeps on smiling at me!"

"What's your mother doing?"

"She's just looking straight ahead, like nothing's happening."

"What's happening now?"

"I pushed his hand away, but –" Again, her story was interrupted by sobs. After a moment, though, she continued. "I tried to push him away, but he pulled out his gun and held it in my face!" Now she burst out crying like a child with a broken heart. I sat with the phone to my ear, hearing what I imagined to be a lifetime of pain, finally being released.

After a few minutes, Mrs. Birch confirmed my guess that her chest pain was gone. I asked her to see me at the end of the day. When we were alone in my office that afternoon, she began to tell me her painful secret. At the age of 16, she had been raped by a friend of her family. Like many women who are raped, she felt somehow culpable. Confused by fear of her parents' disapproval and guilt about whether she had been responsible for the rape, she had kept the secret hidden, all to herself, for 50 years. Adding to her pain, the young man then forced her to have sexual intercourse with him several more times during the next year, until he moved out of town. He threatened to send a letter to her parents unless she acquiesced to his demands.

The dream was, fortunately, a window through which Mrs. Birch gradually came to see a part of herself in a new light. As we continued to meet, over the next several weeks, I attempted to provide a safe and supportive context in which she could feel no longer alone with her pain and in which she could experience, from an adult's point of view, that this adolescent girl was not to blame for the rape. She was finally able to begin healing the pain that had plagued her for so long.

Of course, there had been nothing that any of her many clinicians could do until Mrs. Birch was ready. Her state of readiness depended, presumably, on a multitude of factors – within herself, her family, and her relationships with others.

One may wonder about the process of a patient's developing readiness for therapeutic change. How this state of readiness develops, in any person's life, seems as mysterious as how and at what point a particular blend of ingredients has cooked for exactly the right amount of time to provide tasty relief of hunger. My ability to help Mrs. Birch was, fortunately, not dependent on my initially knowing what her problem was; rather, it required more patience on my part than anything else – patience both with her seeming lack of progress, and with my seeming inability to be helpful. In retrospect, I recall expression of my lack of understanding not as a strategic self-effacing gesture, but as an honest expression of my state of bafflement – combined with a curiosity and a willingness to persist. To be honest, there must have been a part of me that felt some optimism about *something* in our relationship, or I could not have sustained my energy with Mrs. Birch.

Although she was an enigma, Mrs. Birch was not merely a passive recipient of treatment. In retrospect, I now see that she was an active partner in her healing. As much as her understanding allowed, she continued to search for the cause of her suffering – buried for years (literally and symbolically) in a forgotten chest. When her dream occurred, she urged me on, reassuring me that the dream was, in fact, the key to the chest.

This experience also illustrates how imagery can provide a highly effective window for viewing intrapsychic material that is temporarily beyond verbal expression. Having finally been brought to conscious awareness and understanding, the suffering no longer needs to be expressed somatically.

Lest we be too thrilled by the satisfying resolution to this case, we need to remember that not all cases of inexplicable pain complaints can be so pleasingly resolved. In many similar cases, the patient may well have an unidentified medical problem; in the case of a somatoform disorder, the underlying cause may be multifactorial and not readily uncovered by a dream or any other means.

CONCLUSION

Here are some specific psychosocial strategies that are helpful in caring for elders suffering from pain:

1. *Develop a trusting relationship over time.* This means continuity and regular scheduled visits. Make it clear that you will be the caregiver who will work with the patient on the pain problem.
2. *Establish ground rules.* This is especially important when potentially addicting drugs are needed to control of the pain. In addition to coordination of care by the primary physician, there should be agreement that the emergency room is not to be used for obtaining drugs and that any change is the established dose will be made as a joint decision between you and the patient.
3. *Utilize appropriate community resources.* If the elder is isolated, effectiveness of care will be enhanced by addition of a visiting nurse or public health nurse to the team. The local Council on Aging may have a friendly visitor program that can be brought to bear. If the elder is disabled, programs like Meals on Wheels can provide nutritional support and a daily visit.
4. *Pain is a family affair.* "Significant others," family, or friends should be involved with the patient's care. Encouraging a spouse or involved family member to accompany the patient to the office is important. Understanding the involved caregiver's perspective may be extremely valuable in approaching the pain problem.
5. *Utilize physical activities.* Since function is so important, we urge regular physical activities with specific instructions, such as, "I want you to walk around your block twice daily." Use available physical therapy, which will likely involve stretching exercises, to improve strength and range of motion, as well as a specific program for rehabilitation. This may be an indispensable support in enabling the patient to feel better and become more active.

6. *Use relaxation techniques and imaginal or hypnotic techniques.* Help the patient practice deep breathing and relaxation while visualizing serene scenes. Tape record this process, so the patient can practice these techniques at home, using the tape recording as both a motivational tool and a memory aid.

7. *When there is emptiness and a dearth of meaning in the patient's life, help the elder "get a life."* Refer the patient to a social worker, who can, for example, suggest specific volunteer activities.

There is something profoundly sad and unfair about pain in old age – insult really is added to injury. Whether the voice of a wounded heart, opportunities lost, the complaint of tired, crumbling bones, or a merciless cancer, pain is a cruel intruder in what could have been a time of accomplishment, satisfaction, reflection and peace.

Caring for elders and their pain is often discouraging and difficult; at the same time it is work that heals our future self. The process of integrating the emotion of the pain with the medical facts helps us to find a healing path that is at once practical and heart-felt. Youth and renewal in old age are often abandoned beneath a blanket of hopeless gloom or futility sought through medication or empty distraction. Elders in pain deserve our acknowledgment of the sadness that coexists with the dissatisfaction of our best, most optimistic efforts. This sadness is neither depression nor self-pity; rather, it emerges from an honest recognition of the loss brought on by the pain of age. It may be that only through expression of this sadness will we find our way to the compassion and energy necessary to experience renewal and healing.

AFTERWORD: WHEN WE FAIL

Joseph Barber
Samuel LeBaron

TWELVE-YEAR-OLD BILLY hated needles and hated the clinic. But he had acute lymphocytic leukemia, which meant he had to tolerate both needles and the clinic. He came to see me (SL), accompanied by his mother, for help with his pain and anxiety around medical procedures. At first, he listened attentively as I discussed the situation with his mother; gradually, he became talkative and joined the conversation.

He agreed that he would like the pain and worry to be less but said, glumly, "Nothing will help." I described how techniques that used one's imagination had been helpful to other children and offered to help him in the same way. While I spoke with enthusiasm, I had to admit to myself that I had more than the usual doubts in Billy's case. Yet, he agreed to try whatever I had to offer.

When we met the following day, Billy's first comment was, "That tie you're wearing is so ugly! Where did you get it?" He seemed startled and disarmed by my response: I looked down at my tie and told him that it was fun wearing ugly ties and asked him if he would like me to wear an even uglier tie next time. He laughed and said, "Sure. That would be fine."

I noticed with only a little discomfort how smoothly, yet dishonestly, I had deflected his jab. The truth was, I liked my tie and I didn't like a child challenging my taste. Even as I moved the conversation to his family, pets, and favorite TV shows, I vacillated between my sympathies for him and my anger at his impudence.

Anyway, I thought to myself, our work together isn't psychotherapy; however, that's what he needs – somebody with time and a sympathetic ear to listen to his fears and his anger. I began to feel hypocritical, focusing only on his reaction to procedures, when I imagined he must also be struggling with the larger question of dying. I felt a little embarrassed that my reaction had been so facile, sleek – and false. I began to resent Billy for being a part of my confusion.

Awkward and out of sorts, I brushed aside my jumbled thoughts and pressed on. When I asked him whether he could get a picture in his mind of a model train, which I knew he enjoyed, he told me he could, but that he didn't want to. Furthermore, he had changed his mind and decided there was nothing that could help, so there was no point to our meeting anymore.

The truth was that he was right. And the truth about myself was that I felt angry and embarrassed at this dismissal. I continued to make "social calls" when Billy was admitted to the hospital. When I came to his room, he was always cordial and polite, but nothing of significance transpired. During the next several weeks his physical and medical status deteriorated very rapidly; about two months after our first meeting Billy died.

I wish that, at the very least, I had stopped to listen to his anger. If only I had said, "I'm sorry you don't like my tie." Then, instead of being witty, if only I had sat there with him in the midst of his fear and anger. . . .

At present, Billy's needs and my mistakes seem painfully clear to me. But they weren't then.

This chapter explores the experience of treatment failure. Until this chapter, the book has been primarily devoted to the description and exploration of various treatment approaches that are often successful in the treatment of pain and suffering. In fact, most of the clinical literature concerns apparently successful treatments. It is rare to find a discussion of a treatment that was unsuccessful. All clinicians are familiar with the experience of treatment failure, although most, psychotherapists in particular, rarely have an opportunity to discuss a failure with colleagues. In this chapter we describe some of our own treatment failures, in the hope that this will help you learn from your own experiences of failure.

All clinicians have the experience of treating patients successfully only some of the time. In fact, the same treatment is sometimes successful and at other times unsuccessful, depending upon . . . well, that is the question that interests us. What factors lead to therapeutic success, and what factors lead to therapeutic failure? And how much control do we have over any of these factors?

We are interested in exploring therapeutic failures, for four reasons:

1. We want to acknowledge that therapeutic failures are a natural part of clinical practice.
2. We hope that exploration of cases of therapeutic failure might help us identify the cause of the failure, so that we can learn from it.
3. We believe that acknowledgment of our therapeutic failures is a necessary step toward growth as effective clinicians, and we want to take that step and, perhaps, help others to take it as well.
4. Awareness and acceptance of our human limitations allow us to create a place of honesty, contact, and comfort for our patients and ourselves.

WHAT UNDERLIES
TREATMENT FAILURE?

Is it the patient who fails to be successfully treated, or is it the clinician who fails to successfully treat? Or do these questions each miss the complex interaction between clinicians and patients? We will discuss instances in which perhaps it was the patient's own limitations that undermined treatment and made failure more likely. It is important to identify, as early in treatment as possible, what a patient's resources and limitations are. We will also discuss examples of our own limitations, as well as complex clinical circumstances, that determined the failure.

Like all of us, pain patients often have mixed motives when seeking treatment. Whereas the patient suffering acute pain is likely to be unambivalently motivated to seek relief, the patient who has endured pain (and treatment) over time has been changed by that experience, and part of that change is that simple relief from pain is no longer the patient's goal. The pain patient suffers not only from persistent pain but also from the consequences of that pain over time: loss of work productivity—loss of job, even—and the economic disruption that follows; loss of a sense of worth; disruption of marriage and family; loss of social support from friends and coworkers; side-effects of medications; loss of general physical health from simple inactivity; and the psychological effects of these changes as well, particularly in the form of reactive depression.

The patient is often held in a disabling balance between secondary gains, on the one hand, and loss of function, on the other. Any change in the patient's life, including reduction in pain, will necessarily upset that balance. Such an upset may be an opportunity for growth and development; however, if that balance serves to substantially satisfy the patient's deeper psychological needs, the clinician is likely to encounter frustrating obstacles to treatment success.

Essential to the art of effective treatment is the clinician's sensitivity to the balance we have just described and delicacy in promoting shifts that will upset it. Psychological techniques themselves have no inherent sensitivity; that is up to us. We can help the patient become aware of the balance and work toward shifting it. Since no clinician can be unerring in his or her sensitivity and judgment, we inevitably will encounter patients whom we do not help.

Can we become more prescient? Can we reliably judge, early in the evaluation or treatment process, if a patient is likely to benefit from our treatment? How do we determine when and how to correct our therapeutic aims and techniques, to better satisfy the patient's needs? These are easy questions to which there can be no standard answers. In the pages that follow, we propose some tentative answers. Now, let us explore the unpleasant experience of therapeutic failure in some examples of patients whose suffering we failed to relieve. Perhaps there are lessons to be learned here.

CASE EXAMPLE: DOLORES, 34, WITH PAIN
ON THE TOP OF HER HEAD

Dolores walked somewhat forlornly, I (JB) thought, into my office, dressed entirely in black, from her wide-brimmed cloth hat to her platform sandals. Dolores suffered tremendously from pain at the top of her head. She variously described the pain as "tingly," "shocky," "lightning-like," and "burning." Having been evaluated and unsuccessfully treated with cognitive-behavioral techniques at a pain clinic, she had been referred to me for hypnotic treatment of her pain.

The pain had begun some months before, when Dolores thought she noticed a loss of hair at the vertex of her scalp. (Examining physicians could find no significant hair loss.) Since she had dyed her hair a few days before noticing the loss of hair, she believed that her hair and scalp had been inadvertently damaged. She believed that surgery was the only solution to her problem, even though she was unable to specify how that might help.

Because Dolores believed that sunlight was particularly injurious to her scalp, she wore a circle of aluminum foil at the top of her head, secured with bobby pins. She always wore a snug-fitting hat over that, to make sure that no sunlight touched the top of her head.

Dolores was very certain that her scalp had been damaged beyond healing, and that no one was going to help her (except, perhaps, a surgeon).

The intake interview revealed that Dolores was happily married, had two children (aged four and one), and was aware of no source of tension or unhappiness in her life aside from the pain. (She always referred to this as "the pain on the top of my head.") My judgment was that Dolores was entertaining a somatic delusion, which I regarded as a serious problem, but I was unaware of any other psychological symptoms. I did not arrange for psychological testing (as I ordinarily would do), because the pain clinic had already done that, and when I reviewed the evaluation sent from the pain clinic, I found nothing remarkable in this information. The medical evaluation found no cause for Dolores's pain.

I was not sure what would help Dolores, but I thought that hypnotic treatment might serve either to reduce her symptoms or to offer diagnostic information about an alternative approach. Though she was not confident about my ability to help, Dolores consented to treatment, and we agreed that she would return several days later. As she left, however, she reminded me that surgery to remove the "damaged tissue" was the only sure cure.

When Dolores returned for her next visit with me, she was dressed, again, in a striking black outfit, except now she wore bright red boots. This sartorial development seemed significant, although I did not know why. Dolores responded readily to my suggestions for hypnotic induction and demonstrated a variety of hypnotic phenomena, including responses to posthypnotic suggestion. Among the suggestions I offered were those for feeling generally more comfortable and less distressed about the "pain on the top of your head," and for noticing that the sensations would wax and wane, progressively toward less intensity. Afterward, she seemed alert, clear, and pleased with the hypnotic experience. We arranged to meet two days later.

When I saw Dolores two days later, she was still wearing her black hat, a black blouse, and a black jacket, but now the black pants were replaced by red ones, which matched her red boots. This was very striking, but I still did not know what, if anything, to make of her clothing choice.

Dolores reported that she did not feel substantially different from the way she had felt before treatment. Unfazed, I again offered hypnotic suggestions for feeling less bothered by the pain, for feeling curious about the way sensations on the top of her head would begin to change, and for reductions in the intensity of the pain. Afterward, she indicated that she was feeling better. Although the pain was still present, it seemed a little less intense, and she was "a little" less worried about it.

Four days later, Dolores arrived for her next appointment wearing still more red. Now only her blouse and hat were black. Although I had not thought she was depressed, I did wonder if this change from black to red indicated a shift to a less dark mood. Again, she reported that she was not feeling substantially different, although she certainly sounded less obsessed by, and less bothered by, the pain at the top of her head. Further hypnotic suggestions were offered to add to the hoped-for effects of being less troubled by the pain and experiencing it as less intense. We agreed to meet four days later.

As you might predict (though I did not), when Dolores arrived for this appointment, there was no black to be seen among her clothing. She was dressed entirely, strikingly, stunningly – beautifully – in red. I mentioned that I noticed she was not wearing any black, and she replied with a laugh, "I guess it's working, isn't it?" Yet she continued to insist that the pain was precisely the same as when we had begun treatment; she did say, though, that she did not think about the pain as much.

This last report seemed to me to indicate that we were moving in the right direction, therapeutically. For, even if pain sensations are present, if she were less bothered by the pain sensations, she would suffer less, and she could turn her attention more readily and more fully to other things in her life. I offered more suggestions, building on the premise that she could continue to be less bothered by the feelings on the top of her head. And we agreed to meet again, three days later.

However, Dolores must have privately had other plans. The next day, Dolores saw her husband off to work, her son off to daycare, and asked a neighbor who often baby-sat to take care of her one-year-old daughter while she "went shopping." She then apparently returned home, thoroughly cleaned the house, and then lay back in her bed and shot the top of her head off, using the .38 caliber pistol that she and her husband kept for protection. My first thought, on hearing this news from her husband, was that she had finally performed the surgery she insisted would be the only effective remedy—she had removed the offending sensations on the top of her head. My second thought, though, was a little less deft: Surely, Dolores did remove her pain but at terrible cost to herself and to her family. What might I have done to relieve Dolores's suffering? Why did her treatment fail?

Subsequently, I learned that the psychologist at the pain clinic who had referred Dolores to me had felt quite hopeless about Dolores's prospects for treatment. Others on the treatment team in the clinic had felt similarly at a loss. No one had seemed to know how to "get through" to Dolores.

Later, as I thought about Dolores, I wondered if we had all overlooked the implications and possible consequences of her delusional disorder. Why had we not considered the possible benefits of neuroleptic medication? If Dolores's beliefs about her pain had been affected by such medication, and if the energy she spent in obsessing about the dysesthesia on her scalp could have been focused on other issues, perhaps her pain would have abated and she would have been able to benefit from treatment combining psychotherapy and medication. Unfortunately, we will never know. Her husband characterized Dolores as having died from a "terminal illness." Perhaps this is so.

Case Example: Professor Adams, 52, Whose Head Hurt

This geologist and well-known member of the faculty at our university was referred to me (JB) by his neurologist, a headache specialist, with a letter indicating that his case was a puzzlement, but that she thought Professor Adams was "tense" and might respond well to "hypnotic treatment to promote relaxation."

Professor Adams complained of pain that had been diagnosed by the neurologist as "atypical muscle tension headache." Atypical—the word covers a lot of unknown territory without yielding much information. I was a young psychology intern and did not yet have the confidence (or the competence) to ask the neurologist for further information. It would have been helpful to have a clearer understanding, at the outset, of the etiology of Professor Adams's headaches.

This referral reflects a misunderstanding about the nature of hypnotic treatment, namely, that it is a "relaxation technique." As Banyai (1980) and others have reported, relaxation and the hypnotic experience are independent phenomena. Moreover, the notion that relaxation will effectively treat pain is a notion unsupported by any evidence that

I know of. Even if a patient's pain is the result of muscle tension (which is usually the case, of course, in musculoskeletal syndromes), reducing that tension merely for the duration of a treatment session is of little benefit.

In any event, I accepted the referral of Professor Adams with the hope that I might create at least temporary analgesia. (What truly was "atypical" about his headaches was his characterization of them as "unrelenting, unvarying, and unceasing" – such lack of variation is extremely unusual.) I believed that if he could have even a momentary respite from the pain, such relief might create a psychological space within which to place a therapeutic lever, so to speak, in order to create real and lasting treatment gain.

Professor Adams was cooperative but totally unresponsive to my suggestions. I can still see him looking at me, levelly and cooly, as if he were waiting for the show to begin. He was unceasingly polite, he was affable, he did whatever I asked of him, but nothing happened. For example, I suggested that he imagine being in a pleasant sunlit meadow. When he was sitting quietly, eyes closed, I asked him, what he saw in his mind's eye. He said he didn't know about his mind's eye, but his eyes could see only "the insides of my eyeballs."

Day after day we met. We went through hypnotic procedures, he endured my probing questions about what psychological issues might be involved in the headaches – with no effect at all, aside from my growing consternation (and perhaps his own frustration, though he did not reveal this).

Finally, on the ninth visit (the eighth treatment visit), Professor Adams said, "I thank you for your attempt to help me. I think, though, that this will be my last visit." I did not object to his decision; after all, we seemed to be getting nowhere. I would have liked to offer him an alternative, but I really did not know of one. That was the last I saw of him, except in my thoughts, where he has appeared occasionally through the subsequent years, stimulating questions in my mind about how I might have helped him.

Many would argue that the problem was a simple one of hypnotic responsivity. Perhaps they would be correct. What is clear to me is that I never really touched Professor Adams, either physically or psychologically, let alone hypnotically. I do not know what I might have done differently, except perhaps to begin a conversation with him about my sense that I was not touching him. Perhaps that conversation might have been of interest to him.

CASE EXAMPLE: MR. BUTTERWORTH, 79, WHOSE MOUTH HURT

Mr. Butterworth was an exceedingly charming gentleman, a retired art dealer of substantial means, referred by his dentist (a practitioner whose reputation for fitting dentures was exceptional). Unfortunately, Mr. Butterworth's dentures were very painful to him. He was a very handsome man who dressed in a very elegant, "old-world" style, and it mattered to him a lot that he look his best, which he could not without wearing his dentures, but they hurt too much to wear for more than very brief periods.

My (JB) initial conversation with Mr. Butterworth revealed that he fully expected that I would take out a gold watch and use it as a pendulum, commanding that his eyelids would close and his dentures forever after feel terrific. When I told him that, if I used hypnotic methods, they would probably bear little resemblance to what had passed for "hypnosis" at a night club he had attended, he graciously accepted my explanation and consented, perhaps a little begrudgingly, to cooperate with the remainder of the intake interview.

What was most apparent from the interview was that Mr. Butterworth had a narcissistic style of relating to me, which fended off any real emotional contact; he was, nonetheless, insistent that we "get on with the hypnosis" so he could wear his teeth. Also, Mr. Butterworth was very forthright (after reminding me that our conversations were confidential) in letting me know that he still lived "an active romantic life" and enjoyed the company of several young men, an important reason for him to look young and handsome. It was really essential to him that he wear his dentures painlessly and, in his words, "discreetly." In addition, Mr. Butterworth told me that, although he had officially retired over a decade previously, he was involved in several business and charitable ventures, some of which would require 15 to 20 more years of his life for fulfillment. He had no intention of leaving this work unfinished.

It was clear that Mr. Butterworth was denying his age a bit and that the denture problem was an obstacle to that denial. Here is a clear example of how the meaning of pain determines how one copes with it. The denture pain reminded Mr. Butterworth of his advancing age, and such a reminder was itself painful. It is worth noting that, while hypnotic analgesia might well reduce the physical discomfort of dentures, it cannot affect the emotional discomfort of unwanted aging.

Mr. Butterworth was very responsive to hypnotic suggestions; moreover, he was amused at his responsiveness and enjoyed the experiences of arm catalepsy, anesthesia of his mouth and jaw, response to posthypnotic suggestion, and reversible amnesia. (While it is rarely appropriate to demonstrate these phenomena in a clinical setting, I believed the experience would lend him confidence in me and the treatment we were undertaking. Perhaps this demonstration lent me confidence, as well.)

Curiously, Mr. Butterworth was responsive to relevant suggestions, over several treatment appointments, for experiencing comfort in his mouth when wearing his dentures – but only while he was hypnotized in my office. Afterward, he began to feel increasing discomfort from his dentures, so that, after only five minutes, they were as painful as they had been prior to the treatment. He said that the use, at home, of a tape recording of his successful hypnotic experience in the office was "hopeless." As he elaborated on this, it became clear that the prospect of actually listening to the tape recording at home made him agitated, and so he avoided doing so.

Finally, after the sixth treatment appointment, I received a letter from Mr. Butterworth, in elegant handwriting, on beautiful stationery, thanking me for my kind efforts and indicating that he would be traveling out of the country and would "unfortunately be unavailable for further visits with you." Telephoning him at home, I thanked him for the note and expressed my disappointment that we had not been more successful. He was his usual gracious self, expressing (somewhat exaggeratedly, I thought) gratitude for my patience, my kindness, my thoughtfulness (not my effectiveness, unhappily), and wished me luck in my future ventures.

I thought then, and I think now, that if I could have helped Mr. Butterworth to feel more accepting of his aging, I would have stood a better chance of helping him with his dentures. But somehow I was not able to initiate an exploration of that important issue.

Although Professor Adams and Mr. Butterworth had different underlying psychological issues, in retrospect I noticed a similarity. In both cases, these men seemed to be cooperative, and in both I had the impression that they were motivated for pain relief. Unfortunately, it seemed that nothing I said or did really made an impact upon either of them. I am now aware that something about the way I related to each man created an inhibition in me around discussing what may have been a key issue. (In Mr. Butterworth's case, for instance, his aging was a relevant issue, but I felt inhibited to discuss it by his seamless denial of it.) I choose to take this lesson from the experiences: When the pain symptom is not responding well to treatment, this may suggest exploration of the meaning of the pain, or of other, perhaps less obvious psychological issues about the pain, or about the relationship between the patient and myself.

CASE EXAMPLE: MS. WILMINGTON, 46, AND HER PAIN IN THE NECK

Ms. Wilmington was a CPA, divorced, without children, who lived by herself. She came to see me (SL) because of recurring pain in her neck, shoulders, and face. She had already been evaluated by three internists, two neurologists, an ENT specialist, and an orthodontist. She had been given a variety of diagnoses, including trigeminal neuralgia, atypical facial pain, cervical neck strain, and psychogenic pain syndrome.

An MRI of her neck had demonstrated some deterioration of the cervical spine, which could have accounted for some of her symptoms (though not all). She was also noted to have a mild to moderate kyphosis of her spine, which could have contributed somewhat to the symptoms. She noted that these symptoms were worse in times of stress and fatigue and seemed to improve when she was well rested; however, they never went completely away. In fact, even when she was at rest, without any obvious signs of great stress, she continued to have the pain. She described it as a mixture of severe aching with an overlying sharp, stabbing quality that was recurrent and unpredictable. This pain would sometimes attack her shoulders and neck; at other times, it would stab upwards into her jaw and even radiate into her face. Sometimes it seemed to almost explode into her cheekbone on the left side, the explosion sometimes lasting for two to three seconds. On occasion, this pain had been so severe that it caused her to drop to her knees and burst into tears.

Various medical regimens had been tried with little or no success. The side-effects of some of these seemed to her to outweigh any possible benefits. Ms. Wilmington was a pleasant, intelligent woman with a witty sense of humor. For the past three years, she had carried the burden of an older sister who was suffering from multiple sclerosis, and who was also divorced; the two sisters had depended on each other for emotional support and companionship through their difficulties and now, as the sister's condition worsened significantly, she had moved in with Ms. Wilmington. With the help of a live-in housekeeper, she took care of her disabled sister.

When I suggested the possibility of using therapeutic techniques based on the power of her imagination, she was willing to give it a try. She listened intently and complied with all of the requests and suggestions I made; however, none of the suggestions or images seemed to relieve her pain. She reported that it was very pleasant to be so relaxed, and that she enjoyed the beautiful images; on the other hand, she was disappointed that such a pleasant intervention, which had apparently been helpful to other people, did not result relieve her pain.

We continued to try a variety of different suggestions, relaxation techniques and images, both in the office and at home, including many of the suggestions found on standardized scales of hypnotic responsiveness. She accomplished most of these items easily, reflecting her considerable hypnotic talent. She appeared to be very dedicated to trying new techniques and, in spite of repeated failure to achieve a reduction in her pain, continued to express considerable optimism that a different approach might be helpful, even if only a little bit. Yet, while she was able to sleep better at night and she found that she was more relaxed in the day, she continued to suffer from pain.

I was puzzled that Ms. Wilmington was not more disappointed that her pain was not diminished. On the one hand, she was obviously suffering and sincerely hoping for relief; on the other, she appeared to react to this therapeutic failure with unsettling equanimity – as if failure were the only expected outcome.

How curious it seems to me, in retrospect, that I did not explore her wishes and feelings more. (Perhaps her burden of caring for her sister was not accepted unambivalently; perhaps it was an unacceptable burden, but one she did not know how to put down.) At the time, I experienced her as rather stiff and awkward; ironically, however, as I look back on our interaction, I see the same awkward reserve in myself, which inhibited me from addressing the potentially problematic issue of her apparent lack of concern about the failure of therapy. I can only presume, then, that Ms. Wilmington and I contributed jointly to this failure.

CASE EXAMPLE: MR. JACKSON, 42, ALSO SUFFERED FROM PAIN IN THE NECK

Mr. Jackson came to see me (SL) for chronic neck pain. He had received multiple medical evaluations, as well as various types of treatment, for this neck pain, which had been variously described as cervical neck strain, myositis, and fascitis. Treatment modalities had included various medications, massage, physical therapy, and acupuncture; the workup had included evaluations by neurologists, x-rays, and an MRI.

Mr. Jackson was a very pleasant, mild-mannered man, who smiled readily. He struck me as a man who seldom had strong feelings about anything. He did not even seem particularly frustrated by the long and so far futile attempt to treat the pain in his neck. His work was described as satisfactory, varied, and quite rewarding. He had married in the last 12 months and described his relationship with his wife in the same somewhat bland terms that he used to describe everything else, so it was difficult to know whether or not there were strains in their relationship. He did not appear depressed and there were no indications of depression in his history.

Like other complicated pain patients, Mr. Jackson was referred to our pain clinic. Several sessions ensued during which a variety of treatment modalities, including relaxation, exercises, biofeedback, and again, various medical modalities, were attempted without success. After he was seen by a psychotherapist for several sessions, neither he nor the psychotherapist felt that there was any need to continue.

When Mr. Jackson raised the possibility of hypnotic treatment, I agreed to try this with him. At the end of one session, he reported that it was very pleasant and that he had felt considerable reduction in the discomfort for a few seconds at a time. Though it was a minimal change for him, he was eager to try further treatment.

During the second session, he brought his tape recorder and recorded our meeting. At the third meeting, he reported that he became very relaxed while listening to the tape. He seemed enthusiastic about this — in spite of the fact that it did not relieve any of his pain. After a fourth session, he stated that he did not feel any more sessions would be helpful to him, so he discontinued treatment.

I continue to be puzzled by Mr. Jackson. I imagine that there was another, perhaps more important problem waiting to be discovered, attention to which may have helped to resolve his suffering. But he didn't tell, and I didn't ask.

What causes our reluctance as clinicians to ask certain questions? Probably many of the same factors that are a discomfort to us outside our professional roles: fear of hearing an answer that may be too embarrassing, fear of upsetting someone, and fear of setting in motion interactions that are otherwise too challenging for us. We take an easier path, one that is, unfortunately, less helpful to many patients, focusing almost solely on symptomatic relief and excluding more troubling and difficult aspects of the therapeutic relationship.

WHY DO WE FAIL?

What can we learn from reviewing these cases of failed treatment? Let us first face what we find most difficult to acknowledge: As imperfect humans, we sometimes fail and will continue to do so, no matter how hard we try to succeed. Even if both patient and clinician do the best they can, the treatment will sometimes fail. We must acknowledge our fallible humanity, not with dismay or shame, but with benevolent acceptance – just as we encourage our patients to do.

In each of the cases we have described, we failed to "reach" the patient. (Perhaps the patient felt that he or she failed to "reach" the clinician.) Even though the contact was friendly, even though the patient seemed genuinely motivated to be free of pain, even when the patient apparently cooperated with treatment, we felt as if we were being politely, sometimes even graciously, kept at a psychological distance. In each case, we must have contributed to that psychological distance as well, even if we cannot identify our contribution. This distance prevented the therapeutic contact needed for change; somehow we were not able to breach the distance.

Which raises the question: What *is* necessary therapeutic contact? What qualities are required of this contact to make it therapeutically effective? The cliché that the patient must trust the clinician is obviously true, but what, in the contact, establishes such trust? And what prevents its natural development? What is it about our contact with some patients that even raises this question, when with other patients there is no question? What does it take for us to raise an issue that may be very uncomfortable for both patient and clinician?

We know, of course, that some patients are very easy for us to treat. The ease is not a function of their clinical syndrome (though, obviously, some syndromes are easier to treat than others). Upon close inspection, it appears that the ease is dependent, in part, upon our *own* easiness. We feel comfortable, self-confident, and competent with some patients. The feeling is not about our ability to treat a particular syndrome; rather, some quality of the clinical interaction that develops, quite soon in most cases, establishes this feeling within us.

When we feel comfortable, self-confident, and competent with a patient, we are more likely to say what we think needs to be said and to do what we think needs to be done. In the opposite case, unfortunately, we do not. We may not even be aware, except in retrospect, of what we need to say and do. Perhaps this hesitancy is key to understanding the subsequent treatment failure.

This feeling of being comfortable with a patient is difficult to describe fully and accurately. It is opposed to anxiety, intimidation, and powerlessness, which we often experience with difficult-to-treat patients. It is freedom to fully be ourselves with a patient. As such, it may be impossible for a young intern to achieve in the presence of an older patient who conveys a lack of confidence in the clinician.

And yet, this is not the full answer, for, with some patients whom we fail to treat, we may feel comfortable and confident yet have the sense that we are alone in the room, as if the patient is not present with us or does not experience us as present. It seems that the patient does not apprehend us, does not appreciate what we have to offer. The patient may have trouble feeling confident in us, for reasons both real and transferential, and experiencing the safe refuge of our consulting room. Although we wish the patient to feel free to fully be him- or herself, relieved of the ordinary pressures and burdens of the outside world, this freedom is not successfully created or conveyed by us or experienced by the patient (or by us).

We intend to continue to gather material and to one day write a more detailed commentary on issues of failure. Meanwhile, we hope that our discussion here will inspire you to explore what you know, and what you do not know, about the patients with whom you have experienced failure. More, we hope that you will be encouraged to seek consultation with colleagues as a routine part of your professional life. Such opportunities for greater self-awareness are a primary means for personal growth, professional development, and clinical competence. As you think creatively about this issue, perhaps you will have ideas that will lead to more satisfactory future contacts with patients — difficult patients and easy patients both. And, of course, all those patients in between.

REFERENCES

Acute Pain Management Guideline Panel. (1992) Acute Pain Management: Operative or Medical Procedures and Trauma. *Clinical Practice Guideline.* AHCPR Pub. No. 92–0032. Rockville, MD: Agency for Health Care Policy and Research, U.S. Public Health Service.

Ahles, T. A., Blanchard, E. B., & Ruckdeschel, J. C. (1983). The multidimensional nature of cancer-related pain. *Pain, 17,* 277–288.

Alman, B. M., & Carney, R. E. (1981). Consequences of direct and indirect suggestions on success of posthypnotic behavior. *American Journal of Clinical Hypnosis, 213,* 112–118.

American Academy of Pediatrics Committees on Fetus and Newborn and Drugs, Section on Anesthesiology and surgery. (1987). Neonatal anesthesia. *Pediatrics, 80,* 446.

Anand, K. J. S., & Hickey, P. R. (1992). Halothane-morphine compared with high-dose sufentanil for anesthesia and postoperative analgesia in neonatal cardiac surgery. *New England Journal of Medicine, 326,* 1–9.

Anand, K. J. S., Sipple, W. G., Schofield, N. M., et al. (1988). Does halothane anesthesia decrease the metabolic and endocrine stress responses of newborn infants undergoing operations? *British Medical Journal, 196,* 668–672.

Andrykowski, M. A., & Gregg, M. E. (1992). The role of psychological variables in post-chemotherapy nausea: Anxiety and expectation. *Psychosomatic Medicine, 54,* 48–58.

Angell, M. (1982). The quality of mercy. *New England Journal of Medicine, 306,* 98.

Auld, J. M. (1989). Uses of hypnosis in general practice. *Anesthesia Progress, 36,* 127–139.

Avni, J. (1980). The severe burns. *Advances in Psychosomatic Medicine, 10,* 57–77.

Bakan, D. (1976). Pain: The existential symptom. In S. F. Spicker & H. T. Engelhardt, Jr. (Eds.), *Philosophical dimensions of the neuro-medical sciences* (pp. 197–207). Dordrecht, Holland: Reidel Publishing Co.

Banyai, E. I. (1980). A new way to induce a hypnotic-like altered state of consciousness: Active-alert induction. In L. Kardos & C. Pléh (Eds.), *Problems of the regulation of activity* (pp. 261–273). Budapest: Akadémiai Kiadó.

Barabasz, A. F., & Barabasz, M. (1992). Research design and considerations. In E. Fromm & M. R. Nash (Eds.), *Contemporary hypnosis research* (pp.173- 200). New York: Guilford Press.

Barber, J. (1977). Rapid induction analgesia: A clinical report. *American Journal of Clinical Hypnosis, 19,* 138–147.

Barber, J. (1980). Hypnosis and the unhypnotizable. *American Journal of Clinical Hypnosis, 23,*4–9.

Barber, J. (1982). Incorporating hypnosis in the management of chronic pain. In J. Barber & C. Adrian (Eds.), *Psychological approaches to the management of pain* (pp. 40–59). New York: Brunner/Mazel.

Barber, J. (1986). The case of Superman: Integrating hypnosis and gestalt therapy in the treatment of dyssomnia. In E. Dowd & J. Healy (Eds.), *Case studies in hypnotherapy* (pp. 46–60). New York: Guilford Press.

Barber, J. (1989). Suffering children hurt us. *Pediatrician, 16,* 119–123.

Barber, J. (1990). Hypnosis. In J. Bonica (Ed.), *The management of pain* (pp. 1733–1741). Philadelphia: Lea & Febiger.

Barber, J. (1991). The locksmith model. In S. J. Lynn & J. W. Rhue (Eds.), *Theories of hypnosis: Current models and perspectives* (pp. 241–274). New York: Guilford Press.

Barber, J. (1996). Dangers of hypnosis. Sex, pseudo-memories, and other complications. In G. Burrows & R. Stanley (Eds.), *Contemporary international hypnosis* (pp. 13–26). West Sussex: Wiley.

Barber, J, & Adrian, C. (Eds.). (1982). *Psychological approaches to the management of pain.* New York: Brunner/Mazel.

Barber, J., & Mayer, D. (1977). Evaluation of the efficacy and neural mechanism of a hypnotic analgesia procedure in experimental and clinical dental pain. *Pain, 4,* 4–48.

Barber, T. X. (1986). Realities of stage hypnosis. In B. Zilbergeld, G. Edelstien, & D. Araoz (Eds.), *Hypnosis: Questions and answers* (pp. 22–27). New York: Norton.

Barber, T. X., & Hahn, K. W. (1962). Physiological and subjective responses to pain producing stimulation under hypnotically-suggested and waking-imagined "analgesia." *Journal of Abnormal and Social Psychology, 65,* 411–418.

Barber, T. X., & Wilson, S. C. (1977). Hypnosis, suggestions, and altered states of consciousness: Experimental evaluation of the new cognitive-behavioral theory and the traditional trance-state theory of "hypnosis." In W. E. Edmonston, Jr. (Ed.), *Annals of the New York Academy of Sciences, Vol. 296, Conceptual and investigative approaches to hypnotic phenomena* (pp. 34–47). New York: New York Academy of Sciences.

Barbour, A. (1995). *Caring for patients: A critique of the medical model.* Stanford, CA: Stanford University Press.

Bassman, S. W., & Wester, W.C. (1991). Hypnosis and pain control. In W.C. Wester & A.H. Smith (Eds.), *Clinical hypnosis: A multidisciplinary approach* (pp. 271–274). Cincinnati: Behavioral Science Center, Inc., Publications.

Bates, B. L. (1993). Individual differences in response to hypnosis. In J. W. Rhue, S. J. Lynn, & I. Kirsch (Eds.), *Handbook of clinical hypnosis.* Washington, DC: American Psychological Association Press.

Beck, A. T., Ward, C. H., Mendelson, M., et al. (1961). An inventory for measuring depression. *Archives of General Psychiatry, 4,* 561–571.

Bejenke C. J. (1990). Operating room equipment: Useful hypnotic induction aids in anesthesiology. In R. Van Dyck, R. Spinhoven et al. (Eds.), *Hypnosis: Current theory, research, and practice* (pp. 199–205). Amsterdam: V.U. University Press.

Bejenke, C. J. (1993). Hypnosis for surgical interventions. *Hypnos (Swedish Journal of Hypnosis in Psychotherapy and Psychosomatic Medicine and the Journal of the European Society of Hypnosis in Psychotherapy and Psychosomatic Medicine), 20,* 214–220.

Bejenke, C. J. (1995a). Use of hypnosis with surgical oncologic patients. In E. Bölcs, G. Guttmann, M. Martin, M. Mende, H. Kanitschar, & H. Walter (Eds.), *Proceedings of the 6th European congress of hypnosis and psychosomatic medicine* (pp. 186–189). Vienna: Medizinisch-Pharmazeutische Verlagsgesellschaft.

Bejenke, C. J. (1995b). Can patients be protected from the detrimental effects of intraoperative awareness in the absence of effective technology? *Conference on memory and awareness in anaesthesia: Proceedings.* Rotterdam.

Bennett, H. L., Benson, D. R., & Kuiken, D. A. (1986). Preoperative instructions for decreased bleeding during spine surgery. *Anesthesiology, 65,* 245.

Berde, C., Ablin, A., Glazer, J., Miser, A., Shapiro, B., Weisman, S., & Zeltzer, P. (1990). Report of the subcommittee on disease-related pain in childhood cancer. *Pediatrics, 80,* 446.

Berger, K. S.(1991). *The developing person through the life span (3rd).* New York: Worth Publishers, Inc.

Bloch, G. J. (1980). *Mesmerism: A translation of the original medical and scientific writings of F. A. Mesmer, M.D.* Palo Alto, CA: William Kaufmann, Inc.

Blount, R. L., Corbin, S. M., Sturges, J. W., et al. (1989). The relationship between adults and child coping and distress during BMA/LP procedures: A sequential analysis. *Behavior Therapy, 20,* 596–601.

Bonica, J. J. (1990). Cancer pain. In J. J. Bonica (Ed.), *The management of pain: Volume I* (pp.400–460). Philadelphia: Lea & Febiger.

Bonica, J. J., & Loeser, J. D. (1990). Medical evaluation of the patient with pain. In J. J. Bonica (Ed.), *The management of pain: Volume 1* (pp. 563–579). Philadelphi: Lea & Febiger.

Bonke, B. (1990). Psychological consequences of so-called unconscious perception and awareness in anaesthesia. In B. Bonke, W. Fitch, & K. Miller (Eds.), *Memory and awareness in anaesthesia* (pp. 198–218). Amsterdam: Swets & Zeitlinger.

Bowers, K. S. (1978). Responsivity, creativity, and the role of effortless experiencing. *International Journal of Clinical and Experimental Hypnosis, 26*,184-202.

Bowers, K. S. (1983). *Hypnosis for the seriously curious.* New York: Norton.

Bowers, K. S., & LeBaron, S. (1986). Hypnosis and hypnotizability: Implications for clinical intervention. *Hospital and Community Psychiatry, 37*, 457-467.

Brown, D. P. (1992). Clinical hypnosis research since 1986. In E. Fromm & M. R. Nash (Eds.), *Contemporary hypnosis research* (pp. 427-458). New York: Guilford Press.

Brown, D. P., & Fromm, E. (1987). *Hypnosis and behavioral medicine.* Hillsdale, NJ: Erlbaum.

Burish, T. G., & Tope, D. M. (1992). Psychological techniques for controlling the adverse side effects of cancer chemotherapy: Findings from a decade of research. *Journal of Pain & Symptom Management, 7*, 287-301.

Burke, J. F., Quinby, W. C., & Bondoc, C. C. (1976). Primary excision and prompt grafting as routine therapy for the treatment of thermal burns in children. *Surgical Clinics of North America, 56*, 477-494.

Bush, J. P., & Harkins, S. W. (Eds). (1991). *Children in pain: Clinical and research issues from a developmental perspective.* New York: Springer Verlag.

Cash, T. F., & Pruzinsky, T. (1990). *Body images: Development, deviance and change.* New York: Guilford Press.

Chapman, L. F., Goodell, H., & Woff, H. G. (1959). Augmentation of the inflammatory reaction by activity of the central nervous system. *American Medical Association Archives of Neurology, 1*, 557-572.

Choiniere, M., Melzack, R., Rondeau, J., Girard, N., & Paquin, M.-J. (1989). The pain of burns: Characteristics and correlates. *Journal of Trauma, 29* (11), 1531-1539.

Clarke, J. H., & Reynolds, P. J. (1991). Suggestive hypnotherapy for nocturnal bruxism: A pilot study. *American Journal of Clinical Hypnosis, 33*, 248-253.

Clawson, D. K., et al. (1980). Screening examination of the musculoskeletal system. In C. Rosse & D. K. Clawson (Eds.), *The musculoskeletal system in health and disease* (pp. 431-434). Hagerstown, MD: Harper & Row.

Cleeland, C. S., Gonin, R., Hatfield, A. K., Edmonson, J. H., Blum, R. H., Stewart, J. A., & Pandya, K. J. (1994). Pain and its treatment in outpatients with metastatic cancer. *New England Journal of Medicine, 330*, 592-596.

Cleeland, C. S., & Syrjala, K. L. (1992). How to assess cancer pain. In D. C. Turk & R. Melzack (Eds.), *Handbook of pain assessment* (pp. 362-387). New York: Guilford Press.

Coe, W. C., & Sarbin, T. R. (1977). Hypnosis from the standpoint of a contextualist. In W. E. Edmonston, Jr. (Ed.), *Annals of the New York Academy of Sciences, Vol. 296, Conceptual and investigative approaches to hypnotic phenomena* (pp. 2-13.). New York: New York Academy of Sciences.

Craig, K. D. (1986). Social modeling influences: Pain in context. In R. A. Sternbach (Ed.), *Psychology of pain* (2nd Ed.) (pp. 67-95). New York: Raven Press.

Crasilneck, H. B., Stirman, J. A., Wilson B. J., et al. (1955). Use of hypnosis in the management of patients with burns. *Journal of the American Medical Association, 158*, 103-106.

Crasilneck, H. B., & Hall, J. A. (1985). *Clinical hypnosis: Principles and applications* (2nd Ed.). New York: Grune & Stratton.

Crawford, H. J., & Gruzelier, J. H. (1992). A midstream view of the neuropsychology of hypnosis: Recent research and future directions. In E. Fromm & M. R. Nash (Ed.), *Contemporary hypnosis research*. New York: Guilford Press.

Crook, J., Rideout, E., & Browne, G. (1984). The prevalence of pain complaints in a general population. *Pain, 18*, 299–314.

Currerie, P. W., Braun, D. W., & Shires, G. T. (1980). Burn injury: Analysis of survival and hospitalization time for 937 patients. *Annals of Surgery, 192*, 472.

Davis, M.A. (1988). Epidemiology of osteoarthritis. *Clinics in Geriatric Medicine, 4*, 241–255.

De Jong, R. N. (1979). *The neurologic examination*. Hagerstown, MD: Harper & Row.

Diamond, M. J. (1984). It takes two to tango: The neglected importance of the hypnotic relationship. *American Journal of Clinical Hypnosis, 26*, 1–13.

Dick-Read, G. (1959) *Childbirth without fear* (2nd Ed.). New York: Harper & Row.

Disbrow, E. A., Bennett, H. L., & Owings, J. T. (1993). Effect of preoperative suggestions on gastrointestinal motility. *The Western Journal of Medicine, 158*, 488–492.

Donnelly, S., Walsh, D., & Rybicki, L. (1995). The symptoms of advanced cancer: Identification of clinical and research priorities by assessment of prevalence and severity. *Journal of Palliative Care, 11*, 27–32.

DuBreuil, S. C., & Spanos, N. P. (1993). Psychological treatment of warts. In J. W. Rhue, S. J. Lynn, & I. Kirsch (Eds.), *Handbook of clinical hypnosis*. Washington, DC: American Psychological Association.

Dworkin, S. F. (1986). Psychological considerations for facilitating anesthesia and sedation in dentistry. In R. A. Dionne & D. M. Laskin (Eds.), *Anesthesia and sedation in the dental office* (pp. 198–199). New York: Elsevier.

Edelstien, M. G. (1981). *Trauma, trance, and transformation*. New York: Brunner/Mazel.

Egbert, L. D. (1986). Preoperative anxiety. The adult patient. *International Anesthesiology Clinics, 24*, 17–37.

Egbert, L. D., Battit, G. E., Turndorf, H., & Beecher, H. K. (1963). The value of the preoperative visit by the anesthetist. *Journal of the American Medical Association, 185*, 553–555.

Egbert, L. D., Battit, G. E., Welch, C. E., & Bartlett. M. K. (1964). Reduction of postoperative pain by encouragement and instruction of patients. *New England Journal of Medicine, 270*, 825–827.

Eli, I. (1992). *Oral psychophysiology: Stress, pain, and behavior in dental care*. Boca Raton, FL: CRC Press.

Engel, G. L. "Psychogenic" pain and the pain-prone patient. *American Journal of Medicine, 26*, 899–918.

Engrav, L. H., Heimbach, D. M., Reus, J. L., Harnar, R. J., & Marvin, J. A. (1983). Early excision and grafting vs. nonoperative treatment of burns of indeterminant depth. *Journal of Trauma, 23*, 1001–1004.

Enquist, B., von Konow, L., & Bystedt, H. (1995). Pre- and perioperative suggestions in maxillofacial surgery: Effects on blood loss and recovery. *International Journal of Clinical & Experimental Hypnosis, 43*, 3, 284–294.

Erickson, M. H. (1976). Personal communication.

Erickson, M. H. (1980). Further clinical techniques of hypnosis: Utilization techniques. In E. Rossi (Ed.), *The collected papers of Milton H. Erickson on hypnosis. I. The nature of hypnosis and suggestion* (pp. 177–205). New York: Irvington.

Erickson, M. H. (1982). The interspersal hypnotic technique for symptom correction and pain control. In J. Barber & C. Adrian (Eds.), *Psychological approaches to the management of pain.* (pp. 100–117). New York: Brunner/Mazel.

Erickson, M. H. (1990). Erickson's suggestions with bruxism. In D. C. Hammond (Ed.), *Handbook of hypnotic suggestions and metaphors* (p. 184). New York: Norton.

Erickson, M. H., & Erickson, E. M. (1941). Concerning the nature and character of posthypnotic behavior. *The Journal of Genetic Psychology, 24,* 95–133.

Erickson, M. H., Hershman, S., & Secter, I. I. (1990). *The practical application of medical and dental hypnosis.* New York: Brunner/Mazel.

Erikson, E. (1968). *Identity: Youth and crisis.* New York: Norton.

Esdaile, J. (1957). *Hypnosis in medicine and surgery.* Introduction and supplementary reports by W. S. Kroger. New York: Julian.

Evans, M. B., & Paul, G. L . (1970). Effects of hypnotically suggested analgesia on physiological and subjective responses to cold stress. *Journal of Consulting & Clinical Psycholology, 35,* 362–371.

Everett, J. J., Patterson, D. R., Burns, G. L., Montgomery, B., & Heimbach, D. (1993). Adjunctive interventions for burn pain control: Comparison of hypnosis and Ativan. *Journal of Burn Care and Rehabilitation, 14,* 676–683.

Everett, J. J., Patterson, D. R., & Chen, A. C. (1990). Cognitive and behavioral treatments for burn pain. *The Pain Clinic, 3,* 133–145.

Ewin, D. (1979). Hypnosis in burn therapy. In G. D. Burrows, & L. Dennerstein (Eds.), *Hypnosis.* Amsterdam: Elsevier.

Ewin, D. (1984). Hypnosis in surgery and anesthesia. In W. C. Wester, II & A. H. Smith, Jr. (Eds.), *Clinical hypnosis: A multidisciplinary approach.* Philadelphia: J. B. Lippincott Co.

Ewin, D. (1986). Emergency room hypnosis for the burned patient. *American Journal of Clinical Hypnosis, 29,* 7–12.

Fanurik, D., Mizell, T., & Zeltzer, L. (unpublished manuscript). The cold-pressor paradigm with children. Part II: Stability of pain responses over a two-year period.

Fanurik, D., Zeltzer, L. K., Roberts, M. C., Blount, R. L. (1993). The relationship between children's coping styles and psychological intervention for cold pressor pain. *Pain, 52,* 255–257.

Ferrell, B. A. (1991). Pain management in elderly people. *Journal of the American Geriatric Society, 39,* 64–73.

Field, E. S. (1990). Stress reduction trance: A naturalistic Ericksonian Approach. In D. C. Hammond (Ed.), *Handbook of hypnotic suggestions and metaphors* (pp. 170–172). New York: W. W. Norton.

Fields, H. L., & Basbaum, A. I. (1989). Endogenous pain control mechanisms. In P. D. Wall & R. Melzack (Eds.), *Textbook of pain* (pp. 206–217). Edinburgh: Churchill Livingston.

Finer, B. L. (1982). Treatment in an interdisciplinary pain clinic. In J. Barber & C. Adrian (Eds.), *Psychological approaches to the management of pain* (pp. 186–204). New York: Brunner/Mazel.

Finer, B. L., & Nylen, B. O. (1961). Cardiac arrest in the treatment of burns and report on hypnosis as a substitute for anesthesia. *Plastic Reconstructive Surgery, 27,* 49–55.

Finer, B. L., & Terenius, L. (1981, September). *Endorphin involvements during hypnotic analgesia in chronic pain patients.* Paper presented at the Third World Congress on Pain of the International Association for the Study of Pain, Edinburgh, Scotland.

Finkelstein, S. (1991). Hypnosis and dentistry. In W. C. Wester & A. H. Smith (Eds.), *Clinical hypnosis: A multidisciplinary approach* (pp. 337–349). Cincinnati, OH: Behavioral Science Center.

Flowers, C. E., Littlejohn, T. W., & Wells, H. B. (1960). Pharmacologic and hypnoid analgesia. *Obstetrics & Gynecolology, 16,* 210–221.

Fordyce, W. E. (1976). *Behavioral methods for chronic pain and illness.* St. Louis: Mosby.

Fordyce, W. E. (1978). Learning processes in pain. In R. A. Sternbach(Ed.), *The psychology of pain.* New York: Raven Press.

Fordyce, W. E., Fowler, R. S., Jr., Lehmann, J. F., & DeLateur, B. J. (1968). Some implications of learning in problems of chronic pain. *Journal of Chronic Diseases, 21,* 179–190.

Fordyce, W. E., Fowler, R. S., Lehmann, J. F., DeLateur, B. J., Sand, P. I., & Trieschmann, R. B. (1968). Operant conditioning in the treatment of chronic pain. *Archives of Physical Medicine and Rehabilitation, 54,* 399–408.

Fricton, J. (1982). Medical evaluation of patients with chronic pain. In Barber, J., & Adrian, C. (Eds.), *Psychological approaches to the management of pain* (pp. 21–39). New York: Brunner/Mazel.

Fricton, J., & Roth, P. (1985). The effects of direct and indirect hypnotic suggestions for analgesia in high and low susceptible subjects. *American Journal of Clinical Hypnosis, 27,* 226–231.

Frischholz, E. J., Spiegel, D., Spiegel, H., Balma, D. L., & Markell, C. S. (1981). Differential hypnotic responsivity of smokers, phobics, and chronic pain. *Journal of Abnormal Psychology, 91,* 269–272.

Fromm, E., & Nash, M.R. (Eds.) (1992). *Contemporary hypnosis research.* New York: Guilford Press.

Furlong, M. (1990). Positive suggestions presented during anesthesia. In B. Bonke, W. Fitch, & K. Millar (Eds.), *Memory and awareness in anesthesia* (p. 170). Amsterdam: Swets & Zeitlinger.

Genuis, M. L. (1995). The use of hypnosis in helping cancer patients control anxiety, pain, and emesis: A review of recent empirical studies. *American Journal of Clinical Hypnosis, 37,* 316–325.

Gerschman, J. A. (1988). Dental fears and phobias. *Australian Family Physician, 17,* 261–266.

Gfeller, J. D., Lynn, S. J., & Pribble, W. E. (1987). Enhancing hypnotic susceptibility: Interpersonal and rapport factors. *Journal of Personality and Social Psychology, 52,* 586–595.

Ghoneim, M. M., Block, R. I., & Sum Ping, S. T. (1990). Learning without recall during general anesthesia. In B. Bonke, W. Fitch, & K. Millar (Eds.),

Memory and awareness in anaesthesia (p. 160). Amsterdam: Swets & Zeitlinger.

Gift, A. G. (1989). Visual analogue scales: Measurement of subjective phenomena. *Nursing Research, 38,* 286-288.

Gillett, P. L., & Coe, W. C. (1984). The effects of rapid induction analgesia (R.I.A.), hypnotic susceptibility, and the severity of discomfort on the reduction of dental pain. *American Journal of Clinical Hypnosis, 27,* 81-90.

Glazer, D. (1990). TMJ and tension headaches. In D. C. Hammond (Ed.), *Handbook of hypnotic suggestions and metaphors* (pp. 170-172). New York: Norton.

Golan, H. P. (1990). Suggestions with TMJ and bruxism. In D. C. Hammond (Ed.), *Handbook of hypnotic suggestions and metaphors* (p. 182). New York: Norton.

Goldstein, A., & Hilgard, E. R. (1975). Lack of influence of the morphine antagonist naloxone on hypnotic analgesia. *Proceedings of the National Academy of Sciences, 72,* 2041-2043.

Gracely, R. H., & Dubner, R. (1981). Pain assessment in humans – a reply to Hall. *Pain, 11,* 1109-120.

Greene, R. J., & Reyher, J. (1972). Pain tolerance in hypnotic analgesia and imagination states. *Journal of Abnormal Psychology, 79,* 29-38.

Grond, S., Zech, D., Diefenbach, C., & Bischoff, A. (1994). Prevalence and pattern of symptoms in patients with cancer pain: A prospective evaluation of 1635 cancer patients referred to a pain clinic. *Journal of Pain & Symptom Management, 9,* 372-382.

Grossman, S. A., Sheidler, V. R., Swedeen, K., Mucenski, J., & Piantadosi, S. (1991). Correlation of patient and caregiver ratings of cancer pain. *Journal of Pain and Symptom Management, 6,* 53-57.

Hagbarth, K. E., & Finer, B. L. (1963). The plasticity of human withdrawal reflexes to noxious skin stimuli in lower limbs. *Progress in Brain Research,* 65-78.

Haley, J. (Ed.). (1967). *Advanced techniques of hypnosis and therapy: The collected papers of Milton H. Erickson.* New York: Grune & Stratton.

Hammond, D. C., Heye, W. R., & Grant, C. W. (1983). Hypnotic analgesia with burns: An initial study. *American Journal of Clinical Hypnosis, 26,* 56-59.

Hartland, J. (1971). *Medical and dental hypnosis* (2nd Ed.). Baltimore: Williams & Wilkins.

Hassett, L. C. (1994). Summary of the scientific literature for pain and anxiety control in dentistry. *Anesthesia Progress, 41,* 48-57.

Hilgard, E. R. (1965a). Hypnosis. *Annual Review of Psychology, 16,* 157-180.

Hilgard, E. R. (1965b). *Hypnotic susceptibility.* New York: Harcourt Brace Jovanovich.

Hilgard, E. R. (1967a). A quantitative study of pain and its reduction through hypnotic suggestion. *Proceedings of the National Academy of Sciences, 57,* 1581-1586.

Hilgard, E. R. (1967b). Individual differences in hypnotizability. In R. E. Gordon (Ed.), *Handbook of clinical and experimental hypnosis.* New York: Macmillan.

Hilgard, E. R. (1969). Pain as a puzzle for psychology and physiology. *American Psychologist, 24,* 103-113.

Hilgard, E. R. (1973). A neodissociation interpretation of pain reduction in hypnosis. *Psychological Review, 80,* 396–411.

Hilgard, E. R. (1977). *Divided consciousness: Multiple controls in human thought and action.* New York: John Wiley & Sons.

Hilgard, E. R. (1980). Hypnosis in the treatment of pain. In G. D. Burrows & L. Dennerstein (Eds.), *Handbook of hypnosis and psychosomatic medicine.* Amsterdam: Excerpta Medica, Elsevier/North Holland Biomedical Press.

Hilgard, E. R. & Hilgard, J. R. (1994). *Hypnosis in the relief of pain* (Rev. ed.). New York: Brunner/Mazel.

Hilgard, E. R., & Morgan, A. H. (1975). Heart rate and blood pressure in the study of laboratory pain in man under normal conditions and as influenced by hypnosis. *Acta Neurologiae Experimentalis, 35,* 741–759.

Hilgard, E. R., Morgan, A. H., Lange, A. F., Lenox, J. R., MacDonald, H., Marshall, G. D., & Sachs, L. B. (1974). Heart rate changes in pain and hypnosis. *Psychophysiology, 11,* 692–702.

Hilgard, E. R., Morgan, A. H., & MacDonald, H. (1975). Pain and dissociation in the cold pressor test: A study of hypnotic analgesia with "hidden reports" through automatic key pressing and automatic talking. *Journal of Abnormal Psychology, 87,* 17–31.

Hilgard, J. R. (1975). *Personality and hypnosis: A study of imaginative involvement* (Rev. ed.). Chicago: University of Chicago Press.

Hilgard, J. R., & LeBaron, S. W. (1982). Relief of anxiety and pain in children and adolescents with cancer: Quantitative measures and clinical observations. *The International Journal of Clinical & Experimental Hypnosis, 30,* 417–442.

Hilgard, J. R., & LeBaron, S. W. (1984). *Hypnotherapy of pain in children with cancer.* Los Altos, CA: William Kaufman.

Holroyd, J. (1996). Hypnosis treatment of clinical pain: Understanding why hypnosis is useful. *The International Journal of Clinical & Experimental Hypnosis, 44,* 33–51.

Holzman, A. D., & Turk, D. C. (1986). *Pain management.* Oxford: Pergamon Press.

Hughes, S. C., & DeVore, J. S. (1993). Psychologic and alternative techniques for obstetric anesthesia. In S. M. Shnider & G. Levinson (Eds.), *Anesthesia for obstetrics* (3rd Ed.). Baltimore: Williams & Wilkins.

Jacox, A., Carr, D. B., Payne, R., et al. (1994). *Management of cancer pain. Clinical practice guideline, No. 9.* (AHCPR Publication No. 94-0592). Rockville, MD: Agency for Health Care Policy and Research, U.S. Department of Health and Human Services, Public Health Services.

Jay, S. M., Elliott, C. H., Ozolins, M., et al. (1985). Behavioral management of children's distress during painful medical procedures. *Behavior Research and Therapy, 23,* 513–520.

Karlin, R., Morgan, D., & Goldstein, L. (1980). Hypnotic analgesia: A preliminary investigation of quantitated hemispheric electroencephelographic and attentional correlates, *Journal of Abnormal Psycholology, 89,* 591–594.

Katz, E. R., Kellerman, J. & Ellenberg, L. (1987). Hypnosis in the reduction of acute pain in children with cancer. *Journal of Pediatric Psychology, 12,* 379-394.

Katz, J., Kavanagh B. P., Sandler A. N., et al. (1992). Premptive analgesia: clinical evidence of neuroplasticity contributing to postoperative pain. *Anesthesiology, 77,* 439.

Kellerman, J., Zeltzer, L., Ellenberg, L., & Dash, J. (1983). Adolescents with cancer. *Journal of Adolescent Health Care, 4*, 85–90.
Kempe, C. H., & Helfer, R. E. (Eds.). (1980). *The battered child.* (3rd Ed.). Chicago: University of Chicago Press.
Kepes, E. R. (1983). Management of pain. In R. D. T. Cape, R. M. Coe, & I. Rossman (Eds.), *Fundamentals of geriatric medicine* (pp. 247–259). New York: Raven Press.
Kiernan, B. D., Dane, J. R., Phillips, L. H. & Price, D. D. (1995). Hypnotic analgesia reduces R-III nociceptive reflex: Further evidence concerning the multifactorial nature of hypnotic analgesia. *Pain, 60*, 39–47.
Klein, R. M., & Charlton, J. E. (1980). Behavioral observation and analysis of pain behavior in critically burned patients. *Pain, 9*, 27–40.
Kojo, I. (1988). The mechanism of psychophysiological effects of placebo, *Medical Hypotheses, 27*, 261–264.
Kuttner, L., Bowman, M., & Teasdale, M. (1988). Psychological treatment of distress, pain, and anxiety in young children with cancer. *Journal of Developmental and Behavioral Pediatrics, 9*, 374–381.
Lamaze, F. (1958). *Painless childbirth: Psychoprophylactic method.* London: Burke.
LeBaron, S., Reyher, J., & Stack, J. M. (1985). Paternalistic versus egalitarian physician styles: The treatment of patients in crisis. *Journal of Family Practice, 21*, 56–62.
LeBaron, S., Zeltzer, L., & Fanurik, D. (1989). An investigation of cold pressor pain in children. Part I. *Pain, 37*, 161–171.
LeBoyer, F. (1975). *Birth without violence.* London: Wildwood House.
Leriche, R. (1949). *La chirurgie de la doleur* (3rd Ed.). (p. 39). Paris: Masson et Cie.
Levinson, B. W. (1965). States of awareness during general anaesthesia. *British Journal of Anaesthesia, 37*, 544–546.
Lewis, T. (1942). *Pain.* New York: Macmillan.
Lightfoot, G. (1994). An introduction to the psychological concept of control and its application to the dental setting. *Dental Health, 33*, 6–10.
London, P. (1975). Personal communication.
Ludwick-Rosenthal, R., & Neufeld, R. W. J. (1988). Stress management during noxious medical procedures: An evaluative review of outcome studies. *Psychological Bulletin, 104*, 326–342.
Lynn, S. J., & Rhue, J. W. (Eds.). (1991). *Theories of hypnosis: Current models and perspectives.* New York: Guilford Press.
Macleod, A. D., & Maycock, E. (1992). Awareness during anesthesia and post-traumatic stress disorder. *Anaesthesia and Intensive Care, 20*, 378–382.
Mayer, D., Price, D., Barber, J., & Rafii, A. (1976). Acupuncture analgesia: Evidence for activation of a pain inhibitory mechanism of action. In J. Bonica (Ed.): *Pain therapy and research.* New York: Raven Press.
McCarthy, F. M. (1989). *Essentials of safe dentistry for the medically compromised patient* (pp. 41–43). Philadelphia: W. B. Saunders.
McCauley, J. D., Thelan, M. H., Frank, R. G., Willard, R. R., & Callan, K. E. (1983). Hypnosis compared to relaxation in the outpatient management of chronic low back pain. *Archives of Physical Rehabilitation, 64*, 548–552.

McGlashan, T. H., Evans, F. J., & Orne, M. T. (1969). The nature of hypnotic analgesia and the placebo response to experimental pain. *Psychosomatic Medicine, 31*, 227–246.

McGrath, P. A. (1990). *Pain in children: Nature, assessment, and treatment.* (pp. 132–172, 235–250). New York: Guilford Press.

McGrath, P. J., & Unruh, A. (1987). *Pain in children and adolescents.* Amsterdam: Elsevier.

Melzack, R. (1990). The tragedy of needless pain. *Scientific American, 262,* 27–33.

Melzack, R., & Casey, K. L. (1968). Sensory, motivational, and central control determinants of pain. In D. Kenshalo (Ed.), *The skin senses* (pp. 423–443). Springfield: C. C. Thomas.

Melzack, R., & Wall, P. D. (1965). Pain mechanisms: A new theory. *Science, 50,* 971–979.

Melzack, R., & Wall, P. D. (1973). *The challenge of pain.* New York: Basic Books.

Moerman, N., Bonke, B., & Oosting, J. (1993). Awareness and recall during general anesthesia. *Anesthesiology, 79,* 454–464.

Monks, R. (1991). Psychotropic drugs. In J. J. Bonica (Ed.), *The management of pain, Vol. 2.* (pp. 1676–1689). Philadelphia: Lea & Febiger.

Moore, L. E., & Kaplan, J. Z. (1983). Hypnotically accelerated burn wound healing. *American Journal of Clinical Hypnosis, 26,* 16–19.

Morishima, H. O., Pederson, H., & Finster, M. (1978). The influence of maternal psychological stress on the fetus. *American Journal of Obstetrics and Gynecology, 131,* 286–290.

Moya F., & James, L. S. (1960). Medical hypnosis for obstetrics. *Journal of the American Medical Association, 174,* 2026–2032.

Mulligan R., & Lindeman, R. (1979). Behavior modification utilizing hypnosis in a minimal brain dysfunction patient. *Journal of Dentistry for the Handicapped, 4,* 41–43.

Mulligan R., & Clark, G. T. (1979). Effects of hypnosis on the treatment of bruxism. *Journal of Dental Research, 58,* A926.

Myers, R. E. (1975). Maternal psychological stress and fetal asphyxia: A study in the monkey. *American Journal of Obstetrics and Gynecolology, 122,* 47–59.

Nahum, L. H. (1965). Dangers of hypnosis. *Medicine, 767,* 771–778.

Nash, M. (1995). Personal communication.

Neiburger, E. J. (1990). Suggestions with TMJ. In D. C Hammond (Ed.), *Handbook of hypnotic suggestions and metaphors* (p. 183). New York: Norton.

Oleson, J., & Bonica, J. J. (1990). Headache. In J. J. Bonica (Ed.), *The management of pain, Vol 1.* Philadelphia, PA: Lea & Febiger.

Olness, K. (1981). Imagery (self-hypnosis) as adjunct therapy in childhood cancer: Clinical experience with 25 patients. *Journal of Pediatric Hematology/Oncology, 3,* 313–321.

Olness, K., & Gardner, G. G. (1988). *Hypnosis and hypnotherapy with children* (2nd Ed.). Philadelphia, PA: Grune & Stratton.

Orne, M. T. (1959). The nature of hypnosis: Artifact and essence. *Journal of Abnormal & Social Psychology, 58,* 277–299.

Orne, M. T. (1962). On the social psychlogy of the psychological experiment: With particular reference to demand characteristics and their implications. *American Psychologist, 17,* 776–783.

Orne, M. T. (1976). Mechanisms of hypnotic pain control. In J. J. Bonica & D. Albe-Fessard (Eds.), *Advances in pain research and therapy, Vol. 1* (pp. 717–726). New York: Raven Press.

Orne, M. T. (1980). Hypnotic control of pain: Toward a clarification of the different psychological processes involved. In J. J. Bonica (Ed.), *Pain* (pp. 155–172). New York: Raven Press.

Patterson, D. R. (1992). Practical applications of psychological techniques in controlling burn pain. *Journal of Burn Care and Rehabilitation, 13,* 13–18.

Patterson, D. R., Everett, J. J., Burns, G. L., & Marvin, J. A. (1992). Hypnosis for the treatment of burn pain. *Journal of Consulting and Clinical Psychology, 60,* 713–717.

Patterson, D. R., Everett, J. J., Bombardier, C. H., Questad, K. A., Lee, V. K., & Marvin, J. A. (1993). Psychological effects of severe burn injuries. *Psychological Bulletin, 113,* 362–378.

Patterson, D. R., Goldberg, M. L., Ehde, D. M. (in press). Hypnosis in the control of burn pain. *Ericksonian Monographs.*

Patterson, D. R., Marvin, J., Campbell, K. L., Everett, J. J., & Heimbach, D. (1993). *Quantitative and qualitative assessment of pain from burn injuries.* Paper presented at the 25th Annual Meeting of the American Burn Association, Cincinnati, OH, March 24–27.

Patterson, D. R., Questad, K. A., Boltwood, M. D., Covey, M. H., deLateur, B. J., Dutcher, K. A., Heimbach, D. M., & Marvin, J. A. (1987). Patient self-reports three months after sustaining a major burn. *Journal of Burn Care and Rehabilitation, 8,* 274–279.

Patterson, D. R., Questad, K. A., & deLateur, B. J. (1989). Hypnotherapy as an adjunct to narcotic analgesia for the treatment of pain for burn debridement. *American Journal of Clinical Hypnosis, 31,* 156–163.

Patterson, D. R., & Sharar, S. (in press). Treating pain in patients with severe burn injuries. *Advances in Medical Psychotherapy.*

Pekala, R. J., & Kumar, V. K. (1984). Predicting hypnotic responsivity by a self-report phenomenological instrument. *American Journal of Clinical Hypnosis, 27,*114–121.

Pepping, M. (1995). Personal communication.

Perry, S. W. (1984). Undermedication for pain on a burn unit. *General Hospital Psychiatry, 6,* 308–316.

Perry, S. W., Heidrich, G., & Ramos, E. (1981). Assessment of pain by burn patients. *Journal of Burn Care and Rehabilitation, 2,* 322–326.

Perry, S. W., Cella, D. F., Falkenberg, J., Heidrich, G., & Goodwin, C. (1987). Pain perception in burn patients with stress disorders. *Journal of Pain and Symptom Management, 2,* 29–33.

Portenoy, R. K. (1989). Cancer pain: Epidemiology and syndromes. *Cancer, 63,* 2298–2307

Portenoy, R. K., Thaler, H. T., Kornblith, A., Lepore, J. M., Friedlander-Klar, H., Coyle, N., Smart-Curley, T., Kemeny, N., Norton, L., Hoskins, W., & Scher, H. (1994). Symptom prevalence, characteristics and distress in a cancer population. *Quality of Life Research, 3,* 183–189.

Price, D. D. (1983). Roles of psychophysics, neuroscience, and experiential analysis in the study of pain. In L. Kruger & J. Liebeskind (Eds.), *Advances in pain research and therapy, Vol. 6* (pp. 341–355). New York: Raven Press.

Price, D. D. (1988). *Psychological and neural mechanisms of pain.* New York: Raven Press.

Price, D. D., & Barber, J. (1987). A quantitative analysis of factors that contribute to the efficacy of hypnotic analgesia. *Journal of Abnormal Psychology, 96,* 46–51.

Price, D. D., Barber, J. & Harkins, S. (1988). Path analysis of the hypnotic experience. Unpublished manuscript.

Price, D. D., & Barrell, J. J. (1980). An experiential approach with quantitative methods: A research paradigm. *Journal of Humanistic Psychology, 20,* 75–95.

Price, D. D., Barrell, J. J., & Gracely, R. H. (1980). A psychophysical dimension of pain, *Pain, 8,* 137–149.

Price, D. D., & Barrell, J. J. (1990). The structure of the hypnotic state: A self-directed experiential study. In J. J. Barrell (Ed.), *The experiential method: Exploring the human experience* (pp. 85–97). Acton, MA: Copely Publishing Group.

Price, D. D., & Harkins, S. W. (1992a). The affective-motivational dimension of pain: A two-stage model. *American Pain Society Journal, 4,* 229–239.

Price, D. D., & Harkins, S. W. (1992b). Psychophysical approaches to pain measurement and assessment. In D. Turk & R. Melzack (Eds.), *Handbook of pain measurement and assessment* (pp. 111–134). New York: Guilford Press.

Price, D. D., Long, S. P., & Harkins, S. W. (1994). A comparison of measurement characteristics of mechanical visual analogue and simple numerical rating scales of pain. *Pain, 56,* 217–226.

Ptacek, J. T., Patterson, D. R., Montgomery, B. K., & Heimbach, D. M. (1995). Pain, coping, and adjustment in patients with severe burns: Preliminary findings from a prospective study. *Journal of Pain and Symptom Management, 10,* 446–455.

Rausch, V. (1980). Cholecystectomy with self-hypnosis. *The International Journal of Clinical & Experimental Hypnosis, 22,* 124–129.

Reading, A. E. (1982). Chronic pain in gynecology: A psychological analysis. In J. Barber & C. Adrian (Eds.), *Psychological approaches to the management of pain* (pp. 137–149). New York: Brunner/Mazel.

Reaney, J. B. (1990). Hypnosis in the treatment of habit disorders. In W. C. Wester & A. H. Smith (Eds.), *Clinical hypnosis: A multidisciplinary approach.* Cincinnati, OH: Behavioral Science Center.

Reyher, J., & Smeltzer, W. (1968). Uncovering properties of visual imagery and verbal association. *American Journal of Clinical Hypnosis, 26,* 212–225.

Rodolfa, E. R., Kraft, W., & Reilley, R. R. (1990). Etiology and treatment of dental anxiety and phobia. *American Journal of Clinical Hypnosis, 33,* 22–28.

Routh, D. K., & Sanfilippo, M. D. (1991). Helping children cope with painful medical procedures. In J. P. Bush & S. W. Harkins (Eds.), *Children in pain: Clinical and research issues from a developmental perspective* (pp. 397–424). New York: Springer-Verlag.

Sachs, L., Feuerstein, M., & Vitale, J. (1977). Hypnotic self-regulation of chronic pain. *American Journal of Clinical Hypnosis, 20,* 106–113.
Saeger, L. (1992). Choosing appropriate analgesic therapy. In J. Kornell (Ed.), *Pain management and care of the terminal patient.* Seattle, WA: Washington State Medical Association.
Sarbin, T. R., & Slagle, R. W. (1979). Hypnosis and psychophysiological outcomes. In E. Fromm & R. E. Shor (Eds.), *Hypnosis: Developments in research and new perspectives* (pp. 273–303). New York: Aldine.
Scarinci, I. C., McDonald-Haile, J., Bradley, L. A., & Richter, J. E. (1994). Altered pain perception and psychosocial features among women with gastrointestinal disorders and history of abuse: A preliminary model. *American Journal of Medicine, 97,* 108–118.
Schafer, D. (1975). Hypnosis use on a burn unit. *The International Journal of Clinical & Experimental Hypnosis, 23,* 1–14.
Schechter, N. L., Bernstein, B. A., Beck, A., et al. (1991). Individual differences in children's response to pain: Role of temperament and parental characteristics. *Pediatrics, 87,* 171–177.
Schechter, N. L., Berde, C. B., & Yaster, M. (Eds.). (1993). *Pain in children, infants, and adolescents.* Baltimore, MD: Williams & Wilkins.
Schuster, C. S. (1980). Development of a concept of sexuality. In C. S. Schuster & S. S. Ashburn (Eds.), *The process of human development* (pp. 501–516). Boston, MA: Little, Brown, & Co.
Schwender, D., Kaiser, A., Klasing, S., Peter, K., & Pöppel, E. (1994). Midlatencey auditory evoked potentials and explicit and implicit memory in patients undergoing cardiac surgery. *Anesthesiology, 80,* 493–501.
Secter, I. I. (1961). Bruxing. In *A syllabus on hypnosis and a handbook of therapeutic suggestions.* Des Plaines, IL: The American Society of Clinical Hypnosis Education and Research Foundation.
Selby, G., & Lance, J. (1960). Observations on 500 cases of migraine and allied vascular headache. *Journal of Neurology, Neurosurgery, and Psychiatry, 23,* 23.
Shnider, S. M., Wright, R. G., Levinson, G., Roizen, M. F., Wallis, K. L., Rolbin, S. H., & Craft, J. B. (1979). Uterine blood flow and plasma norepinephrine changes during maternal stress in the pregnant ewe. *Anesthesiology, 50,* 524–527.
Shor, R. E. (1959). Hypnosis and the concept of the generalized reality-orientation. *American Journal of Psychotherapy, 13,* 582–602.
Shor, R. E. (1962). Three dimensions of hypnotic depth. *International Journal of Clinical and Experimental Hypnosis, 8,* 151–163.
Shor, R. E. (1965). Hypnosis and the concept of the generalized reality-orientation. In R. Shor & M. Orne (Eds.), *The nature of hypnosis: Selected basic readings* (pp. 288–305). New York: Holt, Rinehart & Winston.
Shor, R. E., & Orne, E. C. (1962). *The Harvard group scale of hypnotic susceptibility, Form A.* Palo Alto, CA: Consulting Psychologists Press.
Shor, R. E., & Orne, M. T. (1965). *The nature of hypnosis: Selected basic readings.* New York: Holt, Rinehart, & Winston.
Siegel, B. S. (1990). *Love, medicine & miracles.* New York: Harper & Row.
Siegel, L. J., & Peterson, L. (1981). Maintenance effects of coping skills in sensory information on young children's response to repeated dental procedures. *Behavioral Therapy, 12,* 530–535.

Simpson, R., Goepferd, S., Ogesen, R., & Zach, G. (1985). *Hypnosis in dentistry: A handbook for clinical use* (pp. 5-30). Springfield: C. C. Thomas.

Singer, J. L. (1973). *The child's world of make-believe: Experimental studies of imaginative play.* New York: Academic Press.

Spangler, D. M. (1982). *Low back pain: Assessment and management* (pp. 9-20). New York: Grune & Stratton.

Spanos, N. P. (1983). The hidden observer as an experimental creation. *Journal of Personality and Social Psychology, 44,* 170-176.

Spanos, N. P. (1986). Hypnotic behavior: A social-psychological interpretation of amnesia, analgesia, and "trance logic." *Behavior and Brain Science, 9,* 440-467.

Spanos, N. P., McNeil, C., & Henderikus, J. S. (1982). Hypnotically "reliving" a prior burn: Effects on blister formation and localized skin temperature. *Journal of Abnormal Psychology, 91,* 303-305.

Spanos, N. P., Kennedy, S. K., & Gwynn, M. I. (1984). Moderating effects of contextual variables on the relationship between hypnotic susceptibility and suggested analgesia. *Journal of Abnormal Psychology, 93,* 285-294.

Spanos, N. P., Radtke-Bodorik, H. L., Ferguson, J. D., & Jones, B. (1979). The effects of hypnotic susceptibility, suggestions for analgesia, and the utilization of cognitive strategies on the reduction of pain. *Journal of Abnormal Psychology, 88,* 282-292.

Spiegel, D., & Albert, A. (1983). Naloxone fails to reverse hypnotic alleviation of chronic pain. *Psychopharmacology, 81,* 140-143.

Spiegel, D., & Bloom, J. R. (1983) Group therapy and hypnosis reduce metastatic breast carcinoma pain. *Psychosomatic Medicine, 45,* 333-339.

Spiegel, D., Sands, S., & Koopman, C. (1994). Pain and depression in patients with cancer. *Cancer, 74,* 2570-2578.

Spiegel, H. (1974). *Manual for hypnotic induction profile.* New York: Soni Medica.

Spiegel, H., & Spiegel, D. (1987). *Trance and treatment: Clinical uses of hypnosis.* New York: Basic Books.

Spira, J. L., & Spiegel, D. (1992). Hypnosis and related techniques in pain management. *Hospice Journal, 8,* 89-119.

Sternbach, R. A. (1974). *Pain patients: Traits and treatment.* New York: Academic Press.

Sternbach, R. A. (1982a). The psychologist's role in the diagnosis and treatment of pain patients. In J. Barber & C. Adrian (Eds.), *Psychological approaches to the management of pain* (pp. 3-20). New York: Brunner/Mazel.

Sternbach, R. A. (1982b). On strategies for identifying neurochemical correlates of hypnotic analgesia. *International Journal of Clinical & Experimental Hypnosis, 30,* 251-256.

Stolzenberg, J. (1961). Age regression in the treatment of two instances of dental phobia. *American Journal of Clinical Hypnosis, 4,* 122-123.

Syrjala, K. L. (1994). *Coping skills for living with cancer.* Seattle, WA: Fred Hutchinson Cancer Research Center.

Syrjala, K. L., & Abrams, J. R. (in press). Hypnosis and imagery in the treatment of pain. In R. J. Gatchel & D. C. Turk (Eds.), *Chronic pain: Psychological perspectives on treatment.* New York: Guilford Press.

Syrjala, K. L., & Abrams, J. R. (1996). Hypnosis and imagery in the treatment of pain. In R. J. Gatchel & D. C. Turk (Eds.), *Psychological approaches to pain management: A practitioner's handbook* (pp. 231–258). New York: Guilford.

Syrjala, K. L., & Chapko, M. E. (1995). Evidence for a biopsychosocial model of cancer treatment-related pain. *Pain, 61,* 69–79.

Syrjala, K. L., Cummings, C., & Donaldson G. (1992). Hypnosis or cognitive behavioral training for the reduction of pain and nausea during cancer treatment: A controlled clinical trial. *Pain, 48,* 137–146.

Syrjala, K. L., Donaldson, G. W., Davis, M. W., Kippes, M. E., & Carr, J. E. (1995). Relaxation and imagery and cognitive-behavioral training reduce pain during cancer treatment: A controlled clinical trial. *Pain, 63,* 189–198.

Syrjala, K. L., Williams, A., Niles, R., Rupert, J., & Abrams, J. (1993). *Relieving cancer pain.* Seattle, WA: Academy Press.

Tellegen, A., & Atkinson, G. (1974). Openness to absorbing and self-altering experiences ("absorption"), a trait related to hypnotic susceptibility. *Journal of Abnormal Psychology, 83,* 268–277.

Tenenbaum, S. J., Kurtz, R. M., & Bienias, J. L. (1990). Hypnotic susceptibility and experimental pain reduction. *American Journal of Clinical Hypnosis, 33,* 40–49.

Traut, E. F., & Passarelli, E. W. (1957). Placebos in the treatment of rheumatoid arthritis and other rheumatic conditions *Annals of the Rheumatic Diseases, 16,* 18–22.

Turner, J., & Chapman, C. (1982). Psychological interventions for chronic pain: A critical review. II. Operant conditioning, hypnosis, and cognitive-behavioral therapy. *Pain, 1,* 23–42.

Turner, J., Deyo, R. A., Loeser, J. D., VonKorff, M., & Fordyce, W. E. (1994). The importance of placebo effects in pain treatment and research. *Journal of the American Medical Association, 271,* 1609–1614.

Turner, J. A. & Romano, J. A. (1991). Psychologic and psychosocial evaluation (pp. 595–609). In J.J. Bonica, (Ed.), *The management of pain,* Vol. 1. Philadelphia, PA: Lea & Febiger.

Tursky, B. (1985). The 55% analgesic effect: Real or artifact? In L. White, B. Tursky, & G. E. Scwhartz (Eds.), *Placebo: Research, theory, and mechanisms.* New York: Guilford Press.

Van der Bijl, P. (1995). Psychogenic pain in dentistry. *Compendium, 16,* 46-54.

Van der Does, A. J., & Van Dyck, R. (1989). Does hypnosis contribute to the care of burn patients? Review of the evidence. *General Hospital Psychiatry, 11,* 119–124.

Wakeman, R., & Kaplan, J. (1978). An experimental study of hypnosis in painful burns. *American Journal of Clinical Hypnosis, 21,* 3–12.

Wall, V. J., & Womack, W. (1989). Hypnotic versus active cognitive strategies for alleviation of procedural distress in pediatric oncology patients. *American Journal of Clinical Hypnosis, 31,* 181–191.

Weitzenhoffer, A. M. (1957). *General techniques of hypnotism.* New York: Grune & Stratton.

Weitzenhoffer, A. M., & Hilgard, E. R. (1959). *Stanford hypnotic susceptibility scale, forms A and B.* Palo Alto, CA: Consulting Psychologists Press.

Wester, W. C. & Smith, A. M. (Eds.). (1990). *Clinical hypnosis: A multidisciplinary approach.* Cincinnati: Behavioral Science Center.

Willer, J. C. (1977). Comparative study of perceived pain and nociceptive flexion reflex in man. *Pain, 3,* 69–80.

Willer, J. C. (1984). Nociceptive flexion reflex as a physiological correlate of sensory pain in humans. In B. Bromm (Ed.), *Pain measurement in man. Neurophysiological correlates of pain* (pp. 87–110). New York: Elsevier.

Willer, J. C. (1985). Studies on pain. Effects of morphine on a spinal nociceptive flexion reflex and related sensory pain in man. *Brain Research, 331,* 105–114.

Wright, M. E. (1990). Example of treating phobic anxiety with individually prepared tapes. In D. C. Hammond (Ed.), *Handbook of hypnotic suggestions and metaphors* (pp. 180–181). New York: Norton.

Youmans, J. R. (1982). *Neurologicalsurgery* (pp. 1–38). Philadelphia, PA: W. B. Saunders.

Zeltzer, L. (1994). Pain and symptom management. In D. Bearison & R. Mulhern (Eds.), *Pediatric Psychooncology: Psychological research in children with cancer* (pp. 61–83). New York: Oxford University Press.

Zeltzer, L., Altman, A., Kohen, D., LeBaron, S., Manuksela, E. L., & Schechter, N. L. (1990). Report of the consensus conference on the management of pain in childhood cancer: Report of the subcommittee on the management of pain associated with procedures in children with cancer. *Pediatrics, 86,* 826–831.

Zeltzer, L., Anderson, C. T. M., & Schechter, N. L. (1990). Pediatric pain: Current status and new directions. *Current Problems in Pediatrics, 20,* 8: 415–486.

Zeltzer, L., Arnoult, S., Hamilton, A., & DeLaura, S. (1994). Visceral pain in children. In P. E. Hyman (Ed.), *Pediatric gastrointestinal motility disorders* (pp. 155–176). New York: Academy Professional Information Services, Inc.

Zeltzer, L., Dash, J., & Holland, J. (1979). Hypnotically induced pain control in sickle cell anemia. *Pediatrics, 64,* 533–536.

Zeltzer, L., Jay, S. M., & Fisher, D. M. (1989). The management of pain associated with pediatric procedures. *Pediatric Clinics of North America, 36:* 1–24.

Zeltzer, L., & LeBaron, S. (1982). Hypnotic and non-hypnotic techniques for reduction of pain and anxiety during painful procedures in children and adolescents with cancer. *Journal of Pediatrics, 101,* 1032–1035.

Zeltzer, L., & LeBaron, S. (1986). The hypnotic treatment of children in pain. In D. Routh & M. Wolraich (Eds.), *Advances in developmental and behavioral pediatrics, Vol. VII.* (pp. 190–234). Greenwich, CT: JAI Press.

NAME INDEX

Ablin, A., 324
Abrams, J., 137, 152
Adrian, C., 13, 291, 325
Ahles, T.A., 123
Albert, A., 13
Alman, B.M., 15, 16
Altman, A., 323
Anand, K.J.S., 308
Anderson, C.T.M., 324
Andrykowski, M.A., 154
Angell, M., 271
Arnoult, S., 307
Atkinson, G., 20, 57
Auld, J.M., 190
Avni, J., 299

Bakan, D., 10
Balma, D.L., 139
Banyai, E.I., 6, 373
Barabasz, A.F., 195
Barbasz, M., 195
Barber, Joseph, viii, ix, xix, 3, 5, 9, 13, 16, 17, 19, 24, 41, 45, 50, 71, 74, 75, 76, 82, 84, 85, 87, 94, 135, 138, 139, 141, 158, 276, 290, 291, 306, 325, 367
Barber, T.X., 4, 69, 81
Barbour, Allen, 351
Barrell, J.J., 70, 77, 83
Bartlett, M.K., 210
Bassman, S.W., 204
Bates, B.L., 277

Battit, G.E., 210
Beck, A.T., 57, 322
Beecher, H.K., 210
Bejenke, Christel, J., xviii, 8, 209, 241, 243, 249
Bennett, H.L., 230
Benson, D.R., 230
Berde, C.B., 306, 324
Bernstein, B.A., 322
Bienias, J.L., 277
Bischoff, A., 122
Blanchard, E.B., 123
Bloch, G.J., 11
Bloom, J.R., 131
Blount, R.L., 322
Bombardier, C.H., 268, 300
Bondoc, C.C., 268
Bonica, John, J., ix, xvii, 33, 48, 50, 51, 123, 159, 172, 181
Bonke, B., 215, 243
Bowers, K.S., 4, 13, 71, 83, 106, 277
Bowman, M., 312, 324
Bradley, L.A., 198
Braun, D.W., 268
Brown, D.P., 87, 199
Browne, G., 342
Burish, T.G., 154
Burke, J.F., 268
Burns, G.L., 276,
Bush, J. P., 324
Bystedt, H., 230

Callan, K.E., 6
Campbell, K.L., 270, 300
Carney, R.E., 15, 16
Carr, D.B., 137
Carr, J.E., 128
Cash, T.F., 300
Cella, D.F., 270
Chapko, M.E., 123
Chapman, C., 14
Chapman, L.F., 278
Charlton, J.E., 270
Chen, A.C., 272
Choiniere, M., 270
Clark, G.T., 200
Clark, J.H., 199
Clawson, D.K., 48
Cleeland, C.S., 122, 131, 140
Coe, W.C., 277
Corbin, S.M., 322
Craig, K.D., 44
Crasilneck, H.B., 13, 17, 275
Crawford, H.J. 81
Crook, J., 342
Cummings, C., 128
Currerie, P.W., 268

Dane, J.R., 13, 81
Dash, J., 14, 324
Davis, M.A., 342
Davis, M.W., 128
De Jong, R.N., 37, 38, 39, 44, 46
DeLateur, B.J., 50, 276
DeLaura, S., 307
DeVore, J.S., 250
Deyo, R.A., 141
Diamond, M.J., 16, 17, 118
Dick-Read, G., 250
Diefenbach, C., 122
Disbrow, E.A., 230, 232
Donaldson, G., 128
Donnelly, S., 122
Dubner, R., 75
DuBreuil, S.C., 278
Dworkin, S.F., 197

Edelstien, M.G., 9
Egbert, L.D., 210, 211
Ehde, D.M., 277
Eli, I., 190
Ellenberg, L., 14, 324

Elliott, C.H., 324
Engrav, L.H., 268
Enquist, B., 230
Erickson, E.M., 95
Erickson, Milton, 87, 95, 111, 190, 200, 207, 297
Erikson, Erik, 310, 354
Esdaile, James, 12
Evans, F.J., 13, 141
Evans, M.B., 69
Everett, J.J., 268, 270, 272, 273, 276, 300
Ewin, D., 278, 282

Falkenberg, J., 270
Fanurik, D., 312, 322, 338
Ferguson, J.D., 138
Ferrell, B.A., 342
Feuerstein, M., 94
Field, E.S., 200
Finkelstein, S., 190
Finer, B.L., 13, 81, 99, 275
Finster, M., 250
Fisher, D.M., 324
Flowers, C.E., 250
Fordyce, Wilbert, 8, 50, 53, 55, 56, 59, 99, 141, 272
Fowkes, William, C., xviii, 14, 341
Fowler, R.S., Jr., 50
Frank, R.G., 6
Fricton, J., 16, 138, 159
Frischholz, E.J., 138
Fromm, E., 4, 5, 87

Gardner, G.G., 13, 14, 324, 325
Genius, M.L., 124
Gerschman, J.A., 197
Gfeller, J.D., 16
Gift, A.G., 276
Gillett, P.L., 277
Girard, N., 270
Glazer, D., 199
Glazer, J., 324
Goepferd, S., 199, 200
Golan, H.P., 200
Goldberg, M.L., 277
Goldstein, A., 13, 80, 81
Goodell, H., 278
Goodwin, C., 270
Gracely, R.H., 75, 77
Grant, C.W., 275

Greene, R.J., 70
Gregg, M.E., 154
Grond, S., 122
Grossman, S.A., 131
Gruzelier, J.H., 81
Gwynn, M.I., 138

Hagbarth, K.E., 81
Hahn, K.W., 69, 81
Haley, J., 17, 87
Hall, J.A., 13, 17
Hamilton, A., 307
Hammond, D.C., 275
Harkins, S.W., 10, 11, 71, 75, 324
Harnar, R.J., 268
Hartland, J., 87
Hassett, L.C., 199
Heidrich, G., 270
Heimbach, D.M., 268, 270, 271, 276
Helfer, R.E., 307
Henderikus, J.S., 278
Hershman, S., 87, 190, 207
Heye, W.R., 275
Hilgard, Ernest, R., ix, 4, 6, 12, 13, 14, 15,
    17, 18, 69, 70, 74, 78, 79, 80, 81, 82,
    87, 195, 197, 201, 202, 277, 292
Hilgard, Josephine, vii, viii, ix, xviii, 12,
    13, 14, 15, 17, 69, 70, 74. 78, 79, 80,
    82, 87, 195, 197, 201, 202, 292, 312,
    314, 320, 324, 325, 334
Holland, J., 14
Holroyd, J., 96
Holzman, A.D., 272
Hughes, S.C., 250

Jacox, A., 137
James, L.S., 250
Janet, Pierre, 24
Jay, S.M., 324
Jones, B., 138

Kaplan, J.Z., 14, 275, 278
Katz, E.R., 324
Kellerman, J., 14, 324
Kempe, C.H., 307
Kennedy, S.K., 138
Kepes, E.R., 342
Kiernan, B.D., 13, 81, 82
Kippes, M.E., 128
Klein, R.M., 270

Kohen, D., 323
Kojo, I., 73
Koopman, C., 123
Kraft, W., 197, 198
Kuiken, D.A., 230
Kumar, V.K., 71, 83
Kurtz, R.M., 277
Kuttner, L., 312, 324

Lamaze, F., 250, 251
Lance, J., 159
LeBaron, S.W., viii, ix, xviii, xix, 14, 27,
    87, 126, 241, 276, 277, 305, 311, 312,
    314, 320, 322, 324, 325, 334, 338, 341,
    367
LeBoyer, F., 250
Lehman, J.F., 50
Leriche, R., 38
Lewis, T., 39, 41
Lightfoot, G., 198
Lindeman, R., 204
Littlejohn, T.W., 250
Loeser, John D., ix, xvii, 33, 48, 141
London, P., 13, 111
Long, S.P., 11
Ludwick-Rosenthal, R., 324
Lynn, S.J., 4, 5, 16

MacDonald, H., 12
Markell, C.S., 139
Marvin, J.A., 268, 270, 276, 300
Mayer, D., 13, 80, 81,
McCarthy, F.M., 189
McCauley, J.D., 6
McDonald-Haile, J., 198
McGlashan, T.H., 141
McGrath, P.A., 324
McNiel, C., 278
Melzack, R., 13, 270, 271
Mendelson, M., 57
Mesmer, Franz Anton, 11
Miser, A., 324
Mizell, T., 322
Moerman, N., 243
Monks, R., 56
Montgomery, B.K., 271, 276
Moore, L.E., 278
Morgan, A.H., 12, 15
Morishima, H.O., 250
Moya, F., 250

Mucenski, J., 131
Mulligan, Roseann, xviii, 185, 199, 204
Myers, R.E., 250

Nahum, L.H., 24
Nash, M.R., 4, 5, 20
Neiburger, E.J., 199, 200
Neufeld, R.W.J., 324
Niles, R., 137
Nylen, B.O., 275

Ogesen, R., 199, 200
Oleson, J., 159, 172, 181
Olness, K., 13, 14, 324, 325
Oosting, J., 243
Orne, E.C., 15
Orne, Martin, 4, 6, 13, 14, 17, 138
Owings, J.T., 230
Ozolins, M., 324

Paquin, M.J., 270
Passarelli, E.W., 73
Patterson, David, R., ix, xviii, 8, 248, 267,
    268, 270, 271, 272, 275, 276, 277, 299,
    300
Paul, G.L., 69
Payne, R., 137
Pederson, H., 250
Pekala, R.J., 71, 83
Pepping, M., 181
Perry, S.W., 270, 308
Peterson, L., 324
Phillips, L.H., 13, 81
Piantados, S., 131
Portenoy, R.K., 122
Pribble, W.E., 16
Price, Donald, D., ix, xviii, 5, 10, 11, 13,
    16, 19, 67, 70, 71, 75, 76, 77, 78, 80,
    81, 82, 83, 84, 138, 139
Pruzinsky, T., 300
Ptacek, J.T., 271

Questad, K.A., 276
Quinby, W.C., 268

Radtke-Bodorik, H.L., 138
Rafii, A., 81
Ramos, E., 270
Rausch, V., 12
Reading, A.E., 115

Reaney, J.B., 200,
Reilley, R.R., 197, 198
Reus, J.L., 268
Reyher, J., 23, 70, 311
Reynolds, P.J., 199
Rhue, J.W., 4, 5
Richter, J.E., 198
Rideout, E., 342
Roberts, M.C., 322
Rodolfa, E.R., 197, 198
Romano, J.A., 51, 52, 53, 54
Rondeau, J., 270
Roth, P., 16, 138
Roth-Roemer, Sari, xviii, 24, 97, 121,
    249
Routh, D.K., 324
Ruckdeschel, J.C., 123
Rupert, J., 137
Rybicki, L., 122

Sachs, L., 94
Saeger, L., 123
Sands, S., 123
Sanfilippo, M.D., 324
Scarinci, I.C., 198
Schafer, D., 14, 275
Schechter, N.L., 306, 322, 324
Scholfield, N.M., 308
Secter, I.I., 87, 190, 207
Selby, G., 159
Sharar, S., 271
Sheidler, V.R., 131
Shires, G.T., 268
Shor, R.E., 4, 5, 6, 13, 15, 77
Siegel, B.S., 352
Siegel, L.J., 324
Simpson, R., 199, 200
Singer, J.L., 314
Sipple, W.G., 308
Smeltzer, W., 23
Smith, A.M., 207
Snider, S.M., 250
Spangler, D.M., 48
Spanos, N.P., 69, 138, 278
Spiegel, D., 13, 123, 131, 139, 195, 277
Spiegel, H., 15, 19, 139, 195, 277
Spira, J.L., 131
Stack, J.M., 311
Sternbach, R.A., xvi, 13, 36, 50, 99
Stirman, J.A., 275

Strauss, Richard, 356
Sturges, J.W., 322
Swedeen, K., 131
Syrjala, Karen, L., xviii, 24, 97, 121, 123, 128, 137, 140, 152, 154, 249

Teasdale, M., 312, 324
Tellegen, A., 20, 57
Tenenbaum, S.J., 277
Terenius, L., 13
Thelan, M.H., 6
Tope, D.M., 154
Traut, E.F., 73
Turk, D.C., 272
Turndorf, H., 210
Turner, J.A., 14, 51, 52, 53, 54, 141
Tursky, B., 75

Van Der Bijl, P., 199
Van der Does, A.J., 278
Van Dyck, R., 278
Vitale, J., 94
von Konow, L., 230
VonKorff, M., 141

Wakeman, R., 14, 275
Wall, P.D., 13
Wall, V.J., 124
Walsh, D., 122
Ward, C.H., 57
Welch, C.E., 210
Weitzenhoffer, A.M., 12, 13, 15, 77, 277
Wells, H.B., 250
Wester, W.C., 204, 207
Willard, R.R., 6
Williams, A., 137
Willer, J.C., 81
Wilson, B.J., 275
Wilson, S.C., 69
Woff, H.G., 278
Womack, W., 124
Wright, M.E., 200

Yaster, M., 306

Zach, G., 199, 200
Zech, D., 122
Zeltzer, L., ix, xviii, 14, 27, 126, 241, 276, 305, 307, 312, 322, 323, 324, 325, 338

SUBJECT INDEX

absorption, 25–26
abuse (physical/sexual), 44, 268, 307
  dental phobias and, 197–98
  gastrointestinal conditions and, 198
acute care, 270, 289–299
  in children, 318–19
  overview of, 289–290
addiction, *see* substance abuse
adolescents, *see* children
alcohol, *see* substance abuse
amnesia, 181, 214, 218, 220, 235, 291, 292, 298–99
amputation, 292, 292, 294
analgesia (hypnotic), 6, 7, 11–20, 67–84
  affective vs. sensory, 82 (*see also* pain)
  with burn patients, 299
  in childbirth, 253–54
  clinical implications of, 82–84
  in dental work, 201–7
  history of, 11–12
  pain processing, influences on, 75–76
  paradox of, 79–80
  placebo vs., 73–74
  sensory mechanisms of, 78–82, 83
  techniques for creating, 87–91, 142–48 (table), 259
anesthesia (hypnotic), 6, 7, 88, 187, 242–43, 248–49
  in childbirth, 250, 253
Anesthesia for Obstetrics, 250

angina pain, 192–96
animal magnetism, 11
anorexia due to cancer treatment, 121–22
anxiety/fear:
  anticipatory, 320, 323, 327, 328
  in burn patients, 268, 284, 290
  in cancer procedures, 126–28
  in children, 307, 317, 320, 323, 324
  in dental work, 200–203
  in hypnotic treatment, 23–24, 28
  pain and, 54
  in surgical patients, 210, 263
"archaic involvement," 5
attention, 25–26, 30, 71, 72, 83
attitudes toward:
  hypnotic treatment, 57
  pain, 55 (*see also* meaning)
audiotapes, use of, 146, 148, 175, 190–91, 200–201, 203, 223, 338, 365, 376
authority, impact on patients, 213–15

Beck Depression Inventory, 57
Birth Without Violence, 250
bladder function, 265 (*see also* catheter)
blood loss, 259–260
bruxism, 199–200
burn injury/pain:
  acute care of, 289–299
  care and treatment, phases of, 268–270, 302

contraindications for hypnosis, 279-280
emergency room interventions, 281-83
hypnoanesthesia and, 248
hypnotic protocols for treating, 290-92
intensive care interventions, 283-89
nature of, 267-68, 270-71, 302
preparing patient, 280-81
rehabilitation, 299-301
wound healing/care procedures, 278,
    290, 291

cancer:
hypnosis, misperceptions of in treating,
    137-38
hypnosis, problems and pitfalls of, 151-
    57 (table)
isolation and dying, coping with, 148-
    150
medical evaluation prior to hypnotic
    treatment, xvii, 33-49, 139-140
pain, 122-23, 124-135 (table)
pain, disease-related, 131-35
pain, procedural, 124-28
pain, treatment-related, 128-131
psychological effects of, 135-37
symptoms of, 122
techniques for pain of, 141-150, 249
*Caring for Patients: A Critique of the Med-
    ical Model*, 351
case examples of:
anesthesia, fear of, 245-46
arthritis, 350-51
bone marrow aspiration, 126-28, 305-6,
    320-21, 325-28
burn pain, 267, 292-97
cancer pain, 111-13, 121-22, 126-28,
    129-131, 132-35, 136-37, 143-46,
    155-57, 342-44
chest pain, 60-62
children, 242, 305-6, 320-21, 325-28,
    329-338, 367-68
dental pain, 185-86, 191-95, 204-6,
    207-8
depression, treatment-related, 136-37
elderly, pain in, 341, 342-44, 345-48,
    350-51, 352, 355-63
facial injury, 330-32
gut pain, 143-46
headache (aneurysm), 97

headache (cluster), 173-76
headache (migraine), 158, 161-67
headache (muscle tension), 169-172,
    329-330, 332-34, 373-74
headache (posttraumatic), 58-60, 181-
    84
headache (vascular), 177-180
hypochondriac, 64-66
joint pain, 62-63, 103-111
knee pain, 350-51
pelvic pain, 115-17
phantom limb pain, 334-38
post-polio syndrome, 115
surgical preparation, 209-210, 217-19,
    226-235, 242
thalamic pain syndrome, 99-103
of therapeutic failure, 367-68, 370-73,
    373-79
treatment-related pain, 129-131
catalepsy, 28, 29, 101
catheter, comfort with, 231-32, 264
chest tubes, comfort with, 230-31
childbirth, natural, 250, 253
children/adolescents:
with burn injuries, 275-76
clinicians' attitudes toward pain in,
    306-7
coping skills of, 319-321
developmental view of fantasy, 313-17
and hypnosis, 27, 275-76, 314-17
imagery, no interest in, 338-340
pain, assessing in, 317-18
pain, misconceptions of adults, 308-310
preparing for surgery, 241-42
psychological approaches to pain in,
    318-324
sleep and coping, 322-23
therapeutic techniques with, 324-338
treatment differences with adults, 310-
    12
undertreatment of, 306-8
choices, need for, 221, 226, 266, 285
chronic benign pain syndrome, 8, 10, 51,
    86
clinicians' issues:
anguish for patients, 98
attitudes toward pain in children, 306-7
beliefs and expectations, 298, 358
frustration toward patients, 354

clinicians' issues (*Cont.*)
  therapeutic failure, *see* separate entry
  treating cancer patients, 151–52
cognitive/behavioral strategies:
  with burn patients, 272–75, 294
  in dentistry, 188
  for pain control, 6, 7, 8, 50
concussion, 180, 181
Consensus Conference on the Treatment
  of Cancer Pain in Children, 323
control, patient's need for, 22, 142, 198,
  211, 266, 350
  anesthesia and loss of, 245
  exercises faciltating, 224–25
  of physiologic functions, 221–22, 230
  see also helplessness
coping:
  children's abilities for, 319–321
  in the elderly, 345, 352
  with isolation and dying, 148–50
  styles in children, 322–24
Council on Aging, 364
countertransference, 118, 152
cultural factors in pain experience, 53,
  126, 307, 342

delirium, 282, 283
delusion, somatic, 370–73
demand characteristics, 68–69
dementia, 53, 103
denial, 284, 342, 345, 356, 375, 376
dentistry:
  dentists' personal issues, 188–89
  expectation of pain, 188
  hypnotic techniques in, 190–96
  origins of fears and phobias, 196–98
  pain management in, 189–190, 198–200
  patient's vs. dentist's perceptions, 192–
    96
  preparation of patient, 200–201
  psychotherapist's role in, 201
  utilizing patients' abilities in, 207–8
dependency needs:
  in burn patients, 279, 284
  in the elderly, 345–48
depression, 52, 54, 57, 62, 121, 123, 129,
  269, 270
desensitization, 324, 328
developmental (levels, issues):
  fantasy, view of, 312–17

and pain treatment in children, 310–12
diagnosis of pain:
  history-taking, 37, 41–45
  location and distribution of pain, 39–40
  medical evaluation, 34–35, 44, 131–32
    (*see also* separate entry)
displacement of pain, 90
dissociation, 6
  hypnotic state, 79, 84
  in induction, 26, 30
  from pain, 90–91, 135, 147 (table)
distancing technique, 135
distraction (techniques), 240, 241–42,
  272, 322, 324, 325, 345
drug-seeking behavior, 318 (*see also* substance abuse)
dying, coping with, 148–150

elderly:
  activity and level of functioning, 345–
    48, 364
  clinicians' issues with, 352–54
  imagination and suggestion in, 354–364
  meaning of pain to, 342–351, 365, 375,
    376
  pain in, neglected, 342
  psychological issues of, 348–49
  psychological strategies for treating,
    364–65
  responsiveness of, 14
  strengths of, 352
empathy, 18 (*see also* rapport)
endorphins and hypnosis, 13
endoscopies, 249
endotracheal tube, *see* ventilation
environmental factors:
  for burn patients, 283, 284, 299
  in evaluating pain, 53–54
eye closure, 28, 195, 202–3
  eye-roll induction, 113, 196

family:
  coping styles of, 322
  history, 44, 105
  hypnosis misused by, 153–57
  involving in care of patient, 319, 364
  suggestions for entire, 228, 288, 294–95
fantasy, 24
  developmental view of, 312–17
  as pain technique, 330–32

Feldenkrais treatment, 115
fractionation, 218, 236, 249

glove anesthesia induction, 203-4,
  206

hallucinations, 5-6, 289
Harvard Group Scale of Hypnotic Susceptibility, 15
headache:
  cluster, 172-76
  migraine, 158-167 (*see also* separate
    entry)
  muscle tension, 167-172, 329-330, 332-
    34, 373-74
  posttraumatic, 180-84
  vascular, 176-180
helplessness, 211, 224, 225, 266, 307, 328,
  348
  see also control
"hidden observer," 79
history:
  of analgesia, 11-12
  in diagnosing pain, 37, 41-45
  family, 44, 105
  for medical evaluation, 36-39, 41-45
  psychological, 44-45, 123-, 332
  -taking, 41-45, 123
hyperemesis, 255
hypervigilance, *see* vigilance
hypnoanesthesia, *see* anesthesia
hypnosis:
  birth of, 12-13
  neurophysiological mechanisms of, 13-
    14
  overview of, 4-8
  suggestion vs., 7-8
  see also hypnotic; pain; suggestion
Hypnosis for the Seriously Curious, 106
hypnotic induction, 6
  of children, 315-16
  emergency room, 282-83
  example of, 106-8
  eye-roll, 113
  intensive care unit, 284, 285-89 (table)
  overview of, 24-32
  pain during, 91-92, 182
  surgical, preprocedure, 235-247 (table),
    262-66
  see also hypnosis; suggestion

hypnotic (method, process, state), xvi
  in analgesia, 69-70
  with burn patients, 275-77
  with cancer patients, *see* cancer
  in children, *see* separate entry
  clinical responses vs., 19
  complications, nonhypnotic, 114-17
  dental pain and, 199-200
  in dentistry, *see* separate entry
  induction, *see* separate entry
  interpersonal nature of, 118
  involvement, degrees of, 77-78
  medical care, integrating with, 135-141,
    152
  not widely used, 117-18
  and obstetrics, 250-55
  phenomena, 5-7
  physical treatment vs., 168
  and preoperative preparation, 235-
    247
  psychological issues and, 171-72, 183-
    84, 362-63
  self-hypnosis, *see* separate entry
  special considerations, 91-96, 161
  spontaneous, 195-96, 222
  state vs. nonstate theories of, 5, 69
  suggestion without, 214-15
  for surgical patients, 211-19
  talking during, 28-29, 169-170, 257
  treatment of pain, *see* separate entry
  see also hypnosis; pain; suggestion
hypnotic responsiveness, ix, 14-15
  analgesia in relation to, 69
  assessment of, 19-20, 57, 105
  automaticity of, 6-7, 71, 73, 83, 93, 237
  in burn patients, 277, 296
  in cancer patients, 139-141
  in the elderly, 14
  individual differences in, 14-15
  locksmith metaphor and, 18
  observing, 27-28, 220-21
  placebo vs., 71-74 (figure), 141, 215, 230
  reduction in pain and, 77-78 (table), 84,
    138-139
  see also suggestibility
Hypnotic Induction Profile, 15, 19, 277
hypnotizability, *see* hypnotic responsiveness
hypochondriasis, 34, 38, 52, 64-66, 116-
  17

iatrogenic complications, 42
imagery, 312, 332–33, 338–340, 363
  see also fantasy; imagination
images, 147 (table), 150
imagination (imaginal focus):
  in children, 313, 314–17, 327, 328
  in elderly, 354–364
  of hypnotic method, 118
  induction, utilizing, 25
  pain treatment utilizing patient's, xvi,
    23, 134, 135, 139,165, 207–8, 240,
    241
  see also fantasy
information for burn patients, 273
information for children, 324
information for surgical patients:
  distressing devices, 230–35
  nonmedical clinician's role, 212, 222
  physician's role, 211–12, 222
  preparing for procedures, 219–223, 262
  as suggestion, 214
instructions for surgical patients, 211
  distressing devices, 230–35
  preparing, 223–25
intensive care, 270
  condition of patient, 285, 289
  environmental considerations, 283, 284
  induction in, 285–89 (table)
International Association for the Study
  of Pain, 50
International Headache Society, 159
intimacy, in hypnotic treatment, 21, 118
intubation, 262 (see also medical procedures; ventilation)

Lamaze, see psychoprophylaxis
litigation, affecting treatment, 56–57, 60,
  300
locksmith metaphor, 18

malingering, 54
McGill Pain Questionnaire, 41
meaning:
  clinician vs. experimenter, 17
  of pain, 10, 55, 78, 82, 83, 96–97, 100,
    111, 112, 114, 140, 181, 182, 342–351,
    365, 375, 376
measurement:
  of experiential factors, 83
  of hypnotic responsiveness, 19–20

of pain, 11, 16, 75, 76–78
  using self-report, 69, 74
medical care:
  hypnotic methods integrating, 135–151,
    152
medical evaluation:
  history-taking, 41–45, 123
  methods of, 35–39
  nonmedical clinician and, 63–66, 131–
    32, 152
  objectives of, 34–35
  physical examination, 45–49
medical procedures:
  information, see separate entry
  instructions, see separate entry
  preoperative hypnotic preparation of pa-
    tient, 235–247, 252, 262–66
  preoperative nonhypnotic preparation
    of patient, 210–12, 212–13, 217–19
  suggestions for, see separate entry
medication, 55–56, 99
  advocating for patient, 154, 271
  for burn patients, 271, 285, 290, 293,
    295, 295
  in childbirth, 252–53
  for children, 306–8, 323, 326, 328
  for cluster headache, 172, 173
  depression, treatment-related, 136–37
  in elderly, 342, 364
  lessened after hypnotic preparation,
    217–19, 244
  for migraine, 160
  for posttraumatic headache, 181
  resistance to taking, 133
  undertreatment of children with, 306–8
  see also opioids
menstrual cycle, headache associated
  with, 177–180
mental status, 54
metaphor, 147 (table), 150
migraine headache:
  hypnotic treatment of, 160–167
  overview of, 159–160
  with aura, 160, 161–64
  without aura, 160, 161, 164–67
Minnesota Multiphasic Personality Inventory (MMPI), 57
motivation, 16, 17, 94, 139, 196, 301
mouth, and emotions in dentistry, 197
musculoskeletal examination, 48

naso-gastric tubes, 232
National Cancer Institute, 121
neodissociation theory of hypnosis, 6-7,
    79-80, 82
neurologic examination, 48
neurotransmitters and hypnosis, 13
nonverbal communications, 215
nurses and hypnotic interventions, 291,
    296

obstetrics, 250-55
operant reinforcement principles (with
    burn patients), 274-75
opioids, 8, 123, 128
    resistance to taking, 111-12, 113
    use of with children, 310
    see also medication
orientation/disorientation, 71
outcomes, assessing, 17

pain:
    affective components of, 10-11, 16, 41,
        55, 74-78, 84, 114, 189, 190, 207
    background, 270-71, 290
    behaviors, 53, 54, 317-18
    burn, *see* separate entry
    cancer, *see* separate entry
    characteristics/nature of, 8-11, 39-41
    in children, *see* separate entry
    chronic benign pain syndrome, 8, 10, 51,
        86
    dental, *see* separate entry
    diary, 55, 59
    duration/periodicity of, 41
    in elderly, *see* separate entry
    expression of, 317-18, 342, 344-45
    failure to treat, *see* failure
    history of, 42-44, 123
    hypnotic induction, during, 91-92, 182
    hypnotic treatment of, 20-24 (*see also*
        separate entry)
    localized, 39
    management strategies, 34, 36
    meaning of, *see* separate entry
    misconceptions about, 308-310
    neuropathic, 123
    nociceptive, 81-83, 123, 159
    nonhypnotic treatment of, xvii, 6, 114-
        17, 141, 210-12, 213-17 (table), 217-
        19, 225-235

physical examination of, 45-49
procedural, 124-28, 270-71, 290
psychological factors/effects, vii, 40, 43,
    48, 51-52, 115, 362-63, 370, 376 (*see
    also* psychological evaluation)
quality of, 40-41, 88, 142-43, 269
recurring syndromes, xvi, 8, 9, 51, 86,
    96-99
referred, 40
reflex sympathetic, 40
responsiveness to hypnotic techniques,
    see responsiveness
sensory components of, 10-11, 16, 41,
    55, 74-82, 84, 88, 114, 189, 190, 207
severity/intensity of, 41, 88, 123, 140,
    269, 302
subjective/objective manifestations of,
    46-48
types of, 9-10, 51, 123, 210
patients:
    burn, unique problems of, 269, 284
    characteristics of, 213, 215
    concerns of, 21-23, 219-220, 223-25
    point of view, 347
    surgical, issues of, 211
    values of, 349-350
personality disorders, 53, 268, 280
phobias (dental), 196-98, 200-201
placebo effect:
    hypnotic analgesia vs., 73-74
    hypnotic responsiveness vs., 71-74 (fig-
        ure), 141, 215, 230
plateau hypnotizability, 19
play:
    hypnotic ability and, 314-17
    objects and, 312-13
    sociodramatic, 313
    therapy, 313
post-concussion headache, 180, 181
posthypnotic suggestions, 26, 32
    for burn patients, 296
    in case examples, 92-93, 101, 102, 108-
        9
    reinforcing, 246-47
    for self-hypnosis, 95-96
posttraumatic stress disorder (PTSD), 54,
    269, 270
projected pain, 39-40
psychological (approaches) to:
    burn injuries, impact of, 300-301

psychological (approaches) to: (*Cont.*)
  cancer, effects of, 135–37
  children in pain, 318–324
  elderly, 364–65
  history, 44–45, 123
  hypnosis, issues in, 171–72, 183–84
  in obstetrics, 250
  pain, factors/effects, vii, 40, 43, 48, 51–
    52, 115
psychological evaluation/issues of pain pa-
    tients:
  basic issues, 52–54
  benefits of, 58–63, 86
  cancer, effects of, 135–37
  in dentistry, 189–190
  effects of pain, 51–52
  elderly, 348–49
  and hypnotic methods, 171–72, 183–84,
    362–63
  interviewing, 54–57
  testing, 57, 116
psychoprophylaxis, 250, 251
psychosocial history, 44–45, 123, 332
pulmonary complications, preventing, 265

R-III spinal reflex, 81, 82
Rapid Induction Analgesia (RIA), 290, 291
rapport, 35, 37 (*see also relationship*)
reflex sympathetic pain, 40
reframing, 141–42, 220, 242, 325, 330
rehabilitation (burn injuries), 270, 299–
    301
rehearsal technique, 236, 239, 245, 256–
    261, 313, 314, 324, 327
reinterpreting pain, 75, 88, 89–90, 141–
    42, 186, 202, 263, 266, 332
relationship in hypnotic experience, 5, 15–
    16, 17 (*see also* rapport)
relaxation, 6, 71, 206–7, 208, 224, 235,
    241, 249, 329, 330, 335, 336, 337, 365,
    373–74
repressors, 272
resistance:
  to evaluation, 53
  to self-hypnosis, 94–95
  to treatment, 54, 280, 297
role enactment theory, 68–69, 82

secondary gains, 54, 89, 140, 370
self-hypnosis, 57, 103, 132
  for back pain, 112
  for burn pain, 281
  for childbirth, 254
  for cluster headache, 172
  for dental work, 200–201, 203, 207–8
  hypnoanesthesia and, 248–49
  for migraine, 163, 166
  misused by patient and family, 153–57
  posthypnotic suggestions for, 95–96
  for posttraumatic headache, 183
  resistance to, 94–95
sensory transformation method, 143–48
social coercion, hypnotic processes and, 4
somatoform disorder, 10, 34, 39, 40, 51, 57
spinal cord mechanisms of hypnotic anal-
    gesia, 80–82, 83, 84
stage hypnosis, 4, 22
Stanford Hypnosis Laboratory, vii, 12
Stanford Scale of Hypnotic Susceptibil-
    ity, 15, 277
storytelling, 150
substance abuse, 53, 54, 268, 279, 310
suffering, 16, 19, 20, 38, 51, 52, 55, 56, 88,
    90, 97, 116, 268, 290, 317, 342, 364
    (*see also* pain)
suggestibility, 255, 282, 284, 302
  see also hypnotic responsiveness
suggestion(s) (hypnotic) for:
  affective vs. sensory pain components,
    74–78, 103
  analgesia, 142–48 (table), 259
  awareness, 113
  beneficial effects of, 215, 217–19
  childbirth, 251–55
  children, 314, 334
  dental-related pain, 192–94, 204–5
  differential effects of, 75–78
  diminution, 100–101, 103, 112
  disease-related pain, 134–35
  displacement, 90
  dissociation, 75, 90–91
  in elderly, 354–364
  ending hypnotic experience, 26, 32,
    203–6
  family participation, 228, 288, 294–95
  "favorite places" technique, 144–45,
    208, 218, 235, 239–240, 282–83, 285
  headache (cluster), 174–75
  headache (migraine), 162–63, 165
  headache (muscle tension), 329–330
  headache (vascular), 178–180
  hope-inspiring, 294

hypnosis vs., 7–8,
incorporation of, 70–74 (figure)
induction, 24–25, 182 (*see also* separate
    entry)
isolation and dying, coping with, 148–
    150
negative, 213–17 (table), 228, 282
neuropathic pain, 123
nonhypnotic, 141, 213–17 (table)
phantom limb pain, 336–37
procedural cancer pain, 127–28
self-perpetuating, 225, 233, 237, 238,
    247, 265
sensitizers, 272–73
sensory substitution, 89–90
surgical patients, *see* suggestions for
    surgical patients
therapeutic, 26, 31
treatment-related cancer pain, 130–
    31
uniqueness of, 73–74
waking, 225–228
see also case examples; hypnosis; hyp-
    notic; posthypnotic
suggestions for surgical patients:
anesthesia (during), 242–43, 258, 262
anesthesia (emerging from), 243
anti-nausea, 260, 264
blood loss, 259–260
children, 242
distressing devices, 230–35, 262, 263
linked to postoperative events, 228–29,
    260–61
linked to remarks, 229–230
operation, during, 243, 262
overview, 211–19
preparing (hypnotic), 235–247 (table)
preparing (nonhypnotic), 225–235
in recovery room, 244–46
special considerations, 246–47
surgery, day of, 239–241
suicide (suicidality), 54, 372–73
surgery:
analgesia (hypnotic), 12
hypnotic applications, 212–19
rehearsal for, 236, 239, 245, 256–261
see also medical procedures; sugges-
    tions for surigcal patients

susceptibility, 213
    see also hypnotic responsiveness
Symptom Check List 90 (SCL-90), 57

talking during hypnosis, 28–29, 169–170,
    257
Tellegen Absorption Scale (TAS), 20, 57
therapeutic:
alliance, 18 (*see also* rapport; relation-
    ship)
contact, 380–81
failure, factors underlying, 379–389
time:
distortion, 236
future orientation, 263, 266
hypnotic condition and, 25
impact of pain, 43
-intensity curve of pain, 41
progression, 237, 263
tracheostomy tube, *see* ventilation
transference, 5, 118, 381
treatment:
choosing criteria for, 20
contraindications of, 24
describing to patients, 23
evaluating, 370
failure, *see* separate entry
fragmentation of, 34, 343
frequency of, 98
interdisciplinary resources for, 52
nurses' role in hypnotic, 291, 296
patients' concerns about, 21–23
requirements, 9
see also hypnotic; suggestions
trigeminal neuralgia, 31, 355

University of Washington Pain Center, 50
utilization, 240–41, 251, 280–81

variables:
dependent, 74–78
independent, 68–74
of subjects' experience, vii–viii
ventilation, mechanical, 232–34, 242, 243,
    244, 263
vigilance, 202–3, 233, 272, 281, 285, 323
visual analogue scale (VAS), 11, 16, 41,
    55, 71, 76–77 (table), 81, 140